WEST ACADEMIC PUBLISHING'S LAW SCHOOL ADVISORY BOARD

PUBLIC HEALTH LAW

IN A NUTSHELL®

FIFTH EDITION

JAMES G. HODGE, JR.
Peter Kiewit Foundation Professor of Law
Sandra Day O'Connor College of Law
Arizona State University

WEST ACADEMIC

860 Blue Gentian Road, Suite 350
Eagan, MN 55121
1-877-888-1330

Published in the United States of America

ISBN: 979-8-89209-210-4

PREFACE/INTRODUCTION

Studying or practicing public health law is challenged by the breadth of the field. As defined in more detail in Chapter 1, public health law includes laws that: (1) are designed primarily to assure the conditions for people to be healthy, or (2) entail rights-based or structural limits on efforts of public or private sectors to protect, promote, or preserve community health.

Public health laws extend to traditional areas such as the prevention and control of communicable diseases (e.g., HIV/AIDS, measles, COVID-19), chronic conditions (e.g., heart disease, cancers, diabetes, Alzheimer's), injuries (e.g., gunshot wounds, vehicular crashes, domestic incidents), and other health threats (e.g., opioids, food-borne illnesses, bioterrorism, environmental health impacts).

Related to these areas are significant legal issues arising from the use of identifiable information for public health surveillance, regulation of property to abate nuisances, inspection of commercial establishments to detect public health threats, and limitations on the dissemination of commercial or other messages that negatively impact community health.

Under even broader conceptions, public health law envelops any legal efforts that address negative effects on human health. These may include various measures to target the underlying causes of poor health outcomes, such as lack of access to health services; socio-economic, racial, ethnic, or other disparities in the distribution of services; homelessness or housing limitations; insufficient food or sustenance; and environmental factors, such as air or water pollution, or global climate change.

Though its scope is comprehensive, the field of public health law also has boundaries for the purposes of this text (and to avoid duplication of material in other NUTSHELL series texts, notably including ADMINISTRATIVE LAW OF HEALTH CARE, BIOETHICS & LAW, DISABILITY LAW, ENVIRONMENTAL LAW, HEALTH CARE LAW & ETHICS, and MENTAL HEALTH LAW). In the interests of presenting a cohesive vision of public health law concentrated on core aspects of the field, this text does not include significant coverage of several legal issues that directly or tangentially affect the public's health. These include laws concerning access and delivery of health care services; national health care reforms; disability law; environmental protection (except as they relate to environmental health); mental health law; reproductive rights; and the licensure or regulation of public health or health care workers (HCWs) and entities.

A. Sources of Public Health Law

As per the following illustration, the primary sources of public health laws in the U.S. are diverse.

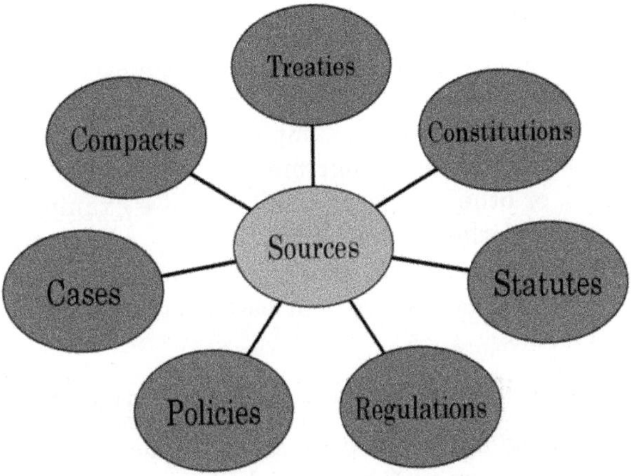

Given the heavy role of government in protecting the public's health, constitutional issues often arise (*see* the U.S. Constitution Bill of Rights and 14th Amendment, restated hereafter, for reference throughout the text). One of the central themes of the field is the consummate need to balance public and private interests in effectuating public health objectives and programs. Federal, state, and local lawmakers promulgate public health statutes or other legislative enactments. Some of these legislative efforts are based on model public health acts or provisions produced via academic or other entities. Legislatures also empower public health and other executive branch agencies to create and enforce regulatory or administrative laws or issue executive orders to advance public health goals.

Courts at all levels of government contribute to the breadth and limits of public health powers through pivotal decisions on constitutional or other challenges. Collectively these cases constitute what is known as the "common law." Finally, public health law includes "soft law" examples, such as memoranda of understanding, departmental policies, advisory letters, or other initiatives. While these examples do not carry the same legal weight as statutes, regulations, or cases, law- and policy-makers may defer to soft law sources in assessing public health legal issues.

B. Teaching & Practicing Public Health Law

Not long ago, core courses in public health law were taught in just a handful of largely graduate-level institutions. Few practitioners nationally identified themselves as "public health lawyers." In the past few decades, however, public health law has emerged as a distinct field of practice and a formal course of academic study. Tens of thousands of practitioners working in public and private sector positions have received comprehensive or selective training in public health legal topics. Hundreds of core courses in public health law are taught annually in lecture, seminar, and clinical formats across the country.

Based on my 2012 survey of public health law academics, core courses in public health law (coupled often with ethics or policy) are offered routinely at many accredited schools of public health, over one-third of American Bar Association (ABA)-accredited law schools, multiple schools of medicine, and select undergraduate institutions. In addition to these core classes, many undergraduate and graduate schools offer courses in health law, bioethics, or other areas that include prominent public health law topics. James G. Hodge, Jr., *A Modern Surv. on Teaching Public Health Law in the U.S.*, 40 JLME 1034 (2013). A 2023 survey of accredited public health schools, however, suggests that just over 1/3 of schools feature broad public health law courses, with considerably fewer of these schools (7%) requiring such courses. Jalayne J. Arias et al., *Centering Law in Public Health Education*, HEALTH AFFAIRS (Apr. 12, 2024).

Whether in schools of law, public health, medicine, or undergraduate programs, students nationally may find this NUTSHELL valuable as a stand-alone guide or complement to other texts used in these courses. Among others, these texts include:

- SCOTT BURRIS ET AL., THE NEW PUBLIC HEALTH LAW: A TRANSDISCIPLINARY APPROACH TO PRACTICE & ADVOCACY (2nd ed. 2022);
- RICHARD J. BONNIE ET AL., PUBLIC HEALTH LAW, ETHICS & POLICY (2nd ed. 2021);
- PUBLIC HEALTH LAW: CONCEPTS & CASE STUDIES (Montrece Ransom et al. eds., 2021);
- WENDY K. MARINER ET AL., PUBLIC HEALTH LAW (3d ed. 2019);
- LAWRENCE O. GOSTIN & LINDSAY F. WILEY, PUBLIC HEALTH LAW & ETHICS: A READER (3rd ed. 2018);
- MARY ANNE BOBINSKI ET AL., BIOETHICS & PUBLIC HEALTH LAW (4th ed. 2018);

- LAWRENCE O. GOSTIN & LINDSAY F. WILEY, PUBLIC HEALTH LAW: POWER, DUTY, RESTRAINT (3rd ed. 2016); and
- WENDY E. PARMET, POPULATIONS, PUBLIC HEALTH & THE LAW (2009).

Major topics in this NUTSHELL feature many of the issues addressed in these texts and courses, although under varied organizational patterns or levels of coverage. The text's Table of Contents and Index facilitate a quick comparison and examination of relevant passages based on study assignments or interest areas.

For public health or legal practitioners seeking a solid introduction or enhanced understanding of the field outside formal coursework, this text is suitable for self-study or as a practical guide on core topics in a condensed format. Considerable content centers on guidance drawn from actual events or issues experienced by legal practitioners in the field.

C. Features & Tools

Like the prior edition, the 5th edition of the Nutshell text features over 150 graphics, images, text boxes, and other tools designed to aid in the learning and comprehension of the material. Extensive references in the text provide additional sources of information for further assessments. The references largely comport with typical legal citations via THE BLUEBOOK: UNIFORM SYS. OF CITATION, with a couple of streamlined adaptations. These include (1) extensive use of abbreviations noted in the Glossary of Acronyms within the citations directly; and (2) deletion of URLs or other web links for specific sources. Separate online searches of most citations noted in the text provide modern web links to access such information.

Each chapter also includes initial statements of Learning Objectives and ending Discussion Questions to provoke assessments and exploration of the core substance of the text. Many of the Discussion Questions center not only on issues raised in the text, but also broader concerns in the field of public health law and ethics. Colleagues teaching courses in public health law may find these questions helpful in providing a platform for in class or online discussions related to each chapter's content. Multiple images throughout the text attempt to graphically portray key legal concepts or ideas to help readers visualize or recall core concepts.

D. Acknowledgments

Many thanks to outstanding colleagues at institutions, agencies, and locations across the country who provided their input, research, or reviews for prior or current editions of this text. They include (in alphabetical order): Asha M. Agrawal, J.D., Leila F. Barraza, J.D., M.P.H., Jennifer Bernstein, J.D., M.P.H., Kyrah Berthiaume, Scott Burris, J.D., Brenna Carpenter, J.D., Veda Collmer, J.D., Alicia Corbett, J.D., Brooke Courtney, J.D., M.P.H., Corey Davis, J.D., M.P.H., Rebecca Freed, J.D., Lance A. Gable, J.D., M.P.H., Richard A. Goodman, M.D., J.D., M.P.H., Monica Hammer, J.D., Kathleen Hoke, J.D., Peter D. Jacobson, J.D., M.P.H., Stacie Kershner, J.D., Kellie Manders, J.D., Greg

Measer, J.D., Chase Millea, J.D., Rose Meltzer, J.D., M.P.H., Sarah A. Noe, J.D., Daniel G. Orenstein, J.D., M.P.H., Wendy E. Parmet, J.D., Jennifer L. Piatt, J.D., Tia Powell, M.D., Clifford M. Rees, J.D., Susan Russo, J.D., Lainie Rutkow, J.D., M.P.H., Ph.D., Matthew Saria, J.D., Stephen P. Teret, J.D., M.P.H., Jon S. Vernick, J.D., M.P.H., Kim Weidenaar, J.D., Sarah A. Wetter, J.D., M.P.H., and Erica N. White, J.D., M.P.H.

Special thanks to Mary Saxon, J.D., Senior Legal Researcher, Center for Public Health Law & Policy, Sandra Day O'Connor College of Law, Arizona State University, for her extraordinary research, editing, and other contributions to the text in 2024.

JAMES G. HODGE, JR., J.D., LL.M.

August 1, 2024

U.S. CONSTITUTION BILL OF RIGHTS & 14TH AMENDMENT

Amendment I. Congress shall make no law respecting an establishment of religion, or prohibiting the free exercise thereof; or abridging the freedom of speech, or of the press; or the right of the people peaceably to assemble, and to petition the Government for a redress of grievances.

Amendment II. A well regulated Militia, being necessary to the security of a free State, the right of the people to keep and bear Arms, shall not be infringed.

Amendment III. No Soldier shall, in time of peace be quartered in any house, without the consent of the Owner, nor in time of war, but in a manner to be prescribed by law.

Amendment IV. The right of the people to be secure in their persons, houses, papers, and effects, against unreasonable searches and seizures, shall not be violated, and no Warrants shall issue, but upon probable cause, supported by Oath or affirmation, and particularly describing the place to be searched, and the persons or things to be seized.

Amendment V. No person shall be held to answer for a capital, or otherwise infamous crime, unless on a presentment or indictment of a Grand Jury, except in cases arising in the land or naval forces, or in the Militia, when in actual service in time of War or public danger; nor shall any person be subject for the same offence to be twice put in jeopardy of life or limb; nor shall be compelled in any criminal case to be a witness against himself, nor be deprived of life, liberty, or property, without due process of law; nor shall private property be taken for public use, without just compensation.

Amendment VI. In all criminal prosecutions, the accused shall enjoy the right to a speedy and public trial, by an impartial jury of the State and district wherein the crime shall have been committed, which district shall have been previously ascertained by law, and to be informed of the nature and cause of the accusation; to be confronted with the witnesses against him; to have compulsory process for obtaining witnesses in his favor, and to have the Assistance of Counsel for his defence.

Amendment VII. In Suits at common law, where the value in controversy shall exceed twenty dollars, the right of trial by jury shall be preserved, and no fact tried by a jury, shall be otherwise re-examined in any Court of the United States, than according to the rules of the common law.

Amendment VIII. Excessive bail shall not be required, nor excessive fines imposed, nor cruel and unusual punishments inflicted.

Amendment IX. The enumeration in the Constitution, of certain rights, shall not be construed to deny or disparage others retained by the people.

Amendment X. The powers not delegated to the United States by the Constitution, nor prohibited by it to the States, are reserved to the States respectively, or to the people.

Amendment XIV. Section 1. All persons born or naturalized in the United States, and subject to the jurisdiction thereof, are citizens of the United States and of the State wherein they reside. No State shall make or enforce any law which shall abridge the privileges or immunities of citizens of the United States; nor shall any State deprive any person of life, liberty, or property, without due process of law; nor deny to any person within its jurisdiction the equal protection of the laws.

Section 2. Representatives shall be apportioned among the several States according to their respective numbers, counting the whole number of persons in each State, excluding Indians not taxed. But when the right to vote at any election for the choice of electors for President and Vice-President of the United States, Representatives in Congress, the Executive and Judicial officers of a State, or the members of the Legislature thereof, is denied to any of the male inhabitants of such State, being twenty-one years of age, and citizens of the United States, or in any way abridged, except for participation in rebellion, or other crime, the basis of representation therein shall be reduced in the proportion which the number of such male citizens shall bear to the whole number of male citizens twenty-one years of age in such State.

Section 3. No person shall be a Senator or Representative in Congress, or elector of President and Vice-President, or hold any office, civil or military, under the United States, or under any State, who, having previously taken an oath, as a member of Congress, or as an officer of the United States, or as a member of any State legislature, or as an executive or judicial officer of any State, to support the Constitution of the United States, shall have engaged in insurrection or rebellion against the same, or given aid or comfort to the enemies thereof. But Congress may by a vote of two-thirds of each House, remove such disability.

Section 4. The validity of the public debt of the United States, authorized by law, including debts incurred for payment of pensions and bounties for services in suppressing insurrection or rebellion, shall not be questioned. But neither the United States nor any State shall assume or pay any debt or obligation incurred in aid of insurrection or rebellion against the United States, or any claim for the loss or emancipation of any slave; but all such debts, obligations and claims shall be held illegal and void.

Section 5. The Congress shall have the power to enforce, by appropriate legislation, the provisions of this article.

OUTLINE

TABLE OF CASES

References are to Pages

GLOSSARY OF ACRONYMS

The following acronyms are used consistently throughout the text:

ABA—American Bar Association

ABLA—Alcoholic Beverage Labeling Act

ACA—Patient Protection & Affordable Care Act

ACIP—Advisory Committee on Immunization Practices

ADA—Americans with Disabilities Act

AHRQ—Agency for Healthcare Research & Quality

AJPH—American Journal of Public Health

AMA—American Medical Association

APA—Administrative Procedure Act

ASPR—Administration for Strategic Preparedness & Response

BLS—Bureau of Labor Statistics

BPA—Bisphenol A

CBRN—Chemical, Biological, Radiological, Nuclear

CDC—Centers for Disease Control & Prevention

CMS—Centers for Medicare & Medicaid Services

COPD—Chronic Obstructive Pulmonary Disease

COVID-19—Coronavirus Disease 2019

CPSA—Consumer Product Safety Act

CPSC—Consumer Product Safety Commission

CRA—Civil Rights Act

CSTE—Council of State & Territorial Epidemiologists

DHS—Department of Homeland Security

DoD—Department of Defense

DOT—Directly-observed Therapy

DUI—Driving Under the Influence

EEOC—Equal Employment Opportunity Commission

EHR—Electronic Health Record

EMAC—Emergency Management Assistance Compact

EMTALA—Emergency Medical Treatment & Active Labor Act

ENDS—Electronic Nicotine Delivery Systems

EPA—Environmental Protection Agency

EPT—Expedited Partner Therapy

EUA—Emergency Use Authorization

EVD—Ebola Viral Disease

FBI—Federal Bureau of Investigation

FDA—Food & Drug Administration

FERPA—Family Educational Rights & Privacy Act

FOIA—Freedom of Information Act

FSPTCA—Family Smoking Prevention & Tobacco Control Act

FTC—Federal Trade Commission

GINA—Genetic Information Nondiscrimination Act

HAI—Health-care Associated Infection

HCW—Health Care Worker

HHS—Department of Health & Human Services

HIA—Health Impact Assessment

HiAP—Health in All Policies

HIE—Health Information Exchange

HIPAA—Health Insurance Portability & Accountability Act

HIV/AIDS—Human Immunodeficiency Virus/ Acquired Immunodeficiency Syndrome

HPV—Human Papillomavirus

HSR—Human Subjects Research

HUD—Department of Housing & Urban Development

IDU—Injecting Drug User

IOM—Institute of Medicine (*see also* **NASEM**)

IRB—Institutional Review Board

JAMA—Journal of the American Medical Association

JLME—Journal of Law, Medicine & Ethics

MCM—Medical countermeasure

MDR—Multidrug-resistant

MMWR—Morbidity & Mortality Weekly Report

MRSA—Methicillin-resistant Staphylococcus Aureus

MSEHPA—Model State Emergency Health Powers Act

MSPHPA—Model State Public Health Privacy Act

NASEM—National Academies of Science, Engineering & Medicine

NCHS—National Center for Health Statistics

NDMS—National Disaster Medical System

NEA—National Emergencies Act

NEJM—New England Journal of Medicine

NEP—Needle Exchange Program

NHTSA—National Highway Traffic Safety Administration

NLEA—Nutritional Labeling & Education Act

NRA—National Rifle Association

NSDUH—National Survey on Drug Use & Health

OCR—Office for Civil Rights

OHRP—Office for Human Research Protections

OSHA—Occupational Safety & Health Administration

PAHPA—Pandemic & All-Hazards Preparedness Act

PCRS—Partner Counseling & Referral Services

PHA—Public Health Authority (as used in reference to HIPAA Privacy Rule)

PHE—Public Health Emergency

PHI—Protected Health Information

PHLR—Public Health Law Research

PHSA—Public Health Service Act

PI—Principal Investigator

PLCAA—Protection of Lawful Commerce in Arms Act

PREP—Public Readiness & Emergency Preparedness

PTSD—Post-traumatic Stress Disorder

RFRA—Religious Freedom Restoration Act

SAMHSA—Substance Abuse & Mental Health Services Administration

SCOTUS—Supreme Court of the United States

SIF—Supervised Injection Facility

SNS—Strategic National Stockpile

SOFA—Sequential Organ Failure Assessment

SSB—Sugar-Sweetened Beverage

STD—Sexually Transmitted Disease

STI—Sexually Transmitted Infection

TB—Tuberculosis

TFAH—Trust for America's Health

UN—United Nations

USDA—U.S. Department of Agriculture

USPSTF—U.S. Preventive Services Task Force

WHO—World Health Organization

XDR—Extreme Drug Resistant

PUBLIC HEALTH LAW

IN A NUTSHELL®

FIFTH EDITION

PART I

CORE STRUCTURE & BASES OF PUBLIC HEALTH LAW

Protecting and promoting the public's health are quintessential functions of government. Public health agencies and officials at the federal, state, and local levels are responsible (albeit in different ways) for accomplishing across societies what no person can secure individually: *assuring the health of communities*. LAWRENCE O. GOSTIN & LINDSAY F. WILEY, PUBLIC HEALTH LAW: POWER, DUTY, RESTRAINT 5–9 (3rd ed. 2016).

Meeting this objective is not easy. It requires significant public and private sector partnerships, constant surveillance, access to accurate and reliable data, state-of-the-art research, enhanced practice methods, effective education and training, ethical guidance, respect for cultural norms, and sufficient financing. *It also requires the law*.

Law is pivotal to nearly every public or private effort to advance the public's health. Understanding the field of public health law begins with an assessment of its core structure and bases. Chapter 1 examines prior and contemporary conceptions of public health law. It also introduces a modern definition of public health law as a guide for the remainder of the text. The source and scope of these laws at each level of government are explored in Chapter 2. This includes a brief overview of structural foundations embedded in constitutional law. Illustrated initially in Figure I.1, below, these structural constitutional principles include federalism, separation of powers, and preemption. As discussed thoroughly in Chapter 2, assessing and applying each of these principles is critical to generating sound public health laws and policies. Understanding how these principles work together within the "constitutional lot" depicted below entails a finer assessment of their impacts collectively.

Figure I.1. The "Constitutional Lot"

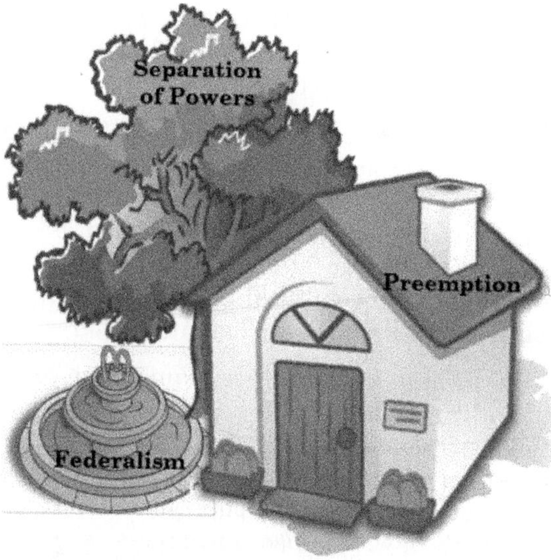

Consistent with an understanding of public health law that regularly balances communal and individual interests, Chapter 3 lays out primary rights-based limitations on the powers of government to protect the public's health. Examples of these rights include due process, equal protection, and freedom of speech. For additional reference, *see also* the U.S. Constitution Bill of Rights and 14th Amendment after the Preface/Introduction. Together with structural principles, these rights present a cohesive, constitutional framework initially described in Chapter 3 and revisited in Parts II and III of the text.

CHAPTER 1

THE FIELD OF PUBLIC HEALTH LAW

	Chapter 1—Learning Objectives
✓	1. Understand historic & modern foundations of U.S. public health practice
✓	2. Assess initial & current definitions of public health law as a field of legal study
✓	3. Explore how law is wielded effectively to assure healthy conditions
✓	4. Recognize the need for efficacy regarding the laws protecting communal health
✓	5. Examine the role of public health ethics in generating public health legal responses

Public health vigilance is essential because the threats to communal health are always changing. Just a century ago, outbreaks of infectious diseases like smallpox, polio, yellow fever, and malaria arose commonly in many U.S. localities. HANS ZINSSER, RATS, LICE & HISTORY: A CHRONICLE OF PESTILENCE AND PLAGUES (1963). Today, natural occurrences of smallpox are globally eradicated, and polio is virtually wiped out. Many other communicable conditions like malaria are controlled and largely forgotten in the U.S., though they continue to plague populations in developing countries. GEORGE ROSEN, A HISTORY OF PUBLIC HEALTH (1993).

Still, new communicable disease threats are always on the horizon. Some like HIV/AIDS in the early 1980s, H1N1 influenza in 2009, Ebola Viral Disease (EVD) in 2014, Zika virus in 2016, and COVID-19 in 2020 emerge from distant locales. Others, like the rapid spread of measles in early 2015 and subsequent years, are homegrown menaces emanating from gaps in vaccination coverage. Jennifer Zipprich et. al., *Measles Outbreak—CA, Dec. 2014–Feb. 2015*, 64 MMWR 153, 153 (2015).

Public health challenges in the U.S. have shifted to include conditions such as cancers and other chronic illnesses, obesity, opioids, injuries, and environmental health risks. A key lesson of the COVID-19 pandemic in 2020–2021 is that the future of public health invariably entails new risks that are either unknown currently or outside the public's view. The history of public health law evinces constant evolution to support public and private approaches to address these ever-changing threats.

A. PUBLIC HEALTH LAW: THEN & NOW

Protecting the public's health once centered largely on the control of infectious diseases and implementation of sanitary practices through federal entities like the U.S. Public Health Service and thousands of state, tribal, and local agencies. FITZHUGH MULLAN, PLAGUES & POLITICS: THE STORY OF THE U.S. PUBLIC HEALTH SERVICE 58 (1989).

As threats to communal health became clearer with significant improvements in epidemiology (i.e., the study of diseases), what it meant to "advance the public's health" surpassed initial conceptions. In 1988, the Institute of Medicine (IOM) (later enveloped into the National Academies of Science, Engineering & Medicine (NASEM)) issued a modern view of public health as ". . . what we, as a society, do collectively to assure the conditions for people to be healthy." IOM, THE FUTURE OF PUBLIC HEALTH 19 (1988).

INSTITUTE OF MEDICINE
OF THE NATIONAL ACADEMIES

IOM's definition reflected a considerable expansion of the mission and objectives of public health. As U.S. Surgeon General Vivek Murthy noted in 2015, "[t]he truth is whenever large numbers of people are dying for preventable reasons, that's a public health issue." Lenny Bernstein, *Surgeon General Vivek Murthy Wants to Move U.S. Health*

Care Toward a "Prevention-based Society," WASH. POST, Apr. 23, 2015.

Under IOM's broad conception, nearly any public or private sector intervention that directly or indirectly affects communal health is within the gambit of modern public health practice, including environmental hazards, injury prevention, occupational safety, and housing. Reflective of this this broad conception, the American Public Health Association has classified "10 Essential Public Health Services," centered around equity (as per Figure 1.1).

Figure 1.1. "10 Essential Public Health Services"

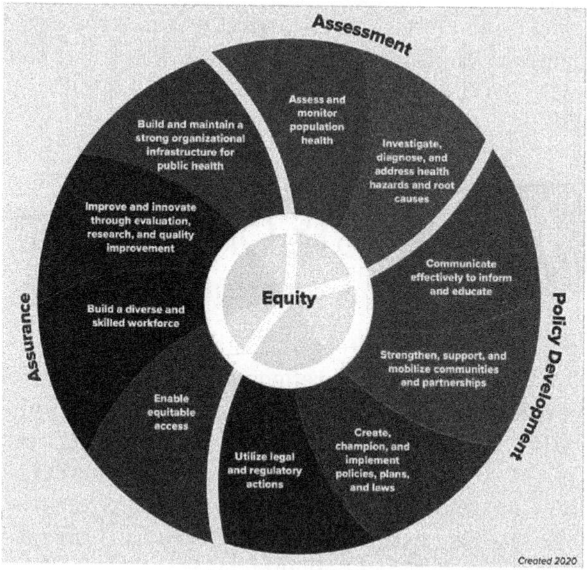

These interventions interplay with individuals' efforts to make healthy choices within a society focused on abating collective risks to individual and community health.

The value of a broader vision for public health in the modern era is undeniable. It has contributed to more sophisticated and sweeping approaches on how to engineer improved public health outcomes, allocate health resources equitably, eliminate health disparities, and counter negative impacts on population health. Public health advocates promote, for example, the concept of "health in all policies" (HIAP) to encourage greater attention to health outcomes related to specific public or private decisions (e.g., the placement, design, and construction of modern housing). WHO, HIAP: TRAINING MANUAL (Vivien Stone ed., 2015); ASTHO, HIAP EVALUATION TOOL FOR STATE & LOCAL HEALTH DEPT'S (2024).

As per Figure 1.2, the Robert Wood Johnson Foundation® has framed its objectives around what it calls a "culture of health." Alonzo L. Plough, *Building a Culture of Health: Challenges for the Public Health Workforce*, 47 AM. J. PREV. MED. S388 (2014). A "culture of health" reflects the collective efforts to improve population-level well-being within a diverse society for long-term benefits to health and health systems.

Figure 1.2. The "Culture of Health"

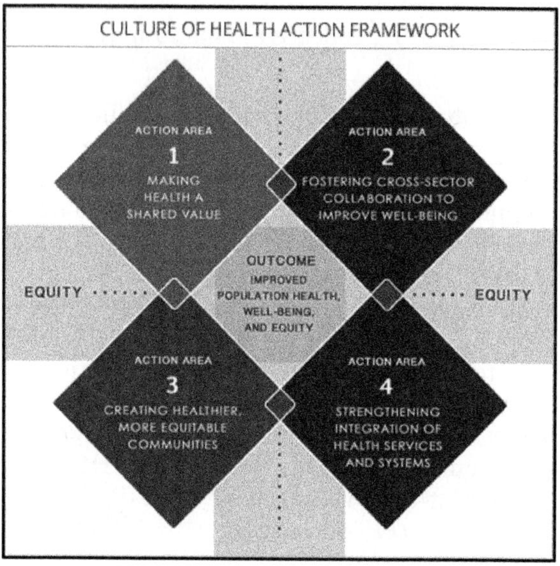

Since health is fundamental to all economic sectors, policies that affect the social determinants of health (including schools, zoning, food, transportation, and workplaces) can be formulated in consideration of their potential positive and negative health impacts. IOM, FOR THE PUBLIC'S HEALTH: REVITALIZING L. & POL'Y TO MEET NEW CHALLENGES (2011). In furtherance of this goal, governmental and private actors have developed innovative health impact assessments (HIAs) (*see* definition in the text box) to better measure the public health ramifications of policies prior to their implementation. NASEM, IMPROVING HEALTH IN THE

U.S.: THE ROLE OF HIAS (2011); JAMES G. HODGE, JR. ET AL., LEGAL REV. CONCERNING USE OF HIAS IN NON-HEALTH SECTORS (2012).

Health Impact Assessments—Defined
"A combination of procedures, methods, and tools by which a policy, program, or project may be judged as to its potential effects on the health of a population, and the distribution of those effects within the population."   *Source*: European Centre for Health Policy, *HIA: Main Concepts and Suggested Approach*, Gothenburg consensus paper, Brussels, 1999.

In the U.S., HIAs have been used to assess the health effects of multiple projects and actions including:

- a bicycle lane proposal to connect off-road bike trails in Washington, DC (2011);
- the impact of sugar-sweetened beverage (SSB) taxes on low income groups and communities of color in Los Angeles County (2013);
- regulations for retail marijuana packaging in Colorado (2013);
- greater access to prison-alternative programs in Wisconsin (2015); and
- a proposal to implement full-day kindergarten in Nevada (2018).

See HIAs in the U.S.: HIA Project, PEW TRUSTS (2018).

Adopting an HIAP approach nationally that incorporates extensive use of HIAs to assess varied interventions consistent with a "culture of health" may invariably contribute to healthier, more equitable societies. Utilization of law as a premier tool toward addressing and ameliorating social determinants of health is a proven intervention capable of substantial health improvements across populations. *See* Lawrence O. Gostin, James G. Hodge, Jr. & Donna E. Levin, *Legal Interventions to Address U.S. Reductions in Life Expectancy*, 324 JAMA 1027 (2020).

Multiple commentators, for example, espouse the effects of national or state laws limiting voting rights of minority or vulnerable populations. Recent U.S. Supreme Court jurisprudence allowing arguably improper racial redistricting under the guise of political gerrymandering strips affected populations from their abilities to vote in favor of public health or other policies. *Alexander v. S.C. Nat. Assoc. for the Advancement of Colored People*, 144 S. Ct. 1221 (2024). Others point to the lack of broadband internet access especially among rural populations as a profound public health threat. Natalie C. Benda, et al. *Broadband Internet Access Is a Social Determinant of Health!*, 110 AJPH 1123 (2020).

These and other examples evince the critical role of laws and policies in promotion of social determinants of health as a public good. Few contest these findings amid emerging social science findings.

Yet, others suggest that a holistic view of the field dilutes the core of what it means to protect the public's health. By spreading thin available resources to address sometimes tangential issues, essential functions of public health (like infectious disease control or food adulteration) may be diminished. In an era in which public health agencies at all levels of government face substantial communicable and chronic disease threats and chronic funding shortages (prior to and after the COVID-19 pandemic—*see* Chapter 12), envisioning a broader mission for public health may be largely beyond reach. *See, e.g.*, David Himmelstein & Steffie Woolhandler, *Public Health's Falling Share of U.S. Spending*, 106 AJPH 56 (2016).

B. DEFINING PUBLIC HEALTH LAW

Just as the practice of public health is not static, neither is public health law. The scope and range of public health laws have expanded over decades. Historic conceptions focused largely on public health powers related to communicable disease control and sanitation. In 1926, Yale University lecturer James Tobey set forth an early definition: "Public health law is that branch of jurisprudence which [applies] common and statutory law to the principles of hygiene and sanitary science." JAMES A. TOBEY, PUBLIC HEALTH LAW: A MANUAL OF LAW FOR SANITARIANS 6–7 (1926). Tobey and other practitioners of this era focused mostly on state and local laws authorizing traditional public health powers of vaccination, isolation, quarantine, testing, screening, treatment, inspection, and abatement of unsanitary conditions or other health nuisances.

As the practice of public health shifted increasingly beyond infectious conditions over several decades, modern assessments of public health law emerged. In the 1st edition of his PUBLIC HEALTH LAW MANUAL in 1965, Columbia Law Professor Frank Grad shared a broader view of public health law as including "provisions [that] have some considerable relationship to the maintenance of health and the prevention of disease." FRANK P. GRAD, THE PUBLIC HEALTH LAW MANUAL 9 (1965).

No longer bound to historic notions of public health functions and core responsibilities, public health law continued to develop as a distinct field. In the 2nd edition of his MANUAL in 1990, Professor Grad noted: "[Public health law] seek[s] to enhance public health not only by prohibiting harmful activities or conditions but also by providing preventive and rehabilitative services to advance the health of the people . . . ." FRANK P. GRAD, THE PUBLIC HEALTH LAW MANUAL 9 (2nd ed. 1990).

Professor Lawrence O. Gostin at Georgetown University Law Center has crafted an influential, modern definition of public health law. In a series of articles and texts on public health law, Professor Gostin lays out a modern conception of the field that incorporates IOM's expansive view of public health:

> Public health law is the study of the legal powers and duties of the state to assure conditions for people to be healthy (to identify, prevent, and

> ameliorate risks to health in the population) and the limitations on the power of the state to constrain the autonomy, privacy, liberty, proprietary, or other legally protected interests of individuals for the common good.

LAWRENCE O. GOSTIN & LINDSAY F. WILEY, PUBLIC HEALTH LAW: POWER, DUTY, RESTRAINT 4 (3rd ed. 2016).

Like Professor Grad, Professor Gostin seeks to extend the reach of public health law well beyond initial conceptions focused on communicable disease control and hygiene. However, Professor Gostin's definition is among the 1st to reflect the compelling balance at work in public health law between the (1) powers of government to act "to ensure the conditions to be healthy" and (2) constraints on these powers to promote or protect individual rights.

Under this view, neither public health powers nor individual freedoms are absolute. Rather, they are consistently at play in determining the breadth and limit of the role of law in the interests of communal health. Professor Wendy Parmet at Northeastern University School of Law recognizes this same dynamic when she notes "[p]ublic health law . . . focuses on the authority of government agencies charged with protecting public health as well as the rights of individuals subject to such regulations." WENDY E. PARMET, POPULATIONS, PUBLIC HEALTH & THE LAW 212–13 (2009).

These sophisticated themes not only raise the scholarly level of study of public health law, they clarify its practice. Public health law is not solely about governments' inherent powers nor individuals' fundamental rights. It is about how these respective components merge to generate meaningful and defensible legal interventions to advance the population's health.

Based on these varied approaches, for the purposes of this text, I define *public health law* as the following:

Public Health Law—Defined
Public health law includes laws (e.g., constitutional, statutory, regulatory, judicial), legal processes, or policies at every level of government (e.g., federal, tribal, state, local) that: 1. are *primarily* designed to assure the conditions for people to be healthy; or 2. concern structural or rights-based limitations on the powers of government to act in the interests of communal health.

At the epicenter of this and other modern definitions of public health law is the dynamic interplay of legal powers and restraints central to the accomplishment of public health objectives through law. Like Professor Gostin, I incorporate IOM's original conception of assuring conditions for people to be healthy. This view intimates a broad and active role for law beyond mere control of communicable diseases and sanitation improvements. The extension of law in diverse areas like education, transportation, and housing to protect and promote health among populations is core to the modern field.

My definition also acknowledges significant limitations on the role of law. While laws can obligate public and private sectors to act in the interests of the public's health, they simultaneously curtail these powers. Unlike Professors Gostin's and Parmet's definitions, which concentrate on rights-based limitations, my definition specifically recognizes rights-based *and* structural limitations on the public health powers of government. Discussed in more detail in Chapter 2, structural limits include principles of *separation of powers* (delineating responsibilities among the 3 branches of government), *federalism* (distinguishing between federal and state governmental authorities), and *preemption* (allowing higher levels of government to abate or override conflicting laws at lower levels). Rights-based limits embedded in constitutional norms and other laws (discussed further in Chapter 3) include individual rights to free expression, freedom of religion, bodily integrity, privacy, equal protection, and due process.

Though still vast in its scope, public health law is corralled by my specification that any such law be ***primarily*** designed to assure healthy conditions. This is meant to rein in the field by excluding from its study those laws that may have only tertiary or unintended effects on the public's health (as per the text box below).

Local Zoning Laws—2 Types

1. A city enacts a zoning ordinance to advance the public's health by limiting the locations of fast food restaurants near elementary or secondary schools. *See, e.g.*, LOS ANGELES, CAL., ORDINANCE 180103 (Sept. 14, 2008) (restricting the placement of new, freestanding restaurants in specific areas of the city). This type of modern zoning law attempts to further the public's health by limiting kids' access to fast food to lower childhood obesity. Consequently, it fits neatly in the field of public health law.

2. Another city enacts a zoning ordinance requiring private planners to limit the size and placement of commercial signage in suburban areas. *See e.g.,* FRANKLIN CNTY., OHIO ZONING RESOL. § 541 (2014) (requiring billboards smaller than 300 sq. ft. to be located at least 200 ft. from residential districts and at least 25 ft. from public streets). The primary objective is to preserve or enhance community aesthetics. An unintended effect is the limiting of commercial visibility of specific businesses (e.g., tobacco shops and liquor stores), leading some consumers to access them less often with tertiary public health benefits. This type of zoning law falls outside the field of public health law.

Distinguishing between these different types of zoning laws may seem non-purposeful when both could positively impact the public's health. Some public health practitioners may strongly advocate for the implementation of aesthetic zoning laws largely because of their community health benefits regardless of whether city council members approve, or even know about, their public health implications. However, broadening the study of public health law to any statute, regulation, or other law having any tangential effect on the health of communities extends the field well beyond the scope of this text.

C. BUILDING EVIDENCE FOR PUBLIC HEALTH LAW

One of the dominant themes emanating from modern conceptions of the field is how law is used as an affirmative tool for public health improvements. *See, e.g.*, Anthony D. Moulton et al., *The Scientific Basis for Law as a Public Health Tool*, 99 AJPH 17, 24 (2009). Like other tools available to public health practitioners such as surveillance, epidemiologic investigations, or educational campaigns, law can be wielded effectively to accomplish communal health goals.

In some cases, law is the principal means to achieve a public health outcome. For years after the advent of effective and safe vaccines for childhood diseases, thousands of children nationally continued to develop preventable conditions. In response, many state legislatures enacted school vaccination laws (conditioning attendance at school upon proof of vaccination for specified conditions) in the early 1900s. As a direct result, childhood vaccination rates climbed and related morbidity and mortality plummeted, demonstrating the efficacy of these laws. *See, e.g.*, James G. Hodge, Jr. & Lawrence O. Gostin, *School Vaccination Requirements: Historical, Social, & Legal Perspectives*, 90 KY. L. J. 831 (2002). School (and day-care) vaccination laws continue to be a core component of child and adolescent health policy (discussed in Chapters 3 and 4).

While the efficacy of vaccination laws is firmly established, many other public health laws lack a sufficient nexus with public health improvements. Reflecting a patchwork approach, many state and local jurisdictions have passed or implemented public health laws over decades that are thought to be functional, but are largely unproven. Though often well-intended, these laws may be supported more so by political guesswork or anecdotes than actual scientific efficacy. Initially, few researchers explored the effectiveness of law as a public health tool even as laws increasingly became a mode of choice to address known public health threats. *See* Scott Burris & Evan D. Anderson, *Legal Regulation of Health-Related Behavior: A Half-Century of PHLR*, 9 ANN. REV. L. & SOC. SCI. 95 (2013).

Mere belief that law is an effective tool for improving public health outcomes is an insufficient basis for legal intervention. Proof of efficacy may be needed increasingly to counteract politicized arguments against the use of law to address public health threats such as COVID-19, obesity, tobacco advertisements, and gun-related violence. Generating greater support on the effectiveness of public health laws is the focus of modern research initiatives launched initially in 2009 through the Public Health Law Research (PHLR) program funded by the Robert Wood Johnson Foundation. Program leaders define "public health law research" as "the scientific study of the relation of law and legal practices to population health." ALEXANDER C. WAGENAAR & SCOTT BURRIS, PHLR: THEORY & METHODS 4 (2013).

PHLR grantees have conducted independent research and examined existing evidence to support the effectiveness of laws and policies related to:

- fluoridating water to reduce tooth decay and improve oral health;
- raising taxes on alcohol to reduce overall consumption;
- requiring directed patrols to lower gun-related crime by uncovering and deterring illegal gun possession in high-risk areas;
- mandating use of child safety seats to substantially reduce injuries to children during vehicular crashes;
- implementing selective breath testing sobriety checkpoints to reduce the harms associated with alcohol impaired driving;
- using red light cameras to lower vehicle crash fatalities; and

- focusing on treatment and rehabilitation through courts to lower recidivism among individuals convicted of drug-related offenses.

D. THE ROLE OF PUBLIC HEALTH ETHICS

Acknowledging an expansive (and increasingly proven) role of law to protect the public's health may suggest that law- and policy-makers can use law at will to motivate or require choices or behaviors among individuals and groups. To be sure, law has been used in heavy-handed ways in the guise of promoting the community's health. Historic examples discussed later in the text include numerous instances in which state and local governments confined, vaccinated, tested, or imposed other measures on unwilling individuals without justification in the name of public health prevention and control.

The legality of public health interventions, however, cannot be divorced from their ethicality. "The prime objective of public health law is to pursue the highest possible level of physical and mental health in the population, consistent with the values of social justice." LAWRENCE O. GOSTIN & LINDSAY F. WILEY, PUBLIC HEALTH LAW: POWER, DUTY, RESTRAINT 4 (3rd ed. 2016).

Principles of ethics influence the development and enforcement of law, often providing guidance where the law cannot. For example, public health law may allow for the confinement of persons with infectious diseases like tuberculosis (TB) when they present a threat to others. *See* SHEILA M. ROTHMAN, LIVING IN

THE SHADOW OF DEATH: TB & THE SOCIAL EXPERIENCE OF ILLNESS IN AM. HISTORY (1994). An individual's liberties may unquestionably be curtailed legally when they pose serious risks to others related to infectious diseases (*see* Chapter 5).

However, ethical norms guide appropriate uses of these legal authorities to those rare cases where individuals refuse either to voluntarily participate in treatment programs or defuse the risks of transmitting TB to others. Increasingly, modern TB control laws reflect what is known as an "ethic of voluntarism" to respect individual autonomy even when others' health may be at some slight risk.

Framed by the utilitarian goal of achieving the greatest health outcomes for the most persons possible, public health ethics reflect other norms (such as bioethics principles of autonomy, beneficence, non-maleficence, and justice), but are in fact distinct. In 2002, the Public Health Leadership Society enunciated a series of 12 core public health ethics principles.

Core Public Health Ethics Principles

Public health actors and entities should:

1. address principally the fundamental causes of disease and requirements for health, aiming to prevent adverse health outcomes;
2. achieve community health with respect for the rights of individuals in the community;

3. be evaluated through processes that ensure opportunities for community input;
4. empower disenfranchised communities to assure basic health resources/conditions for all;
5. seek information needed to implement effective health policies and programs;
6. provide communities with needed information and obtain community consent;
7. act expeditiously on information within available resources and public mandates;
8. respect diverse community values, beliefs, and cultures;
9. implement programs that most enhance the physical and social environment;
10. protect confidentiality of information that can harm individuals or communities;
11. ensure professional competence of personnel; and
12. engage in collaborations that build the public's trust and institutional effectiveness and obtain community's consent for their implementation.

Principles of public health ethics center on the inherent moral responsibilities of providing for the public's health through government and the private sector. James C. Thomas et al., *A Code of Ethics for*

Public Health, 92 AJPH 1057 (2002); James C. Thomas et al., *Code of Ethics for Public Health*, in INT'L ENCYCLOPEDIA OF PUB. HEALTH 71–74 (2nd ed. 2016). They pertain not merely to those who practice public health sciences or deliver services (many of whom may also adhere to ethics codes for their respective medical or other professions), but also to how public health initiatives are applied. Public health actors must assure their interventions are effective, necessary, proportional, equitable, and transparent. Consistent with modern social justice theory and principles of health equity, limited resources must be fairly allocated and communal burdens adequately shared. MADISON POWERS & RUTH FADEN, SOCIAL JUSTICE: THE MORAL FOUNDATIONS OF PUBLIC HEALTH & HEALTH POLICY (2006).

Applying principles of public health ethics can be complicated, especially if government acts in paternal ways to the detriment of individual freedoms or choices. Though often legally sound and democratically-driven, programmatic decisions via government that dictate the terms in which autonomous persons must behave or adhere to specific protocols are ethically suspect. James Childress et al., *Public Health Ethics: Mapping the Terrain*, 30 JLME 170, 175–176 (2002).

Thus, while government can require children to be vaccinated as a condition of school attendance, legally mandating that adults (e.g., emergency room nurses) be vaccinated is ethically challenging. Alexandra M. Stewart et al., *Mandatory Vaccination of Health-Care Personnel: Good Policy, Law & Outcomes*, 53 JURIMETRICS J. 431 (2013); *see also* Chapter 12 for discussion of COVID-19 vaccine mandates). Many health professionals view government's issuance of vaccine mandates as coercive even though providers may have a duty to protect patient safety. *See* Richard K. Zimmerman et al., *Hosp. Policies, State Laws & HCW Influenza Rates*, 34 INFECTION CONTROL & HOSP. EPIDEMIOLOGY 854 (2013).

In *Horvath v. City of Leander*, 946 F.3d 787 (5th Cir. 2020), a federal appellate court affirmed a policy of the City of Leander (TX) resulting in the termination of a fire department/EMS employee seeking a religious exemption from a vaccine requirement. The employee refused multiple alternative job accommodations with the same employer that presented fewer risks for unvaccinated personnel. Such accommodations were sufficient, ruled the court.

A year later, in *Labarbera v. NYU Winthrop Hospital*, No. 18–cv–6737, 2021 WL 980873 (E.D.N.Y. 2021), a New York federal district court rejected discrimination claims brought by a pregnant employee fired for non-compliance with her hospital's employee flu vaccination requirement. She alleged that the hospital did not consider pregnancy an acceptable medical contraindication under its vaccine mandate. The court concluded that federal determinations that vaccines are safe for pregnant women invalidated her claims of unwarranted discrimination.

Other measures, such as laws requiring seatbelt use in vehicles or helmets when operating motorcycles or bicycles, may be viewed as overly paternalistic (*see* discussion in Chapter 7). Under an alternative view known as *libertarian paternalism*, institutions can "self-consciously [attempt] to move people in directions that will make their lives better," without having to curb individual choices. RICHARD H. THALER & CASS R. SUNSTEIN, NUDGE: IMPROVING DECISIONS ABOUT HEALTH, WEALTH & HAPPINESS 6 (2009). For example, instead of government making people purchase broccoli (which was famously argued as part of federal health care reform debates in 2011–2012), it might consider requiring the placement of healthier foods like broccoli in higher traffic areas of stores to encourage their purchase and consumption. *Id.*

Public health ethics ultimately incorporate substantive and procedural elements to advance communal health. Professor Nancy E. Kass at the Johns Hopkins Bloomberg School of Public Health lays out a series of ethical steps to consider before implementation of any public health program or intervention:

- Identify goals that aid in decreasing morbidity or mortality;
- Determine whether data exist to indicate that tactics will be effective;
- Consider potential burdens, particularly risks to privacy, liberty, and justice;

- Examine whether alternatives would mitigate these burdens while maintaining effectiveness;
- Distribute benefits and burdens fairly based on data rather than arbitrary or stereotypical reasons; and
- Analyze whether the benefits outweigh the burdens.

Nancy E. Kass, *An Ethics Framework for Public Health*, 91 AJPH 1776 (2001).

Consistent with Professor Kass' approach and guidance from countless others, multiple model principles of public health ethics have been extensively generated and applied especially in emergencies. During the COVID-19 pandemic (*see* Chapter 12), for example, extensive ethical guidance on allocations of scarce resources including tests, personal protective equipment, treatments, and vaccines were generated to help set priorities.

The National Academies of
SCIENCES · ENGINEERING · MEDICINE

A NASEM committee, for example, rapidly studied and produced real-time guidance on COVID-19 vaccine distributions that were heavily relied on by policymakers. NASEM framed allocations in terms of phased approaches designed to assure fair and equitable access to those in greatest need of vaccines initially, with additional distributions to others as supplies increased. *A Framework for Equitable Allocation of Vaccine for the Novel Coronavirus*, NASEM (Sep. 1, 2020).

Beyond early views that limited the role of law to traditional public health areas of infectious disease control and sanitation, the field of public health law has matured to align public health practice, science, politics, and ethics to promote community health and safety. Relying on more than historic tradition and modern guesswork, new research reveals the efficacy of specific public health legal interventions. Law can be an affirmative tool for positive public health outcomes. Realizing its full potential, however, requires a strong understanding of the source and scope of public health laws at the federal, state, and local levels. This is the focus of Chapter 2.

	Chapter 1—Discussion Questions
?	1. How has the definition of public health law changed over the last century?
?	2. How might public health law be defined 50–100 years from now based on these or other changes?
?	3. What are the core constitutional components in public health law & policy?
?	4. Why is it essential to demonstrate efficacy in the use of law to promote the public's health?
?	5. How do principles of public health ethics supplement or influence public health laws & policies?

CHAPTER 2

SOURCE & SCOPE OF PUBLIC HEALTH LEGAL POWERS

	Chapter 2—Learning Objectives
✓	1. Explore the theories & applied facets of core structural principles of constitutional law
✓	2. Determine how differing levels & branches of government collaborate on public health laws
✓	3. Understand how principles of preemption can help or hinder public health laws
✓	4. Assess how specific applications of structural principles impact public health innovations
✓	5. Ascertain legal distinctions among federal, state & local public health powers

The source and scope of governmental powers to address communal health are core to the definition of public health law. As per the discussion in Chapter 1, protecting the population's health is a fundamental responsibility of government. However, determining which level of government is empowered to implement and enforce public health laws can be challenging. Federal, state, and local governments often work together to address public health issues. Yet, sometimes they clash over who is in charge, or refuse to address public health initiatives even though they clearly have the legal power to act. Public health authority hinges on the proper distribution and allocation of powers outlined in the U.S. Constitution.

Constitutional obligations of government to protect individuals and populations from communal health threats vary extensively due in part to government's responsibility to differing persons in society. Government's health responsibilities related to specific persons (e.g., prisoners, institutionalized persons with mental disabilities) are linked to these persons' non-autonomous status. Prisoners, for example, are considered wards of the state by virtue of their incarceration. Federal constitutional principles prohibiting cruel and unusual punishments via the 8th Amendment necessitate the provision of basic health and public health services within correctional facilities. *Brown v. Plata*, 563 U.S. 493 (2011) (medical and mental health care provided in California's prisons fell below the standard of decency required by the 8th Amendment due in part to overcrowding).

Protecting the health of other vulnerable persons or the general public, however, is not constitutionally guaranteed. In most cases, government is not required to assure the health of specific individuals, much less the public. In *DeShaney v. Winnebago County Department of Social Services*, 489 U.S. 189 (1989), SCOTUS considered a child's claim against Wisconsin county agencies. Joshua DeShaney was mercilessly abused by his father while supposedly under the watchful eye of local child welfare services. Eventually, the child suffered permanent physical and mental injuries. Joshua and his mother sued multiple governmental agents, alleging Wisconsin officials deprived Joshua of his liberty under the Due Process Clause of the 14th Amendment.

Dismissing the claim, Chief Justice William Rehnquist (*see* Figure 2.1 below) famously concluded that absent a "special relationship" (e.g., such as the relationship between government and prisoners or other wards), "a State's failure to protect an individual against private violence simply does not constitute a violation of [due process]." *Id.* at 197.

Figure 2.1. Chief Justice William Rehnquist

As a result, Joshua and his mother could not recover damages from government officials even though their acts or omissions may have contributed to the child's long-term disabilities. As Justice Blackmun lamented in his dissent, "Poor Joshua." *Id.* at 213.

In 2005, the Supreme Court clarified that due process rights also did not confer a property interest sufficient to assure government action concerning a woman seeking enforcement of a restraining order issued by a local court in Colorado. *See Castle Rock v. Gonzales*, 545 U.S. 748 (2005). Based on these and related decisions, the U.S. Constitution has not been interpreted to require federal, state, or local governments to actually assure communal health, or even at times the health and safety of specific persons. *See, e.g., Bush v. City of Utica*, 948 F. Supp.2d 246 (D.N.D. NY 2013) (rejecting due process claim alleging failure to provide life-saving, fire protection efforts); James G. Hodge, Jr. et al., *Constitutional Cohesion & the Right to Public Health,* 53 MICH. J. L. REFORM 173, 179–188 (2019) (discussed in Chapter 3).

Even abject failures to act in the interests of at-risk individuals rarely lead to legal action against government agencies or officials, often due to statutory immunities protecting them from liability. For example, in *City of Los Angeles v. Superior Court*, 276 Cal. Rptr. 3d 332 (Ct. App. 2021), a police officer's wife sued the City of Los Angeles for negligence and "a dangerous condition of public property" after her husband contracted typhus from "unsanitary conditions" at the police station and later transmitted it to her. Although the trial court determined the City owed a duty of care to the officer's wife, on appeal the higher court found the city was immune on the grounds that "[a] public entity's liability must be based on statute," which was unsatisfied in this case.

Beginning in June 2017, however, multiple state and local health officials in Flint, Michigan were charged with various crimes, including involuntary manslaughter, for their alleged failures to properly alert the public about the potential for contracting Legionnaire's disease, exposure to lead, and other public health harms from faulty public water systems. Brakkton Booker, *Ex-Michigan Gov. Rick Snyder & 8 Others Criminally Charged in Flint Water Crisis*, NPR (Jan. 14, 2021). Multiple illnesses and at least 12 deaths within the affected community ensued over months before health officials properly informed the public of the risks.

While initial charges were dropped against officials in 2019, in January 2021, a Michigan grand jury announced the indictment of 9 officials on 42 criminal counts. Mich. Att'y Gen., *Flint Water Prosecution Team Expands Investigation Based on New Evidence, Dismisses Cases Brought by Former Special Counsel*, MICHIGAN.GOV (June 13, 2019); *see also Guertin v. Michigan*, 912 F.3d 907 (6th Cir. 2019), *cert. denied sub nom. City of Flint v. Guertin*, 140 S. Ct. 933 (2020) (allowing due process and other claims brought by injured Flint residents to proceed against the state and select agents). Ultimately, these charges against officials were dismissed in 2022 by the Michigan Supreme Court. In October 2023, the state's Attorney General dropped plans to prosecute officials. Danny Wimmer, *Flint Water Prosecution Team Responds to Michigan Supreme Court's Decision on Last Remaining Flint Water Crisis Charges Against Rick Snyder*, MICH. DEP'T OF ATT'Y GEN. (Oct. 31, 2023).

In 2023, however, 2 municipally-employed paramedics in Colorado were found guilty of criminally-negligent homicide after they injected Elijah McClain with a lethal dose of ketamine during an arrest in 2019. One of the paramedics was also found guilty of associated assault charges. McClain was apprehended on a cold night on the street in his Denver-area community initially by law enforcement who received reports of his allegedly erratic behavior. McClain had a known history of mental health issues. His death attributed to forcible treatment during his arrest led to specific reforms nationally on how law enforcement and emergency workers handle similar cases. Colleen Slevin & Matthew Brown, *Paramedics Were Convicted in Elijah McClain's Death. That Could Make Other First Responders Pause*, AP NEWS, Dec. 23, 2023.

A. THE CONSTITUTIONAL FOUNTAIN OF PUBLIC HEALTH POWERS

The U.S. Constitution may not require government to assure the conditions for people to be healthy, but it does set the legal foundation for public and private health interventions. Principles of constitutional design (1) allocate power between the federal government and the states (federalism); (2) divide power among the 3 branches of government (separation of powers); (3) prioritize higher governments' laws over lower levels of government (preemption); and (4) impinge governmental powers to protect individual freedoms (examined in Chapter 3)). In these ways, the Constitution originates the flow of power to protect the public's health and simultaneously curbs such authorities to protect individual interests.

1. FEDERALISM

Among the unique facets of American democracy is the Constitutional principle of federalism. As per Figure 2.2, federalism distinguishes powers among the levels of governments.

Figure 2.2. Constitutional Fountain of Federalism

Like pools in a fountain, federal powers are separate and distinct from state and local powers. As explained below, the powers of the national government are enumerated and limited. Through the 10th Amendment, states are reserved sovereign power over "all the objects, which, in the ordinary course of affairs, concern the lives, liberties and properties of the people; and the internal order, improvement, and prosperity of the State." U.S. CONST. amend. X. These residual powers broadly authorize states to regulate matters affecting the health, safety, and general welfare of the public and their citizens.

Though ingenious as a structural principle of constitutional design, federalism applies in unpredictable ways. There is no bright line separating federal and state authorities. In reality, governments' respective powers have historically overlapped, especially in areas like public health. In many cases, principles of cooperative federalism render agreeable compromises. Yet, when federal and state powers collide or clash, the application of federalism takes on many shades and near imperceptible gradations. James G. Hodge, Jr., *The Role of New Federalism & Public Health Law*, 12 J. L. & HEALTH 309, 316 (1998).

For example, states may (a) seek to invade areas set aside for exclusive federal interventions (e.g., enacting laws which interfere with Congress' regulation of interstate commerce) or (b) fail to recognize federal supremacy or authority (e.g., attempting to impose taxes on federal goods). States' resistance to exercises of federal authority were common in the nation's early history as they tested the limits of their sovereign powers (discussed in sections below). Debates about the scope of Congress' powers to increase access to health services through the Patient Protection and Affordable Care Act (ACA) and various "repeal and replace" bills introduced during President Donald Trump's administration reflect similar themes. *NFIB v. Sebelius*, 567 U.S. 519 (2012) (discussed below); *see also* PATIENT CARE

& PROFESSIONALISM (Catherine D. DeAngelis ed., 2014).

Conversely, the federal government may attempt to intrude on state duties. Historically, federal exercises which interfered with traditional state powers were politically volatile. They were struck down routinely by courts assigning considerable weight to sovereign state police powers under the 10th Amendment. *See Hammer v. Dagenhart*, 247 U.S. 251 (1918) (federal statute prohibiting the interstate commerce of child labor products infringed on states' power to regulate child labor hours); *overruled by U.S. v. Darby*, 312 U.S. 100 (1941).

In theory, federal laws which moved into areas traditionally left to the states were beyond Congress' jurisdiction and thus unconstitutional under principles of federalism. Federal expansion during the New Deal Era (1933–1938) relaxed traditional conceptions of federalism, ushering in numerous federal interventions in public health and other areas. *See, e.g.*, James G. Hodge, Jr., *Federalism & Liberty: Reaching Constitutional Accord*, 72 KANSAS L. REV. 163 (2023). These include establishment of the U.S. Public Health Service in 1939 (*see* image in Chapter 1) and the Centers for Disease Control in 1946 (later renamed the Centers for Disease Control and Prevention (CDC), as per the image below).

Supreme Court jurisprudence accommodated these changes in many ways. In 1941, the Court observed in *Darby* that Congress' power may be "attended by the same incidents [as the] exercise of the police power of the states." 312 U.S. at 115. Later years saw the introduction of sweeping federal health care reforms through the Social Security Act Amendments of 1965, 42 U.S.C. § 1395 (2010), establishing Medicare and Medicaid programs, as well as significant environmental laws and policies.

Following decades of federal expansion into the public health sphere, political and judicial actors rediscovered and advocated for core principles of federalism. Collectively labeled "new federalism" among constitutional scholars in the 1990s, a series of influential decisions resulted in the Supreme Court's:

- adoption of a strong rule against federal invasion of "core state functions;"
- presumption against application of federal statutes to state and local political processes;
- disdain for federal actions that "commandeer" state governments into the service of federal regulatory purposes;

- rejection of federal claims brought by private parties against states; and
- application of a plain statement rule that Congress must "make its intention . . . unmistakably clear in the language of the statute" whenever it seeks to preempt state law so as to alter the balance of federalism. *Gregory v. Ashcroft*, 501 U.S. 452, 460 (1991).

See, e.g., James G. Hodge, Jr., *The Role of New Federalism*, 12 J. L. & HEALTH 309, 335 (1998).

Principles of new federalism re-opened state challenges of some federal public health laws on 10th Amendment grounds. ERWIN CHEMERINSKY, CONSTITUTIONAL LAW: PRINCIPLES & POLICIES 269–74 (4th ed. 2011). The Supreme Court's decision in *United States v. Lopez*, 514 U.S. 549 (1995), is illustrative. It held that Congress exceeded its Commerce powers by statutorily making gun possession within a local school zone a federal criminal offense. Finding a lack of "substantial affects" on interstate commerce, the Court declared the statute unconstitutional despite Congress' laudable, underlying public health objective in preventing gun-related violence at or near schools. *Id.* at 567.

Federalism continues to dominate political and judicial processes. In 2012, the Supreme Court opined that Congress lacked the Commerce power to require individuals to purchase health insurance (through what is known as the "individual mandate") via the ACA. Writing for the Court, Chief Justice

John Roberts (Figure 2.3) found instead that Congress' power to tax was sufficiently broad to justify the mandate. *Sebelius*, 567 U.S. at 570.

Figure 2.3. Chief Justice John Roberts

As a result, the ACA's individual mandate was upheld under federal tax authority, but not through Congress' power to regulate interstate commerce, thus preserving some traditional state-based authorities under principles of new federalism.

When Congress passed the Tax Cuts and Jobs Act, signed by President Trump on December 22, 2017, the penalty supporting the ACA's individual mandate provision was "zeroed" out. H.R. 115–97, 115th Cong. (2017). This meant that no American would be penalized for failing to secure health insurance despite the ACA's mandate provision. Absent the penalty, argued officials in Texas and 17 other states, the continued use of Congress' tax power in support of the provision must be unconstitutional. After years of contested litigation, the case was ultimately resolved by the Supreme Court on June 17, 2021. *California v. Texas*, 593 U.S. 659 (2021).

Writing for a 7–2 majority, Justice Stephen Breyer determined that all of the parties to the case, including 2 individuals and multiple states, lacked standing to raise their claims. Dismissing the case, he surmised "the plaintiffs . . . failed to show a concrete, particularized injury fairly traceable to enforcement of the individual mandate provision of the ACA."

2. SEPARATION OF POWERS

As depicted in Figure 2.4, federal and state constitutions explicitly separate governmental powers into 3 branches: (a) the legislative branch (with the power to create laws); (b) the executive branch (with the power to enforce laws); and (c) the judicial branch (with the power to interpret laws). Constitutional separation of governmental powers provides a system of checks and balances to help stymie the potential for government oppression. Each branch of government has unique constitutional authority to create, enforce, or interpret public health law and policy.

Figure 2.4. Separation of Powers

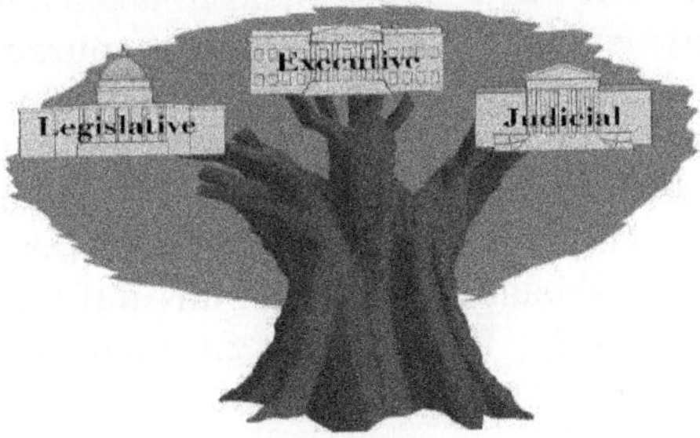

Legislative Branch. Federal and state legislatures largely create health policy and allocate necessary resources to effectuate it through introduction and passage of legislation. Legislative enactments are invariably the product of negotiations and compromise inherent in the political process. Once enacted and approved by the elected head of the executive branch (e.g., President or Governor), legislation takes precedence over competing laws and policies (often including prior legislation). Based on "conflicts of laws" principles, legislation can override executive or judicial actions so long as it is constitutionally-sound (among other factors).

To assure legislation furthers communal health objectives, legislators need reliable, accurate information on public health threats and interventions to make complex decisions that are also consistent with their constituents' interests and competing claims. *See* Chapter 8 for a considerable examination and discussion of public health data needs.

Executive Branch. The executive branch (primarily through public health departments or agencies) enforces health policy pursuant to delegated legislative authority. Such delegations can be extensive or narrow. For example, in creating a state public health agency, a state legislature may bestow it with broad powers to protect the public's health. The legislature may later direct the agency to perform specific functions (e.g., conduct disease surveillance, vaccinate specific populations, or conduct an HIA related to a transportation project). Under either broad or specific delegations of power, public health agencies take direction from the legislature and must act accordingly within the scope of their delegated powers consistent with principles of separation of powers.

Federal and state executive agencies may work in tandem with lawmakers to determine the extent and course of public health policies. Conflicts can arise when public health agencies attempt to create and administer complex health regulations which some legislators may not agree with in principle or policy. Concerning federal agencies, provided Congress articulates standards for issuance and enforcement of these regulations, the U.S. Supreme Court historically approved such delegations with related deference to agency interpretations.

In 2024, however, SCOTUS overturned its long-standing approach concerning judicial deference to reasonable interpretations of ambiguous statutory terms under *Chevron, U.S.A., Inc. v. NRDC, Inc.*, 467 U.S. 837 (1984). In 2 companion cases, *Loper Bright Enters. v. Raimondo*, 144 S.Ct. 2244 (2024) and *Relentless, Inc. v. U.S. Dep't of Com.*, 144 S.Ct. 2244 (2024) (hereinafter referred to collectively as *Loper*), the Court rejected Chevron deference as antiquated and inconsistent.

Characterizing agency deference under *Chevron* as a "legal fiction," Chief Justice John Roberts clarified in 6–3 majority decision that federal courts "may not" defer outright to agencies' interpretations of ambiguous statutes. Instead, courts must exercise their own independent judgment in determining the scope of federal agency authorities in the face of statutory ambiguities under Congressional direction via the Administrative Procedure Act (APA) of 1946 and principles of separation of powers.

Loper essentially abandoned *Chevron* deference once and for all after 40 years of divergent applications. In its place, Chief Justice Roberts proffered new guidance for courts reviewing ambiguous statutory authorities for agency regulations as follows:

1. "Courts must exercise their independent judgment in deciding whether an agency has acted within its statutory authority. . . ."

2. While "[c]areful attention to the judgment of the Executive Branch may help inform that inquiry," courts should not rely on agency interpretations in cases of ambiguities.

3. In specific instances where Congress statutorily "delegates authority to an agency consistent with constitutional limits, courts must respect the delegation, while ensuring that the agency acts within it." *Id.*

Stated succinctly, under *Loper* (1) sheer reliance on agency interpretations in cases of ambiguous Congressional delegations is out; (2) courts exercising their own independent judgements about the meaning of federal statutory law are in.

As per a scathing dissent by Justice Elena Kagan, abandoning *Chevron* deference carries profound consequences for federal public health agencies. Even though *Loper* does not apply directly in cases where agencies are interpreting their own regulations, the decision "puts courts at the apex of the administrative process . . . because there are always gaps and ambiguities in regulatory statutes." *Id.* What's "ambiguous" in Congressional statutory authorizations, concludes Justice Kagan, is always subject to interpretation.

The Court's decision in *Loper* comes on the heels of its diminution of agency regulatory authorities 2 years prior. In *West Virginia v. EPA*, 597 U.S. 697 (2022), the Court introduced what is referred to as the "major questions doctrine." Under this doctrine, Congress must explicitly authorize federal agency actions on substantial issues of "economic and political significance." *Id.* Federal agencies seeking to regulate in such areas must act under clear legislative delegation to avoid separation of powers violations. Under *West Virginia* federal health and environmental agencies' capacities to generate equitable, evidence-based regulations (absent express Congressional authorization) were curbed. *See, e.g.*, Erica N. White, *Overcoming the Major Questions Doctrine with Public Health Authorities*, 18 HARV. L. & POL'Y REV. 183 (2023).

Coupled with *Loper*, federal administrative regulatory powers are inhibited as federal courts take on enhanced responsibilities as public policy decision-makers (despite lacking subject-matter expertise). *See, e.g.*, James G. Hodge, Jr., Jennifer L. Piatt, Erica N. White, et al., *Supreme Court Impacts in Public Health Law: 2023–2024*, 52(3) JLME 482 (2024). SCOTUS' deregulation of administrative powers includes decisions extending the period of time for bringing challenges, *Corner Post, Inc. v. Bd. of Governors of the Fed. Rsrv. Sys.*, 144 S.Ct. 2440 (2024), as well as limitations on the scope of agencies' adjudicatory authorities. *Sec. & Exch. Comm'n v. Jarkesy*, 144 S.Ct. 2117 (2024).

State or local public health agencies may face similar challenges and standards subject to each state's own judicial review. As with federal agencies, state or local executive agencies that exceed the bounds of their delegated authorities may find their public health regulations or policies negated. In *Boreali v. Axelrod*, 71 N.Y.2d 1 (Ct. App. N.Y. 1987), for example, New York State's Public Health Council promulgated a comprehensive code to govern tobacco smoking in public areas. Although the New York State legislature authorized the Council to regulate generally in the interests of the public's health, the court found the Council overstepped its authority when it attempted to more closely regulate tobacco. Over 25 years later, a New York appellate court took the same approach in *Boreali* to strike down New York City's proposed ban on large portion sizes of SSBs. *N.Y. Statewide Coal. of Hispanic Chambers of Com. v. N.Y. Dep't of Health & Mental Hygiene*, 970 N.Y.S.2d 200 (App. Div. 2013); *see* Chapter 9 for additional discussion.

Similarly, in 2013, the Kentucky Supreme Court admonished an effort of a local county board of health to curb indoor smoking. Bullitt County's Board of Health passed a regulation prohibiting tobacco smoke in all enclosed public locations and places of employment. When challenged on appeal, the Supreme Court found that the regulation was unconstitutional because the Board exceeded its statutory authority (even though prior decisions affirmed that state law did not preempt local smoking ordinances). The problem with the Board's regulation stemmed from how it was enacted, suggested the court, and not what it pertained to. *Bullitt Fiscal Ct. et. al v. Bullitt Cnty. Bd. of Health*, 2012 WL 6062751 (Ky. June 19, 2013).

In an unreported decision, *Vapor Technology Association v. Oregon Health Authority*, No. A172417 (Or. Ct. App. Nov. 14, 2019), the court blocked an effort by Oregon's health department to promulgate a temporary rule banning the sale of nicotine products. Although Oregon law gave the department "direct supervision of all matters relating to the preservation of life and health of the people," neither these powers, nor Oregon Governor's prior executive order, granted the department such broad rulemaking authority. The court rejected arguments that the public would be harmed if the rule was blocked, assessing such harms as speculative (for additional discussion of the harms of nicotine products, *see* Chapter 6).

Judicial Branch. The judiciary is tasked generally with interpreting the law to resolve disputes pursuant to "cases or controversies" that arise when individuals or groups disagree. As per the case examples above, courts exert substantial influence in public health law and policy. Among other issues, they decide whether:

(1) specific persons or other parties have jurisdiction to contest legislative or executive actions;

(2) public health statutes or regulations are constitutionally-sound;

(3) agency actions are legislatively authorized;

(4) public health officials have gathered sufficient evidence to support their interventions; and

(5) public or private actors are negligent.

Courts are typically bound by precedent (i.e., prior judicial decisions) and tend to defer to the policy decisions of lawmakers consistent with separation of powers principles. As a result, judges often strive to decide cases based on the underlying intent of statutory or administrative laws. Still, judicial decisions on public health matters vary extensively for many reasons.

Precedent extends only as far as a court's jurisdiction. Thus, while the U.S. Supreme Court's decisions on federal constitutional law have precedential value nationally, a state supreme court's decision on a matter of state law only applies within that state. Other state courts may weigh another state court's opinion on similar laws or facts, but are not required to decide in the same way.

Divergent judicial results also arise from the fact that some judges are politically elected (rather than appointed) or because of the unique facts of a particular case. Courts less familiar with public health issues or data may decide cases in reliance on different information. *See, e.g.,* N.Y. STATE PUBLIC HEALTH LEGAL MANUAL (Michael Colodner ed., 2011). Nationally, courts struggle at times to distinguish valid scientific evidence (*see Daubert v. Merrell Dow Pharm., Inc.*, 509 U.S. 579 (1993)) from "junk science" advanced by "denialists." *See* Leila Barraza et al., *Denialism & Its Adverse Effect on Public Health*, 53 JURIMETRICS J. 307 (2013).

In New Mexico, for example, several courts weighed highly-suspect evidence of whether low frequency electromagnetic waves emanating from a neighbor's Wi-Fi and cell phones may have harmed the plaintiff's health. *See* George Johnson, *Science, Lost in a Legal Maze*, N.Y. TIMES, Mar. 24, 2015. For an illustration of divergent court decisions on the constitutionality of tobacco warning labels based on conflicting evidence, *see* Chapter 9.

3. PREEMPTION

As an embedded legal theory within the U.S. constitutional system, preemption refers to how state or local laws may be averted, displaced, or negated by conflicting laws at a higher level of government. Thus, federal laws can preempt state, tribal, or local laws and state laws can preempt local laws (*see* Figure 2.5).

Figure 2.5. Preemption Conceptually

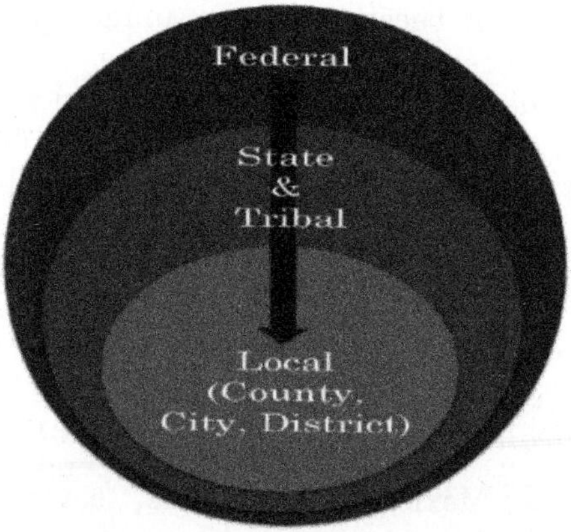

The notion that a higher level of government may override the laws of a lower level of government is easy in theory but complicated as applied. As discussed later in this chapter, the U.S. Constitution grants the federal government limited, defined powers (e.g., to regulate interstate commerce, to tax, and set conditions on the receipt of federal funds). By design, federal legislators, officials, and judges are constrained to act pursuant to the powers specifically granted to them by the Constitution and federal law.

To preserve federal exercises of powers from intrusion or interference by state and local governments, the Supremacy Clause of the Constitution (art. VI, cl. 2) provides that federal constitutional, statutory, regulatory, and judicial laws preempt state and local laws. *See* CHEMERINSKY, CONST. LAW, at 402–27. So long as federal laws are constitutionally authorized, they prevail over any conflicting state or local statutes, regulations, judicial decisions, or other laws.

This same basic constitutional scheme plays out at the state level, subject to a key distinction. State legislation, regulations, and judicial decisions preempt conflicting local laws. However, while federalism restrains the federal government from directing state governments, no similar principles limit state controls over local governments. As sovereign governments, state allocations of powers to counties, cities, or other municipalities can generally be withdrawn or tied to other stringent conditions impacting local authority (a.k.a. "home rule").

In sum, federal laws are supreme and can override conflicting state or local laws. State laws cannot preempt federal laws, but can negate conflicting local laws (such as a local ordinance prohibiting public health practices that state law requires). As applied, preemption offers additional nuances. Congress can expressly (via specific legislative language) or impliedly (based on Congressional intent as interpreted by courts) preempt state or local laws completely, partially, or not at all. *See, e.g.*, James G. Hodge, Jr. & Alicia Corbett, *Legal Preemption & the Prevention of Chronic Conditions*, 13 PREVENTING CHRONIC CONDITIONS 1 (2016).

As illustrated in Figure 2.6, and described further below, federal or state laws may preempt laws at lower levels of government in 3 primary ways:

1. *Ceiling:* State or local laws imposing stricter standards than those at the federal level can be preempted if the federal standard is meant to act as a "ceiling," which lower level governments cannot exceed.

2. *Floor:* State or local laws providing less restrictive standards may also be preempted if meeting a lower standard defeats the purpose of federal law. In this way, federal actors create a legal "floor," for which state or local laws cannot go below but can surpass via greater requirements.

3. *Field:* Federal law may "occupy a field" so completely as to preempt similar state or local laws altogether (even if federal law insufficiently achieves essential public health outcomes). In this way, federal preemption can essentially strip state or local governments of their ability to address public health issues.

Figure 2.6. Preemption

Preemption can help or hinder public health goals and objectives. Federal preemption has been used positively to create a national floor for public health policies (e.g., menu labeling provisions discussed in Chapter 9). Conversely, preemption can be used to thwart state or local public health legal and policy routes and objectives to promote the public's health. In the past decade, state legislatures have preempted local innovations in diverse public health areas including gun control, food policies, and employment protections (*see* text box below).

Graham v. R.J. Reynolds Tobacco Co.
In *Graham v. R.J. Reynolds Tobacco Co.*, 857 F.3d 1169 (11th Cir. 2017), a panel of judges on the 11th Circuit Court of Appeals reviewed a state-based litigation claim against the tobacco industry seeking compensation for the untimely death of a woman from lung cancer.

The claim was based on a prior court finding that cigarettes are defective and inherently dangerous. The tobacco industry argued:

- Congress had not banned cigarettes (choosing instead to regulate them in specific settings);
- Congress intended for cigarettes to remain on the market; and
- State-based tort claims based on the dangerousness of cigarettes (that could inhibit future sales) were effectively preempted.

The court disagreed, finding that existing federal law (discussed in more detail in Chapter 9) does not preempt state law tort claims.

Through what may be labeled broadly as "preemption plus" strategies, law- and policy-makers increasingly seek to control lower levels of government through actions that exceed traditional boundaries or targets of preemption. James G. Hodge, Jr. et al., *Public Health Preemption Plus: Constitutional Affronts to Public Health Innovations*, 79 OHIO ST. L. J. 685 (2019). These schemes are most prominent in public health areas impacting big industries (e.g., tobacco, fast food) or specific interests (e.g., rights to bear arms, religious freedom). As illustrated in Figure 2.7, they include direct threats of government officials, fines assessed against government agencies, loss of funds, and de-authorizations of traditional public health powers.

In 2011, for example, Florida revised its firearm preemption statute to allow penalties (up to $5,000 per violation) against appointed or elected officials in local jurisdictions that enacted or enforced contrary gun control laws. FL. STAT. § 790.33 (2011). Florida's anti-gun provisions also deny local elected officials indemnification from liability if they violate the statute in their formal capacities. Florida's Governor can remove from office or terminate from employment any local official who enforces a preempted local gun measure. In 2014, Florida Carry, a pro-gun non-profit, sued the City of Tallahassee and its mayor for failing to remove preempted gun ordinances from local codes. State sanctions were avoided only when the court determined Tallahassee's ordinances were not actually promulgated or enforced.

Figure 2.7. Preemption Plus

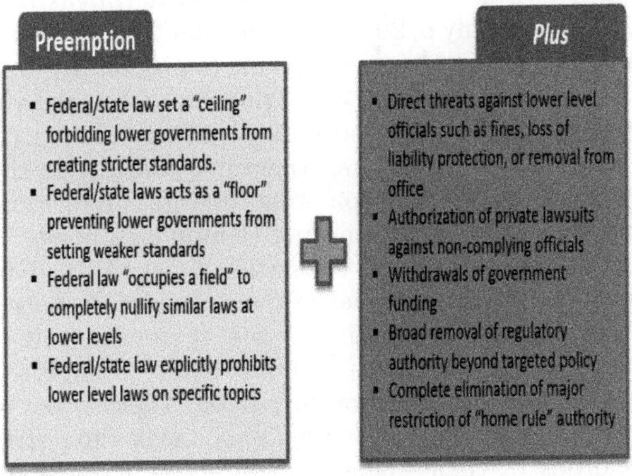

Authorizing withdrawals of government funding, even for funds unrelated to the target of preemption policies, is another way to control state or local actions. Arizona Senate Bill 1487, A.R.S. § 41–194.01 (West 2021), allowed the state Attorney General to link state funding allocations to local government compliance with state laws. In 2016 the City Council of Tempe (AZ) withdrew consideration of a policy to mandate paid sick and safe time for employees against a threat of loss of all state funding. Tucson (AZ) lost its challenge against the State regarding the potential withdrawal of $176 million in state funds related to Tucson's ordinance requiring the melting down of guns in the City's possession. *State ex rel. Brnovich v. City of Tucson*, 399 P.3d 663 (Ariz. 2017).

States have also threatened municipalities with a loss of local regulatory authority in pursuit of strengthening preemption efforts. Emily Badger, *Red States & Blue Cities: A Partisan Battle Intensifies*, N.Y. TIMES, July 6, 2017. In November 2014, the City of Denton, Texas banned fracking (a process through which sub-surface rock formations are fractured via pressurized fluids to stimulate natural gas or oil flows). The city's ban was viewed as contrary to the state's interest in promoting energy production. Instead of simply preempting Denton's authority to ban fracking, the Texas legislature passed H.B. 40 in 2015 to strip all localities of their broader authority to regulate oil and gas industries. It simultaneously introduced (but did not pass) H.B. 540 to prohibit the adoption of local laws on any issue. These types of "blanket preemption" proposals seek to strip localities of their home rule authority to regulate generally in the interests of health, safety, and welfare.

Absent effective counter-arguments, "preemption plus" strategies can force state or local compliance with policies set by higher level governments that are antithetical to the public's health. James G. Hodge, Jr. et al., *Public Health "Preemption Plus,"* 45(1) J. OF L., MED. & ETHICS 156 (2017). As a result, many policymakers view these tactics as contrary to public health legal innovations.

B. FEDERAL PUBLIC HEALTH POWERS

In theory, the federal government has limited, defined powers. Consistent with principles of federalism, Congress draws its authority to act from specific, enumerated powers granted pursuant to Article II of the Constitution. These include the powers to regulate interstate commerce, tax, and set conditions on federal spending. The aforementioned political and judicial expansion of these powers (through what is known as the doctrine of implied powers) allows the federal government considerable authority to act in the interests of public health and safety. The federal government may employ all means reasonably appropriate to achieve the objectives of its listed powers, including raising revenue for public health services and regulating private activities that endanger human health.

Congressional passage of key pieces of legislation concerning vehicle safety, food policy, national security, environmental protection, transportation, and access to health services, among other areas, establishes national, uniform standards essential to achieving public health objectives. As noted above, conflicting state or local laws are typically preempted depending on the specifics of the underlying legislation.

In the context of public health, federal preemption (noted above) can be a double-edged sword. The supremacy of federal law allows Congress or executive agencies to address public health issues in broad strokes with national applications and inherent benefits to the public's health. Conversely, in some areas, such as environmental protection, federal law may "occupy the field" so completely as to negate any state or local regulations in the same area. If federal law is insufficient to fully achieve essential public health outcomes, the resulting vacuum of state and local regulations can inhibit improved health outcomes. *See, e.g., U.S. v. City & Cty. of Denver*, 100 F.3d 1509 (10th Cir. 1996) (Comprehensive Environmental Response, Compensation, and Liability Act preempted Denver's zoning ordinance prohibiting the maintenance of hazardous waste).

Prior debates in 2017 concerning President Trump's unilateral decision to withdraw the U.S. from the 2015 Paris climate change agreement are illustrative. *See* Paris Agreement to the UN Framework Convention on Climate Change, Apr. 22, 2016. The federal government alone (and not the states) has legal authority to negotiate treaties and other transnational agreements. While the Paris Agreement does not constitute a formal treaty among nations, U.S. participation is contingent on Presidential acquiescence and other voluntary measures adhered to among federal agencies.

Even though President Trump's withdrawal never materialized with the reversal of his policies by President Joe Biden in 2021, multiple sub-national entities in the public and private sectors in the U.S. reaffirmed their commitment to global climate change. The U.S. Climate Alliance, comprised of 12 states and Puerto Rico, thousands of municipal leaders, and hundreds of universities and private businesses, committed to upholding the Paris Agreement. *See* Camila Domonoske, *Mayors, Companies Vow to Act on Climate, Even as U.S. Leaves Paris Accord*, NPR (June 5, 2017, 4:41 PM). In addition, over half the states and D.C. set legal or voluntary standards for meeting renewable energy targets. Editorial, *Filling the Void on Climate Change*, N.Y. TIMES, June 7, 2017. Public health legal activism at state and local levels reflects the dynamic nature underlying federal-state balances of power.

C. STATE PUBLIC HEALTH POWERS

Unlike the federal government's enumerated, limited powers, states have extensive authority to protect the public's health. Their public health powers derive largely from their reserved sovereign powers via the 10th Amendment (and may extend to local governments through state delegations). The expansive role of state governments in public health is directly related to the breadth of their police and *parens patriae* powers, as defined and explained below.

1. POLICE POWERS

Often misconstrued as the powers of government to conduct law enforcement activities, state "police powers" are much broader in scope. They represent the state's primary source of power to promote the general welfare of society. Historically, police powers have been defined as "the inherent authority of the state to enact laws and promulgate regulations to protect, preserve and promote the health, safety, morals, and general welfare of the people." ERNST FREUND, THE POLICE POWER: PUBLIC POLICY & CONSTITUTIONAL RIGHTS 3–4 (1904). In 2006, the U.S. Supreme Court noted how principles of federalism "allow the States great latitude under their police powers to legislate [to protect] the lives, limbs, health, comfort, and quiet of all persons." *Gonzales v. Oregon*, 546 U.S. 243, 270 (2006).

Police powers are an original source of public health laws designed to prevent morbidity and mortality across populations. Police powers support public health measures to test, screen, vaccinate, treat, quarantine, and isolate individuals. They authorize the creation of state and local public health agencies and empower them to conduct educational campaigns, surveillance, and epidemiological investigations. Many additional public health authorities discussed later in the text are supported directly by state police powers. In furtherance of these powers, states may restrict (within constitutional limits) private interests in liberty, autonomy, and privacy, as well as economic interests in freedom to contract and use of property. *Allied Structural Steel Co. v. Spannaus,* 438 U.S. 234, 241 (1978); *see also* discussion of emergency public health powers in Chapters 11 and 12.

2. PARENS PATRIAE POWERS

In addition to their sovereign police powers, states also possess *parens patriae* powers. Translated literally as the "parent of the country," these powers authorize state government not only to act in the interests of the community's well-being, but also in relation to individuals' own best interests. LAWRENCE O. GOSTIN, PUBLIC HEALTH LAW: POWER, DUTY, RESTRAINT 95–96 (2nd ed. 2008).

Parens patriae powers are invoked in 2 major ways. First, the state may seek legal standing in cases supporting the community's health and welfare (e.g., the state sues the federal government on behalf of the state's citizens to compel specific public health goals). *See, e.g., Massachusetts v. EPA*, 549 U.S. 497 (2007) (requesting EPA to regulate emissions of greenhouse gases). Second, the state may serve as guardian of, or provide protections for, persons who may otherwise lack capacity to look after their own interests or welfare. *Parens patriae* powers in this context allow the state to step in for the benefit of minors, persons with mental disabilities, the elderly, prisoners, or other wards of the state to avert or correct known physical or mental harms.

For example, state government may rely on its *parens patriae* powers to:

1. protect a child from mental or physical abuse or neglect (*see Santosky v. Kramer*, 455 U.S. 745 (1982));
2. institutionalize a person with mental instabilities who poses a risk to him- or herself (*see Mezick v. State*, 920 S.W.2d 427 (Tex. App. 1996)); or
3. prevent harms to incapacitated older persons from their caretakers (*see Congress Care Ctr. Ass'n v. Chi. Dep't of Health*, 632 N.E.2d 266 (Ill. App. Ct. 1994)).

Use of state-based *parens patriae* powers can be controversial when constitutional rights are at stake (*see* the text box below).

Clark v. Cohen

In *Clark v. Cohen*, 794 F.2d 79 (3rd Cir. 1986), Carolyn Clark was confined at a state-run mental institution for 28 years without notice or a hearing despite her repeated requests to receive training on how to live independently. After her release, she sued various public officials and contractors of the Pennsylvania Department of Public Welfare and County of Philadelphia. The federal court of appeals affirmed that Clark's involuntary confinement violated her constitutional right to liberty and procedural due process, noting:

> "To deprive any citizen of his or her liberty upon the altruistic theory that the confinement is for humane therapeutic reasons and then fail to provide adequate treatment [violate] the very fundamentals of due process."
>
> *Id.* at 94 (citing *Wyatt v. Stickney*, 325 F. Supp. 781, 785 (M.D. Ala. 1971)).

D. LOCAL PUBLIC HEALTH POWERS

County, city, or other local public health officials are on the front line of public health practice. They are directly responsible for conducting public health surveillance, implementing health programs funded by federal and state governments, operating health clinics, and setting public health policies for their specific populations. Performance of local (and state) public health agencies may be evaluated consistent with national accreditation standards. Kim Krisberg, *Eleven Health Departments First to Attain Public Health Accreditation*, 43 THE NATION'S HEALTH 1 (2013).

Local governments' authorities to act in the interests of the public's health extend largely from broad or narrow delegations of police powers via state constitutional, legislative, or executive means. Such delegations provide local governments with a limited realm of powers, or "home rule," over public health matters of local concern within their jurisdiction. ANTIEAU ON LOCAL GOVERNMENT LAW § 21.01 (2d ed. 2006); *see also City of Chi. v. Taylor*, 774 N.E.2d 22,

26–27 (Ill. App. Ct. 2002) (home rule is premised on the idea that local governments are best-positioned to assess their communities' needs and enact laws addressing local concerns). State legislatures may modify, clarify, preempt, or remove home rule at will, unless it is protected by provisions embedded in state constitutions.

Exercises of local authority in the interests of public health can neither extend beyond limited jurisdictional boundaries nor conflict with or impair federal or state law. In 2001, for example, the City of Cleveland relied on its home rule powers to pass an ordinance prohibiting liquor advertising on billboards and other public signs. When an outdoor advertising firm sued to enjoin the city from enforcing the provisions, the court found that the ordinance was preempted by state law allowing alcohol advertising (and in violation of constitutional commercial speech protections, discussed in Chapter 9). *See Eller Media Co. v. City of Cleveland,* 161 F. Supp. 2d 796 (N.D. Ohio 2001).

Local governments' home rule authority may also be limited judicially. Through what is known as "Dillon's Rule" (based on the holdings and scholarship of Iowa Supreme Court Justice John F. Dillon in the late 1800s), local governments are limited to those authorities expressly granted to them by state legislatures. Dillon's Rule suggests that local governments may exercise only those powers expressly granted or necessarily implied via statute, unless it is vested with broad home rule.

JOHN F. DILLON, THE LAW OF MUNICIPAL CORPORATIONS 173 (2d ed. 1873).

Modern applications of Dillon's Rule are muted. For example, the Tennessee Supreme Court opined in 2001 that strict construction of the limits of local power is only appropriate when there is a complete lack of, or ambiguity in, state legislative intent. Thus, Dillon's Rule may not apply whenever a state legislature clearly grants comprehensive authority to a local government in the interests of the public's health. *Southern Constructors, Inc. v. Loudon Cty. Bd. of Educ.*, 58 S.W.3d 706 (Tenn. 2001).

As discussed in this chapter, the powers of government to protect the public's health are extensive and overlapping. Inevitable conflicts between governmental levels (federal, state, and local) and branches (legislative, executive, judicial) evoke constitutional principles of federalism and separation of powers. These structural principles determine which level or branch is authorized to act in the interests of the public's health. Preemption principles dictate when a higher level of government overrides the laws at lower levels.

Assessing the full constitutional limits of public health powers, however, requires further exploration. Chapter 3 introduces how individual rights counter-balance governments' broad powers to protect the public's health, and then explains how structural and rights-based norms are interconnected through what is labeled as "constitutional cohesion."

	Chapter 2—Discussion Questions
?	1. How do core structural constitutional principles affect public health legal options?
?	2. How have interpretations & conceptions of constitutional structural principles changed?
?	3. Why is federalism important in the field of public health law?
?	4. When might a subsidiary state or local public health law not be preempted by federal law on the same topic?
?	5. What are the primary differences between state police & *parens patriae* powers?

CHAPTER 3

CONSTITUTIONAL RIGHTS & THE PUBLIC'S HEALTH

	Chapter 3—Learning Objectives
✓	1. Understand essential constitutional rights implicated in public health laws & policies
✓	2. Examine how individual rights are understood & balanced to advance public health goals
✓	3. Assess varying levels of scrutiny through which infringements of rights are assessed
✓	4. Explore one of the seminal cases in public health law focused on state & local governmental vaccination powers
✓	5. Integrate individual rights & structural principles to more fully comprehend the legality of public health policies

In addition to creating a structural foundation for assigning and executing governmental public health powers, the federal Constitution limits these powers through affirmative protections of individual rights and liberties. The Bill of Rights (the first 10 amendments to the Constitution), the 14th Amendment, and other constitutional provisions create a zone of individual rights that government may not infringe or invade absent justification. At the crux of public health practice in theory and practice is the need to constantly balance tensions between population-based laws and individual rights.

As per Figure 3.1, individual rights are core constitutional components. Illustrated as pickets of a fence, individual rights are part of the "Constitutional Lot" (initially introduced in Part I). Understanding how individual rights are counterweighed with public health powers is complex. Even more complicated is how structural principles and individual rights interrelate. These issues are discussed later in this chapter through the seminal case, *Jacobson v. Massachusetts*, and principles of constitutional cohesion.

Figure 3.1. The Constitutional Lot—Reframed

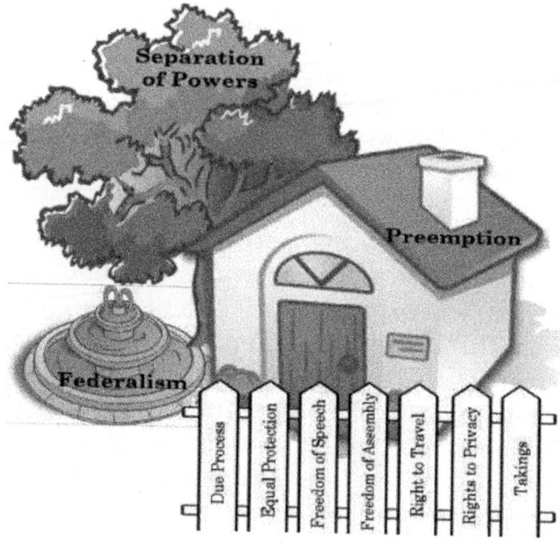

A. FOUNDATIONS OF RIGHTS-BASED LIMITATIONS

An extensive array of constitutionally-protected individual rights affects how government regulates in the interests of the public's health. Unlike the private sector (which does not generally owe individuals respect for their constitutional rights), government cannot infringe on fundamental individual rights without sufficient reasons. As courts regularly considered during the COVID-19 pandemic, constitutional rights are not absolute, but rather are subject to constant balancing under varying rules and tests (*see* Chapter 12). The U.S. Supreme Court has developed different levels of scrutiny, or standards, that it and other courts apply in assessing potential infringements of individual rights depending on multifarious factors. Illustrated succinctly in Figure 3.2, these levels include:

Strict Scrutiny. When fundamental rights (e.g., bodily privacy) or "suspect classes" (e.g., race, ethnicity, alienage, national origin) are implicated, government's action must (1) be narrowly tailored to serve a compelling government interest and (2) often represent the least restrictive means for accomplishing government's objective. *Adarand Constructors, Inc. v. Pena*, 515 U.S. 200 (1995) (federal program that incentivized hiring subcontractors based on racial classification was subject to strict scrutiny). Whenever strict scrutiny is invoked, it is exceedingly difficult for government interests to prevail. As a result, they are typically struck down by courts.

Take, for example, a public health regulation or policy that discriminates openly (or what courts sometimes refer to as "on its face") against persons on the basis of race by denying them access to public health services. Following a devastating hurricane in Galveston, Texas in September 1900 that killed thousands of persons, essential supplies were reportedly distributed first to the city's White residents; whatever was left each day was later handed out to Blacks. *See* PATRICIA B. BIXEL & ELIZABETH H. TURNER, GALVESTON & THE 1900 STORM: CATASTROPHE & CATALYST 80 (2000). Such a law or policy is contrary to equal protection principles (discussed below). Absent a compelling governmental interest (which is highly unlikely given patent discrimination), it is unconstitutional.

Intermediate (or Heightened) Scrutiny. In other instances in which government actions or laws implicate individuals on grounds of gender, legitimacy of birth, sexual orientation, or other bases, courts will assess whether there is a substantial relationship with important government interests. *See U.S. v. Virginia*, 518 U.S. 515 (1996) (state-run military institute's policy of admitting only male students was unconstitutional). Meeting this intermediate standard is easier than under strict scrutiny, but is still difficult when government action lacks a close nexus with public health objectives.

In some cases, such as implementation of maternal health interventions, public health agencies may have sufficient justification for discriminating on the basis of gender. *See, e.g., Geduldig v. Aiello*, 417 U.S.

484 (1974) (California disability insurance program which failed to cover pregnancy did not violate equal protection principles because men and women are not similarly situated).

In 2015, the Supreme Court extended the fundamental right to marry to same-sex couples in *Obergefell v. Hodges,* 576 U.S. 644 (2015). Some scholars thought the Court might reason that sexual orientation is classifiable as a "suspect class." Instead, it identified violations of substantive due process and equal protection principles to overturn state laws that denied same-sex couples' rights to marry.

Rational Basis Scrutiny. In most other instances in which governments' actions infringe on individual rights or interests, a minimal level of scrutiny is applied. Government need only demonstrate that there is some rational basis for its expressed actions by showing a reasonable relationship to a legitimate government interest. *Vance v. Bradley*, 440 U.S. 93, 96–97 (1979) (government had a rational basis for implementing mandatory retirement age for Foreign Service employees which did not contravene principles of equal protection). Contrasted with strict scrutiny, whenever courts employ the rational basis test, they tend to defer to legislative or executive prerogatives consistent with separation of powers. So long as government can show some legitimate purpose, individual rights may be curtailed. As a result, public health laws measured under this standard usually survive scrutiny.

In limited cases, the Supreme Court may apply a more stringent form of rational basis review. In *City of Cleburne v. Cleburne Living Center, Inc.*, 473 U.S. 432 (1985), the Court invalidated a local zoning ordinance that attempted to restrict placement of a mental institution within a local community. It found there was no legitimate government interest underlying the ordinance that otherwise discriminated against persons with mental disabilities in violation of principles of equal protection.

Figure 3.2 summarizes levels of scrutiny applied to rights to equal protection and substantive due process.

Figure 3.2. Constitutional Levels of Scrutiny

Level of Scrutiny	Equal Protection	Substantive Due Process	Requires
STRICT	Race, national origin/ethnicity, Suspect classes	Fundamental rights; procreation, travel, marriage	Compelling government interest + narrow tailoring
HEIGHTENED (INTERMEDIATE)	Gender, illegitimate children; quasi-suspect classes	Quasi-fundamental rights (bodily integrity)	Substantially related to an important gov't objective
MINIMAL (RATIONAL BASIS)	Any other classifications	Any other infringement	Rational relationship to a legitimate state interest

B. BRIEF OVERVIEW OF SPECIFIC RIGHTS

The Constitution protects individuals and groups from unwarranted exercises of government, largely through the Bill of Rights and the 14th Amendment. As per the picket fence illustration in Figure 3.1, these include fundamental rights to protect core freedoms (e.g., free speech), generalized rights to inhibit government oppression (e.g., due process), and rights designed to obviate government favoritism or discrimination (e.g., equal protection), as examined briefly below.

1. FIRST AMENDMENT RIGHTS

Public health practice may implicate 1st Amendment rights, specifically rights to free speech and expression, rights to assemble, and religious freedoms. These rights are held not only by individuals, but also corporations or other legally-recognized entities (e.g., associations, unions, and partnerships). SCOTUS closely guards freedoms of speech and expression against government intrusion. *Tinker v. Des Moines Indep. Cmty. Sch. Dist.*, 393 U.S. 503 (1969); *Texas v. Johnson,* 491 U.S. 397 (1989). Still, 1st Amendment freedom of speech does not equate to saying whatever one wants. Manifold restrictions may be set via government for public actors voicing hate speech, dangerous or reckless rhetoric, false or misleading information, or "true threats" of violence against others.

In *Counterman v. Colorado*, 600 U.S. 66 (2023), SCOTUS considered whether a defendant who sent multiple disturbing social media messages directed at a public figure could be prosecuted under state law that forbid menacing communications. Counterman claimed his conviction was unconstitutional under the 1st Amendment because the state did not prove he knew or intended that his messages were threatening. Writing for a 7–2 majority, Justice Elena Kagan agreed. Government must prove a mental state of recklessness—that is, a speaker is aware that his statements could be interpreted as threatening—to sustain a "true threat" prosecution under free speech protections. The Court's "recklessness" requirement complicates future prosecutions for domestic violence, cyber-harassment and other acts impacting public health and safety. Alison Durkee, *Supreme Court Overturns Stalker's Conviction in First Amendment Case Over "True Threats,"* FORBES, June 27, 2023.

First Amendment protections for political, religious, and commercial speech range in their scope and application.

Political Speech. Laws that directly impact political speech are subject to review under the Court's highest level of scrutiny. *Citizens U. v. Fed. Elec. Comm'n*, 558 U.S. 310 (2010). Political speech is "interactive communication concerning political change." *Buckley v. Am. Const. L. Found., Inc.*, 525 U.S. 182, 186 (1999) (citing *Meyer v. Grant*, 486 U.S. 414, 422 (1988)). This includes not only politics and candidates in general, but also "structures and forms of government, the manner in which government is operated . . . , and all such matters relating to political processes." *Mills v. Alabama*, 384 U.S. 214,

218–19 (1966). So long as such speech is covered (that is, it is not false, misleading, defamatory, implicating national security threats, or falls under other limited contexts), the 1st Amendment assures individuals their right to speak publicly or privately.

Commercial Speech. Government infringements on commercial speech, or "expressions related solely to the economic interests of the speaker and its audience," garner their own unique review. *Central Hudson Gas & Elec. Corp. v. Pub. Serv. Comm'n of N.Y.,* 447 U.S. 557 (1980). Infringements on commercial speech emanate typically from government attempts to (1) limit the time, place, and manner of advertising of specific, lawful products (e.g., SSBs, tobacco) generally or to specific audiences (e.g., minors); or (2) require commercial entities to provide truthful information (e.g., warnings about known or potential product harms) or counter information (e.g., calorie labeling on menus). In such cases, the Supreme Court assesses each potential infringement typically under a 4-part test set forth in *Central Hudson,* discussed in Chapter 9.

Freedom of Assembly. Individuals also have the right to gather, or assemble, for lawful purposes subject to reasonable restrictions. Freedom of assembly may not extend to group activities that negatively impact the community or the public's health or safety (as discussed in Chapter 12 related to the COVID-19 pandemic).

For example, political protesters who erected tents and accumulated garbage and human waste in New York City in 2011 were lawfully dispersed by the city and park owner in the interests of maintaining hygiene and public safety. *In re Waller v. N.Y.C.*, 933 N.Y.S.2d 541 (N.Y. Sup. Ct. 2011). Similar outcomes were experienced among protesters on dozens of colleges in the Spring 2024 as students and others pitched tents and occupied campuses in objection to the Israeli-Palestine war. After allowing protests initially, university officials and police began disassembling protesters. Jeremy W. Peters, *Encampment Is Testing College's Commitment To Ideals of Free Speech*, N.Y. TIMES, May 7, 2024. Government may impose restrictions provided they are narrowly tailored, serve a compelling government interest, and provide alternative channels for individuals to communicate or associate. *Clark v. Cmty. for Creative Non-Violence*, 468 U.S. 288 (1984).

Freedom of Religion. The 1st Amendment Establishment Clause ["Congress shall make no law respecting an establishment of religion . . ."] and Free Exercise Clause ["or prohibiting the free exercise thereof . . ."] protect religious freedoms. They work in tandem to prohibit government from endorsing or "establishing" specific religious faiths and support individuals' freedom to practice their chosen religion. In many ways, these 2 facets of religious freedom are compatible to the extent they allow individuals to believe as they choose without governmental interference or influence through support for 1 religion over another. In the public health context, however, sometimes they are at odds, as explained further in relation to vaccination laws and policies in Chapter 4 and the COVID-19 pandemic in Chapter 12.

2. DUE PROCESS

Additional rights implicated through public health powers include principles of due process. Pursuant to the 5th Amendment (and later the 14th Amendment, which applies the Bill of Rights to the states) government shall not "deprive any person of life, liberty, or property, without due process of law." There are 2 major types of due process protections:

1. ***Procedural.*** Prior to or coextensive with deprivations of life, liberty, or property, government must provide individuals with some procedural steps or assurances (e.g., notice, right to counsel, right to an appeal). The level and extent of process due depend on the scope and duration of deprivation of rights involved. *Mathews v. Eldridge*, 424 U.S. 319 (1976).

2. ***Substantive.*** Due process principles also require government to have a sufficient justification for depriving individuals' life, liberty, or property interests. CHEMERINSKY, CONST. LAW at 558. Any time government infringes on these basic interests in arbitrary, vague, or capricious ways, such infringements violate substantive due process. *Foucha v. Louisiana*, 504 U.S. 71 (1992) (state law committing a person acquitted from insanity charges violates substantive due process).

Additional rights flow from court interpretations of the breadth of "life, liberty, or property," such as the right to travel, discussed below.

3. RIGHT TO TRAVEL

Although the U.S. Constitution does not expressly provide for a right to travel, it is firmly embedded in fundamental liberties (*see* CHEMERINSKY, CONST. LAW, at 879), and the Privileges & Immunities Clause, which helps assure state citizens share similar benefits and protections in other states. U.S. CONST. art. IV, § 2, cl. 1. This Clause is a primary basis for protecting persons against (1) the erection of "actual barriers to interstate movement" and (2) disparate treatment for intrastate travelers. *Doe v. Miller,* 405 F.3d 700, 711 (8th Cir. 2005).

Government cannot prevent individuals from entering or leaving a state (absent justification) or mistreat state visitors. It must also extend similar benefits to persons choosing to reside in a state. *Saenz v. Roe,* 526 U.S. 489 (1999). Additional parameters related to the right to travel are discussed in the text box below.

Limitations on the Right to Travel
A Florida law that required sex offenders to notify law enforcement when they permanently or temporarily change their address was approved against a right to travel challenge in *Doe v. Moore,* 410 F.3d 1337, 1348 (11th Cir. 2005). The 11th Circuit Court of Appeals found that there was a

compelling state interest in "preventing future sexual offenses and alerting local law enforcement and citizens to the whereabouts of those that could reoffend." *Id. See also Burman v. Streeval*, No. 4:11CV0569, 2011 WL 3562999 (N.D. Ohio Aug. 11, 2011) (prisoner's segregation for not consenting to TB test does not infringe his right to travel).

In 2019, SCOTUS upheld the prosecution of a convicted sex offender for failing to register pursuant to the Sex Offender Registration & Notification Act of 2006, 34 U.S.C. § 20913 (2020). The offender alleged Congress failed to properly delegate its authority to the U.S. Attorney General, whose regulations applied the Act to the offender. Justice Elena Kagan for the majority found Congress' delegation "falls well within constitutional bounds." *Gundy v. U.S.*, 588 U.S. 128, 137 (2019).

4. EQUAL PROTECTION

Principles of equal protection, derived from the 14th Amendment, generally require similar treatment for like individuals. They apply automatically to state and local governments via the 14th Amendment, and to the federal government through the 5th Amendment. *Bolling v. Sharpe,* 347 U.S. 497 (1954) (federal government must adhere to same equal protection requirements as states to avoid a denial of due process under the 5th Amendment).

Equal protection may be invoked by public health laws or policies that classify specific persons or groups. People with certain conditions or living in particular areas may be targeted for government public health interventions. Older adults may be entitled to special services not provided to younger persons. Children may benefit from public health programs for which adults are left out. None of these examples presents equal protection violations so long as government has some rational basis for distinguishing individuals in the interests of the public's health.

However, when classifications are based on "suspect classes" (e.g., race, ethnicity, national origin) or other questionable grounds (e.g., gender), the level of scrutiny ramps up (as discussed above), and the intervention may be found contrary to principles of equal protection. CHEMERINSKY, CONST. LAW, at 684–801. In *Students for Fair Admission, Inc. v. President & Fellows of Harvard Coll.*, 600 U.S. 181 (2023), SCOTUS overruled longstanding precedent enabling higher education institutions to consider race as a factor in student admissions through their affirmative action programs, citing 14th Amendment equal protection principles. It held that collegiate admissions programs may "never use race as a stereotype or negative," subjecting affirmative action programs to strict judicial scrutiny. The Court's renouncement of higher education admissions policies may extend to race-based determinations in other settings, including public health data collections, allocations of health resources, and distribution of government benefits.

Kim Krisberg, *Changes to Race, Ethnicity Data Collection Will Impact Health*, 53 THE NATION'S HEALTH 1 (2023).

Some public health laws violate equal protection because they openly authorize discrimination. For example, a state quarantine order that applied solely to persons of Asian descent, even though the communicable disease targeted by the order was transmissible among all races, was viewed as patently unconstitutional in 1900. *Jew Ho v. Williamson*, 103 F. 10 (N.D. Cal. 1900).

Other laws are neutral as stated, but discriminatory in their administration. Sometimes "the impact of a law may be so clearly discriminatory as to allow no other explanation than that it was adopted for impermissible purposes." CHEMERINSKY, CONST. LAW, at 732. Concerning laws which have a disparate impact, discriminatory purposes (and likely effects) must be proven for an equal protection violation to arise. *Id.* at 713, 730. As observed by the U.S. Supreme Court in *Yick Wo v. Hopkins*, 118 U.S. 356 (1886) (determining unconstitutional local regulations governing laundry operations applied to persons of Chinese descent in San Francisco):

> "Though the law itself be fair on its face, and impartial in appearance, yet, if it is applied and administered by public authority with an evil eye and an unequal hand . . . the denial of equal protection is still within the prohibition of the constitution. . . ."

In *Village of Arlington Heights v. Metropolitan Housing Development Corp.*, 429 U.S. 252 (1977), a city council in Illinois refused to rezone an area of land to allow low and moderate income housing construction. Blacks alleged the zoning policy effectively denied them community access. The Supreme Court agreed. "Sometimes a clear pattern, unexplainable on grounds other than race, emerges from the effect of the state action even when the governing legislation appears neutral on its face." *Id.* at 266.

A more contemporary example extends from allegations in 2021 that long-standing distributions of emergency funds following natural disasters by the Federal Emergency Management Agency (FEMA) contributed to racial disparities. Christopher Flavelle, *Arrival of FEMA Aid Widens Racial Disparities*, N.Y. TIMES, June 8, 2021. Though FEMA officials did not likely engage in intentional acts of discrimination in allocating recovery resources, repeated patterns emerged of Blacks and Latinos struggling to access federal funds or receiving less resources for similar property damages than similarly-situated Whites. *Id.*

Equal protection principles are reflected in multiple federal, state, and local anti-discrimination laws. The federal Civil Rights Act (CRA) of 1964 bans discrimination on the grounds of race, ethnicity, and national or religious origins (as well as sex in many, but not all, sectors). Pub. L. No. 88–352, 78 Stat. 241 (codified as amended in scattered sections of 42 U.S.C. (2009). Private membership clubs and public international organizations, for example, may discriminate on the basis of sex. EEOC COMPLIANCE MANUAL § 2–III(B)(4) (2009).

On June 15, 2020, the U.S. Supreme Court extended CRA Title VII protections against discrimination based on sexual orientation or gender identity in *Bostock v. Clayton County*, 590 U.S. 644 (2020). Discriminating on the basis of one's sexual orientation or gender identity invariably entails sex-based discrimination in violation of Title VII. An employer who terminates an employee for "merely for being gay or transgender defies the law." *Id.* at 1755.

On April 24, 2024, SCOTUS held that employees do not need to show "significant" harms pursuant to identifiable terms or conditions of employment to establish a claim for discrimination challenging job transfers under CRA Title VII. In *Muldrow v. City of St. Louis*, 144 S. Ct. 967 (2024), the Court reversed lower courts' dismissals of Muldrow's alleged sex-based discriminatory job transfer via the St. Louis Police Department on grounds she did not incur a materially-adverse action (under Title VII's "significant disadvantage" requirement). Just because she did not lose salary or benefits via the transfer did not mean she was preempted from a claim. Under *Muldrow*, federal courts may allow plaintiffs to recover in workplace discrimination suits based on sex and other protected characteristics.

In *EEOC v. Houston Funding*, 717 F.3d 425 (5th Cir. 2013), a woman who was fired for lactating was successful in her claim against her employer for sexual discrimination under CRA Title VII (as amended by the Pregnancy Discrimination Act of 1978, 42 U.S.C. § 2000e(k) (2008)). Additional protections for breastfeeding women are provided via the ACA, Pub. L. No. 111–148, § 4207 (amending 29 U.S.C. § 207), as well as state laws. In combination, these laws help promote maternal and child health by helping to eliminate discrimination against women.

5. PRIVACY

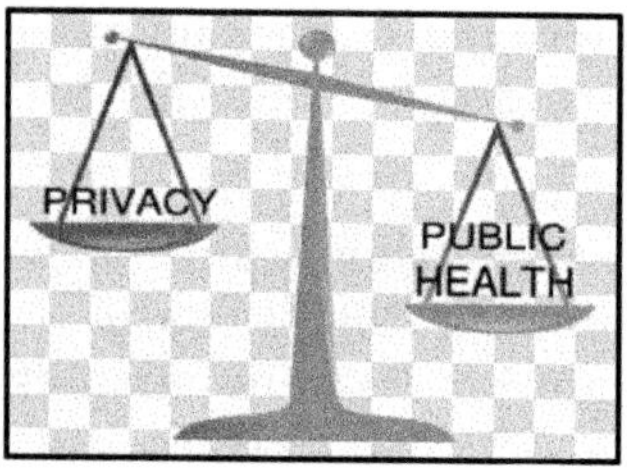

Rights to privacy extend from multiple parts of the Constitution and are constantly implicated in public health policies and practices. As Professor Anita Allen describes, there are 3 primary types of privacy: bodily, decisional, and informational. Anita L. Allen, *Taking Liberties: Privacy, Private Choice, & Social Contract Theory*, 56 U. CIN. L. REV. 461, 464–66 (1987).

1. ***Bodily*** privacy extends principally from liberty principles inherent in due process as well as freedoms from unreasonable searches and seizures via the 4th Amendment. As discussed in Chapter 4, respect for bodily privacy prevents

government from forcing an autonomous individual to receive treatment or undergo intrusive public health screening and testing without compelling justification.

2. ***Decisional*** privacy concerns individuals' interests in making core, personal decisions about their health or other status without unwarranted governmental interference. This facet of privacy supports persons' interests in making reproductive or other medical choices, determining the extent of medical or other care they desire, and deciding how best to parent their children. *See Prince v. Massachusetts*, 321 U.S. 158 (1944) (appealing child labor conviction on parental rights basis). This latter "right to parent" arises concerning public health programs that mitigate parental choices (*see* Chapter 4 for additional discussion).

3. ***Informational*** privacy rights apply to persons' sensitive information, including health data. A bevy of privacy statutes and regulations laws govern access, use, and disclosure of one's personally-identifiable medical data, but constitutional protections are fairly lax. If government can demonstrate a rational, public health basis for accessing or requesting identifiable data, as well as reasonable security measures, such uses are constitutionally permitted. *See Whalen v. Roe*, 429 U.S. 589 (1977) (discussed in Chapter 8).

6. ADDITIONAL RIGHTS

Freedom from Cruel and Unusual Punishment. The 8th Amendment prohibits government from inflicting "cruel and unusual punishment," based on evolving standards set in part by the Supreme Court. *Roper v. Simmons*, 543 U.S. 551 (2005).

Though more often implicated in criminal cases related to the death penalty (*see Stanford v. Kentucky*, 492 U.S. 361 (1989)), and other punitive cases, the 8th Amendment also applies to some public health measures. In *Estelle v. Gamble*, 429 U.S. 97 (1976), the Court required provision of medical care to prisoners via the 8th Amendment. *Id.* at 103.

Respect for constitutional rights is often synergistic with advancing the public's health, but some conflicts lead to difficult tradeoffs and balances. Despite years of law and policy interventions offering short- and long-term solutions, over 650,000 people were homeless across the nation on average each night in 2023, representing a 12% increase since the start of the COVID-19 pandemic in 2020. *HUD Releases January 2023 Point-in-Time Count Rep. Rep.*, HUD (Dec. 15, 2023).

Homeless populations have been targeted nationally for interventions that can be discriminatory, degrading, or unconstitutional. State and local laws banning panhandling prevailed, for example, until SCOTUS expanded free speech interests in *Reed v. Town of Gilbert*, 576 U.S. 155 (2015), leading to a spate of lower court decisions striking down such laws. *See* James G. Hodge, Jr. et al., *Homelessness & the Public's Health: Legal Responses*, 45(SI) JLME 28 (2017).

As per the text box below, 8th Amendment rights of homeless persons are implicated against the backdrop of societal efforts to address their plight in the interests of the public's health and safety.

Assessing 8th Amendment Rights of Homeless Persons

In *City of Boise v. Martin,* 920 F.3d 584 (9th Cir. 2019), a federal appellate court held that the 8th Amendment bars localities from prosecuting people for sleeping outside on public property when they have no other shelter options. Boise officials suggested the decision "effectively creates a constitutional right to camp." *City of Boise Formally Asks U.S. Supreme Court to Hear Martin Case*, CITY OF BOISE (Aug. 22, 2019).

While SCOTUS denied Boise's request for review, it would have the last word on the 9th Circuit's determination. In *Grants Pass v. Johnson*, 144 S.Ct. 2202 (2024), Justice Neil Gorsuch determined for the Court's majority that anti-camping and loitering ordinances targeting homeless populations in the City of Grants Pass (OR) did not in fact violate 8th Amendment rights against cruel and unusual punishments. Prior treatment of such laws as implicating 8th Amendment protections was inherently flawed, concluded Justice Gorsuch, as generally-applicable anti-camping laws do not criminalize the mere status of being homeless.

Justice Sotomayor dissented that Grants Pass' ordinances unconstitutionally targeted homeless persons. As per the Court's decision in *Robinson* v. *California*, 370 U.S. 660 (1962) (invalidating law criminalizing the mere status of drug addiction), she concluded that Grants Pass' laws punished "people with no access to shelter" for essentially "being homeless," which is "cruel and unusual" under the 8th Amendment.

The majority's rejection of 8th Amendment protections for homeless populations raises substantial legal uncertainties over the scope of state and local interventions classifying public spaces off-limits to persons exercising basic human necessities like overnight sleep.

Some constitutional rights may deter or defeat core public health legal interventions designed to prevent excess morbidity and mortality, including rights to bear arms and limitations on government takings of private property.

Right to Bear Arms. The 2nd Amendment guarantees that the "right to keep and bear arms . . . shall not be infringed." This strongly-held right directly collides with public health interventions designed to curb gun-related violence and death in the U.S. Epic political and constitutional battles arise over the balance between efforts to prevent gun violence nationally and individual interests in owning and using firearms. IOM, PRIORITIES FOR RSCH. TO REDUCE THE THREAT OF FIREARM-RELATED VIOLENCE (2013).

U.S. Supreme Court jurisprudence on the scope of 2nd Amendment protections is cloudy at best. In *District of Columbia v. Heller*, 554 U.S. 570 (2008), the Court held that the District's attempt to prohibit the possession and use of handguns at home was unconstitutional. Despite its holding, the Court clarified that federal, state, or local laws may:

1. prohibit "possession of firearms by felons and the mentally ill;"
2. forbid "the carrying of firearms in sensitive places such as schools and government buildings;"
3. set "conditions and qualifications on the commercial sale of firearms;" and
4. outlaw the "carrying of 'dangerous and unusual weapons.' " *Id.* at 626–27.

Two years later, the Court rejected a similar local hand gun law in Chicago, clarifying that the 2nd Amendment applies to states and localities through the 14th Amendment. *McDonald v. City of Chi.*, 561 U.S. 742 (2010).

Then, on June 23, 2022, the Court decided *N.Y. State Rifle & Pistol Ass'n v. Bruen*, 597 U.S. 1 (2022). In *Bruen*, it determined that states cannot deny applications for concealed carry permits to persons lacking "proper cause" given historic 2nd

Amendment self-defense guarantees. Since *Bruen* months of confusion arose across lower courts as to how to apply the Court's standard of review of purported 2nd Amendment violations. On June 21, 2024, an 8–1 majority of the Court determined in *U.S. v. Rahimi,* 144 S.Ct. 1889 (2024), that federal law requiring the removal of firearms from dangerous persons subject to domestic violence restraining orders was constitutional. In so doing, Chief Justice John Roberts clarified that "appropriate analyses involves considering whether the challenged regulation is consistent with principles that underpin our regulatory tradition," and not exact matches with historic laws at the time of constitutional construction as seemingly called for in *Bruen*. Many view *Rahimi* as allowing continued enforcement of reasonable gun control laws as per *Heller* without the specter of comparable historic analogues seemingly required in *Bruen*.

Takings. Pursuant to its powers of eminent domain, government can take private property for public use. However, the 5th Amendment requires that any government taking be accompanied by "just compensation." Stated simply, government cannot take private property for public use without paying for it, subject to determinations of its economic value. As discussed in Chapter 10, compensating owners is not required when government legitimately exercises its power to abate public health nuisances.

Furthermore, what qualifies as a "public use" varies, but most definitely includes public health purposes. For example, a local government may justifiably take privately-held resources during a public health emergency (PHE) so long as it pays for them later. The Supreme Court also recognizes a broader realm of qualifying uses. In *Kelo v. City of New London*, 545 U.S. 469 (2005), New London, Connecticut addressed "economic distress" in its downtown and waterfront areas by taking private land for redevelopment. *Id.* at 472. The Court upheld the city's plan, acknowledging that economic development alone can actually constitute a "public purpose." *Id.* at 485.

C. BALANCING INDIVIDUAL & COMMUNITY INTERESTS

At the heart of public health law are struggles to determine the point at which government authority to promote the population's health must yield to individual constitutional rights. For much of this nation's history, this balance was firmly weighted in favor of public health interventions. Countless court decisions through the early 20th century found in favor of state or local governments seeking to protect the public's health, sometimes to the detriment of individual rights. James G. Hodge, Jr., *The Role of New Federalism & Public Health Law*, 12 J. L. & HEALTH 309 (1998).

Courts justified these decisions in part by the strong need for public health measures to control infectious and chronic conditions for which there were no cures and scant, incomplete, or inaccurate epidemiologic data. Public health actors were granted substantial deference to stymie significant threats to the health and economy of the community often with no or little recourse among affected persons.

Seavey v. Preble (1874)

In *Seavey v. Preble,* 64 Me. 120 (1874), the Supreme Judicial Court of Maine reversed a lower court ruling allowing a homeowner to recover funds from a city-employed physician. As a preventive measure (lacking in a strong scientific basis), the physician ordered the removal of wallpaper from a home after persons expired there from smallpox. Responding to the homeowners' objections, the court observed in relation to smallpox how "the law demands the utmost vigilance to prevent its spread. . . To accomplish this object . . . many other things [may be] done which under the circumstances would be considered a gross outrage upon the rights of persons and property. . . *Salus populi suprema lex*—the safety of the people is the supreme law—is the governing principle in such case."

Yet other legal factors were also at play. In the early 1900s, Congress and the Supreme Court had yet to fully recognize the application of the Bill of Rights to state and local governments. CHEMERINSKY, CONST. LAW, at 511–19. Thus, for example, the protections of the 1st Amendment did not fully apply to state and local governments via the "incorporation doctrine" until 1925. *Gitlow v. N.Y.,*

268 U.S. 652, 666 (1925). Furthermore, courts' deference to public health legislation (through separation of powers principles) and respect for varying authorities among the levels of government (via federalism) were different.

Each of these issues is on display in 1 of the most famous and oft-cited public health cases in Supreme Court jurisprudence, *Jacobson v. Massachusetts*, 197 U.S. 11 (1905). The Commonwealth of Massachusetts legislature enacted a law empowering local boards of health to require the vaccination of residents if necessary for the public health or safety. Facing a potential outbreak of smallpox impacting Boston and other localities, the City of Cambridge Board of Health issued a vaccination requirement in 1902 that all persons be inoculated or face a $5 fine (the equivalent of about $140 in 2021).

Henning Jacobson, a local reverend, refused the smallpox vaccination (*see* Figure 3.3). He was convicted by a local court and ordered to pay the fine. On appeal, the Massachusetts Supreme Judicial Court upheld the conviction. Jacobson took his case to the U.S. Supreme Court, arguing that Cambridge's compulsory vaccination law was "unreasonable, arbitrary, and oppressive," and thus "hostile to the inherent right of every freeman to care for his own body and health." *Id.* at 26. His claim was grounded mainly in constitutional liberty interests which, he asserted, supported natural rights of persons to bodily integrity and decisional privacy (although he also argued unsuccessfully on grounds of equal protection and other legal bases).

Figure 3.3. Reverend Henning Jacobson

Rejecting Jacobson's appeal, the Supreme Court adopted a narrower view of individual liberty under substantive due process. It took a more community-oriented approach in which citizens owe duties to each other and society as a whole. Justice John Marshall Harlan (*see* Figure 3.4), writing for the Court, stated:

> [T]he liberty secured by the Constitution ... does not import an absolute right in each person to be, at all times and in all circumstances, wholly freed from restraint. There are manifold restraints to which every person is necessarily subject for the common good. On any other basis

> organized society could not exist with safety to its members. . . .

Id. at 26. Under the social contract theory advanced by the Court, a community has the right to implement public health requirements to protect itself against threatening diseases consistent with state police powers. The legacy of *Jacobson* is seen most clearly in the Court's defense of the breadth and necessity of public health authority under the police power (discussed in Chapters 2 and 12).

Figure 3.4. Justice John Marshall Harlan

Yet the Court continued its analysis, offering a seminal change in the prior balance of police power authorities and individual rights. While acknowledging the extent of public health authority, Justice Harlan recognized specific limits to such exercises. As explained by Professor Lawrence O. Gostin, utilizing state police powers in support of vaccination requirements or other compulsory public health initiatives is constitutionally permissible when exercised in conformity with the principles of:

(1) ***Public Health Necessity***—police powers used in the interests of communal health must be justified, and not exercised in arbitrary ways beyond what is reasonably required for the safety of the public;

(2) ***Reasonable Means***—there must be some reasonable relationship between the public health intervention and the achievement of a legitimate public health objective that does not plainly invade individual rights;

(3) ***Proportionality***—public health powers that are arbitrary and oppressive in particular cases may require judicial intervention to prevent injustices or "absurd consequence[s]." *Id.* at 39. Even efficacious public health interventions may be unconstitutional if they are onerous or unfair; and

(4) ***Harm Avoidance***—no compulsory public health measure should pose direct risks to specific persons with known adverse reactions. Thus, while persons may be required to be vaccinated for the common good, those who can demonstrate they are "unfit subjects" for vaccination because of the potential for adverse health consequences may not be subjected to the intervention. *Id.* at 12. Jacobson argued that he was not fit for vaccination, but the Court found he failed to present sufficient medical evidence in support of his claim. Requiring a person to be immunized despite knowing harm, concluded the Court, would be "cruel and inhuman in the last degree." *Id.* at 39; *see also* LAWRENCE O.

GOSTIN, PUBLIC HEALTH LAW: POWER, DUTY, RESTRAINT 126–28 (2nd ed. 2008).

Jacobson stands firmly for the proposition that police powers authorize states to require vaccination for the public good, but such powers must be exercised reasonably consistent with due process or other individual rights. Yet, there is another side to the case that reflects the Court's appreciation of structural constitutional constraints at the time.

Concerning Jacobson's rights-based claims, attorneys for the Commonwealth of Massachusetts argued in essence that the state and its legislative bodies have: (1) unquestionable powers and duties to protect the public's health (to which courts must defer); and (2) reasonably determined that smallpox vaccinations in affected communities further the public's health. In prior cases with similar facts, courts typically adjudicated in favor of government. However, the Commonwealth also recognized the nature and force of Jacobson's objections. The "antivaccination" movement during this period was vocal and strong (even if the minority). *See, e.g.*, Michael R. Albert et al, *The Last Smallpox Epidemic in Boston & the Vaccination Controversy, 1901–1903*, 344 NEJM 375 (2001) (noting unsuccessful efforts of the Anti-Compulsory Vaccination League and others to repeal the state's vaccination laws in 1902). As well, the Cambridge Board of Health regulation failed to specify its lawful support. *See* Wendy E. Parmet et al., *Individual Rights vs. the Public's Health—100 Years After Jacobson v. Massachusetts*, 352 NEJM 652 (2005).

The Commonwealth attempted to circumvent Jacobson's liberty-based claim with arguments grounded in structural principles of constitutional law, including separation of powers, federalism, and social contract theory under Massachusetts' constitution. The Commonwealth argued that courts cannot contravene public health legislative judgments unless such were utterly arbitrary and unreasonable. Neither the Cambridge vaccination requirement nor the lower court's refusal to allow Jacobson's evidence of his fitness for vaccination was improper in light of the exercise of the state's overwhelming police powers.

Massachusetts' attorneys intimated that courts should not question the rational judgments of a local legislative body acting under a proper delegation of police power from the Commonwealth, which the Supreme Court acknowledged. "[The] [C]ourt would usurp the functions of another branch of government if it adjudged, as a matter of law, that the mode adopted under the sanction of the state, to protect the people at large was arbitrary and not justified by the necessities of the case." *Jacobson*, 197 U.S. at 28. Both the Court and the Commonwealth agreed in principle that when the legislature has spoken, it is entitled to significant judicial deference (even if constitutional rights are implicated). As Justice Harlan noted, "no court . . . is justified in disregarding the action of the legislature simply because in its . . . opinion [a] particular method was—perhaps or possibly—not the best." *Id.* at 35.

Principles of federalism also come into play. Though these principles undulate over time between state sovereignty and federal supremacy, in 1905 they were pointed firmly in the direction of the states. The Court acceded. "The safety and health of the people of Massachusetts are, in the first instance, for that Commonwealth to guard and protect. They are matters that do not ordinarily concern the national government." *Id.* at 38. It, however, also recognized its own judicial role. "While this [C]ourt should guard with firmness every right appertaining to life, liberty, or property . . . , it is of the last importance that it should not invade the domain of local authority except when it is plainly necessary to do so . . . ." *Id.* Clearly the Court respected principles of federalism in support of states' public health powers, but retained its authority to arbitrate potential constitutional violations of individual freedoms.

Finally, the Supreme Court acknowledged the Commonwealth's presentation of principles of communal responsibility inherent in social contract theory. The Massachusetts constitution sets forth "as a fundamental principle of the social compact that the whole people covenants with each other and that all should be governed by certain laws for the common good," *id.* at 27, notably including public health laws, observed the Court.

These structural principles (separation of powers, federalism, and social contract theory) shed greater light on how and why *Jacobson* was decided. Sovereign states are instituted to, among other things, protect the public's health for the benefit of their citizens. The Commonwealth used its broad police powers in the pursuit of protecting the community. The federal judicial branch must respect exercises consistent with separation of powers and federalism. To the extent the Commonwealth's actions furthered the public's health, they counter-balance potential infringements of individual constitutional rights.

As constitutional norms change, these observations may not always govern review of modern public health cases involving the juxtaposition of state police powers and individual rights, especially in emergencies like the COVID-19 pandemic (*see* Chapter 12). Yet, *Jacobson* must be read more broadly than it is oft-cited in support of (1) government regulation of persons in the interests of public health and safety, (2) limitations on individual liberty interests as needed to protect communal health, and (3) various school vaccination requirements, isolation, quarantine, fluoridation, and other public health measures.

As per Figure 3.5, Henning Jacobson has long since passed away, but his case before the Supreme Court continues to be influential in public health law and policy. The true legacy of *Jacobson* is its historical and modern guidance on when and how to balance the states' use of public health powers with individual rights and interests. Though constantly subject to legal challenges and reassessments, the case remains good law because of the Court's essential recognition that protecting the public's health is synergistic with respecting individual liberties. *See* James G. Hodge, Jr., *Jacobson v. Massachusetts: Alternate Perspectives*, 33(S) JLME 26 (2005).

Figure 3.5. Gravestone of Rev. Henning Jacobson

Source: Clifford M. Rees (2012)

D. CONSTITUTIONAL COHESION

Jacobson represents one of many SCOTUS decisions recognizing the cohesiveness of structural and rights-based principles embedded in the U.S. Constitution. Conventional legal reasoning tends to approach the Constitution as serving 2 distinct purposes:

(1) creating structural interventions (e.g., federalism, separation of powers, preemption) to guide and limit governmental powers; and

(2) conferring specific rights to protect individuals and entities from unwarranted governmental actions. *See, e.g.*, Rebecca L. Brown, *Separated Powers & Ordered Liberty*, 139 U. PA. L. REV. 1513, 1531 (1991).

In reality, as the Court has repeatedly acknowledged, these 2 primary objectives are actually "mirror images" of each other in a cohesive constitutional design. Ozan O. Varol, *Structural Rights*, 105 GEO. L. J. 1001, 1004–05 (2017). In *San Antonio Independent School District v. Rodriguez*, 411 U.S. 1 (1973), for example, the Court ties principles of federalism with equal protection in assessing right to education claims.

> "[E]very claim arising under the Equal Protection Clause has implications for the relationship between national and state power under our federal system. Questions of federalism are always inherent in the process of determining whether a State's laws are to be accorded the traditional presumption of constitutionality, or are to be subjected instead to rigorous judicial scrutiny." *Id.* at 43.

In *Gregory v. Ashcroft*, 501 U.S. 452, 453 (1991), Justice Sandra Day O'Connor notes how "[t]he 'constitutionally mandated balance of power' between the States and the Federal Government was adopted by the Framers to ensure the protection of 'our fundamental liberties.' " (quoting *Atascadero State Hosp. v. Scanlon*, 473 U.S. 234, 242 (1985)). Invalidating federal firearm purchase background checks in *Printz v. United States*, 521 U.S. 898, 921 (1997), the Court expressly observes how constitutional structural components (e.g., separation of powers and federalism) protect individual liberty.

In *Bond v. U.S.,* 564 U.S. 211 (2011), Justice Anthony Kennedy elucidates the interconnectivity of federalism and liberty. At question was whether private individuals can raise federalism-based claims challenging a federal statute as exceeding Congress' constitutional authority. *Id.* at 214. After Carole Anne Bond learned her close friend was impregnated by her husband, Bond allegedly exposed her friend to caustic substances, who was injured as a result. Bond was charged under the federal Chemical Weapons Convention Implementation Act of 1998 with possession of chemicals that "can cause death, temporary incapacitation or permanent harm to humans or animals." 18 U.S.C. § 229F. Resonating a legal argument advanced in *U.S. v. Lopez,* 514 U.S. 549 (1995) (*see* Chapter 2), Bond's attorneys challenged the application of the federal bioterrorism law to her situation on federalism grounds under the 10th Amendment. *Bond,* 564 U.S. at 215.

Finding unanimously in favor of Bond, the Court explained how the benefits of federalism do not pertain solely to the states but rather extend to individuals. As Justice Kennedy explains: "[I]ndividual liberty secured by federalism is not simply derivative of the rights of the States. *Federalism also protects the liberty of all persons within a State by ensuring that laws enacted in excess of delegated governmental power cannot direct or control their actions.*" *Id.* at 221–22 (emphasis added).

As the Court affirms in *Bond,* the protections of liberty extending from federalism accrue to the individual directly to ward against laws that exceed constitutional boundaries. *See, e.g.*, James G. Hodge, Jr., *Federalism & Liberty: Reaching Constitutional Accord*, 72 KANSAS L. REV. 163 (2023). As SCOTUS later observes in *National Labor Relations Bd. v. Canning*, 573 U.S. 513 (2014), structural concepts are "no less critical to preserving liberty than the later adopted provisions of the Bill of Rights."

Illustrated in Figure 3.6, below, principles of *constitutional cohesion* refer to how structural facets and rights-based principles are interwoven within the Constitution to protect individuals and groups from governmental vices like oppression, overreaching, tyranny, and malfeasance.

Figure 3.6. Constitutional Cohesion

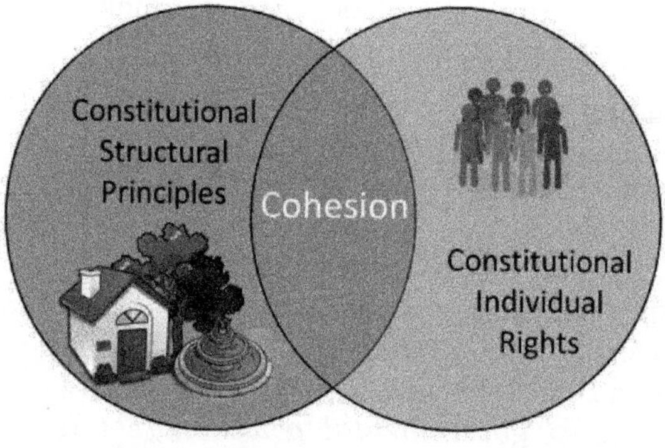

Source: James G. Hodge, Jr. et al., *Constitutional Cohesion*, 53 MICH. J. L. REFORM at 181.

From a public health point of view, these principles offer legal opportunities with accompanying drawbacks. Consistent with a cohesive constitutional view, structural and rights-based arguments can be interchangeable. Federalism arguments, for example, may arise to address alleged rights-based infringements. In *U.S. v. Lopez* (noted above and in Chapter 2), attorneys representing a minor criminally charged with gun possession in violation of the federal Gun Free School Zones Act bypassed rights-based arguments to build a successful federalism challenge to Congress' commerce authority to implement the Act.

More aggressive interpretations of constitutional cohesion recognize additional rights unspecified in plain text, but ensconced in national protections. Take, for example, the Court's assessment of rights to travel (noted above). For decades, the Court acknowledged specific aspects of a constitutional right to travel, but did not link them to explicit constitutional language. In *Saenz v. Roe*, 526 U.S. 489 (1999), the Court re-examines 3 components of the right to travel. Two applications of the right—to be treated as (1) a welcome visitor and (2) like other citizens when traveling across states—have constitutional textual sources. *Id* at 500–03. The 3rd prong, Americans' rights to ingress and egress across state borders, lacks any direct constitutional support. In *Saenz*, the Court determines this 3rd component of the right to travel "may simply have been 'conceived from the beginning to be a necessary concomitant of the stronger Union the Constitution created.'" *Id.* at 501, citing *U.S. v. Guest*, 383 U.S.

745, 758 (1966). The right exists, it seems, despite any explicit constitutional support.

Taken to its apex, constitutional cohesion may arguably be interpreted to support governmental duties to protect the public's health. *See* Hodge, Jr. et al., *Constitutional Cohesion,* 53 MICH. J. L. REFORM at 179–188. While the Supreme Court is unlikely to stretch the reach of constitutional duties to recognize an affirmative right to public health, it has repeatedly opined how public health protections are an essential role of government. *See Gibbons v. Ogden*, 22 U.S. 1, 92–93 (1824) (noting how states and localities have a fundamental role in protecting public health); *Phalen v. Virginia*, 49 U.S. 163, 168 (1850) ("[T]he suppression of nuisances injurious to public health or morality is among the most important duties of government."); and *Stone v. Mississippi*, 101 U.S. 814, 819 (1880) ("No legislature can bargain away the public health or the public morals. . . . Government is organized with a view to their preservation, and cannot divest itself of the power to provide for them.").

Irrespective of government's affirmative public health duties, additional take-aways from principles of constitutional cohesion directly implicate public health policies. As the Court opined in *Jacobson*, individual rights are not rigid or static. Rather, they are sufficiently flexible to adapt or adjust within a federalist infrastructure in which government must act in the interests of public health and safety. In *Dobbs v. Jackson Women's Health Org.*, 597 U.S. 215 (2022), Justice Samuel Alito for the majority rescinded the constitutional right to abortion, in part, on the guise that federalism principles supported a return to states of their inherent authority to regulate. In *Grants Pass v. Johnson*, 144 S.Ct. 2202 (2024) (noted above), Justice Neil Gorsuch relied on similar reasoning to reject the notion that 8th Amendment rights against cruel and unusual punishment did not deter local laws prohibiting camping or loitering on public lands by homeless persons.

A key final take-away from principles of constitutional cohesion is the recognition that as contexts change so do rights. As discussed later in Chapter 12 focusing on critical legal responses during the COVID-19 pandemic, altered perceptions of rights and freedoms especially during emergencies may be constitutional because rights flex along with governmental responsibilities to protect the public's health. James G. Hodge, Jr. et al., *COVID's Constitutional Conundrum: Assessing Individual Rights in PHEs*, 88 TENN. L. REV. 837 (2021).

Understanding the breadth of the field of public health law coupled with the limits of governments' public health powers provides an appropriate backdrop for further study. In Part II, specific legal authorities to prevent and control public health conditions, including communicable and chronic diseases as well as avoidable injuries and corresponding deaths, are examined. At all levels of government, these conditions not only justify the use of significant public health powers, but also raise difficult tradeoffs with respect to individual rights and structural norms.

	Chapter 3—Discussion Questions
?	1. How do court-approved levels of scrutiny impact the interpretation of individual rights?
?	2. How are fundamental individual rights balanced with public health objectives?
?	3. What are the distinctions between procedural & substantive due process?
?	4. How can respect for individual rights inhibit protection of the public's health?
?	5. How do cohesive structural & rights-based principles interplay in *Jacobson v. Massachusetts* as well as modern cases & controversies?

PART II

LEGAL AUTHORITY TO PREVENT & CONTROL PUBLIC HEALTH CONDITIONS

Threats to the public's health are numerous and diverse. Long-standing (e.g., TB) and emerging (e.g., COVID-19) communicable diseases remain a scourge on populations. Chronic conditions, including heart disease, cancers, and diabetes, afflict millions of Americans. Preventable injuries and concomitant deaths negatively impact or cut short the lives of children and adults globally. Core to the mission of public health is the mitigation of the effects of these and other threats to individuals and communities.

American government at all levels has numerous, traditional, and long-standing powers available to address public health risks. It may exercise these public health powers directly, or defer to partners in the private sector for their execution or assistance. So long as these powers are properly grounded in constitutional authorities and limits, the legal options are extensive. When wielded in the interests of community wellness, public health legal powers can be an effective tool for improving outcomes. However, if exercised (1) with impunity for individual liberties or other constitutionally-protected rights, (2) counter to core principles of public health ethics or equity, or (3) in politically insensitive ways, public health authorities may lack legal and practical justifications for their actions.

This Part discusses the legal bases for interventions to address major challenges to communal health stemming from communicable diseases (Chapters 4 and 5), chronic conditions (Chapter 6), and injuries and deaths (Chapter 7). Public health powers used to address some communicable conditions, such as testing, screening, vaccination, or treatment, may equally apply to chronic illnesses, such as cancers. However, some of these powers are used almost exclusively in response to a particular type of threat (e.g., use of expedited partner therapy (EPT) to address sexually-transmitted diseases).

Execution of public health powers to address any condition implicates careful tradeoffs and constant balancing between individual freedoms and community needs. As in Part I, these themes are revisited in many contexts throughout the illustration of public health powers and their related impacts on individual rights.

CHAPTER 4

PREVENTING & TREATING COMMUNICABLE CONDITIONS

	Chapter 4—Learning Objectives
✓	1. Review the major sources & causes of communicable conditions in the U.S.
✓	2. Explore differences between voluntary, mandatory & compulsory public health powers
✓	3. Assess the array of traditional & emerging powers to control communicable diseases
✓	4. Investigate specific legal implications raised by the use of public health powers
✓	5. Consider how public health communicable disease practices are improved through law

The global history of public health practice is intrinsically tied to the prevention and control of communicable diseases. From the founding of the U.S. to modern times, curbing the threat of illnesses spread between and among individuals is a constant governmental objective. Even as the mission of public health has expanded to assuring the conditions for people to be healthy (discussed in Chapter 1), controlling the spread of communicable diseases remains a focal point for federal, state, and local public health agencies. They are equipped with preventive tools, techniques, and data stemming from considerable advances in public health surveillance and control practices. As displayed throughout the COVID-19 pandemic of 2020–2022, effective prevention and control of communicable diseases rely heavily on the law.

Legal interventions to respond to communicable disease threats are multifarious. Intermixed with some of the most ancient of communal health authorities (e.g., isolation and quarantine) are relatively new public health powers (e.g., directly-observed therapy (DOT)) that together comprise the bastion of public health abilities to address communicable conditions. Exploration of these powers and associated trade-offs begins with an assessment of the scope and impact of communicable conditions on human health in the U.S. and abroad.

A. COMMUNICABLE CONDITIONS—DEFINED

WHO defines a "communicable condition" as an illness "caused by microorganisms such as bacteria, viruses, parasites and fungi that can be spread, directly or indirectly, from one person to another. Some are transmitted through bites from insects while others are caused by ingesting contaminated food or water." WHO, COMMUNICABLE DISEASES: OVERVIEW (2021). Similarly, New York City's Health Code defines such conditions as "caused by an infectious agent or its toxins that occurs through the direct or indirect transmission of the infectious agent or its products" from different sources. N.Y.C.

HEALTH CODE tit. 24, § 11.01 (2010). The breadth of what constitutes communicable conditions complicates efforts to predict their spread (a main focus of epidemiology) and control their impacts on populations.

Many communicable diseases are transmitted between humans through air-borne agents (e.g., influenza, COVID-19), casual contact (e.g., chicken pox), from mother to child (e.g., HIV), or via the transfer of blood or other bodily fluids from unprotected sexual contact (e.g., gonorrhea). Some infectious diseases are contracted through other living vectors such as animals (e.g., rabies), insects (e.g., Lyme disease), or plants/fungi (e.g., Valley Fever). Environmental sources such as water (e.g., cryptosporidium) and food (e.g., salmonella) also serve as dominant modes of transmission of infectious diseases. In 2015, dozens of patrons at Chipotle®, a national Mexican restaurant chain, were sickened by the bacteria, E. coli, circulated via contaminated food. Stephanie Strom, *Chipotle E. Coli Cases Rise, with 5 More Ill in Midwest*, N.Y. TIMES, Dec. 22, 2015. In 2023, Quaker Oats® issued a national recall of multiple products over concerns they were contaminated with salmonella. Emmanuel Felton, *Quaker Oats recalls dozens of granola bars, cereals over salmonella fears*. WASH. POST, Dec. 17, 2023.

Communicable conditions present enormous public health challenges. Some infectious agents may be primary bioterrorism threats (e.g., smallpox, anthrax, tularemia, plague, and botulism). NASEM

& DHS, BIOLOGICAL ATTACK: HUMAN PATHOGENS, BIOTOXINS & AGRICULTURAL THREATS (2004). As discussed in Chapter 11, their emergence in any individual or group in the U.S. garners immediate and substantial public health investigation and control efforts because of the likelihood of bioterrorist activity.

Other diseases that transmit easily between humans can also wreak havoc on populations. The 1918–1919 "Spanish flu" pandemic killed upwards of 100 million people globally. JOHN M. BARRY, THE GREAT INFLUENZA 397 (2005) (*see* Figure 4.1).

Figure 4.1. Spanish Flu

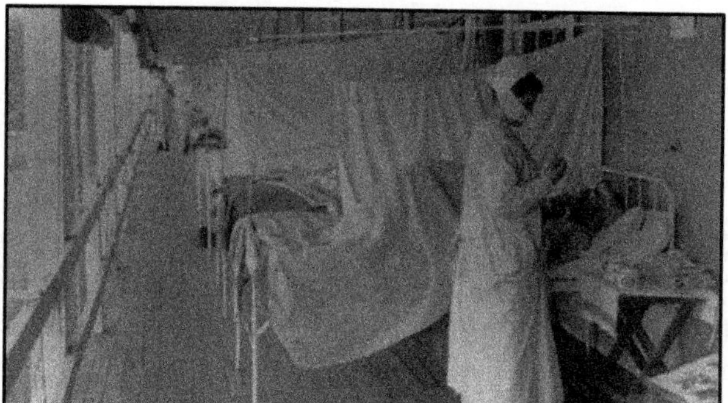

Source: Library of Cong., Apr. 7, 2020.

According to WHO the 2009–2010 H1N1 pandemic flu infected millions and killed tens of thousands worldwide. WHO, EVOLUTION OF A PANDEMIC: A(H1N1) 2009 (2013). The global death toll from the COVID-19 pandemic exceeds multiple millions. Even annual flu outbreaks can be lethal, lending to preventable mortality ranging from 4,900–52,000 deaths per year in the U.S. alone. CDC, *Figure 1: Estimated Range of Annual Burden of Flu in the U.S. from 2010–2022* (2024).

Many infectious conditions are less easily transmitted or detected, but still necessitate public health attention. In 2019, approximately 10 million people globally contracted TB, multidrug resistant (MDR-) TB, or extreme drug resistant (XDR-) TB (*see* Figure 4.2). Nearly 1.4 million people died from TB-related causes. WHO, GLOBAL TB REPORT 7 (2020).

Figure 4.2. TB Bacteria

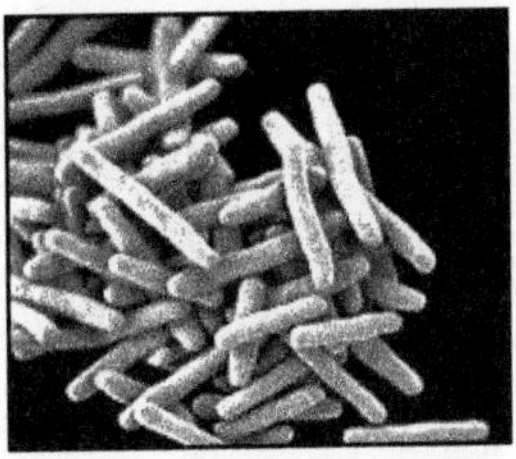

Source: CDC, TB Image ID# 16881, Pub. Health Image Library (2013).

Dwindling resources and continued global migration suggest more persons may perish from this centuries-old disease (previously known as consumption) in the years ahead.

Local TB Outbreaks

Localized outbreaks of TB still occur in the U.S., mostly in urban environments. Kiren Mitruka et al., *TB Outbreak Investigations in the U.S., 2002–2008*, 17 EMERGING INFECTIOUS DISEASES 425 (2011).

- In 2015, over 24 persons in a Kansas town were diagnosed with TB largely through exposure to a single source. Liz Szabo, *27 Kansas Students Test Positive for TB*, USA TODAY, Mar. 19, 2015.
- That same year, hundreds were exposed to TB through a single, infected nurse at the Santa Clara (CA) Valley Medical Center. Liam Stack, *Nurse With TB May Have Exposed Over 1,000, Including 350 Infants*, N.Y. TIMES, Dec. 14, 2015.

In 2016, about 2.4 million persons in the U.S. were infected with hepatitis C according to CDC; half of them were unaware of their infections. CDC, HEPATITIS C QUESTIONS & ANSWERS FOR HEALTH PROFESSIONALS (2021). Despite the availability of efficacious treatment, the deaths of nearly 15,000 Americans in 2019 were associated with this infectious condition. CDC, *Viral Hepatitis Surveillance* (2019). Hepatitis C was spread for decades largely through contaminated blood transfusions (prior to enhanced testing in the 1990s).

Increasingly it is communicated through injecting drug practices and unsafe sexual behaviors.

Sexually-transmitted infections (STIs) present significant, often undetected risks internationally and in the U.S. Since its emergence in the early 1980s, HIV/AIDS has claimed over 40.4 million lives globally. WHO, HIV & AIDS (2023). Global deaths of persons with HIV/AIDS may have accelerated during the COVID-19 pandemic with some reports alleging greater risks of mortality among patients with both diseases. Apoorva Mandavilli, *COVID-19 Poses Particularly High Risks for People With HIV, a Large Study Finds*, N.Y. TIMES, July 16, 2021.

CDC estimates over 1.2 million Americans are living with HIV infection, including 156,000 (13%) whose infections are undiagnosed. CDC, *Monitoring Selected National HIV Prevention & Care Objectives by Using HIV Surveillance Data*, 19 HIV SURVEILLANCE SUPPLEMENTAL REP. 3 (2019). Almost 36,000 persons in the U.S. contracted the disease in 2021 alone. CDC, HIV INCIDENCE (2021).

The most common STI is genital human papillomavirus (HPV). Nearly 79 million Americans are infected with HPV according to CDC estimates. CDC, GENITAL HPV INFECTION—FACT SHEET (2017). Nearly all sexually-active men and women will get at least 1 type of HPV at some point in their lives. Though the condition is largely asymptomatic in most persons, some strains can lead to genital warts as well as cervical and other cancers. CDC, *STD Treatment Guidelines, 2010*, 59 MMWR 1, 69–70 (2010).

Hundreds of thousands of individuals are infected with 2 other prominent STIs, specifically gonorrhea and Chlamydia. CDC received reports of over 1.8 million new cases of Chlamydia alone in 2019, mostly among women. Nearly 130,000 new infections of syphilis were also reported in 2019. CDC, FACT SHEET: REPORTED STDS IN THE U.S. (2019). Left untreated, each of these STIs can lead to significant long-term disabilities, including cancers and infertility, or death.

Improper food handling practices and questionable sanitation from farms to factories also contribute significantly to the spread of infectious diseases. Over 25,000 lab-confirmed cases of food-related illness were reported to CDC in 2022. The actual number of cases is likely many times higher. Salmonella poisonings led to 2,228 hospitalizations and 62 deaths that same year. Miranda J. Delahoy et. al., *Preliminary Incidence & Trends of Infections Caused by Pathogens Transmitted Commonly Through Food*, 72 MMWR 701, 704 (2023).

Water-borne infectious agents, including the sometimes deadly agent, cryptosporidium, cause hundreds of infections annually. They arise predominantly through exposure to microorganisms in recreational water or contaminants in public or private water supplies. CDC, *Surveillance for Waterborne Disease Outbreaks & Other Health Events*, 60 MMWR 1 (2011). In 1993, undetected cryptosporidium contaminations in the city water supply of Milwaukee, Wisconsin led to 69 deaths. Phaedra S. Corso et al., *Cost of Illness in the 1993*

Waterborne Cryptosporidium Outbreak, Milwaukee, WI, 9 EMERGING INFECTIOUS DISEASES 426, 430 (2003); *Markweise v. Peck Foods Corp.*, 556 N.W.2d 326 (Wis. Ct. App. 1996) (resulting litigation against the city and others was dismissed due to failure to provide advance notice of claim as required via statute when suing municipalities).

B. VOLUNTARY, MANDATORY & COMPULSORY POWERS

Whether spread via air-borne, casual or sexual contact, or other vectors, communicable conditions remain a challenge despite public health victories over many diseases that once plagued populations (e.g., smallpox, polio). To combat these threats, U.S. public health authorities rely on a series of public health powers classifiable broadly as voluntary, mandatory, or compulsory in nature.

Voluntary interventions refer generally to public health measures that elicit the participation of individuals or groups acting on their own volition. Lawful efforts to address communicable diseases, for example, may include education campaigns. *See, e.g.*, *Doe v. Irwin*, 615 F.2d 1162 (6th Cir. 1980) (family planning center offering voluntary sex education classes and contraceptives to minors); *see also* Chapter 9. They may also include vaccine drives, testing or screening programs, and treatment options. *See, e.g.*, *Parents U. for Better Sch., Inc. v. Sch. Dist. of Phila. Bd. of Edu.*, 148 F.3d 260 (3rd Cir. 1998); *Curtis v. Sch. Comm. of Falmouth*, 652 N.E.2d 580 (S.J.C. Mass. 1995) (optional school condom distribution programs approved against familial privacy, religious freedom, and other legal challenges).

In each instance, individuals seek information or public health services based on their own choice, often reflected through informed consent (such as prior to testing or treatment). Exercises of voluntary public health powers are ethically-sound (*see* Chapter 1) and highly favored in practice so long as they are efficacious.

Mandatory public health powers raise the stakes. When legally authorized, practitioners may implement public health interventions that no longer seek the voluntary actions of individuals. Rather, they set conditions on participation to encourage or require individuals or groups to protect the public's health to avoid penalties or loss of privileges. Requiring citizens to be vaccinated or else be fined, as described in *Jacobson v. Massachusetts* in Chapter 3, is illustrative. So are mandatory COVID-19 vaccination requirements set by hundreds of universities for returning students in the Fall 2021 (*see* Chapter 12).

Other examples include testing, screening, and treatment programs that mandate individual compliance subject to varying conditions, such as receipt of treatment or other services. Participation in a treatment program may be conditioned on one's avoidance of more intrusive public health measures, such as quarantine or isolation (*see* Chapter 5). In each of these and other instances, mandatory public health powers are often challenged based on infringements of individual freedoms and rights even though individuals ultimately retain a choice of participating.

With the exercise of ***compulsory*** public health powers, individual choice is no longer an option, nor is government offering the chance to participate to avoid penalties or receive valued services or benefits. One's participation will be garnered by force of varying magnitude as necessary. Jennifer L. Piatt, James G. Hodge, Jr. & Leila Barraza, *When Can You Be Required to Get a COVID-19 Vaccine*, SLATE-FUTURE TENSE (2021). Compulsory interventions require individuals to participate or change their behaviors irrespective of their consent. In the early 1900s, New York City public health officials went door-to-door to forcibly vaccinate adults against smallpox or other infectious diseases. Implementation of the Chamberlain-Kahn Act of 1918, 42 U.S.C. §§ 24–25e (1918), as amended in 1938, involved the forcible detention of known or suspected commercial sex workers (or "prostitutes" as they were labeled in the Act) for treatment and study. The Act was repealed in 1944. *Id.* at § 1313.

A vestige of public health practice from bygone eras, compulsory public health powers are seldom used today (outside PHEs) because they run counter to public health ethics and can infringe on individual liberties. Exercises of compulsory powers may fail to survive constitutional scrutiny even if government has compelling interests (often because there are less restrictive alternatives available). Yet, select examples of the use of compulsory powers in the control of infectious diseases remain. For example, forcible testing of persons charged with criminal transmission of HIV may be allowed to determine whether the individual is infected and protect others who may have been exposed. *In re Multimedia KSDK, Inc.*, 581 N.E.2d 911 (Ill. App. Ct. 1991).

Social distancing measures, including quarantine, isolation, and curfews (discussed in Chapter 5), may be implemented voluntarily, but when necessary, government can require affected persons to adhere to such measures especially in PHEs. *See* TURNING POINT MODEL STATE PUB. HEALTH ACT § 5–101 (2003) and Chapter 12. During the COVID-19 pandemic, thousands of examples of persons subjected to compulsory social distancing interventions arose when they failed to comply with express governmental preventive measures. Compulsory powers may also be used to protect the health of minors, prisoners, or others pursuant to *parens patriae* powers (discussed in Chapter 2).

C. TESTING & SCREENING

Public health powers to test and screen (*see* definitions below) for communicable conditions are authorized generally or for specific conditions via statute or regulation in all states and many localities. *See, e.g.*, Ronald Bayer et al., *HIV Antibody Screening: An Ethical Framework for Evaluating Proposed Programs*, 256 JAMA 1768 (1986).

Testing	***Screening***
Diagnostic tests (or procedures) are used to ascertain the presence or absence of a particular disease or condition in an individual	Screening involves the application of specific tests or procedures to ascertain the presence or absence of a disease or condition in groups or populations

Stated succinctly, a person who is a member of a high-risk population for a specific infectious condition may be subjected to *screening* that may lead to administration of a diagnostic *test* to confirm infection. During the 2014 global Ebola pandemic, for example, U.S. authorities screened over 30,000 air travelers arriving from West African "hot zones" for symptoms; those with initial symptoms (e.g., high fever) could be asked to submit to further testing. Sabrina Tavernise & Anemona Hartocollis, *Monitoring Sys. Is Criticized as Rare Virus Causes a Death in New Jersey*, N.Y. TIMES, May 27, 2015. Of note, ultimately no new cases of Ebola from incoming travelers were detected through these screening efforts.

Multiple practical factors militate whether public health authorities may engage testing or screening programs or initiatives, including their affordability, accuracy, efficacy, ethicality, and potential for positive interventions based on results. The U.S. Preventive Services Task Force (USPSTF), for example, rejected proposals in 2017 for wider screening of persons for celiac disease (a potentiallydebilitating condition tied to consumption of gluten). It noted the questionable accuracy of current tests, potential harms underlying mass screening, and lack of efficacy of screening persons for a condition with differing (or no) symptoms and affects. *See, e.g.*, Jane Brody, *Who Really Needs to Be Gluten-Free?*, N.Y. TIMES, June 20, 2017.

Some screening programs may lack efficacy simply because their underlying tests are untrustworthy. *See, e.g.*, Bob Ortega, *FDA to Scrutinize HPV Test Linked to False Readings*, ARIZ. REP., July 31, 2013, at A1 (FDA reviewed laboratory use of specific HPV test based on reported high rates of false positive results). Other screening efforts may insufficiently address at risk populations. In 2023, for example, the American Cancer Society sought to substantially expand the numbers of Americans screened for lung cancer (due largely to tobacco use) against the backdrop of historically-low rates of early detection under extant screening guidance. Leana S. Wen, *New guidance for lunch cancer screenings will save more lives*. WASH. POST, Nov. 29, 2023. Conversely, some question whether broader screenings actually encourage risky behaviors or misallocate limited resources if smokers are regularly screened for lung cancer (despite no signs of illness). Negative test results may lead them to falsely believe their behavior is not as risky after all. *See* Jane E. Brody, *Screening & Enabling Smokers*, N.Y. TIMES, Sept. 8, 2015.

Screening Compensation

Compensating persons to encourage their participation in public health screening programs is controversial.

- For years health plans and employers have offered incentives (e.g., cash payments, gift cards) to women getting mammograms. Some argue that these incentives may be wasteful because women may seek screenings more often than actually needed. *See* Harald Schmidt, *Rewards of Ambiguous Merit*, N.Y. TIMES, Jan. 19, 2016.
- In 2015, local health authorities in Marion (AL) (pop. 3,600) used federal funds to provide cash incentives for residents willing to submit to blood tests for TB. Rates of TB in the community of largely Black residents were nearly 100 times greater than the state average. *See* Alan Blinder, *Outbreak Is Fueled by Mistrust in AL*, N.Y. TIMES, Jan. 18, 2016.

Testing and screening programs that (1) include pre- and post-counseling, (2) seek voluntary compliance expressed through advance informed consent, (3) avoid coercive tactics, and (4) elude unwarranted classification of protected groups are legally acceptable (even if non-efficacious). Each year USPSTF issues a series of national guidelines determining whom should be tested for varied communicable conditions which may be followed at the discretion of HCWs and their patients. USPSTF, THE GUIDE TO CLINICAL PREVENTIVE SERVICES (2012).

Even voluntary testing and screening programs can still raise legal concerns over privacy. In 2006, CDC adjusted its national recommendation for the administration of HIV/AIDS tests to include all persons ages 13–64 seeking routine physicals or other treatment. Bernard M. Branson et. al., *Revised Recommendations for HIV Testing of Adults, Adolescents & Pregnant Women in Health-Care Settings*, 55 MMWR 1, 7 (2006). CDC's recommendation included an "opt-out" feature, meaning testing would be done automatically unless rejected by the patient. In 2013, President Obama expressed continued support for the voluntary HIV testing of Americans to facilitate advance detection and treatment. OFF. OF NAT'L AIDS POL'Y, NAT'L HIV/AIDS STRATEGY: UPDATE OF 2014 FED. ACTIONS TO ACHIEVE NAT'L GOALS & IMPROVE OUTCOMES ALONG THE HIV CONTINUUM 3, 7 (2014).

While some have raised privacy concerns related to this opt-out mode of implementation, CDC's recommendation reflects a watershed shift in national HIV/AIDS strategy following nearly 2 decades of various testing and screening programs focused on high-risk groups (e.g., homosexual men, pregnant women, injecting drug users (IDUs), sex offenders). IOM, HIV SCREENING & ACCESS TO CARE: EXPLORING BARRIERS & FACILITATORS TO EXPANDED

HIV TESTING (2010). These types of screening efforts were challenged legally based on their potential to infringe the bodily and informational privacy of at-risk individuals. *See In re Juveniles A, B, C, D, E*, 847 P.2d 455 (Wash. 1993) (HIV screening of juvenile and adult sex offenders is not a violation of constitutional right to privacy).

Additional challenges arose over the use of named-based reporting of test results to local, state, and federal public health authorities. *See Middlebrooks v. State Bd. of Health*, 710 So. 2d 891 (Ala. 1998) (state statute requiring name-based reporting of HIV/AIDS patients by physicians does not violate informational privacy rights) (discussed further in Chapter 8).

Newborn Screening in Minnesota

Like most states, Minnesota public health authorities oversee a screening program to search for initial, potential genetic or other conditions among newborns. In *Bearder v. State*, 806 N.W.2d 766 (Minn. 2011), parents of 25 children sued Minnesota's health department for "collecting, using, storing, and disseminating the children's blood samples and test results without obtaining written informed consent in violation of the Genetic Privacy Act." To the extent that authorities used blood samples for unrelated research, they exceeded their authority under the state's screening statutes.

Government requirements that persons be tested or screened without consent for public health purposes can also implicate 4th Amendment prohibitions of "unreasonable searches and seizures." The U.S. Supreme Court has clarified that the 4th Amendment applies to physical searches of one's person, effects, or property as well as bodily searches (e.g., blood or DNA tests). *See Skinner v. Ry. Labor Execs. Ass'n,* 489 U.S. 602 (1989) (alcohol and drug testing of railway employees is reasonable and consistent with need for public safety); *Maryland v. King*, 569 U.S. 435 (2013) (DNA testing of arrestees via cheek swabs presents only a minimal intrusion on defendants' expectation of privacy).

Under the 4th Amendment government must generally issue a warrant based on probable cause prior to initiating a search, including blood or other diagnostic tests. Pursuant to what is known as the "special needs doctrine," however, government may conduct warrantless searches (generally outside the context of law enforcement) when requiring a warrant would be impractical or impossible (*see* discussion of searches of premises in Chapter 10.

In *Ferguson v. City of Charleston*, 532 U.S. 67 (2001), a local policy requiring the non-consensual testing of pregnant women or new mothers for drug-related conditions (notably cocaine) at the state-supported Medical University of South Carolina (Figure 4.3) was challenged as an unlawful search. Initially implemented in the 1990s during what some called an epidemic of "crack babies," the public health purpose of the screening program was to identify women who exposed their fetuses or infants to illicit drugs through maternal-child transmission. Yet, test results were also reported to local law enforcement for potential prosecution of the mothers.

Figure 4.3. Medical University of South Carolina

Source: College of Health Professions, Med. Univ. S.C., (2016), http://academicdepartments.musc.edu/chp/.

The end result was pernicious, noted the U.S. Supreme Court, in linking unsuspecting women (often minorities seeking publicly-funded maternal care) with criminal charges. As a result, the testing policy did not comport with the special needs doctrine, and was declared unconstitutional. *Id.* at 84. *See also Glover v. Eastern Neb. Cmty. Off. of Retardation*, 867 F.2d 461 (8th Cir. 1989) (public agency employees serving mentally-disabled persons cannot be required to be tested for Hepatitis B and HIV; risks to patients were insufficient to justify the intrusion on privacy).

D. TREATMENT & RELATED THERAPIES

One of the primary benefits of public health testing and screening programs is the potential to match positive cases with available treatments. Treatment services are provided typically through private sector health practitioners, although many states continue to fund government-run public health clinics that deliver basic health services often to the most needy in the community. Funding crises threaten the future existence of public health clinics in many jurisdictions. *See, e.g.*, Bobby Kerlik, *Pennsylvania Supreme Court Halts Corbett Plan to Close Health Centers,* PITTSBURGH TRIB.-REV., July 18, 2013 (temporary injunction of Governor's plan to shut down 26 of the state's public health centers).

When effective treatments exist, failing to make them available for persons who are tested or screened via public health programs is unethical. STEPHEN HOLLAND, PUBLIC HEALTH ETHICS 162 (2007). Voluntary treatment programs are generally permissible, however, so long as options are explained to individuals and they are given meaningful opportunities for informed consent. *See Canterbury v. Spence*, 464 F.2d 772 (D.C. Cir. 1972).

Legal issues related to consent concerning treatment of minors may arise. In *Anspach v. City of Philadelphia,* 503 F.3d 256 (3rd Cir. 2007), parents objected to the provision of contraceptives to their 16-year-old daughter at a local public health clinic. The court rejected their claim that the clinic's services were coercive and contrary to their constitutional parental rights, deeming the services as voluntary in nature.

Significant constitutional questions can arise when treatment for communicable diseases is no longer optional either because government sets significant conditions for its receipt (e.g., release from isolation) or attempts to force a person to be treated. The U.S. Supreme Court has espoused that individual liberty interests via substantive due process include rights to refuse treatment and sustenance. *Cruzan v. Mo. Dep't of Health*, 497 U.S. 261 (1990). Compelled medication of prisoners or other wards related to communicable diseases may be permissible provided it is appropriate and essential for the health or safety of the individual or others in the absence of less intrusive alternatives. *See Riggins v. Nevada*, 504 U.S. 127 (1992).

Whether public health powers are sufficiently broad to require individuals to complete treatment as a condition of participation in specific activities or release from confinement may depend on whether:

- absent treatment, the individual's communicable condition and behaviors present significant health risks to others;
- treatment options do not place the individual at greater risk of harm;
- requirements for completion of treatment are reasonable, appropriate, and consistent with the current standard of care; and
- adequate procedural due process protections are followed (as discussed in Chapter 3).

1. DIRECTLY-OBSERVED THERAPY

One prominent example of conditional treatment predominately used in treating persons with TB (and potentially other communicable diseases requiring long treatment regimens) is DOT. *See, e.g.*, Michael J. Booker, *Compliance, Coercion & Compassion: Moral Dimensions of the Return of TB*, 17 J. MED. HUMAN. 91 (1996). It is designed to assure an infected individual is fully and successfully treated by requiring a public health worker, HCW, or a family member to administer or observe the individual receiving regular treatments (e.g., ingesting pills or receiving injections). Observations may be conducted in person or via telecommunications.

DOT has proven efficacious in administering TB treatment by (1) limiting the potential development of drug resistant strains (which may stem from incompletions of drug regimens); and (2) lowering the potential for further transmission. It is legally authorized in many states, particularly concerning voluntary compliance. N.M. STAT. ANN. § 24–1–15.1 (2009). Sometimes, participation in DOT is mandated concerning (1) recalcitrant patients (*see City of Newark v. J.S.*, 652 A.2d 265 (N.J. Super. 1993); *City of Milwaukee v. Washington*, 735 N.W.2d 111 (Wis. 2007)), or (2) prisoners (*see De Gidio v. Pung*, 704 F. Supp. 922 (D. Minn. 1989)).

2. EXPEDITED PARTNER THERAPY

Another type of conditional treatment is known as EPT. CDC endorsed the use of EPT first in 2006 for national implementation. CDC, *STD Treatment Guidelines,* 55 MMWR 5, 5–6 (2006). As per Figure

4.4, the public health concept of EPT is straightforward: when treating patients with STIs like Chlamydia or gonorrhea, sufficient doses of safe, prescribed antibiotics should be provided not just for patients, but also for their close sexual partners. Providing treatment for both patient and partner expedites treatment to the partner, resulting in reduced infections and lowered spread of STIs. CDC researchers have demonstrated the efficacy of EPT related to specific STIs. *See* Matthew Golden et. al., *Uptake & Population-Level Impact of EPT on [Chlamydia & Gonorrhea]*, 12 PLOS MED. (2015).

Figure 4.4. EPT in Practice

Source: CDC, *EPT: An Important STD Prevention Tool*

Legal dilemmas related to EPT principally concern the provision or dispensing of a drug to the partner who has not been diagnosed by a HCW or received a prescription in the normal course of health or pharmaceutical care. Additional legal issues concern

(1) the potential for adverse events (though rare) for the partner, (2) misuse of the antibiotics (leading to potential drug resistance), and (3) liability for issuing prescriptions without physically examining an individual (i.e., the partner).

These issues are overcome in multiple states through direct legislative or regulatory authorizations for the practice of EPT. In other states, EPT is incorporated by reference into existing CDC STI guidance. *See* MONT. ADMIN. R. §§ 37.114.515, 37.114.530 (2013). An extensive assessment of state public health laws conducted initially in 2008 (and regularly updated by CDC) found that most states' laws support, or at least do not prevent, EPT in practice. James G. Hodge, Jr. et al., *EPT: Assessing the Legal Environment,* 98 AJPH 23, 23–28 (2008). As of 2023, EPT is legally permissible in 46 states. *STDs: Legal Status of EPT*, CDC (2023). In many jurisdictions, EPT is thus considered the prevailing standard of practice in the provision of care for patients with specific STIs. *Expedited Partner Therapy*, CDC (2023).

E. PARTNER NOTIFICATION

Testing, screening, and treatment are essential tools to find and address "index cases" (i.e., persons that have specific communicable conditions). An additional practice often coupled with these interventions, especially with conditions like HIV/AIDS, TB, or bioterrorism agents, is what is known traditionally as "contact tracing," and modernly as "partner notification" or "partner counseling and referral services" (PCRS). E. Foust et. al., *PCRS to Identify Persons with Undiagnosed HIV—N.C., 2001,* 52 MMWR 1181 (2014).

The public health premise of PCRS is to seek the assistance of infected persons to help locate and notify their contacts or partners of potential exposure. Partner notification generally entails infected individuals working with their health providers or public health officials to identify prospective partners. For example, following confirmation of a positive HIV test, a doctor or practitioner at a local public health clinic may ask an individual if she has had any recent, unprotected sexual contact with others. Based on this information, she may be encouraged to (1) notify her partners of their potential exposure, (2) seek the doctor's assistance in notifying them, or (3) permit the local public health department to provide this information.

In the latter 2 instances, notification of the partners is combined typically with testing, counseling, and treatment referrals. In each case, notice is intended to be non-identifiable (i.e., a practitioner does not directly identify the index case who exposed a partner to HIV). In reality, some partners inevitably identify the source of their exposure. For example, a person who is in a long-term monogamous sexual relationship may clearly know who exposed her to HIV through partner notification. Although unintended, the potential for identification of index cases via partner notification raises significant health information privacy issues (discussed further in Chapter 8). Some index cases have faced physical or mental abuse from their partners after they were notified of their exposure. Andrea Gielen et. al., *Women Living with HIV: Disclosure, Violence & Social Support,* 77 J. URB. HEALTH 480 (2000).

When conducted via government, PCRS participation may also implicate rights against self-incrimination protected by the 5th Amendment. A local public health official may ask an adult with HIV to identify potential sexual contacts, which could include minors, a criminal offense in several jurisdictions. Zita Lazzarini et al., *Criminalization of HIV Transmission & Exposure*, 103 AJPH 1350 (2013). In 2004, local public health and law enforcement authorities aligned to alert the public of the intentional acts of Nushawn Williams (*see* Figure 4.5), who was HIV+. Mr. Williams knowingly engaged in unprotected sexual acts with multiple partners, including minors, resulting in several partner infections.

Figure 4.5. Nushawn Williams Criminal Profile

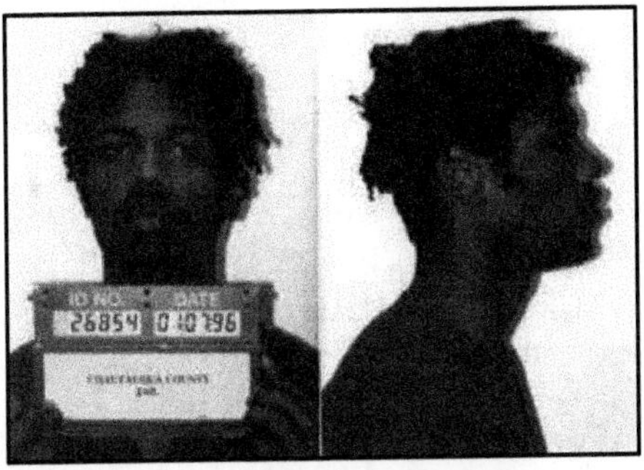

See Thomas Shevory, Notorious H.I.V.: The Media Spectacle of Nushawn Williams (2004) (documenting prosecution of Williams for allegedly having unprotected sex with multiple minors after having received HIV+ test results); Jay Tokaz, *Jury Rules Nushawn Williams Has Condition Making Him Likely to Commit More Sex Crimes,* Buffalo News (June 28, 2013) (Williams completed his 12-year prison sentence in 2010 but remains imprisoned under a N.Y.S. law allowing confinement of dangerous sex offenders).

For these reasons, partner notification practices almost always involve the voluntary assent of index cases. Still, access to specific information about others' exposure might be deemed essential to thwart major threats to the public's health such as during an outbreak of smallpox caused by bioterrorists.

F. VACCINATION

Widespread vaccination of the population is one of the premier public health achievements of the 20th century due in part to legal support at all levels of government. CDC, *Achievements in Pub. Health, 1900–999 Impact of Vaccines Universally Recommended for Children*, 48 MMWR 243 (1999). The federal Food and Drug Administration (FDA) is authorized to approve vaccines for use in the population. 42 U.S.C. § 262 (2012).

CDC's Advisory Committee on Immunization Practices (ACIP) annually sets vaccination requirements and recommendations, which most states follow in part as a condition of the receipt of federal vaccine funds.

HHS uses these recommendations and other data to provide financial incentives for the manufacture of vaccines and set expectations for public or private insurance coverage. Steven H. Woolf & Doug Campos-Outcalt, *Severing the Link Between*

Coverage Policy and the USPSTF, 309 JAMA 1899 (2013).

All states legally require vaccination of children and adolescents for a host of communicable diseases (e.g., mumps, measles, rubella) as a condition of attendance at elementary, secondary, and often institutes of higher education. Local and state departments of education and health collaborate to monitor the administration of school vaccination requirements. Increasingly states also tie attendance at day-care or other operations to completion of vaccination regimens. *See* CDC, SCHOOL & CHILDCARE VACCINATION SURVS. 1 (2007–2008).

As discussed below, vaccine mandates are overwhelmingly approved by courts. An attempt by the New York City Board of Health to require annual influenza vaccines for children, however, was rejected by a court in 2015. The court found that the Board's unilateral addition of influenza to the list of conditions for which kids must be vaccinated prior to day-care or school entry exceeded the Board's delegated authority from the State legislature. *Garcia v. N.Y.C. Dep't of Health & Mental Hygiene*, No. 161484, 2015 WL 9215585 (N.Y. Sup. Dec. 16, 2015). On appeal, New York's highest court reversed, finding that the lower court was wrong to stop enforcement of the flu vaccine rules, which were promulgated within the scope of the city's authority. *Garcia v. N.Y.C. Dep't of Health & Mental Hygiene*, 106 N.E.3d 1187, 1190 (N.Y. 2018).

Public health authorities routinely operate vaccine information campaigns in response to annual influenza, help set policies for vaccinating public and private HCWs, and encourage or require vaccination in real-time during outbreaks or emergency events. In most cases, vaccines are administered with consent of the individual or a minor's parent or guardian, although the scope of consent varies. In a Louisiana case, for example, a court held that informed consent did not have to include notice of a 1 in 8 million risk of contracting polio from a vaccine because a reasonable person with knowledge of this risk would still get vaccinated. *Boyd v. La. Med. Mut. Ins. Co.*, 593 So. 2d 427 (La. Ct. App. 1991).

The U.S. Supreme Court approved government's imposition of vaccines to control epidemic diseases in 1905 in *Jacobson* (discussed in Chapter 3), and separately endorsed school vaccination programs in 1922. *Zucht v. King*, 260 U.S. 174 (1922) (allowing to stand a San Antonio, Texas requirement that children be vaccinated as a condition of school attendance against due process and equal protection challenges). Still, vaccination implementation across jurisdictions is inconsistent in part because of legal exceptions. Based on respect of 1st Amendment freedom of religion principles (discussed initially in Chapter 3), nearly all states (except CA, CT, ME, MS, NY, and WV) allow religious exemptions from school vaccination or child care requirements. Fifteen states still also recognize philosophically-based exceptions. *States with Religious & Philosophical Exemptions from School Immunization Requirements*, NAT'L CONF. OF STATE LEGISLATURES (Aug. 3, 2023).

Standards for administering these exceptions vary. In some states, parents seeking exemptions for their children must (1) provide significant, notarized documentation of their sincere religious beliefs and proof of their denomination's rejection of vaccine; (2) participate in an education session on childhood vaccines; or (3) seek state health department or court approval. In many states, such as Arizona, however, receiving an exception to vaccination mandates is as easy as completing and filing a form through school administration.

Ease of obtaining vaccination exemptions is problematic in an era where misinformation widely circulated through social media or other sources raises concerns over vaccine safety. In 2019, WHO classified vaccine hesitancy as a major threat to global health. Lawrence O. Gostin et al., *The Public Health Crisis of Underimmunisation: A Global Plan of Action*, 20(1) LANCET INFECTIOUS DISEASES E11 (2020). As per Figure 4.6, vaccine hesitancy is a major factor in the U.S. as well.

Figure 4.6. Surveillance of Vaccine Hesitancy

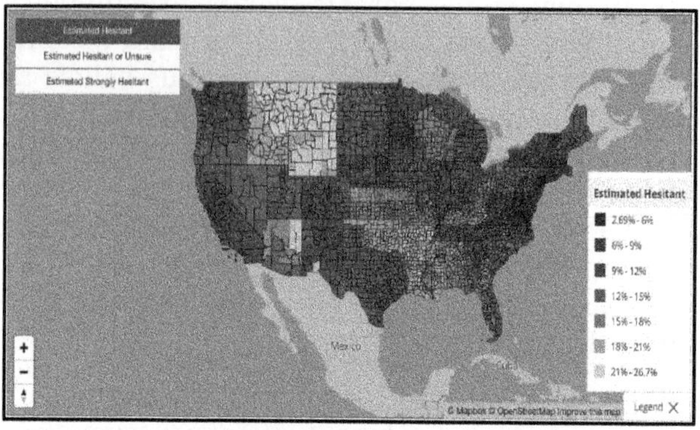

Source: *CDC, Estimates of Vaccine Hesitancy for COVID-19* (June 7, 2021).

Some believe childhood vaccinations cause autism or other conditions based in part on debunked scientific reports and political influences. After meeting with President Donald Trump in January 2017, vaccine critic and 2024 Presidential candidate Robert F. Kennedy Jr. announced he would lead a commission exploring links between vaccines and autism. Editorial, *Trump's Vaccine-Commission Idea Is Biased & Dangerous*, 541 NATURE 259 (Jan. 19, 2017). The commission never materialized, although Kennedy remains an anti-vax advocate. Roni Caryn Rabin, *On Vaccines 'He Is Wrong,' Family Says of Kennedy*, N.Y. TIMES, May 9, 2019.

Lax requirements for religious or philosophical exemptions can compromise vaccination compliance rates. *See LePage v. Dep't of Health*, 18 P.3d 1177 (Wy. 2001) (invalidating health department assessments of claims of religious support for exemption). CDC recorded the highest national rate of vaccine exemptions among kindergarten students ever (3%) in 2022–2023. Lena H. Sun, *Vaccine exemptions for kindergartners hit highest level yet, CDC data shows*, WASH. POST, Nov. 9, 2023. Routine outbreaks of preventable conditions can result from low vaccine uptakes (as per the case study below).

Measles Outbreak—Disneyland

In December 2014, a measles outbreak beginning from a single infected person at Disneyland, California led to the infection of 117 people in 7 states. Most of these infected persons were unvaccinated for measles due to religious or philosophical exemptions or were too young to be vaccinated. Nakia S. Clemmons et al., *Measles—U.S., Jan. 4–Apr. 2, 2015*, 64 MMWR 373, 373–76 (2015).

In response, California enacted legislation on June 30, 2015 to eliminate most religious or philosophical exemptions to childhood vaccine requirements by 2016. Charlotte Alter, *California Governor Jerry Brown Signs Mandatory Vaccine Law*, TIME (June 30, 2015). It became the largest U.S. state by population to require all school children to receive vaccinations except those seeking medical exemptions.

Additional outbreaks of preventable childhood diseases have since arisen nationally. In New York State, vaccine hesitancy particularly among Orthodox Jewish communities within and outside New York City led to significant rises in cases of measles in 2019. Lawrence O. Gostin & James G. Hodge, Jr., *Potential Discrimination in New York City's Measles PHE Order*, THE HILL, Apr. 11, 2019. The city and surrounding municipalities declared a PHE in the Spring 2019 to address burgeoning cases, enforce vaccination requirements, and temporarily close schools and limit public gatherings. Tyler Pager, *'Monkey, Rat & Pig DNA:' Vaccine Fears Drive a Measles Surge*, N.Y. TIMES, Apr. 10, 2019.

A judge in Rockland County (outside N.Y.C.) voided a PHE declaration issued by a county executive as unlawful and unwarranted. *Rockland County Measles Outbreak: Judge Lifts Ban on Unvaccinated Children, but Not Because Outbreak Ended*, CBS NEWS (Apr. 5, 2019). Like California, soon after the measles outbreak, New York State legislatively eliminated religious exemptions from childhood vaccination requirements. Assemb. B. 2371A, 2019–2020 Gen. Assemb., Reg. Sess. (N.Y. 2019).

While most state or federal courts approve statutory or regulatory vaccination exceptions, constitutional conundrums under the 1st and 14th Amendments have led to varying decisions. In *Brown v. Stone*, 378 So. 2d 218 (Miss. 1979), the Mississippi Supreme Court invalidated the state's religious exemption on equal protection grounds because most parents would not qualify for it. When the New York State legislature repealed a religious exemption applied to school vaccination mandates in 2019, parents sued in *F.F. v. State*, 108 N.Y.S.3d 761 (Sup. Ct. 2019), claiming religious discrimination and equal protection violations. The New York Supreme Court, Albany County denied their claims, favoring "public health concerns" over "respect for religious beliefs."

In *Boone v. Boozman*, 217 F. Supp. 2d 938 (E.D. Ark. 2002), a federal district court demonstrated how the companion portions of the 1st Amendment to protect religious freedom can be interpreted inappositely. The court struck down Arkansas' religious-belief exemption as a violation of the Establishment Clause (because it had the purpose or effect of advancing religion) as well as the Free Exercise Clause (because it supported the religious rights of those within a "recognized church or religious denomination" but not others). Overriding the court's decision, the Arkansas legislature reformed its statutes to include religious and philosophical exemptions. ARK. CODE ANN. § 6–18–702(d) (2005).

While these cases diverge from most courts' permissive view of the constitutionality of religious or philosophical vaccine exemptions, they reflect the considerable legal tensions at stake in the implementation of vaccines against the backdrop of religious beliefs and public misperceptions about vaccines' risks. *See, e.g.,* James G. Hodge, Jr. & Lawrence O. Gostin, *School Vaccination Requirements: Historical, Social & Legal Perspectives*, 90 KY. L.J. 831 (2002).

Religious Freedom Restoration Act

The Religious Freedom Restoration Act (RFRA), 42 U.S.C. § 2000cc et seq. (2015), passed by Congress in 1993 (and later by 23 states) provides additional protection beyond the 1st Amendment for individuals' religious beliefs. RFRA may be used to (1) expand already permissive religious-based vaccine exemptions; and (2) undermine immunization requirements. Broad definitions of who constitutes a "person" under the Act, as well as how one may "exercise" religion, may lend to religious-based objections to vaccine requirements. Under RFRA, a person need only demonstrate that a particular vaccine mandate substantially burdened one's exercise of religion.

Government can override these objections by demonstrating a compelling governmental interest furthered through the least restrictive means. *See e.g.,* James G. Hodge Jr., *Protecting*

Religious Freedoms & the Public's Health, 130 PUB. HEALTH REP. 1, 8–11 (2015).

Vaccines are extremely safe when used consistent with FDA approvals for specific populations. Still, the potential for adverse reactions to vaccines among select patients may arise. The National Vaccine Injury Compensation Program, created in 1986, provides no-fault relief for affected persons provided they can show their injuries or deaths are related to the administration of a vaccine listed by the Program. National Childhood Vaccine Injury Act of 1986, 42 U.S.C. §§ 300aa–1 to 300aa–34 (2012). To date, nearly 20,000 claims have been adjudicated through appointed Special Masters. HRSA, NAT'L VACCINE INJURY COMPENSATION PROG. DATA (June 1, 2021). Primary recourse through the Program is necessitated in part by the Act's limitation on state-based claims for damages related to design defects of vaccines (discussed in Chapter 7). *See Brusewitz v. Wyeth*, 562 U.S. 223 (2011). Additional vaccine-related liability protections in declared emergencies are examined in Chapters 11 and 12.

The legal powers to prevent and control communicable diseases through testing, screening, treatment, and vaccination are core facets of public health practice. Sometimes public health authorities must respond through powers designed not only to detect and deter infectious diseases, but also to separate individuals and populations who pose risks to others. Through social distancing measures, examined more closely in Chapter 5, public health agents create space among individuals and groups to thwart the spread of communicable conditions. In so doing, they can raise dynamic and controversial issues in how to use law effectively, fairly, and constitutionally in the promotion of the public's health.

	Chapter 4—Discussion Questions
?	1. When do public health agencies appropriately use voluntary, mandatory & compulsory powers?
?	2. How does law support core communicable disease control powers like testing & screening?
?	3. How are individual & communal interests balanced to control diseases?
?	4. What are some legal solutions to complex issues related to permissive vaccination policies?
?	5. When may disease control powers be altered or limited via public health ethics?

CHAPTER 5
SOCIAL DISTANCING MEASURES

	Chapter 5—Learning Objectives
✓	1. Compare & contrast differing types of social distancing powers
✓	2. Assess the implementation & use of these powers among different levels of government
✓	3. Examine potentially significant infringements of individual rights to liberty & due process
✓	4. Determine lawful paths to properly balancing social distancing powers & individual rights
✓	5. Understand the legal & ethical elements supporting voluntarism in public health practice

In addition to public health powers to test, screen, treat, and vaccinate, other powers are also available to control communicable conditions. Social distancing powers including quarantine, isolation, curfew, and closure are among the oldest (and some may say the most antiquated) public health measures. Although wielded historically in ways that occasionally castigated affected persons, social distancing powers are not punitive *per se*. Rather, they are designed solely to limit the spread of air-borne or other easily-transmitted conditions through infected or exposed individuals. As seen during the COVID-19 pandemic (explored in Chapter 12), these powers continue to be relied on in furtherance of the public's health often when other interventions are unavailable or ineffective.

Application and enforcement of social distancing can be highly controversial in large part because of their effects on constitutional rights to freedom of movement, assembly, bodily integrity, and privacy (as discussed initially in Chapter 3). Purported infringements on civil liberties among individuals and groups can arouse legal and ethical challenges. For these reasons, such measures may be administered or enforced sparingly despite broad legal authorization for their use at the federal, state, or local levels.

As examined below, what may be legally authorized in creating social distances between individuals does not always comport with what is practiced in the field of public health. For example, federal health or state authorities may legally-apprehend and isolate an individual suspected of carrying any of a number of highly-infectious conditions. In practice, however, they may defer to ethical principles supporting voluntary compliance of individuals whose lives and families may be at risk from serious infectious diseases due to their unintended exposures.

Beginning with the dynamic and controversial powers of quarantine and isolation, legal authority and challenges to implementing social distancing measures are examined closely in the following sections.

A. STATE/LOCAL QUARANTINE & ISOLATION

The primary objective underlying the powers to quarantine and isolate individuals or groups is the separation of at-risk and infectious individuals from healthy persons to limit further transmission within communities. Though often used interchangeably by law- and policy-makers, quarantine and isolation are distinct legal powers. Isolation involves separating known, infected persons while quarantine involves separating persons who are merely exposed to infectious conditions (*see* the definitions in the text box below).

Quarantine	*Isolation*
Separation of a person or group of persons presumed or known to have been exposed to a communicable disease to avoid infections with those not exposed	Separation of a person or group of persons known or suspected to be infected with a communicable disease to prevent further spread of infection

All states' public health laws authorize the isolation or quarantine of individuals for varied communicable diseases. TFAH, READY OR NOT? PROTECTING THE PUBLIC'S HEALTH IN THE AGE OF

BIOTERRORISM (2004). Figure 5.1 illustrates an historic quarantine posting authorized via law.

Figure 5.1. Quarantine Posting

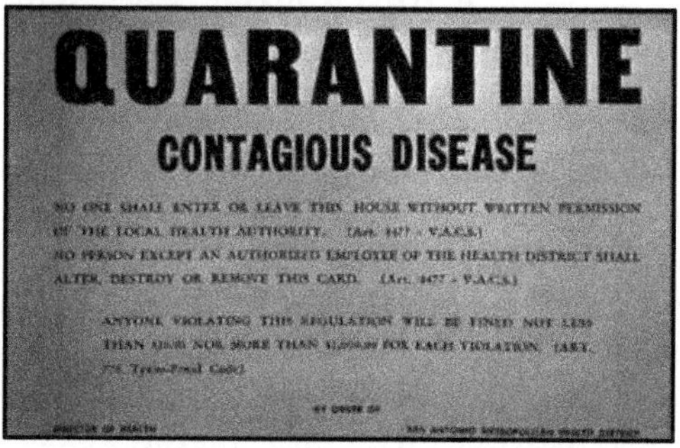

Delaware state law, for example, authorizes that "[p]ersons shall be isolated or quarantined if it is determined by clear and convincing evidence that the person . . . poses a significant risk of transmitting a disease to others with serious consequences." DEL. CODE ANN. tit. 20, § 3136(2) (West 2002). Absent clear and convincing evidence supporting such measures, Delaware law clarifies: "[a] person's refusal to accept medical examination, vaccination or treatment . . . shall constitute prima facie evidence that said person should be quarantined or isolated." Subject to varied degrees of specificity, many tribal and local governments include similar provisions in their respective laws.

Quarantine or isolation powers are used routinely across the U.S., particularly involving persons with active cases of TB or other airborne, infectious conditions. During the COVID-19 pandemic of

2020/2021, hundreds of thousands of Americans were subjected to formal quarantine and isolation orders across all levels of government (*see* Chapter 12). Early in the pandemic, for example, CDC quarantined thousands of Americans aboard specific flights returning from affected regions of China on U.S. military bases in California, Texas, and other locales. Bill Chappell, *Coronavirus Update: 346 Americans Emerge from Quarantine at California Military Bases*, NPR (Feb. 18, 2020).

Implementation of these powers varies based on specific circumstances and other factors, including the:

- *underlying infectious condition*—deadly or non-treatable disabling conditions (e.g., COVID-19, EVD) or bioterrorism agents (e.g., smallpox) may garner considerably more attention than other non-deadly diseases;
- *mode of transmission*—in general the greater the communicability of a condition, the more likely specific interventions designed to curtail its spread may be used;
- *duration*—these powers are typically limited to the period of time in which a person may actively communicate a disease to others;
- *setting*—which may include homes, workplaces, schools, health care facilities, transportation hubs, or other off-site environments; and

- *need for varied medical treatment*—persons requiring significant medical care may be quarantined or isolated in an equipped hospital or specialty treatment center.

With some exceptions, routine (e.g., non-emergency) exercises of these powers do not generate significant legal or political controversies. Katherine T. Rooney, *U.S. Biological Quarantine: A Look at the Legal Framework*, 42 J. LEGIS. 101 (2016). This is due, in large part, to the fact that (1) most state or local public health agencies seek to respect the interests of those subject to quarantine or isolation; and (2) affected persons often voluntarily comply with efforts undertaken by state or local public health agencies. There are, however, multiple reported case decisions to the contrary.

On June 17, 2005, Ruby Washington was diagnosed with noninfectious pulmonary TB. She received TB medication initially via a clinic in Wisconsin, but did not show up for her follow up appointments. Concerned that her condition may become infectious and she might flee the area, Milwaukee's Health Department ordered Ms. Washington to submit to ongoing DOT. Most persons subject to these orders comply voluntarily without further incident. Not Ruby, however. She failed repeatedly to adhere to its terms or show up for specific appointments. Consequently, the health department petitioned the court for her long-term confinement in a local jail against her objections. The court held that Wisconsin's TB control statute authorizes long-term confinement (even in jail if necessary) of a person infected with active TB who fails or refuses to comply with a prescribed treatment regimen. *In re Washington*, 735 N.W.2d 111 (Wisc. 2007).

Washington's treatment and confinement of a recalcitrant TB patient in jail facilities are not unprecedented. In a widely-publicized case 2 years later in Arizona in 2007, Robert Daniels became ill in the Phoenix metropolitan area after he contracted XDR-TB in Moscow. He was placed initially in a county sanitarium, but health officials claimed he willfully failed to take his medication and appeared in public without wearing a required mask intended to limit his risk of transmission to others. As a result, Daniels was isolated involuntarily for 10 months during which time he was allegedly subjected to inhumane treatment. A high profile challenge of his confinement was brought by the American Civil Liberties Union, lending to national media attention. Richard Nox, *Arizona TB Patient Jailed as a Public Health Menace*, NPR, (June 11, 2007). A federal district court in Arizona later dismissed the claim. *Daniels v. Maricopa County, et al.*, No. 2:07–cv–01080–SRB (D. Ariz. 2009).

In a similar case in Texas nearly a decade later, *In re Commitment of J.S.T.*, 478 S.W.3d 856 (Tex. Ct. App. 2015), J.S.T. tested positive multiple times for TB, but refused to take his medication consistently. The Galveston County Health District ordered him to "implement and carry out measures" applied to other TB patients. When J.S.T. refused, the district sought his involuntary commitment to the Texas Center of Infectious Disease in San Antonio for treatment. As in the *Washington* case, the court approved the isolation proceedings based on evidence that J.S.T. was infected with a long-term communicable disease that presented a real threat to the public's health if left untreated.

TB is not the only condition for which restrictive quarantine or isolation measures may be undertaken. In 2014, nurse Kaci Hickox (*see* Figure 5.2) was quarantined in New Jersey and Maine during the Ebola outbreak. She was initially targeted for interventions after showing an elevated fever via a standard Ebola screening at Newark's airport following her work abroad treating EVD patients in Sierra Leone. On October 24, 2014, New Jersey Governor Chris Christie and state health authorities determined that she must be quarantined based on her temperature reading and travel history. For over 60 hours, Hickox was physically separated from others in a tent adjacent to a local hospital in Newark and monitored for additional signs of EVD infection. Anemona Hartocollis & Emma G. Fitzsimmons, *Tested Negative for Ebola, Nurse Criticizes Her Quarantine*, N.Y. TIMES, Oct. 25, 2014. She later sued Governor Christie (among others) for her temporary confinement. As a result the State of New Jersey agreed to abide by a series of enhanced quarantine rights in the future. Marc Santora, *New Jersey Accepts Quarantine Rights to End Ebola Suit*, N.Y. TIMES, July 28, 2017.

Figure 5.2. Nurse Kaci Hickox

Source: Illustration by Avery M. Hodge

On October 27, 2014, Hickox was allowed to return to her residence in Maine after objecting to her situation in New Jersey. Soon after her arrival, however, Maine Governor Paul LePage (*see* Figure 5.3) and Health Commissioner Mary Mayhew attempted to impose a mandatory 21-day "home quarantine" court order on Hickox. Jennifer Levitz, *Nurse Defies Ebola Quarantine in Maine*, WALL ST. J. (Oct. 30, 2014). After another HCW, Dr. Craig Spencer, was determined to be EVD+ just 24 hours after visiting varied public destinations in New York City, Maine's limited quarantine against Hickox was framed as a public health necessity. Faith Karimi, *From Guinea to the U.S.: Timeline of First Ebola Patient in N.Y.C.*, CNN (Oct. 25, 2014). Hickox challenged the quarantine order in court.

Figure 5.3. Maine Governor Paul LePage

On October 31, a federal district court judge found that the State lacked "clear and convincing evidence" that Hickox posed sufficient risks to the community to support her mandatory home quarantine. *Mayhew v. Hickox*, No. FORDC–CV–2014–36, 2014 U.S. Dist. (D. Maine 2014). Her initial high temperature reading at the Newark airport proved to be an anomaly. She evinced no further EVD symptoms. Lacking any additional proof of harm, Hickox's quarantine order was deemed unnecessary and unlawful. Though released from restrictive home isolation, Hickox was required by the court to complete a self-monitoring program for signs of Ebola infection until mid-November 2014. Dave Sherwood & Colleen Jenkins, *Nurse Kaci Hickox and State of Maine Settle Quarantine Lawsuit*, SCI. AM. (2014).

B. FEDERAL QUARANTINE & ISOLATION

As per the cases summarized above, most exercises of quarantine and isolation powers in the U.S. are conducted by state, tribal, or local authorities who typically are on the frontlines of such cases. Federal agents do not usually get involved directly in administering social distancing powers, even though they may have authority to do so. CDC has long been empowered under statutory law (PHSA, 42 U.S.C. § 6A (2016)) to quarantine or isolate individuals who are (1) traveling into the U.S. or between states and (2) suspected of carrying a communicable disease.

As per Figure 5.4, the list of diseases for which CDC may quarantine individuals is limited via Executive Order to conditions like measles, plague, smallpox, EVD, and "severe acute respiratory syndromes," like SARS or COVID-19. Exec. Order No. 13295, 68 Fed. Reg. 17255 (Apr. 4, 2003), amended by No. 14047, 86 Fed. Reg. 52591 (Sept. 22, 2021).

Figure 5.4. List of Quarantinable Diseases

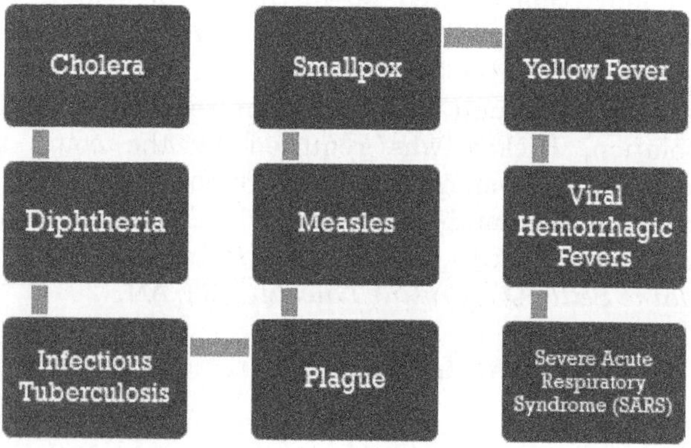

To monitor for persons with these conditions, and intervene in cases where infected individuals may arrive or circulate within the U.S., CDC operates several quarantine stations in major transportation hubs across the country (*see* Figure 5.5). CDC medical and public health personnel are authorized to investigate and determine whether ill persons can enter or travel in the U.S. They may also screen cargo, inspect animals, and conduct public health surveillance and monitoring activities of immigrants, refugees, asylees, and parolees. Where quarantine of individuals is warranted CDC officers may issue orders and align with state and local health officials to assure their successful completion. James J. Misrahi et al., *HHS/CDC Legal Response to SARS Outbreak*, 10 EMERGING INFECTIOUS DISEASES 353 (2004).

Figure 5.5. CDC Quarantine Stations

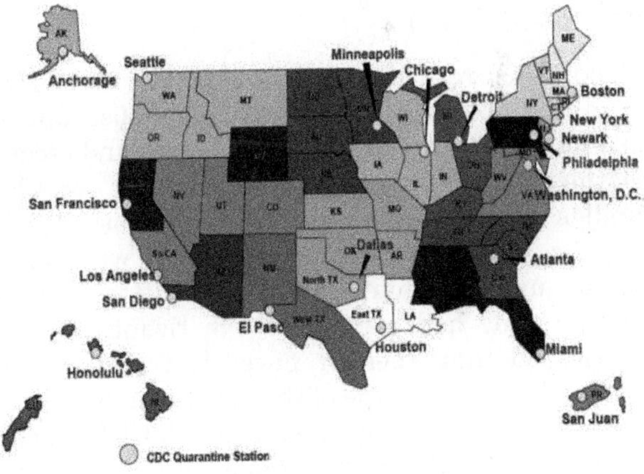

CDC's limited quarantine authority was thoroughly tested in a well-publicized case in 2007 involving a recalcitrant individual with TB. Andrew Speaker, an attorney practicing in Atlanta, Georgia (CDC's home base), contracted TB during his prior travels. Although local health authorities in Georgia asked him to limit his future travel, Speaker left Atlanta's international airport for an extensive European trip with his recent bride. After Speaker departed (despite local orders not to go), CDC determined from lab samples that he may have XDR-TB. Federal officials notified Speaker overseas and asked him to report to health authorities in Italy where he was located at the time. When he refused, an international media storm erupted. Speaker eventually returned to the U.S. days later by flying into Canada and driving across the border into New York State. David P. Fidler et al., *Through the Quarantine Looking Glass: Drug-Resistant TB & Public Health Governance, Law & Ethics,* 35 JLME 526, 526–33 (2007).

Upon his return, CDC issued its 1st federal quarantine order since the early 1960s. Speaker surrendered to public health authorities and received treatment at a Denver hospital that regularly handles TB patients. Multiple persons close to Speaker during his extensive travels were briefly placed under limited quarantine to ascertain whether they had contracted TB. Eventually CDC determined that Speaker never had XDR-TB, but rather a less severe type of the disease. A subsequent lawsuit brought by Speaker against CDC alleging privacy and other violations was summarily dismissed on September 14, 2012. *Speaker v. CDC*, 489 F. App'x 425 (11th Cir. 2012).

The incidents surrounding Speaker, as well as prior PHE events nationally, illustrated the limits of CDC's antiquated disease control regulations which it had repeatedly sought to amend. In 2005, CDC proposed a comprehensive series of regulations to allow individuals to be detained up to 3 business days pending an order for quarantine, isolation, conditional release, or a "finding of no infection." Control of Communicable Diseases, 70 Fed. Reg. 229 (proposed Nov. 30, 2005). These proposed regulations were never implemented. In 2012, the agency slightly amended its regulations to broaden their scope and revamp definitions of quarantine, isolation, and other existing terms. Control of Communicable Diseases: Interstate; Scope & Definitions, 77 Fed. Reg. 247 (proposed Dec. 26, 2012).

Additional reforms, however, were needed. After months of deliberations, CDC published a sweeping final rule to clarify and enhance its powers on January 19, 2017, a day prior to the inauguration of President Donald J. Trump. Control of Communicable Diseases, 82 Fed. Reg. 6890 (Jan. 19, 2017). These new regulations support upgraded prevention measures at U.S. airports and other transit locations where individuals engage in international, interstate, or even purely intrastate travel. Measures include active screening techniques (e.g., observation, questioning, and review of suspect travelers' documents and health records) and social distancing powers including apprehension, quarantine, and isolation.

To facilitate early detection, CDC's measures extend to anyone "reasonably believed" to have a "quarantinable communicable disease," listed via Executive Order noted above (*see* Figure 5.4). "Ill persons" include those with signs (e.g., fever, rash, headache, persistent cough) or "any other symptoms or indications" as determined by CDC. Federal officials may issue orders for apprehension, isolation, quarantine, or conditional release of affected individuals for up to 72 hours without a formal hearing.

To assist in the agency's determinations, an affected individual may be required to undergo a medical examination by a licensed HCW. Examinations may include testing as reasonably necessary to confirm or rule out the presence of a quarantinable condition. Those determined to be infected may be isolated and prohibited from engaging in interstate or international travel (with some exceptions) without a federal travel permit. Lawrence O. Gostin & James G. Hodge, Jr., *Reforming Fed. Pub. Health Powers: Responding to Nat'l & Global Threats*, 317 JAMA 1211 (2017).

The expansive scope and breadth of CDC's revised social distancing powers were relied on during the COVID-19 pandemic to quarantine and isolate thousands of persons aboard planes returning from affected regions overseas over a period of several weeks beginning in late January 2020. CDC, *COVID-19 Timeline* (2020).

As planes carrying Americans arrived from China and other locales, federal authorities directed them to land typically on U.S. military basis in several states including Alabama, California and Texas. Passengers were deplaned, housed on military bases, and subjected to 14 day quarantine orders. Individual rights-based objections arose focused on temporary due process violations.

However, surrounding communities where CDC quarantined individuals also raised legal objections to their release. On February 28, 2020, city officials in Costa Mesa, California obtained a temporary injunction from a federal court to block CDC's transfer of individuals housed at a nearby military base who were exposed to or infected with COVID-19. CDC was forced to drop its plans to relocate persons to a former state facility in the area. Hillary Davis & Faith E. Pinho, *Fed. Gov't Says It Won't Put Coronavirus Patients in Costa Mesa*, L.A. TIMES (Feb. 28, 2020).

On March 2, local officials in the City of San Antonio and Bexar County sued CDC and others to attempt to block CDC from releasing 120+ COVID-19 evacuees from quarantine at the nearby Joint Base San Antonio-Lackland. Lauren Caruba & Sig Christenson, *San Antonio, Bexar Cnty. in Battle with CDC over Evacuees in Coronavirus Quarantine*, SAN ANTONIO EXPRESS News (Mar. 3, 2020). Concerns arose over whether the release of such persons following quarantine might result in unintentional spread of COVID-19 in the community. One woman previously released from the base tested positive for

COVID-19. U.S. district court Judge Xavier Rodriguez (*see* Figure 5.6) denied the local governments' request while admonishing CDC for "washing its own hands further of this quarantine." *See* Roseanna Garza, *City Sues Feds for Stricter Quarantine Measures; Judge Denies Request*, SAN ANTONIO REP. (Mar. 2, 2020).

Figure 5.6. Judge Xavier Rodriguez

CDC's reliance on determinations grounded in officers' "reasonable beliefs" of an individual's infection to support one's apprehension, quarantine or isolation may lead to additional objections outside declared emergencies like COVID-19. Utilization of lax criteria to warrant interventions like apprehension or limited duration quarantine falls below the "clear and convincing" standard of evidence generally applied to justify deprivations of liberty interests. Broadly defining "ill persons" allows federal officials wide discretion to make initial determinations of a traveler's health status, but could also lead to unjustified orders imposed on individuals with relatively minor conditions. To the extent CDC's regulations do not require external assessments or reviews via a neutral decision maker, individuals may arguably be denied procedural due process.

C. CURFEWS & CLOSURES

Outside of formally-declared emergencies, curfews and closures are typically used in response to perceived or actual threats to communities stemming from acts of violence, loitering, epidemics, mass disasters, or outbreaks of food-borne illnesses from commercial or other sources. They are designed to set temporary limits on the time or place of assembly of individuals so as to mitigate the spread of disease or minimize risks of harm.

State or local public health officers may, for example, order curfews for communities affected by disease to disassociate individuals from gathering in large groups. Utilization and application of such orders to entire communities were heavily relied on during the COVID-19 pandemic (*see* Chapter 12) pursuant to extensive emergency declarations. Routine, non-emergency use of curfews may include standing orders for specific persons or groups to avoid gatherings in certain places during set times (*see* Figure 5.7).

Figure 5.7. Curfew Sign

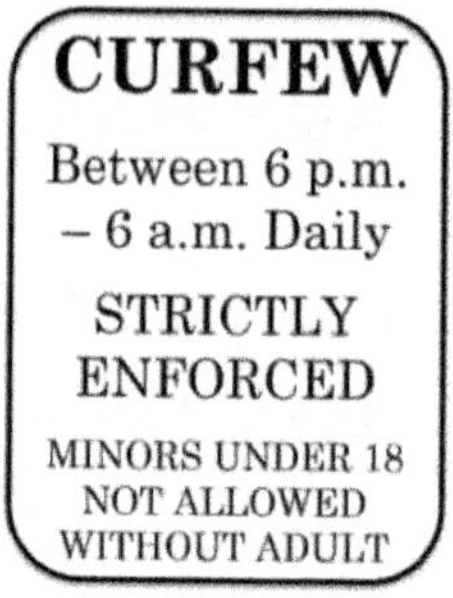

Provided orders for curfews are warranted by demonstrated public and safety concerns, temporary infringements on individuals' liberty or rights to travel are allowed. *See In re Juan C.*, 33 Cal. Rptr. 2d 919, 922 (Ct. App. 1994) ("Though the right to travel . . . is constitutionally protected, [it] may be legitimately curtailed [via curfew] when a community has been ravaged by flood, fire or disease, and its safety and welfare are threatened." (citing *Zemel v. Rusk,* 381 U.S. 1, 15–16 (1965)).

People v. Liccione

In *People v. Liccione,* 39 Misc. 3d 838, 964 N.Y.S.2d 405 (Just. Ct. 2013), a New York juvenile, age 17, was charged with violating a curfew law in the Village of Hilton (in western N.Y. near Rochester).

The law was enacted by the Village Board because it determined that large numbers of minors were congregating after dark and disturbing residents. Stated purposes of the curfew were to reduce juvenile crime and vandalism, protect children, and reinforce parental authority.

The juvenile moved to dismiss the charge arguing that the law "violate[d] . . . due process rights to enjoy freedom of movement and a parent's right to control the upbringing of [his or her] children." The court disagreed, holding that the curfew law was a necessary response to reported disturbances from the presence of minors in public areas after dark.

Closure orders may be implemented by public health agencies (often with law enforcement) to shut down places that either are:

- the source of an outbreak (e.g., a restaurant responsible for serving contaminated food). In September 2023, local health officials in Seattle ordered the closure of a restaurant after nearly 3 dozen patrons were sickened with gastrointestinal illnesses. Paige Cornwell, *Health Officials Close Kirkland Restaurant after 34 People Sickened*, SEATTLE TIMES, Sept. 21, 2023; or

- an environment where disease may be easily spread (e.g., a school where student gatherings may further influenza infections). In March 2023, an elementary school in Long Beach, CA was closed temporarily in the backdrop of a norovirus outbreak among students and staff. Fernando Haro Garcia, *Carver Elementary School Ordered to Close Amid Norovirus Outbreak*, LONG BEACH POST NEWS, Mar. 16, 2023.

New Jersey statutory law provides, for example, that the Commissioner of Health in an emergency may "close [or] direct and compel the evacuation of . . . any facility [for] which there is reasonable cause to believe that it may endanger the public health." N.J. STAT. ANN. § 26:13–8 (West 2005). Every state executed these types of powers during the COVID-19 pandemic (*see* Chapter 12).

D. PERSONAL LIBERTIES

Intrusions on personal liberties stemming from social distancing measures vary. As noted above, isolation or quarantine orders can significantly restrict individual movement by authorizing the forcible removal of persons from their homes for the duration of their infectivity. In most cases, however, these orders typically seek voluntary compliance in alignment with public health ethics and principles of health justice. Public health officials encourage affected individuals to remain at home and utilize universal precautions to prevent the spread of disease, unless specific medical care warrants one's placement in a health care setting.

In cases where uses of coercive public health powers may be needed or relied on, public health authorities must be prepared to demonstrate to courts assessing potential challenges that:

- the subject of social distancing measures is actually, or is reasonably suspected of, being infectious (re: isolation) or exposed to infectious conditions (re: quarantine);

- the subject poses a specific threat to other's health. Temporary quarantine of a group of persons after their exposure to an infectious condition, such as smallpox, is justified to prevent the transmission of a deadly pathogen. Quarantine of a group of persons exposed to annual influenza (which does not substantially threaten most persons' health) may be unlawful except in specific settings (e.g., long-term care or nursing facilities); *see* W. VA. CODE R. 64–13–8 (2017) (allowing isolation or transfer of nursing home residents to prevent the spread of infection));

- the terms of placement are safe and habitable. In 1909, the South Carolina Supreme Court struck down a quarantine order served on an older woman with leprosy in part because she was removed from her comfortable "cottage" home in town to a "pesthouse, coarse and comfortless" near the municipal landfill. *Kirk v. Wyman*, 65 S.E. 387 (S.C. 1909);

- individual or group confinement is warranted. In 1892, about 1,200 Russian Jews were quarantined unjustifiably outside New York City. Most (about 1,150) were healthy people who unfortunately lived in proximity to 50 ship passengers who had developed typhus. HOWARD MARKEL, QUARANTINE! 59 (1997). In *Jew Ho v. Williamson*, 103 F. 10 (N.D. Cal. 1900), a federal district court outlawed a plague-related quarantine order over several blocks of modern-day Chinatown in San Francisco as "unreasonable, unjust, . . . oppressive," and discriminatory. *Id.* at 26; and
- adequate procedural due process is provided (as noted in Chapter 3 and discussed further in the text box below).

Greene v. Edwards

In *Greene v. Edwards*, 263 S.E.2d 661 (W. Va. 1980), the West Virginia Supreme Court required public health authorities to apply the same procedural protections concerning the involuntary commitment of persons with mental illness to those confined due to TB infection. These due process protections include:

1. adequate notice;

2. right to a hearing;
3. right to counsel;
4. right to present and confront witnesses;
5. right to a verbatim transcript; and
6. clear and convincing evidence to justify isolation. *Id.* at 663.

Unlike in *Greene*, so long as appropriate procedures are followed in the implementation of quarantine or isolation measures, courts are typically deferential to state or local public health authorities. In *Levin v. Adalberto M.*, 67 Cal. Rptr.3d 277 (Ct. App. 2007), a Ventura county public health officer sought enforcement of a civil order of detention against Aldalberto M, a TB patient. The California Court of Appeals affirmed the detention, noting that the patient was treated fairly and with compassion at each stage of the process by local public health authorities, law enforcement, and judicial actors. He was provided with medical care, a suitable location, an attorney, and a meaningful opportunity to be heard in court. Under California state and local laws, noted the court, the isolation order must inform affected persons (among other details) of their rights to:

- request release (including identification of local officials through which such request may be made);
- be represented by legal counsel appointed on request; and

- a review of the order within 60 days, even if such review is not specifically requested.

Additional procedural elements may be required in other settings depending on specific state or local legal requirements or practices.

In summary, modern courts tend to closely scrutinize impositions of social distancing measures that affect individual liberties and bodily privacy. Public health authorities must demonstrate a strong governmental interest in support of a well-targeted intervention for which often there is no less restrictive alternative. LAWRENCE O. GOSTIN & LINDSAY F. WILEY, PUBLIC HEALTH LAW: POWER, DUTY, RESTRAINT 430 (3rd ed. 2016). Even though courts tend to defer to the judgments of legislators or health officials as to the need for specific public health interventions (under separation of powers principles noted in Chapter 2), constitutional requirements can limit the use of significant public health powers to control infectious diseases, a persistent theme throughout the COVID-19 pandemic as discussed in Chapter 12.

Communicable diseases will always be a primary part of the public health agenda, but additional legal challenges arise from the emergence of chronic conditions. Collectively, these conditions comprise major foci for public health improvement. Some traditional legal powers, such as testing and screening, are aptly applied to non-communicable conditions. Other powers, like quarantine and isolation, have little use related to chronic conditions. As a result, new legal routes to counter varying threats to community health must be considered. Exploration of these paths begins in Chapter 6.

	Chapter 5—Discussion Questions
?	1. What are the legal or practical differences between quarantine & isolation?
?	2. How might social distancing laws fail to comport with ethical principles of voluntarism?
?	3. What due process requirements are involved in implementing social distancing powers?
?	4. What are potential structural legal challenges to the use of federal social distancing powers?
?	5. What other variables should be considered as to the legality of social distancing powers?

CHAPTER 6

ADDRESSING CHRONIC CONDITIONS

	Chapter 6—Learning Objectives
✓	1. Explore the diverse types & causes of chronic conditions across the U.S.
✓	2. Identify existing uses of traditional public health powers to counter chronic conditions
✓	3. Ascertain the powers to tax, spend & regulate to address chronic conditions nationally
✓	4. Assess the legal & political trade-offs to greater use of laws to prevent chronic conditions
✓	5. Examine how disability rights may support or stigmatize persons with chronic illnesses

Controlling communicable diseases discussed in Chapters 4 and 5 entail considerable public health efforts, but even greater impacts on population health in the 21st century emanate from chronic conditions. Sensational diseases like COVID-19, Zika virus, EVD, H5N1 (avian) flu, or HIV/AIDS grab the public's attention as to how public health authorities intervene, but heart disease, cancers, diabetes, and other conditions are the real killers annually across societies.

Communicable and chronic conditions are often intertwined with sometimes deadly consequences. The heavy focus on controlling EVD in West Africa over multiple months, for example, stripped resources away from other public health measures to address chronic (and other communicable) conditions, leading to deleterious impacts on populations. As Harvard public health professor Dr. Paul Farmer concluded in 2015, "There are more people who are going to die from Ebola, but not have Ebola." Betsy McKay, *Ebola Casts A Long Shadow*, WALL ST. J., June 5, 2015, at A1. After Congress failed for months to authorize major funds to respond to Zika virus infections in 2016, CDC and additional public health agencies had to tap funds from other dedicated sources, including EVD prevention, to respond. *See* James G. Hodge Jr., *Generation Zika*, 57 JURIMETRICS J. 25 (2017).

Multi-year, extensive response efforts devoted to combatting COVID-19 (discussed in Chapter 12) required public health and medical officials to turn away from prior, existing chronic health issues among Americans to address the even more immediate risks to morbidity and mortality presented by infectious diseases. Declinations in Americans' life expectancy inevitably resulted during and after COVID-19, although not entirely to deaths resulting from infectious conditions. ELIZABETH ARIAS ET AL., CDC, PROVISIONAL LIFE EXPECTANCY ESTIMATES FOR 2022 (2023).

Though defying precise definition, chronic conditions are at the source of millions of deaths in the U.S. each year and contribute to massive disability among the living. Joel Achenbach et al, *Chronic Illness Are Killing Us Too Soon*, WASH. POST, Oct. 22, 2023. They are caused by multiple factors, many of which are preventable. Assessing how law can be a tool in the fight against avoidable morbidity and mortality stemming from chronic illnesses requires a close examination of the breadth of public health efforts to alter individual and population-based behaviors.

A. CHRONIC CONDITIONS—DEFINED

Unlike communicable conditions, most chronic conditions are not transferred directly between humans or from other vectors to humans. Beyond this distinction, defining chronic conditions is subject to interpretation. Richard A. Goodman et al., *Defining & Measuring Chronic Conditions: Imperatives for Rsch., Pol'y, Prog. & Practice*, 10 PREVENTING CHRONIC DISEASE E66 (2013).

Chronic conditions are generally characterized by their "uncertain etiology, multiple risk factors, . . . long latency period, . . . prolonged course of illness, noncontagious origin, functional impairment or disability, and incurability." Matthew McKenna & Janet L. Collins, *Current Issues & Challenges in Chronic Disease Control*, *in* PATRICK L. REMINGTON ET AL., CHRONIC DISEASE EPIDEMIOLOGY & CONTROL 1–24 (2nd ed. 2010). These characterizations, however, do not necessarily clarify what conditions are (or are not) classifiable as chronic.

HHS defines chronic illnesses generally as those "conditions that last a year or more and require ongoing medical attention and/or limit activities of daily living." HHS, MULTIPLE CHRONIC CONDITIONS: A STRATEGIC FRAMEWORK 2 (2010). The National Center for Health Statistics (NCHS) defines chronic illnesses as including conditions that are (1) not cured once acquired or (2) present for 3 months or longer. Concerning infants, any conditions present since birth are categorized as chronic, such as Zika-related microcephaly. NCHS, *Def. of "Condition,"* 486–7 app. (2011). Under these dual conceptions, chronic conditions thus include heart disease, many cancers, diabetes, and clinical depression, but not the common cold or temporary injuries.

No matter how defined, the health care costs and public health impacts of physical or mental chronic conditions in the U.S. are staggering. Chronic illnesses are the nation's leading contributor to death and disability. According to CDC:

- 60% of all adults have at least 1 such condition (and more than ½ of them have multiple conditions);
- 26% of the American population is limited in their daily activities by these conditions;
- 70% of all deaths annually are attributable to chronic conditions; and
- 90% of health care costs each year are devoted to their treatment.

CDC, CHRONIC DISEASES & HEALTH PROMOTION (2021).

Worse yet, "[t]he number and proportion of Americans living with chronic conditions [are] increasing" as the population ages. Professor Gerry Anderson predicts that over 170 million Americans will have multiple chronic conditions by 2030. GERARD ANDERSON, CHRONIC CARE: MAKING THE CASE FOR ONGOING CARE 9 (2010). The types and impacts of chronic conditions vary extensively by population (e.g., children, young adults, elderly), but major examples include:

Heart Disease. Nearly one-fifth of U.S. deaths annually (~695,000) are caused by heart disease. CDC, *Heart Disease Fact Sheet* (2023). Costs of health care services, medications, and lost productivity related to coronary heart disease alone were estimated at $407.3 billion in 2018. Connie W. Tsao et al., *Heart Disease and Stroke Statistics—2023 Update: A Report from the American Heart Association*, 147 CIRCULATION e93, e101 (2023).

As per Figure 6.1, mortality from heart disease ranges across the U.S. based on geography and age.

Figure 6.1. Heart Disease Death Rates

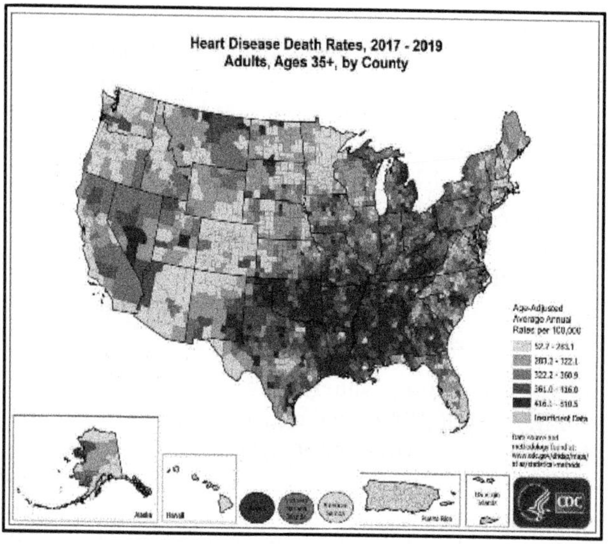

Cancers. Even though the definition of cancer is constantly evolving as scientists unravel more about its properties, its collective impacts on human health are immense (*see* Figure 6.2, below). In general, "cancer" refers to a wide array of illnesses involving the development of abnormal cells that can divide rapidly and infiltrate and destroy bodily tissues. Mayo Clinic Staff, *Cancer*, MAYO CLINIC (May 23, 2015). In 2023, over 1.9 million new cases of cancer arose in the U.S., with projected deaths in excess of 609,000, many by lung cancers caused by smoking (127,070). Am. Cancer Soc., CANCER FACTS & FIGURES (2023).

Figure 6.2. Top 3 Cancers in the U.S. by Sex 2021

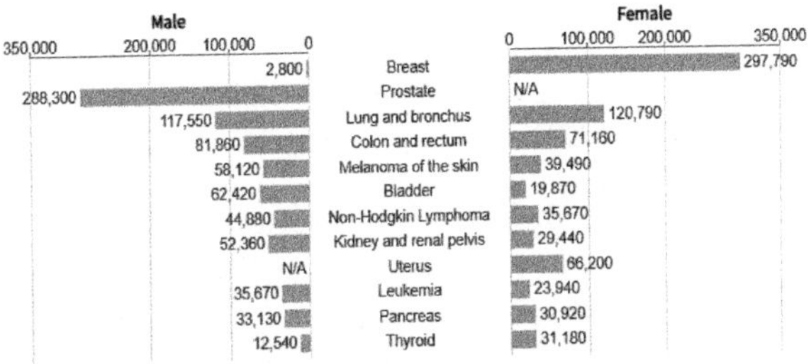

Source: Am. Cancer Soc. (2023)

In 2023, President Biden vowed to "end cancer as we know it" through his "moonshot" initiative designed to cut the cancer death rate by 50% or more by 2047. Dan Diamond, *Biden picks Vanderbilt physician to lead National Cancer Institute*, WASH. POST, Nov. 18, 2023. Still ongoing, annual risks of cancer are profound for 5,000+ Americans who learn they have cancer each day in 2023. Additional concerns arise over increasing rates of colorectal and multiple, other cancers among persons under the age of 50. Heidi Ledford, *Why Are So Many Young People Getting Cancer? What the Data Say*, 627 NATURE 14 (2024). Some scientists have examined whether cancer cells in the future may be communicated from animal to person or directly between persons. George Johnson, *Scientists Ponder Contagious Cancer*, N.Y. TIMES, Feb. 23, 2016.

Diabetes. Type 1 and 2 diabetes affect over 14% of American adults. Over 1.2 million people 18 years and older were newly diagnosed with diabetes in

2021. In addition to requiring daily monitoring and management for many patients, diabetes is also the leading cause of kidney failure, non-traumatic lower limb amputations, and new cases of blindness among adults. CDC, NAT'L DIABETES STAT. RPT. (2023).

Figure 6.3. CDC Snapshot of Diabetes

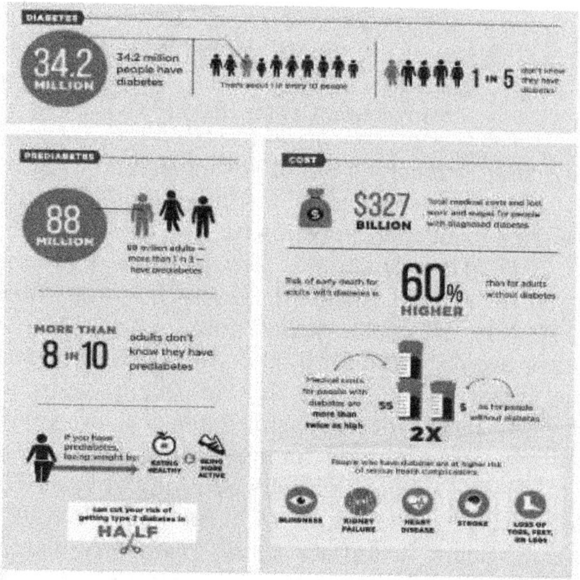

Alzheimer's Disease. Up to 6.7 million Americans age 65 or older are living with Alzheimer's disease, facing an average 4–8 years between diagnosis and death. In 2019, the disease was the official cause of death for 121,499 individuals. ALZHEIMER'S ASSOC., 2023 ALZHEIMER'S DISEASE

FACTS & FIGURES 20, 33 (2023). Death rates vary extensively via age, as per Figure 6.4 below.

Figure 6.4. Age-Adjusted Death Rates for Alzheimer's Disease in the U.S.

Table 6. U.S. annual Alzheimer's death rates (per 100,000 people) by age and year

Age	2000	2002	2004	2006	2008	2010	2012	2014	2016	2017
45-54	0.2	0.1	0.2	0.2	0.2	0.3	0.2	0.2	0.2	0.2
55-64	2.0	1.9	1.8	2.1	2.2	2.1	2.2	2.1	2.7	2.8
65-74	18.7	19.6	19.5	19.9	21.1	19.8	17.9	19.6	23.6	24.5
75-84	139.6	157.7	168.5	175.0	192.5	184.5	175.4	185.6	214.1	219.7
85+	667.7	790.9	875.3	923.4	1002.2	987.1	936.1	1006.8	1216.9	1244.7

Created from data from the National Center for Health Statistics [248].[A12]

Mortality rates related to Alzheimer's disease, however, may be historically under-reported. At least 1 study estimated that over 500,000 deaths in 2010 were attributable to the spectrum of Alzheimer's disease (over 5 times greater than numbers reported via official death certificates). If this study is accurate, Alzheimer's disease was actually the 3rd leading cause of death in the U.S. in 2010. Bryan D. James, et al., *Contribution of Alzheimer Disease to Mortality in the U.S.*, 82 NEUROLOGY 1045 (2014).

Irrespective of the specific numbers of deaths, mortality impacts are significant. One study found that 61% of patients with Alzheimer's disease at age 70 are expected to die before 80 (compared with only 30% of such individuals without the disease). Henry

Michael Arrighi et al., *Lethality of Alzheimer Disease and Its Impact on Nursing Home Placement*, 24 ALZHEIMER DISEASE & ASSOC. DISORDERS 90 (2010).

As with communicable conditions, the sheer numbers of health threats from multiple sources and types of chronic conditions are vast. While the chronic conditions noted above constitute a substantial majority of annual deaths, additional chronic conditions with catastrophic effects on the population's health include arthritis, asthma, chronic obstructive pulmonary disease (COPD), depression, epilepsy, glaucoma, hemophilia, hypertension, osteoporosis, post-traumatic stress disorder (PTSD), and stroke.

B. CAUSES OF CHRONIC CONDITIONS

The causes of chronic conditions are as diverse as the conditions themselves. Contributing factors include genetics, stress, occupation, socioeconomic status, environmental exposures, medical errors or other adverse events, and lack of access to public health or health care services. Even factors outside the norm may contribute to the onset of chronic conditions. In 2024, researchers revealed how specific conditions (e.g., high blood pressure, diabetes) experienced by pregnant women led to increased risks of chronic conditions (e.g., heart disease) of their children nearly a decade after their birth. Roni Caryn Rabin, *Children Born to Mothers With Pregnancy Complications Face Higher Heart Risk*, N.Y. TIMES, Feb. 12, 2024.

Dietary factors are also at play. Three of the 4 primary modifiable health risk behaviors at the source of most chronic conditions relate to what Americans consume. These 3 behaviors are poor nutrition, tobacco use, and excessive alcohol consumption (physical inactivity is the 4th). Regular ingestion and use of "consumable vices," including tobacco, alcohol, sugar, salt, caffeine, nicotine, and high-fat or processed foods, contribute significantly to the development of chronic diseases. *See* James G. Hodge, Jr. et al., *The Consumable Vice: Caffeine, Public Health & the Law*, 27 J. CONTEMP. HEALTH L. & POL'Y 76 (2010); DAVID A. KESSLER, THE END OF OVEREATING: TAKING CONTROL OF THE INSATIABLE AMERICAN APPETITE (2009).

Obesity. CDC suggests that poor dietary choices coupled with low levels of physical activity are among the leading causes of death annually in the U.S. This comports with major increases in rates of obesity among children, adolescents, and adults over the decades. As per Figure 6.5, when CDC first began to measure national obesity rates in 1960, rates of obesity among Americans steadily climbed. By 2017–2020, 43% of men, 42% of women, and 19.7% of children and adolescents aged 2–19 years, were obese. Another 30.7% of Americans were overweight. NCHS, NAT'L HEALTH & NUTRITION EXAMINATION SURV., 2017–2018; CDC, CHILDHOOD OBESITY FACTS (2022).

Figure 6.5. Obesity Prevalence in the U.S.

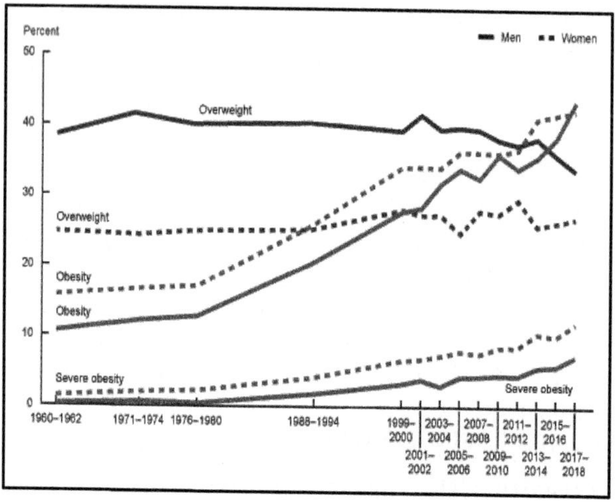

Source: NCHS, NAT'L HEALTH EXAM. SURV. & NAT'L HEALTH & NUTRITION EXAM. SURV. (2018).

Absent substantial changes, the future of Americans' battle with obesity is bleak. Over a decade ago, authors of 1 study suggested nearly all American adults would be overweight by 2048. Youfa Wang et al., *Will All Americans Become Overweight or Obese?*, 16 OBESITY 2323 (2008). This seems possible given current trends which only worsened during the COVID-19 pandemic. A 2021 study suggests American adults facing months of social distancing and isolation may have averaged weight gains of 2 pounds per month. Roni Caryn Rabin, *How Much Did We Gain During the Lockdown?*, N.Y. TIMES, Mar. 23, 2021. Existing obesity among patients was a major contributing factor to COVID-related deaths as well.

As with many medical conditions suffered by millions, pharmaceutical interventions are increasingly available. FDA approvals of Novo Nordisk's Wegovy® (2021) and Lilly's Mounjaro® (2023), which are designed to treat obesity by regulating one's appetite, hold promise for some patients. Some health insurers, including Medicare, however, are reluctant to cover the costs of these drugs. Daniel Gilbert & David Ovalle, *FDA approves Lilly diabetes drug Mounjaro for weight loss*, WASH. POST, Nov. 9, 2023. New obesity drugs are demonstrating promise as treatments for other conditions antecedent to overweightness. Gina Kolata, *Doctors Test the Limits of New Obesity Drugs*, N.Y. TIMES, June 18, 2024. As Lilly® touted in its June 2024 print advertisement, its obesity drugs are "about health," and not just cosmetic weight loss. Lilly, *We Are Making Obesity Medications*, N.Y. TIMES, June 25, 2024.

Tobacco and Nicotine. Tobacco products used regularly by nearly 20% of Americans (and many more in decades past) are a major contributing factor to roughly 480,000 annual deaths in the U.S. *Burden of Cigarette Use in the U.S.*, CDC (2023). As per Figure 6.6 below, mortality impacts of tobacco use across U.S. populations vary based on numerous factors, including age, gender, and education.

Figure 6.6. Average Life Expectancy for Smokers/Nonsmokers by Gender & Education

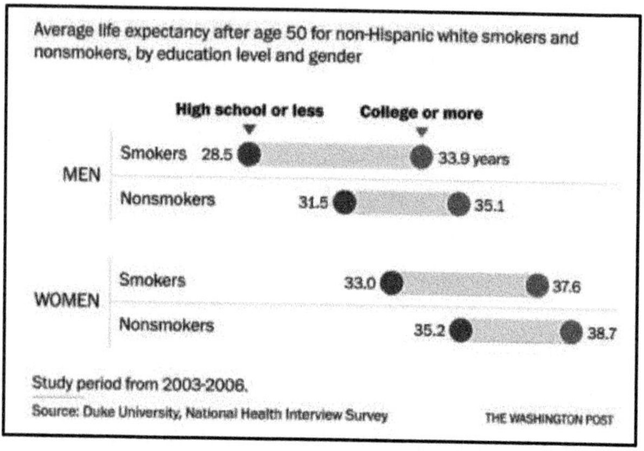

Source: William Wan, *America's New Tobacco Crisis: The Rich Stopped Smoking, the Poor Didn't*, WASH. POST, June 13, 2017.

Increasing use of e-cigarettes, vaping, and other Electronic Nicotine Delivery Systems (ENDS) products incur additional risks, particularly among minors. Exposure to nicotine or toxins through inhalation or byproducts of e-cigarettes assimilate some of the same exposures in tobacco cigarettes. Rachel Grana et al., *E-Cigarettes: A Scientific Rev.*, 129 CIRCULATION 1972 (2014).

Over 19.5% of American high school students and over 4.5% of middle school students reported e-cigarette use in 2020. *Youth Tobacco Use: Results from the National Youth Tobacco Surv.*, FDA (2020). These statistics represent an 1800% increase from prior figures in 2011. *Vaping Statistics 2021*,

SINGLECARE (Jan. 21, 2021). Whether teens' greater use of e-cigarettes displaces or contributes to their tobacco consumption later is not fully known. Sabrina Tavernise, *E-Cigarettes Aren't Getting Youths Hooked on Tobacco, Study Suggests*, N.Y. TIMES, Apr. 15, 2016. Evidence to this effect, however, is mounting. Authors of a 2021 study concluded that youths using e-cigarettes were at least 7 times more likely to smoke cigarettes 1 year later compared to young individuals who had never vaped. Elizabeth C. Hair et al., *Ass'n Between E-Cigarette Use & Future Combustible Cigarette Use*, 112 ADDICTIVE BEHAVS. 1, 5 (2021).

Besides tobacco and ENDS, other consumable vices such as alcohol, salt, and sugar present additional, significant health risks.

Alcohol. Excessive alcohol consumption contributes to over 50 different diseases and injuries that in sum constitute the 3rd greatest preventable causes of death in the U.S. CDC, ALCOHOL USE & HEALTH (2013). Based on a 2015 national survey conducted by the federal Substance Abuse and Mental Health Services Administration (SAMHSA), over 80% of all persons aged 18 and older drank alcohol at some point in their lifetime. No less than 42% of all persons drank regularly and nearly 55% of persons aged 18–65 years drank in the last month. *See* SAMHSA, 2015 NSDUH (2016). Alcohol use increased further among many impacted groups during the COVID-19 pandemic. Nambi Ndugga & Austin Fraukt, *Alcohol Consumption Has Risen Amid Pandemic*, N.Y. TIMES, Apr. 21, 2021.

Alcohol use among minors and college age adults is particularly concerning. In its 2015 assessment, SAMSHA reported that 28.4% of minors ages 12–17 said they drank alcohol at some point in their lifetime; and over 13% indicated that they drank in the past month. *Id.* Other research suggests that approximately 65% of college students consume alcohol regularly; 43% of males and 32% of females binge drink at least once over a 2 week period. Aaron White & Ralph Hingson, *The Burden of Alcohol Use Excessive Alcohol Consumption & Related Consequences Among College Students*, 35 ALCOHOL RES. 201 (2014). While most of these persons may not be dependent, significant negative health effects surface or accumulate over their lifetimes. Marissa B. Esser et al., *Prevalence of Alcohol Dependence Among US Adult Drinkers, 2009–11*, 11 PREVENTING CHRONIC DISEASE 206 (2014). As WHO concluded in 2023, "when it comes to alcohol consumption, there is no safe amount that does not affect health." WHO, *No Level of Alcohol Consumption is Safe for our Health* (2023).

Salt. Unlike alcohol, sodium is essential to human life, but its over-consumption (primarily through salt) carries significant public health complications. Theodore A. Kotchen, *Salt in Health & Disease—A Delicate Balance,* 368 NEJM 1229 (2013). In the U.S., tens of thousands perish each year from heart disease, stroke, and other chronic conditions tied to hypertension (high blood pressure) from long-term, over-consumption of sodium compounds. Thomas R. Frieden, *Sodium Reduction—Saving Lives by Putting Choice Into Consumers' Hands*, 315 JAMA

579 (2016). Subject to debate as to how much salt is too much, in 2012 more than 90% of American children and close to 90% of adults ingested salt in excess of standard dietary guidelines. James G. Hodge, Jr. & Leila F. Barraza, *Legal Regulation of Sodium Consumption to Reduce Chronic Conditions*, 13(E26) PREVENTING CHRONIC CONDITIONS 1 (2016); Lash S. Clarke et al., *Temporal Trends in Dietary Sodium Intake Among Adults Aged ≥19 Years—United States,* 2003–2016. 60 MMWR 1478, 1479 (2021).

Sugar. Studies concerning the impacts of over-consumption of sugar in American's diets led 1 observer to conclude that "[s]ugar is indeed toxic." Mark Bittman, Editorial, *It's The Sugar, Folks*, N.Y. TIMES, Feb. 28, 2013. Mark Moss in his 2021 text, HOOKED, argues that sugars as an additive in processed food are actually addictive, perhaps even more so than nicotine or other drugs. Moss and others claim the U.S. food industry intentionally manipulated the contents of highly-processed foods, including SSBs, to appeal to Americans' insatiable taste for sugars (and other additives). *See* Anahad O'Connor, *This Is Your Brain On Processed Food*, N.Y. TIMES, Apr. 6, 2021.

Researchers conservatively linked ingestion of sugar, largely through beverages, to 25,000 deaths in the U.S. in 2010 (and 180,000 deaths globally). Gitanjali M. Singh et al., *Mortality Due to SSB Consumption: A Global, Regional & National Comparative Risk Assessment,* 127 CIRCULATION 22 (2013). In 2019, researchers suggested ingestion of

SSBs led to a 21% increased risk of death among adults consuming more than 2 beverages a day as compared to those drinking less 1. Vasanti S. Malik et al., *Long-Term Consumption of Sugar-Sweetened and Artificially Sweetened Beverages & Risk of Mortality in U.S. Adults*, 139 CIRCULATION 2113 (2019). In another global study, researchers conclusively tie increased ingestion of sugar with higher rates of diabetes, independent of obesity rates. Sanjay Basu et al., *The Relationship of Sugar to Population-Level Diabetes Prevalence: An Econometric Analysis of Repeated Cross-Sectional Data*, 8 PLOS 1 e57873 (2013).

In 2014, researchers compared thousands of adults who consumed 17–21% of their daily intake from added sugars to those who consumed about 8% over 2 decades. They found that the group consuming more sugar had a 38% higher risk of cardiovascular disease mortality even after controlling for overall diet quality. This suggests that the risks of added sugar intake are independent from the effects of a generally unhealthy diet. Quanhe Yang, PhD, et al., *Added Sugar Intake & Cardiovascular Disease Mortality Among U.S. Adults,* 174 JAMA INTERNAL MED. 516 (2014). A 2017 study coupled excessive sugar intake with higher pre-clinical indicators of Alzheimer's disease. Matthew P. Pase et al., *Sugary Beverage Intake & Preclinical Alzheimer's Disease in the Community*, 13(9) ALZHEIMER'S & DEMENTIA 955 (2017).

Under these and multiple, additional studies, researchers are revealing how over-indulgence in sugars contribute extensively to varying chronic conditions. Questions arising from these findings concerning sugars and other consumable vices include critical assessments of exactly what governmental or private sector health proponents can do to control for these types of risks as major causes of chronic conditions.

C. LEGAL AUTHORITIES

Chronic conditions differ from communicable ones in many ways, but similar public health powers can be used to address their incidence. *See, e.g.*, Wendy C. Perdue et al., *A Legal Framework for Preventing Cardiovascular Disease*, 29 AM. J. PREVENTIVE MED. 139 (2005). Public health laws authorizing counseling, testing, screening, and treatment are used extensively to counteract chronic conditions. Federal and state recommendations for testing and screening of various cancers (e.g., breast, prostate, colon, lung), often based on guidance from medical and public health organizations, are routinely followed by health care practitioners and patients.

Vaccinations may help stymie the rate of some chronic conditions. New evidence in 2023 suggests the potential for cancer vaccines to obviate substantial risks of increased morbidity and mortality even among actual cancer patients with melanoma who were administered the vaccine as part of initial clinical trials. Jade Cobern, *Cancer Vaccine with Minimal Side Effects Nearing Phase 3 Clinical Trials*, ABCNEWS, Jan. 20, 2024. Additional studies may support further applications of vaccines to ward off known health impacts of an array of cancers in the 21st century.

Of course, existing vaccines are already known to help prevent the onset of cancers among specific populations. To the extent that HPV vaccine deters infection, individuals can avoid related cancers of the reproductive organs and other parts of the body tied to their infection with the communicable condition. Consequently, CDC recommends HPV vaccines for boys and girls beginning at ages 11–12. Mark H. Sawyer et al., *Recommendations on the Use of Quadrivalent HPV in Males—ACIP, 2011*, 60 MMWR 1705, 1707 (2011). Though safe and efficacious, uptake of HPV vaccinations nationally has been curtailed by political and other views focused on the proper age in which an STI-related threat should be addressed via vaccine. *See* James Colgrove et al., *HPV Vaccination Mandates—Lawmaking amid Political & Scientific Controversy*, 363 NEJM 785, 787 (2010); Shannon Stokely et al., *HPV Coverage Among Adolescent Girls, 2007–2012*, 62 MMWR 591, 594 (2013).

Education campaigns alert the public to risks (sometimes through graphic illustrations) of chronic conditions related to tobacco, alcohol, or drug use. A New York City health department education campaign in 2009 targeted the ingestion of SSBs through advertisements depicting consumers gulping down thick globs of fat. Sewell Chan, *New Targets in the Fat Fight: Soda & Juice*, N.Y. TIMES, Sept. 1, 2009. Another campaign in 2015 focused on labeling restaurant menu items containing excessive amounts of salt with a simple, easy-to-see icon (*see* Figure 6.7).

Figure 6.7. New York City Salt Icon

Source: NYC Health Dep't (2015)

This labeling requirement was challenged unsuccessfully in New York courts. *Nat'l Rest. Ass'n v. N.Y.C. Dep't of Health & Mental Hygiene*, 148 A.D.3d 169, 49 N.Y.S.3d 18 (1st Dep't 2017). Additional discussion of public health education efforts is noted in Chapter 9.

Not all public health powers used to prevent communicable diseases apply to chronic conditions. Social distancing measures (e.g., isolation, quarantine, curfews) discussed in Chapter 5 typically lack utility (and constitutionality) as applied to most chronic conditions. To this end, other public health powers are relied on to: (1) alter individual and group behaviors contributing to the onset of chronic illness; (2) change environmental impacts that lend to their proliferation; or (3) prevent factors in which chronic illnesses may arise or result in significant harms to individuals or the public. Core among these legal strategies, examined below, are the powers to tax and spend; regulatory laws directly governing the environment and private sector; and anti-discrimination protections.

1. THE POWER TO TAX

Governments' powers to tax involve more than raising revenue. These powers are used strategically and lawfully to change or alter behaviors, often in the interests of preventing or treating chronic conditions. The power to tax necessarily includes the power to spend, including setting significant conditions on how governmental resources may be used when doled out to public or private entities (discussed below). At its core, government's "power over the purse" allows it considerable discretion in collecting and disbursing individual and corporate resources for the betterment of society. CHEMERINSKY, CONST. LAW, at 279–80.

While each level of government has some authority to tax, the federal government's taxing prowess (pursuant to U.S. CONST. art. I, § 8) is considerable. Particularly since the institution of national income taxes in 1913, Congress has used its taxing authority extensively. ROY G. BLAKEY & GLADYS C. BLAKEY, THE FEDERAL INCOME TAX 71 (2006). As Chief Justice John Roberts noted in 2012 in SCOTUS' decision on the constitutionality of the ACA, the power to tax includes the power to "affect individual conduct." *NFIB v. Sebelius,* 567 U.S. 519, 567 (2012).

So long as it acts consistent with principles of federalism and individual rights, Congress can (and regularly does) use its taxing power in the interests of the public's health. Related to the prevention and control of chronic illnesses, for example, the federal government (and many states and localities) tax products like tobacco to help discourage their consumption. In 2023, New York City charges taxes in the amount of $6.85 per pack of cigarettes, constituting over 1/2 of the average base cost per pack of $13. *N.Y. Cigarette & Tobacco Products Taxes*, DEP'T OF TAX. & FIN. (2023). Such taxes are based on the proven economic theory that to the extent they substantially raise the price of cigarettes, people will smoke less, and their overall health and risk of developing chronic conditions will improve. HHS & CDC, REDUCING TOBACCO USE: A REP. OF THE SURGEON GENERAL 337, 359 (2000).

In *Guns Save Life, Inc. v. Ali*, No. 1–18–1846, 2020 WL 1285619 (Ill. App. Ct. Mar. 13, 2020), *appeal allowed,* 154 N.E.3d 778 (Ill. 2020), an Illinois appellate court upheld a Cook County (Chicago area) ordinance taxing the sale of firearms and ammunition. Cook County passed an ordinance in 2013 imposing a tax of $25 per firearm, later taxing ammunition as well. Revenues were allocated toward public safety efforts. A gun-rights advocacy group, retailer, and consumer, challenged the taxes as proscribed via the 2nd Amendment and state laws regulating the sale of firearms. In 2021, the Illinois Supreme Court held that the tax ordinances were unconstitutional not so much on 2nd Amendment grounds as the tax was deemed insufficiently tied to the county's objective of "ameliorating costs of gun violence." *Guns Save Life, Inc. v. Ali*, 190 N.E.3d 139, 147 (Ill. 2021).

In general, the 2nd Amendment allows taxes that do not fully restrict who may purchase a weapon or ammunition. Standard sales taxes on consumer products that are neither prohibitory or exclusionary do not interfere with 2nd Amendment rights just because a lawful product costs more. Multiple municipalities have proposed specific gun taxes on purchases at dealers or shows. Zusha Elinson, *Cities Target Guns Sales for New Tax,* WALL ST. J., Oct. 29, 2019, at A3.

Similarly some states and localities have taxed junk foods or high-calorie beverages to limit consumption. Michael F. Jacobson & Kelly D. Brownell, *Small Taxes on Soft Drinks & Snack Foods to Promote Health,* 90 AJPH 854 (2000). In 2015, the Navajo Nation (pop.~400,000) approved implementation of a 2% tax on all junk food sold on its reservation spanning across Arizona, New Mexico, and Utah. Revenues are to be devoted to healthy eating and other public health programs. Implementation of the Healthy Diné Nation Act, NAVAJO NATION CODE ANN. tit. 24 (2014), includes eliminating a 5% sales tax on healthy foods which was shown to discourage their purchase compared to perceived less expensive processed foods. Sabrina Toppa, *This Place Just Became the 1st Part of the U.S. to Impose a Tax on Junk Food,* TIME, Mar. 30, 2015).

In 2014, Berkeley, California passed a tax on SSBs, including a 1¢ per ounce tax on soda. Laura Mandaro, *Nation's First Soda Tax is Passed*, USA TODAY, Nov. 5, 2014. Berkeley's ordinance assimilated provisions of Mexico's SSB tax which some assert has helped to lower national consumption. *See* Eliza Barclay, *Mexico's Sugary Drink Tax Makes a Dent in Consumption, Study Claims,* NPR (June 19, 2015). Four months after implementation of Berkley's tax, authors of 1 study found that self-reported consumption of SSBs in Berkeley fell by 21%; consumers indicated they were drinking more water in place of SSBs. Margot Sanger-Katz, *Faced With a New Tax, Berkeley Drinks Less Soda*, N.Y. TIMES, Aug. 25, 2016.

Some evidence suggests that increasing taxes on SSBs directly lowers children's BMIs, saving billions on health care costs nationally while also generating considerable state and local tax revenues. *See* Jane E. Brody, *Prudent Ways to Fight Childhood Obesity*, N.Y. TIMES, June 23, 2015. In 2016, WHO recommended taxing sugary beverages to raise their price by 20% to lower consumption. Sabrina Tavernise, *WHO Recommends Taxing Sugary Drinks*, N.Y. TIMES, Oct. 12, 2016. As of May 2022, 85 countries have implemented some form of a tax on SSBs. WHO, SUGAR-SWEETENED BEVERAGE TAXATION POLICIES 9 (2022).

The City of Philadelphia passed a SSB tax of 1.5¢ per ounce in 2016 to generate millions of dollars for childhood education. Merrit Kennedy, *Philadelphia Becomes 1st Major U.S. City to Pass a Tax on Soda*, NPR (June 16, 2016). Though subject to legal challenges, Philadelphia successfully defended its local authority to tax SSBs. *Williams v. City of Philadelphia*, Nos. 2 & 3 EAP 2018 (Pa. July 18,

2018); Dep't of Revenue, *Philadelphia Beverage Tax*, CITY OF PHILA. (Feb. 16, 2021). Three California cities (San Francisco, Oakland, and Albany) as well as Cook County, Illinois, passed 1¢ per ounce taxes in 2016. On November 30, 2017, Cook County's SSB tax was repealed by its Board of Commissioners amid public criticism and the filing of a lawsuit brought by the Illinois Retail Merchants Association. Associated Press, *Judge in Illinois bars implementation of proposed tax on SSBs*, AZ. REP., July 1, 2017.

In addition to municipal SSB taxes, multiple states including Hawaii, Massachusetts, New York, Rhode Island, Washington, and West Virginia considered these taxes since 2020. *State & Local Backgrounders, Soda Taxes*, URBAN INST. (2024). Hawaii contemplated a 2¢ per ounce tax. A proposed bill in New York would levy a graduated excise tax on SSBs. Ulrik Boesen, *Sugar Taxes Back on the Menu*, TAX FOUND. (2021). The District of Columbia taxes SSBs at a 8% sales tax rate, which is 2% higher than the general sales tax rate. *State & Local Backgrounders, Soda Taxes*, URBAN INST. (2024). After Arkansas initially levied a per gallon excise tax on sodas, lawmakers considered repealing the tax in 2021. Michael R. Wickline, *State Panel Looks at Ending Soda Tax,* ARKANSAS DEMOCRAT GAZETTE, Mar. 8, 2021. Other states, including Washington (2010) and West Virginia (2024), repealed their SSB taxes. CARBONATED BEVERAGE TAX REPEALED, WASH. STATE DEP'T REV. (2010); W. VA. CODE § 11–19–3.

The flip-side of direct taxation to change consumer behaviors is the use of tax subsidies or credits to encourage product purchases or other market factors in the interests of the public's health. Congress, for example, created positive tax incentives for individuals to purchase individual health insurance through the ACA (later negated via Congress by the Tax Cuts and Jobs Act of 2017, discussed in Chapter 2). By encouraging employees to obtain insurance, access to preventive and other health services may be expanded with direct public health benefits.

Taxes designed to shape or alter behaviors antithetical to individual or community health are lawful in most cases, but also contentious. Even though multiple California cities had already begun taxing SSBs, in July 2018, the California state legislature preempted existing and future local SSB taxes. S.B. 872, 2017–2018 Reg. Sess. (Cal. 2018). Raucous political debates often accompany the passage and implementation of many tax-related measures in Congress and across the states. They reflect political realities underlying the creation of new tax schemes to positively change consumer behaviors. The public and its legislative representatives often disdain tax hikes, especially when government attempts to change behaviors of autonomous individuals in paternalistic ways. Yet, when politically satiable, government's use of its direct power to tax to address chronic conditions is virtually without limit.

2. THE POWER TO SPEND

Collecting revenues through taxes also allows governments to disburse resources in ways that promote the "general welfare," notably including communal health. And whenever government, (particularly at the federal level) has money to spend, it may set conditions on its receipt. Through its constitutional powers to spend, Congress may lawfully impose a myriad of conditions on the disbursement of federal funds to which tribal, state, or local governments (or private entities) generally must adhere. CHEMERINSKY, CONST. LAW at 285–86. Of course, any public or private entity can always reject specific conditions attached to funding streams, but they will lose access to sometimes significant public health resources.

Examples of Congress' use of its spending power to address chronic (or other) conditions are broad. They range from the setting of conditions on the receipt of basic health care resources (e.g., Medicaid) to specific allotments for public health surveillance (e.g., HIV/AIDS reporting, discussed in Chapter 8) and research on chronic conditions like obesity and Alzheimer's disease. Though Congress' power is extensive, the U.S. Supreme Court has set some limits on the use of conditional spending, particularly between federal and state governments.

In *South Dakota v. Dole*, 483 U.S. 203 (1987), the Court approved Congress' condition that states seeking select highway transportation funds upgrade their drinking age to 21 (largely to reduce alcohol-related crashes and fatalities on federal highways). Rejecting a federalism-based challenge, Chief Justice William Rehnquist clarified that Congress' exercise of its conditional spending power is constitutional as applied to the states so long as:

(a) it serves some general purpose (the Court has typically deferred to Congress' stated purposes consistent with principles of separation of powers);

(b) the choices and conditions are clear and unambiguous;

(c) the conditions are related to some national project or program;

(d) states are not induced to engage in unconstitutional acts. For example, in *Agency for Int'l Dev. v. Alliance for Open Society Int'l*, 570 U.S. 205 (2013), the Court struck down an "anti-prostitution pledge," which prohibited the issuance of HIV-related grants to U.S.-based recipients who did not affirmatively state their opposition to prostitution and sex trafficking. Such conditions violated the free speech rights of recipients under the 1st Amendment; *contra Agency for Int'l Dev. v. All. for Open Soc'y Int'l*, 591 U.S. 430 (2020) (determining the same policy as constitutional when applied to foreign affiliates who lack similar constitutional rights as U.S. recipients); and

(e) states are not compelled to accept the funds. *Dole*, 483 U.S. at 207–11.

For years following the Supreme Court's decision in *Dole*, virtually no Congressional exercise of conditional spending power was adjudged by courts to "compel" states to accept federal funds. States always have the option of rejecting federal dollars if they do not like the terms underlying a conditional spending proposal. However, in the Court's aforementioned decision on the constitutionality of the ACA, Congress' plan to add millions of new beneficiaries to the Medicaid program (which provides health services to largely low-income families) was rejected. *Sebelius*, 567 U.S. at 585.

The ACA provided each state the option of expanding its Medicaid population to include a larger proportion of low-income adults by 2014, or else face the loss of all its federal Medicaid funds. In response to states' federalism-based challenges, Chief Justice Roberts opined that this choice unconstitutionally compelled states to comply due in large part to (a) the enormous sums at stake if states chose not to expand their programs; and (b) a significant "shift in kind, not merely degree" of the original purposes of the Medicaid program via expansion. *Id.* at 2604–06. Though the Court rejected the ACA's compelled conditions, it crafted a constitutional compromise. HHS' Centers for Medicare and Medicaid Services (CMS) can only condition states' receipt of expansion funds (instead of their entire Medicaid budget) on states' willingness to extend their Medicaid populations.

By limiting Congress' use of its spending power to condition receipt of federal funds, the *Sebelius* case tamped down Congress' ability to extend access to basic health insurance to more Americans, a primary public health objective of the ACA. *See, e.g.*, Nicole Huberfeld et al., *Plunging Into Endless Difficulties: Medicaid & Coercion in* [*NFIB v. Sebelius*], 93 BOS. L. REV. 1 (2013). No longer facing the threat of losing their entire Medicaid budget, 10 states have failed to expand their programs, even though the federal government pays the bulk of the costs for new Medicaid enrollees under the ACA over several years. *Status of State Medicaid Expansion Decisions: Interactive Map*, KAISER FAM. FOUND. (2024). As a result of SCOTUS' opinion, millions of Americans are denied access to publicly-funded, basic health services, including preventive care. The Court's decision also opens new possibilities for state and local governments to challenge other federal public health spending programs, including long-standing environmental laws, on similar grounds that the terms of receipt of federal funds are onerous and unconstitutional.

3. THE POWER TO REGULATE

The potential to influence individual and governmental choices through the powers to tax and spend is commanding. Yet, government also has the power to directly regulate private entities and individuals consistent with prevention and control strategies related to chronic conditions. As discussed in Chapter 2, so long as legislative bodies provide clear and articulable standards for executive agencies to regulate, public health officials can generally administer and enforce laws to further the public's health. Through public health regulation, for example, government can:

Ban or Limit the Sale of Products Deemed Harmful to the Public's Health (among other purposes). *See, e.g.*, James G. Hodge, Jr. & Megan A. Scanlon, *The Legal Anatomy of Product Bans to Protect the Public's Health*, 23 ANNALS OF HEALTH L. 20 (2014). Following discovery of the harmful effects of lead largely on child development, its removal from paint, gasoline, and other products is now mandated. Shana R. Cappell, *Lead Paint Poisoning & the Resource Conservation & Recovery Act*, 35 COLUM. J. L. & SOC. PROBS. 175, 178 (2002). More recently, in early 2024, FDA noted its intent to ban the use of formaldehyde in hair straightening products following years of evidence of advanced risks of multiple cancers tied to exposure to this chemical. Ronnie Cohen, *FDA's Plan to Ban Hair Relaxer Chemical Called Too Little, Too Late*, KAISER FAM. FOUND. HEALTH NEWS (2024).

In 2015 multiple states considered regulatory bans of "palcohol," a powdered form of alcohol proposed for market release following federal review and approval. Rachel Abrams, *Powdered Alcohol Meets Resistance in the U.S. Before it Ever Comes to Market*, N.Y. TIMES, Apr. 3, 2015. In a 2017 study, researchers positively correlated trans-fat bans (or other legal restrictions) with improved heart health in affected communities. Eric J. Brandt et al., *Hosp. Admissions for Myocardial Infarction & Stroke Before & After Trans-Fatty Acid Restrictions in N.Y.*, 2(6) JAMA CARDIOL. 627 (2017).

Explicit calls for FDA to ban menthol tobacco products has persistently surfaced given known harmful impacts of this specific tobacco product, which is particularly popular (and deadly) among Black Americans. Still, in 2023, President Biden's administration shelved plans to ban the product entirely. Anne Flaherty, *Biden Administration Pulls Back from Banning Menthol Cigarettes,* ABCNEWS, Dec. 6, 2023. Some allege the Administration's decision was politically motivated in an election year. Christina Jewett & Noah Wieland, *Biden Delaying A Menthol Ban for Cigarettes*, N.Y. TIMES, Apr. 27, 2024. Some advocacy groups sued to push FDA to ban these products. Emily Field, *FDA Sued Again Over Years Of Delays On Menthol Ban*, LAW360, Apr. 3, 2024. Undeterred, on June 21, 2024, FDA approved menthol-flavored e-cigarettes despite known risks of potential youth use. Michael Levenson, *After U.S. Delay on Ban, FDA Allows the First Menthol-flavored E-Cigarettes*, N.Y. TIMES, June 24, 2024.

During the COVID-19 pandemic, FDA (together with the Federal Trade Commission (FTC)) systematically addressed false, misleading, and dangerous claims that specific drugs or other products were effective cures. In California, for example, Dr. Juli A. Mazi was charged by federal agents with selling pellets online that were allegedly capable of triggering an immune response to COVID-19. Derrick Bryson Taylor, *Officials Say Woman Sold Fake Remedy for COVID-19*, N.Y. TIMES, July 16, 2021. Hundreds of thousands of Americans pursued false remedies, including malaria drugs chloroquine and hydroxychloroquine once touted by President Trump, for treatment (*see* Figure 6.8).

Figure 6.8. WHO Warning Regarding False COVID-19 Treatments

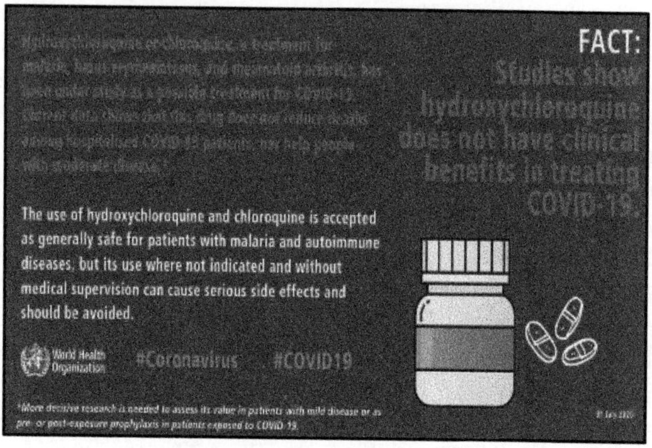

Source: WHO, COVID-19 Advice for the Pub.: Mythbusters (May 5, 2021).

Many who could not access or afford traditional health services purchased drugs and herbal remedies from unscrupulous sources (e.g., websites, flea markets, charlatans, pop-up sites, unlicensed clinics). FTC explicitly threatened hundreds of companies making "deceptive claims related to the treatment, cure, or prevention of" COVID-19 with penalties exceeding $40,000 per violation. Amy Maxmen, *Desperate to Receive COVID Care*, N.Y. TIMES, June 22, 2021.

Limit Possession of Products That May Harm Specific Populations. In June 2024, California Governor Gavin Newsom proposed banning use of smartphones among children while in school. The public health premise for his proposal extended from direct harms to children attributable to excessive use of such devices. Shawn Hubler, *Governor Calls for Ban on Use of Smartphones in California Schools*, N.Y. TIMES, June 20, 2024. It assimilates the legal premises for banning any product among particular populations: when a product causes demonstrable harms, public health authorities may seek to limit its access or prohibit its use altogether.

For decades, federal and state governments have uniformly prohibited persons under the age of 18 from purchasing tobacco products.

More recently, researchers found that 75% of adults favored increasing the legal minimum age to purchase all tobacco products from 18 to 21 years old. Tanya Basu, *Majority of Americans Agree You Should be 21 to Buy Tobacco*, TIME (July 7, 2015). In 2015, Hawaii raised the minimum age to purchase tobacco products to 21, S.B. 1030, 28th Leg., 2015

(Haw. 2015). California followed suit in 2016. S.B. 5, 2015–2016 Leg., 2d Extra. Sess. (Cal. 2016).

Other states and localities have similarly acted. As of September 30, 2023, 41 states, 3 territories, and D.C. have raised their tobacco purchase age to 21. *STATE System Minimum Legal Sales Age Laws for Tobacco Products Fact Sheet*, CDC (2024). On July 19, 2021, Brookline, Massachusetts purportedly became the 1st locality to ban tobacco sales to "anyone born in the 21st century." Laurent Huber, *Brookline, MA Becomes 1st City in the U.S. to Ban Tobacco Sales to Anyone Born in the 21st Century*, ACTION ON SMOKING & HEALTH, July 19, 2021.

In *RPF Oil Company v. Genesee County*, 330 Mich. App. 533 (2019), however, the Michigan Court of Appeals held that the state's Age of Majority law (establishing that individuals age 18+ are entitled to all rights, privileges, and responsibilities allowed via constitution or statute) preempted localities from prohibiting the sale of tobacco products to persons under the age of 21. Michigan state law affords certain rights or privileges that cannot be contravened by local laws. Consequently, Genesee County's law restricting access to tobacco for those 18–20 years old was preempted.

Similar efforts to restrict minor access and use apply to ENDS. In 2016, FDA proposed significant regulations governing the sale of these nicotine delivery devices. Leila Barraza et al., *Regulations & Policies Regarding E-Cigarettes,* CANCER (Apr. 25, 2017). Among other measures, FDA's regulations would (1) require photo ID checks of everyone under age 27 who attempts to purchase ENDS; (2) prohibit sale of ENDS to minors; (3) eliminate vending machine sales (unless in an adult-only facility); and (4) cease free ENDS samples. *See* Restrictions on the Sale & Distribution of Tobacco Products et seq., 21 C.F.R. §§ 1100, 1140, 1143 (2020).

On December 10, 2019, the U.S. Court of Appeals for the D.C. Circuit upheld FDA's authority to directly regulate ENDS products against industry challenges in *Nicopure Labs, LLC v. FDA*, 944 F.3d 267 (D.C. Cir. 2019). The court found that FDA lawfully requested manufacturers to demonstrate how allowing ENDS products on the market is consistent with public health given evidence of the addictiveness of nicotine and related harms.

Based on this and other decisions, FDA oversight of ENDS sales intensified during President Biden's administration. Initial warning letters from FDA to ENDS manufacturers with unauthorized products on the market were issued in January 2021. *Perspective: FDA's Progress on Review of Tobacco Product Applications*, FDA (Feb. 16, 2021). Later that spring, FDA launched a multimedia e-cigarette education campaign targeting individuals aged 12–17. *FDA Commits to Evidence-Based Actions Aimed at Saving Lives & Preventing Future Generations of Smokers*, FDA (Apr. 29, 2021). Coextensively, multiple state and local governments are regulating the distribution, use, and sale of ENDS.

FDA is also considering outright bans of ENDS, including Juul® products, given their appeal to minors despite allegations by manufacturers that these products also help tobacco users cease smoking. Sheila Kaplan, *Juul's Survival Rides on Fight to Sway FDA*, N.Y. TIMES, July 6, 2021. All states legally restrict youth access to ENDS, and 30 states tax e-cigarettes and regulate e-cigarette product packaging. *U.S. E-Cigarette Regulations—50 State Review (2021)*, PUB. HEALTH L. CTR. (as of Mar. 15, 2021). Litigation against industry leaders, including Juul®, also seeks to curb access and use (*see* text box below).

Juul® Products in Litigation

In June 2021, Juul® reached a $40 million settlement agreement with the North Carolina Attorney General who sued the company claiming it intentionally targeted youths through its marketing, leading to heightened cases of nicotine addiction. Without admitting fault, the company agreed to fund addiction prevention and treatment programs, avoid using models younger than 35 years old to advertise its products, and cease placing ads near schools.

Together with the U.S. Attorney General, 39 state Attorneys General investigated Juul's® marketing and sales practices, resulting in a $438.5 million settlement with 33 states in 2022. Christina Jewett, *Juul Settles Multistate Youth Vaping Inquiry for $438.5 Million*, N.Y. TIMES, Sept. 6, 2022. Additional lawsuits in 14 states and D.C. allege similar claims.

In December 2022, Juul® agreed to pay $1.2 billion to settle 10,000 consolidated cases through multidistrict litigation in California centered on personal injury, consumer class actions, and public entities seeking reparations for vaping-related injuries. Christina Jewett, *Vaping Settlement by Juul is Said to Total $1.7 Billion*, N.Y. TIMES, Dec. 10, 2022.

Control How Products Are Manufactured or Sold. In many places, the sale of alcohol is restricted to certain locations during set days and hours. *See, e.g.*, S.C. CODE ANN. § 61–6–1500(A)(1)(a) (2012). Many of the 36 states and D.C. legalizing the sale of marijuana for medicinal or recreational (18 states) purposes set narrow manufacturing and licensing requirements to help assure the product does not find its way to unlawful purchasers or users (in violation of the federal Controlled Substances Act, 21 U.S.C. §§ 801–971 (2012)). MARIJUANA POL'Y PROJECT, KEY ASPECTS OF STATE & D.C. MEDICAL MARIJUANA LAWS (2020); Jeremy Berke et al., *Marijuana Legalization Is Sweeping the US. See Every State Where Cannabis Is Legal.*, BUS. INSIDER, July 9, 2021.

Still, proliferation of marijuana retailers lawfully selling products of all types across multiple states has generated substantial concerns over ease of access to these products and extensive regulatory responses. In May 2024, the U.S. Department of Justice called for a rescission of long-standing federal laws and policies banning marijuana use as a controlled substance. Federal legislation introduced that same month proposed new regulations for the drug, as well as tax policies for its lawful sale, expungement of records of certain marijuana-related criminal offenses, and increased funds to study public health impacts of widespread use. Kayla Guo, *Senate Democrats Reintroduce Legislation to End Federal Prohibition of Marijuana*, N.Y. TIMES, May 2, 2024.

Require Entities to Create or Sell Products in Conformity with Public Health Mandates. As discussed in Chapter 9, FDA (via the ACA) requires chain restaurants across the U.S. to post calorie counts for their menu items similar to practices implemented already in several state and local jurisdictions. With ready access to calorie data at the point of sale, consumers can make healthier choices and potentially lower their overall calorie consumption.

Set Meaningful Restrictions on Consumer Uses of Products in Public Places. Federal, state, and local smoke-free laws over several decades have targeted public environments from cars to planes to public squares to eradicate public exposures to second-hand smoke. *See, e.g.*, Amy R. Confair et al.,

Factors Affecting Successful Enactment of Legislation Prohibiting Smoking in Cars with Children, 53 JURIMETRICS J. 375 (2013). In 2015, the University of California-San Francisco completely removed all SSBs from its vendors on campus and launched a study of its employees to assess related health effects. Anahad O'Connor, *Setting Limits on Soda*, N.Y. TIMES, Nov. 8, 2016.

Create Safer Workplaces That Reduce Exposures to Harmful Elements or Practices. Federal and state regulations governing coal mines have significantly reduced the incidence of "black lung" deaths. Federal workplace standards issued via the Occupational Safety and Health Administration (OSHA) have not only helped reduce injuries (discussed in Chapter 7), but also lowered chronic conditions through workplace safety initiatives. During the COVID-19 pandemic, OSHA issued several guidance documents denoting varied safety measures in health care and other workplaces to help protect workers (and others) from preventable infections. OSHA, Subpart U—COVID-19 Emergency Temporary Standard (June 2021).

These notable examples are merely illustrative. Governmental regulatory powers to address chronic (and other) conditions extend into multiple facets of public and private life. Though capable of heavy-handed enforcement, public health agencies typically seek cooperative and contributive efforts among public and private actors to conceive, draft, and implement regulatory controls.

Legality of Public Health Regulations

In summary, public health regulations are lawful and viable so long as administrative agencies:

- act within the scope of their delegated powers;
- adhere to procedural requirements in creating and enforcing regulatory provisions;
- have legitimate public health support for the need to regulate;
- survive sometimes aggressive counter-campaigns among industry or other entities seeking to derail regulations; and
- do not otherwise offend constitutional or other principles of law.

Particularly at the local level, avoiding potential conflicts of regulatory laws and structural principles issues can be dubious. In April 2011, for example, the Cleveland City Council enacted an anti-obesity ordinance to ban trans fats in foods served in restaurants and other food shops. A few months later, the Ohio legislature amended state law to prohibit municipalities from regulating the ingredients used by food servers. The net effect of the Ohio legislature's amendment was to preempt Cleveland's trans fats ordinance. The City sued the State claiming that the amendment unconstitutionally stripped the City of its home rule (discussed in Chapter 2). After the trial court decided in favor of the City, the Ohio Court of Appeals affirmed that the legislature's amendment unlawfully overrode Cleveland's home rule. Consequently, it reinstated the City's trans-fat ordinance. *City of Cleveland v. Ohio*, 989 N.E.2d 1072 (Ohio Ct. App. 2013).

4. ADDRESSING DISABILITY BIAS

Many chronic conditions are also disabling. Persons who are impaired in their major life activities due to their chronic illness may be entitled to special protections from discrimination under the federal Americans with Disabilities Act (ADA), 42 U.S.C. §§ 12101–12213 (2012), and additional laws at the federal, state, and local levels.

ADA.gov
United States Department of Justice
Civil Rights Division

Implemented pursuant to Congress' interstate commerce powers, the ADA protects persons with actual disabilities as well as those who are simply regarded by others as having a disability. *Id.* at § 12102(1). *See, e.g., EEOC v. W. Meade Place, LLP*, 841 F. App'x 962 (6th Cir. 2021) (allowing a jury determination as to whether an employee with anxiety disorder who was terminated from a nursing home meets the ADA definition of "disabled." A jury could reasonably find that the employer perceived the employee as having an "impairment," which is sufficient to garner ADA protections irrespective of its severity).

Collectively, disability laws help to eliminate discrimination against some persons with chronic conditions in the workplace and many other settings. The U.S. Supreme Court has clarified that the ADA does not require employers to hire persons whose known disabilities would lend to specific harms of the employee on the job. *See Chevron U.S.A., Inc. v. Echazabal*, 536 U.S. 73 (2002) (rejecting ADA claim of prospective employee whose liver condition would be aggravated through employer's available positions at a refinery). Nevertheless, proof of adverse employment decisions may not be essential to raise ADA claims. *See Exby-Stolley v. Bd. of Cnty. Comm'rs*, 979 F.3d 784 (10th Cir. 2020) (a blind law clerk could invoke ADA protections whether or not she suffered an adverse employment action. Such a requirement contravenes prior decisions, ADA's remedial purposes, and EEOC interpretations of the elements of an ADA failure-to-accommodate claim). While the scope of individual disability protections via the ADA exceeds this text, disability laws can contribute to the reduction of chronic illness in key ways. ADA requirements to support reasonable accommodations in many settings directly benefit persons with disabilities, but also have reciprocal benefits for others. Building redesigns (e.g., to include elevators or lifts) and retrofitting of community plans (e.g., to include sidewalk ramps or paved trails) consistent with the ADA have transformed the built environment across the country, leading to safer communities that help reduce injuries and diminish chronic conditions.

Universal precautions in health care settings, ushered in part via the ADA's requirements to accommodate patients and HCWs with disabilities, have lowered infectious disease transmission, upgraded care for chronic conditions, and improved the efficiency of care in some instances. For example, the ADA mandates that hospitals receiving federal funding assist deaf patients to ensure effective communication through on-site and remote interpretation, handwritten notes, and captioned telephones. *See, e.g.*, Leila Miller, *'I was panicked': Deaf Patients struggle to get interpreters in medical emergencies*, STAT (May 22, 2017).

Outside the health care setting, 1 survey suggests that over 42% of U.S. businesses report enhanced workplace safety based in part on ADA-influenced improvements. Helen A. Schartz et al., *Workplace Accommodations: Evidence Based Outcomes*, 27 WORK 345, 349 (2006). Protecting disabled workers underlies indoor smoking bans to accommodate persons with asthma or other conditions, as well as improve air quality for all workers. Lainie Rutkow et al., *Banning Second-hand Smoke in Indoor Public Places Under the ADA: A Legal & Public Health Imperative*, 40 CONN. L. REV. 409, 409 (2007).

Telecommuting options to assist disabled workers under the ADA help reduce commute times, lower accident rates, decrease the spread of infectious diseases, and minimize work-related stress. Brianne M. Sullenger, *Telecommuting: A Reasonable Accommodation under the ADA as Technology Advances*, 19 REGENT U. L. REV. 537, 542–43 (2006). Disabilities protections are even considered in relation to emergency legal preparedness plans and policies to assure adequate safeguards for persons with physical and mental impairments. U.S. GOV'T ACCOUNTABILITY OFF., FED. DISASTER ASSISTANCE: FEMA'S PROGRESS IN AIDING INDIVIDUALS WITH DISABILITIES COULD BE FURTHER ENHANCED (Feb. 2017).

Anti-discrimination protections may, however, be contravened by other public health laws that directly or indirectly reflect bias related to the causes of chronic conditions, or persons who suffer from them. For example, anti-tobacco policies at the federal and state levels authorize discrimination against smokers and other tobacco consumers in the interest of protecting the public's health. Smokers may not light up in many public places, can be denied life insurance outright or charged more for health insurance, or be restricted in their employment options (or not hired at all for that matter). Each of these policies have underlying legal support grounded in protecting the public's health by discouraging smoking. Yet persons with chronic illnesses, including many smokers, are largely disadvantaged.

Persons who use illicit drugs may be addicted to these substances and, consequently, are greatly limited in their major life activities. However, the ADA expressly excludes illicit drug use among those items classifiable as disabilities. 42 U.S.C. § 12114 (2013). Few may agree that users of heroin, fentanyl, cocaine, crystal meth, or other dangerous drugs are entitled to disability protections, but policies related to their treatment are beginning to change. Once castigated and charged criminally, users of addictive drugs are now provided options to avoid prosecution so long as they participate in drug treatment programs. In Connecticut, courts are statutorily authorized to order offenders who are drug- or alcohol-dependent into treatment in lieu of prosecution or incarceration. CONN. GEN. STAT. §§ 17a–692 to 17a–701 (2013).

In June 2013, the American Medical Association (AMA) called for a reclassification of obesity as a disease. Andrew Pollack, *A.M.A. Recognizes Obesity as a Disease*, N.Y. TIMES, June 18, 2013. If broadly adopted, this might help qualify all forms of obesity, like its associated condition, Type II diabetes, for disability protections and related health insurance coverage. Currently only "severe obesity" (when body weight is more than 100% over norm) may qualify as a disability under the ADA. EEOC COMPLIANCE

MANUAL § 902.2(c)(5)(ii) (2009). Despite AMA's recognition of obesity as a disease, it is still viewed largely as a risk factor for other chronic conditions, but not as a distinct disease. *Recognition of Obesity as a Disease H–440.842*, AM. MED. ASSOC. (2023).

As a result, obesity remains a major public health target with some policies having potentially deleterious impacts on affected individuals. Consider proposals in some states or localities to (a) authorize charging obese persons more for their health insurance premiums (*see, e.g.*, TENN. CODE ANN. § 56–7–3013 (2013) (insurers can establish premium schedules based on obesity); or (b) set workplace wellness bonuses based on levels of physical activity (*see, e.g.*, MASS. GEN. LAWS ANN. tit. IX, ch. 62 § 6N (2013) (establishing a $10,000 tax credit for employers seeking to create a wellness program); MISS. CODE ANN. § 41–97–9 (2012) (creating model program for employee wellness including incentives).

Each of these incentive-driven policies may negatively impact persons who are overweight or obese to the extent they are charged more for similar services, cannot participate fully to garner benefits, or simply lose opportunities because of their weight. Disability protections may prevent some of these impacts (e.g., ADA employment protections apply to persons simply "regarded as" having a disability). Conversely, some public health laws and policies represent an affront to equality of persons with conditions that are, or will soon be, chronic.

Addressing chronic conditions through law requires creative options and resulting trade-offs. Implementing public health laws to deter individual behaviors that lead to chronic illnesses seems overly paternalistic to some. For others, application of such laws is unfair related to their own conditions, the onset of which may not be of their own doing. Still, at the source of government regulatory approaches related to chronic conditions is the laudable goal of preventing excess morbidity and mortality. Achieving this same objective concerning injury prevention entails extensive use of additional legal tools, namely civil litigation and criminal enforcement, as discussed in Chapter 7.

	Chapter 6—Discussion Questions
?	1. How do public health practitioners distinguish communicable & chronic conditions?
?	2. What public health powers can help change negative behaviors that lead to the onset of chronic conditions?
?	3. What are the practical & political realties or limits to greater use of tax & spend powers?
?	4. How can regulatory laws be used effectively to address causes of chronic conditions?
?	5. How may public health laws intended to prevent chronic conditions stigmatize persons?

CHAPTER 7

MITIGATING THE INCIDENCE & SEVERITY OF INJURIES & OTHER HARMS

	Chapter 7—Learning Objectives
✓	1. Understand the diverse array of preventable injuries & related deaths in the U.S.
✓	2. Assess & compare the varied causes of injuries & related deaths
✓	3. Explore the broad use of tort laws to address preventable causes of morbidity & mortality
✓	4. Review the dominant product liability themes designed to compensate injured persons
✓	5. Consider how criminal laws & policies impact injury prevention & control methods

In addition to communicable and chronic conditions, a 3rd major focus of public health agencies, advocacy organizations, and other partners is the prevention of injuries and related harms or deaths. Public health practitioners define injuries broadly as "any unintentional or intentional [bodily] damage . . . resulting from acute exposure to thermal, mechanical, electrical, or chemical energy or from the absence of . . . essentials as heat or oxygen." NAT'L

COMM. FOR INJURY PREVENTION & CONTROL, INJURY PREVENTION: MEETING THE CHALLENGE 4 (1989).

Coupled with these acute harms are long-term, chronic injuries related to repeated exposures to products like tobacco, alcohol, or drugs. Injuries arise from multiple sources and causes. Some are unintentional (e.g., many vehicle crashes). Others are not (e.g., direct assaults). The collective impacts of injuries on the population each year are significant, as explained in section A, below.

The public health tragedy underlying many injuries, harms, and related deaths is that most are preventable through changes in behaviors, products, and the environment via public health education (*see* Chapter 9), engineering, and the law. Many types of laws, including themes discussed already in Part II (e.g., screening, treatment, powers to tax and spend, regulations) are used effectively to prevent injuries and deaths. Two additional areas of law to avert injuries include tort and criminal law.

Deleterious practices leading to unintentional injuries are intrinsically tied to "tort" laws (laws addressing civil wrongs). Through actual or threatened tort litigation, the design, manufacture, sale, and use of an array of products including food, drugs, tobacco, toys, and vehicles have changed to prevent injuries. How tort actions lead to product changes over time in the interests of consumer safety and the public's health is discussed further in section B.

Criminal law presents a different and controversial approach to address injuries and related deaths. By penalizing individual or corporate behaviors that contribute to injuries, the underlying public health premise of criminal law (and tort law for that matter) is to deter dangerous, reckless, or harmful acts. This premise may be suspect. Take, for example, strict laws prohibiting illicit drug possession to protect individuals from potentially fatal drug overdoses. Persons prosecuted under these laws may receive what some may deem as just punishments, namely criminal fines and incarceration. Yet, without additional interventions (e.g., drug rehabilitation and treatment programs), these punishments may (1) negatively impact their health and their families' well-being, particularly among lower socio-economic groups, and (2) largely fail to treat the underlying addiction. The extent to which such laws deter others from similar behaviors is often presumed, but not always well-known. As discussed in section C, the traditional use of criminal law to punish behaviors that cause or lead to injuries to oneself or others is evolving toward rehabilitation.

A. PRIMARY SOURCES OF INJURIES, HARMS & DEATHS

Sources and impacts of preventable injuries, harms, and deaths in the U.S. are attributable to 3 major sources: (1) occupational or environmental hazards, (2) products, and (3) risky behaviors. In 2022, for example, occupational hazards (e.g., fires, falls, harmful substances) led to ~2.3 million nonfatal injuries and 5,486 deaths. BLS, EMPLOYER REPORTED

WORKPLACE INJURIES & ILLNESSES-2021–2022 (2023); BLS, NAT'L CENSUS OF FATAL OCCUPATIONAL INJURIES IN 2022 (2023). Other substantial causes of injuries and deaths in the U.S. are noted below.

Vehicular Collisions. Vehicular crashes are a leading cause of preventable injuries and deaths outside the workplace. CDC estimates 2.1 million adults required emergency treatment following such crashes in 2020. CDC, *Transportation Safety* (2023). Transportation-related incidents (including cars, large trucks, buses, and other vehicles) caused 42,795 deaths in 2022. NHTSA, EARLY ESTIMATE OF MOTOR VEHICLE TRAFFIC FATALITIES IN 2022 (2023).

Figure 7.1. Reasons for Driver-Related Collisions

DRIVER-RELATED COLLISIONS—REASONS	%
RECOGNITION ERROR (driver's inattention, internal/external distractions, inadequate surveillance)	**41%**
DECISION ERROR (driving too fast for conditions or curves, false assumption of others' actions, illegal maneuvers, misjudgments)	**33%**
PERFORMANCE ERROR (overcompensation, poor directional control)	**11%**

NON-PERFORMANCE ERROR (sleep)	**7%**
OTHER	**8%**

Source: SANTOKH SINGH, NHTSA, TRAFFIC SAFETY FACTS: CRITICAL REASONS FOR CRASHES INVESTIGATED IN THE NAT'L MOTOR VEHICLE CRASH CAUSATION SURV. (2018).

As per Figure 7.1, many factors contribute to vehicular crashes, including driver errors, road conditions, alcohol and drug use, highway design, and weather-related hazards. At the top of this list is "distracted driving," predominantly including use of cellular or navigation devices while operating vehicles. A 2015 study of over 1,200 drivers in Texas found that persons under the age 25 are 4 times more likely than others to use a cellular device while driving. Female drivers are 63% more likely to speak on their phones than males. Michelle L. Wilkinson, et al., *Prevalence & Correlates of Cell Phone Use Among Texas Drivers,* 2 PREVENTATIVE MED. REP. 149, 150 (2015).

Since 2015, the use of handheld devices among drivers has increased from 2.2% to 3.41% in 2022. More alarming, an estimated 6.5% of 16–24 year old drivers use their handheld devices while driving. NHTSA, DOT HS 813 531, DRIVER ELECTRONIC DEVICE USE IN 2022 (2024). Some suggest the risks of being in a vehicle collision while using a cellular device (even hands-free devices) are approximately the same as driving drunk. Sumie Leung et al., *A Comparison of the Effect of Mobile Phone Use & Alcohol Consumption on Driving Simulation*

Performance, 13 TRAFFIC INJ. PREVENTION 566 (2012).

In 2021, the National Highway Traffic Safety Administration (NHTSA) conservatively estimated 3,211 Americans perished due to distracted driving. NHTSA, DOT HS 813 443, DISTRACTED DRIVING IN 2021 (2023). Although most states ban or limit use of cellular devices while driving (especially among minors), accurate assessments are hampered by significant difficulties in detecting unlawful cellular use. Denise Lavoie, *Police losing battle to stop texting behind the wheel*, ARIZ. REP., Sept. 6, 2016, at 8A. In 2016, New York State legislators proposed use of a "textalyzer" designed to scan cellular devices at the scene of a collision to determine if drivers were using them just prior to the incident. Matt Richtel, *On Your Phone at the Wheel? Watch Out for the Textalyzer*, N.Y. TIMES, Apr. 28, 2016. The New York legislation and a similar proposal in Nevada ultimately failed. Hamza Shaban, *'Breathalyzer for Texting': Nevada Weighs Controversial Technology to Curb Distracted Driving*, WASH. POST, Mar. 18, 2019.

Toys, Foods & Other Products. Products used or consumed regularly also pose substantial risks of injury to human health. In 2019, for example, an estimated 224,200 toy-related injuries were treated in emergency departments nationally. ANGIE QIN & CSPC, TOY-RELATED DEATHS & INJURIES CALENDAR YEAR 2019 8 (2020). Some products like fireworks can be especially dangerous, contributing to nearly 10,200 injuries and 11 deaths in 2022. U.S. CPSC, 2022 FIREWORKS ANNUAL REPORT 2 (2023). On July

4, 2021, National Hockey League® goalie, Matiss Kivlenieks, age 24, died in Michigan after being struck in chest by a fallen fireworks mortar. Claire Fahy, *Promising Goalie for Blue Jackets Dies After Being Hit by Fireworks*, N.Y. TIMES, July 6, 2021.

In addition to the risks of food-borne illnesses (discussed in Chapter 4) and "consumable vices" (discussed in Chapter 6), foreign objects (e.g., bones, glass, plastics, shells, stones) found in packaged and prepared foods injure thousands of Americans each year. *See, e.g.*, Frederick N. Hyman et al., *FDA Surveillance of the Role of Foreign Objects in Foodborne Injuries*, 108 PUB. HEALTH REP. 54, 55 (1993); Kimberly Kindy, *Processed Meat Recalls Rise Dramatically as Consumers Bite Down on Metal, Plastic & Glass*, WASH. POST, Dec. 23, 2019.

Poisons present another distinct threat. In 2022, there were 2,064,875 human exposures to poisons reported nationally in the U.S. and 2,622 related fatalities. David B. Gummin et al., *2022 Ann. Rep. of the Nat'l Poison Data Sys. (NPDS) from America's Poison Centers: 40th Annual Report*, 61 CLINICAL TOXICOLOGY 717, 717, 740 (2023). Deaths related to poison exposures, especially among kids, were considerably higher in past decades. Significant reductions may be attributed in large part to packaging redesigns to eliminate unintentional exposures, as well as national poison control centers offering real-time emergency information and guidance to callers online and via emergency call centers. LEWIN GROUP, INC., FINAL REP. ON THE VALUE OF THE POISON CTR. SYS. (2012).

Arsenic in Wine?

Trace levels of poisons may be within consumable products themselves. A class action lawsuit filed in 2015 in Los Angeles County Superior Court alleged that wineries bottled products with significantly higher levels of arsenic than are safe for consumption. *Charles v. The Wine Group, Inc.*, No. BC576061 (Cal. Super. Ct. 2015), *appeal filed sub nom. Charles v. Sutter Home Winery, Inc.*, No. B275295 (Cal. App. Dep't Super. Ct. May 26, 2016); Ben O'Donnell, *Wineries Fight Arsenic Lawsuit Claims*, WINE SPECTATOR, June 15, 2015, at 15. The case was dismissed in 2016 after an appellate court found that wine providers were not required to provide additional warning labels for arsenic. *See Charles v. Sutter Home Winery, Inc.*, 23 Cal. Rptr. 3d 513 (Ct. App. 2018) (de-published).

Violence. Injuries and deaths tied to horrific acts of gun-related violence are highly-publicized (e.g., shooting rampages in Monterey Park, CA (2023, 12 dead); Lewiston, ME (2023, 19 dead); Uvalde, TX (2022, 21 dead); Boulder, CO (2021, 10 dead); Atlanta, GA (2021, 10 dead); Dayton, OH (2019, 9 dead); El Paso, TX (2019, 23 dead); Virginia Beach, VA (2019, 12 dead); Odessa, TX (2019, 8 dead)); Orlando, FL (2016, 49 dead); Charleston, SC (2015, 9 dead); Newtown, CT (2012, 27 dead); and Virginia Tech University (2007, 32 dead). *See, e.g.*, Daniel

Victor & Jenny Gross, *A List of Recent Mass Shootings in the U.S.*, N.Y. TIMES, Apr. 16, 2021.

In March 2021 the White House acknowledged gun violence was a "public health crisis." The House of Representatives passed the Bipartisan Background Checks Act of 2021, H.R. 8, 117th Cong. (2021), to expand background checks for firearm sales, but it was never fully enacted. Three years later, with little improvement nationally, U.S. Surgeon General Dr. Vivek Murthy again declared gun violence a public health crisis. His advisory suggested manifold interventions including greater prevention research, safe storage laws (and related HCW guidance to patients), assault weapons bans, and universal background checks. Ellen Barry, *Surgeon General Declares Gun Violence a Public Health Crisis, Like Smoking*, N.Y. TIMES, June 26, 2024.

On February 4, 2024, in one of the most high profile cases of its kind nationally, Michigan parents were found guilty of involuntary manslaughter in the gun-related deaths of 4 persons—all committed in a school-related rampage by their 15-year old son. James and Jennifer Crumbley were convicted of allowing their disturbed son to readily access guns within their family's household. Jacey Fortin & Anna Betts, *Parents of School Shooter Who Killed 4 Are Sentenced to 10–15 Years in Prison,* N.Y. TIMES, Apr. 10, 2024.

Behind the headlines of these horrific acts of mass shootings and deaths, tens of thousands of instances of gun-related morbidity and mortality occur each year largely out of the "media spotlight" due to individual risky or criminal acts. *See, e.g.*, Wendy E. Parmet, *Valuing the Unidentified: The Potential of Public Health Law*, 53 JURIMETRICS J. 225 (2013). In 2015, over 84,000 individuals were treated in emergency departments for nonfatal gunshot wounds. CDC NAT'L CTR. FOR INJURY PREVENTION & CONTROL, *Overall Firearm Gunshot Nonfatal Emergency Dep't Visits & Rates per 100,000* (2015). In 2022, over 48,000 deaths resulted from gunshot wounds in the U.S. (far exceeding rates per capita in other industrialized countries). CDC, FIREARM VIOLENCE PREVENTION—FAST FACTS (2023).

Domestic and interpersonal violence, including abuse, stalking, rape, and bullying, impose additional threats of injury or deaths. Millions of American women are victims of physical violence by an intimate partner each year. More than 25% of women and 10% of men in the U.S. experience rape, physical violence, and/or stalking by an intimate partner at some point in their lives. CDC, NAT'L INTIMATE PARTNER & SEXUAL VIOLENCE SURV.: 2015 DATA BRIEF (Nov. 2018).

In 2022, over 558,899 cases of child abuse and neglect were reported, including 1,990 fatalities of children ages of 0–17 years old. HHS et al., CHILD MALTREATMENT 2022, at ii (2022). Youth violence is the second leading cause of death for people ages 15–24. In 2019, 20% of high school students reported being bullied on school grounds; 16% reported cyber bullying. CDC, *Preventing Bullying* (2020). That same year, over 420,000 persons between the ages of 10–24 years old received emergency treatment for injuries sustained from physical assaults. CDC, NONFATAL INJURY REPORTS, 2000–2019.

Suicide. Across the U.S., 49,449 persons committed suicide in 2022. CDC, SUICIDE DATA & STATISTICS (2023). The causes and contributing factors to these deaths are many, but access to firearms is a primary one. Public health research shows that suicide rates are higher in states where gun ownership is more prevalent. *See, e.g.*, Matthew Miller et al., *Firearms & Violent Death in the U.S.*, *in* REDUCING GUN VIOLENCE IN AMERICA, at 11; Sabrina Tavernise, *With Guns, Killer & Victim Are Usually Same*, N.Y. TIMES, Feb. 14, 2013.

According to CDC, 13.3% of female students and 6.6% of male students nationally attempted suicide in 2021. CDC, *Suicidal Thoughts and Behaviors Among High School Students—Youth Risk Behavior Survey, U.S., 2021*, 72 MMWR 45, 48 (2023). These trends only worsened during the COVID-19 pandemic. CDC reported substantial increases in mental health emergency treatments among kids aged 5–11 years between April–October 2020 (compared to the prior year) due in part to extensive, long-term social distancing and school closures (*see* Chapter 12). Christina Caron, *A Mental Health Crisis Flares Among Young Children*, N.Y. TIMES, June 30, 2021. Increasingly, parents of children whose suicides may coincide with bullying or other abusive acts have sued to hold schools accountable in part for these deaths. Donna St. George, *Parents hold schools accountable for suicides,* WASH. POST, Nov. 13, 2024 (reporting multiple school systems nationally settling wrongful death claims with families for millions).

Drugs. Use of illicit and prescription drugs leads to hundreds of thousands of injuries or harms and tens of thousands of deaths each year. The April 21, 2016 death of the musician, Prince (Figure 7.2), due to his overdose of the prescription synthetic opiate painkiller, fentanyl, underscores the severity of the problem. Jan Hoffman, *In Prince's Battle With Opioids, A Familiar Narrative That Begins With Pain*, N.Y. TIMES, May 6, 2016. In 2018, musician, Tom Petty, died via accidental overdose of multiple opioids, including fentanyl. Marwa Eltagouri, *Tom Petty died of an accidental drug overdose*, WASH. POST, Jan. 19, 2018.

Figure 7.2. Prince

Source: *ZIFF's 'USA Night' honors Prince*, U.S. EMBASSY ZIM., (Oct. 2016).

Beyond celebrity deaths due to opioids, millions of drug users suffer direct or indirect injuries, lost days of productivity, and profound economic and social impacts. Hundreds of thousands have perished.

Between 1999–2019, the number of drug-induced deaths (largely comprised of opioid-related fatalities) surpassed 1 million, exceeding the number of deaths by vehicle crashes nationally during the same period. Over the course of the COVID-19 pandemic drug-related deaths rose significantly, exceeding 111,000 persons in 2022 alone, Noah Weiland, *U.S. Recorded Nearly 110,000 Overdose Deaths in 2022*, N.Y. TIMES, May 17, 2023, before slightly tapering off to less than 108,000 in 2023. Jan Hoffman, *Overdose Deaths Dropped for the First Time in 5 Years*, N.Y. TIMES, May 16, 2024.

Governments have engaged in significant law and policy reforms and objectives to quell the opioid epidemic. Lawrence O. Gostin et al., *Reframing the Opioid Epidemic as a National Emergency*, 318 JAMA 1539 (2017); RICHARD J. BONNIE ET AL., PUBLIC HEALTH LAW, ETHICS & POLICY 646–660 (2nd ed. 2021). Presidents Obama, Trump, and Biden proposed major funding and other initiatives to curb illicit drug and opioid misuses. Gardener Harris, *Obama Seeks $1.1 Billion To Help Fight Opioid Abuse*. N.Y. TIMES, Feb. 3, 2016. On October 26, 2017, HHS issued a national PHE in response to the opioid epidemic. *HHS Acting Secretary Declares PHE to Address National Opioid Crisis*, HHS.GOV (2017). This initial PHE was renewed for over 24 consecutive 90-day periods.

Governors in Alaska, Arizona, Maryland, Massachusetts, and Virginia, among other jurisdictions, have similarly declared states of emergency. *See, e.g.*, Ariz. Gov. Doug Ducey,

Declaration of Emergency & Notification of Enhanced Surveillance Advisory (June 5, 2017). In November 2023, D.C. Mayor Muriel E. Bowser declared a public health emergency in response to the continued "opioid crisis" in the District. Jenna Portnoy, *D.C. mayor declares opioid crisis emergency*, WASH. POST, Nov. 14, 2023. States have implemented bipartisan reforms to make available essential life-saving drugs, such as naloxone, for victims of overdoses. Naloxone temporarily blocks opioid receptors in the brain to restore breathing in overdose patients until emergency medical assistance can be provided. On March 29, 2023, FDA reclassified naloxone as an over-the-counter drug, allowing persons nationally to access it with considerably fewer barriers than prescription drugs. German Lopez, *Treating Overdoses Over the Counter*, N.Y. TIMES, Sept. 11, 2023.

Figure 7.3. Naloxone

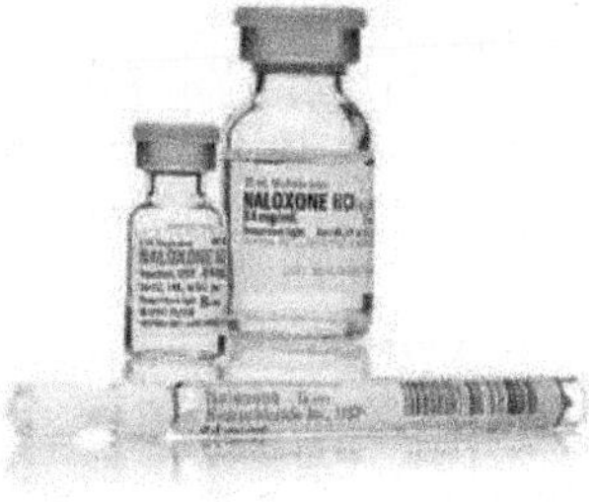

Source: NHTSA, *Federal EMS Advisory Bd. Asked to Address Response to Opioid Overdoses* (2016).

States like Massachusetts have reported reduced death rates due to opioid overdose in communities that have implemented community-based naloxone distribution programs. NETWORK FOR PUB. HEALTH L., LEGAL INTERVENTIONS TO REDUCE OVERDOSE MORTALITY: NALOXONE ACCESS & GOOD SAMARITAN LAWS 2 (2015). Good Samaritan laws have been reformed or clarified to apply liability protections to persons attempting to quell immediate risks to victims. In D.C. naloxone is available through vending machines in select locations. John Kelly, *Vending machine is designed to safeguard addicts' health*, WASH. POST, Nov. 14, 2023.

Congress passed major funding and other initiatives through the CARE Act of 2016, H.R. 4553, 114th Cong. (2016), and 21st Century Cures Act, H.R. 6, 114th Cong. (2015). That same year, CDC published national guidelines regarding prescription painkillers, emphasizing significant reductions in their use for common conditions and recommending that doctors encourage patients to initially use non-addictive painkillers like ibuprofen. Deborah Dowell et al., *CDC Guideline for Prescribing Opioids for Chronic Pain—U.S., **2016***, 65 MMWR 1 (2016); Liz Szabo, *Doctors told not to prescribe opiates for chronic pain,* USA TODAY, Mar. 16, 2016.

In 2020, federal authorities sought to improve access to evidence-based, opioid use disorder treatment during the COVID-19 pandemic, including allowing (1) persons to seek buprenorphine treatment via telemedicine and (2) methadone treatment programs to give up to 28 days of medication to patients rather than requiring them to visit clinics daily (which was highly impractical or impossible during the pandemic). *See* SAMHSA, OPIOID TREATMENT PROG. GUIDANCE (2020).

States and localities have explored more aggressive legal tactics. New York State passed its Opioid Stewardship Act which imposed $600 million in payments on several opioid distributers. The act was left undisturbed on appeal. *Ass'n for Accessible Med. v. James,* 974 F.3d 216 (2nd Cir. 2020). Viewing the required payments under the act as a state tax (and not a regulatory penalty), the federal court refused to intervene.

Seattle-King County (WA) proposed opening the nation's first supervised injection facilities (SIFs) for users. S.B. 5223, 2017 Leg., 65th Reg. Sess. (Wash. 2017) (as passed by Senate, Mar. 2, 2017). Multiple additional cities and counties announced their own SIFs leading to considerable controversies. *See, e.g.*, Bonnie Miller Rubin, *A Battle Rages Over Safe-Injection Sites*, WALL ST. J., Apr. 30, 2019, at R8; Lawrence O. Gostin, James G. Hodge, Jr. & Chelsea Gulinson, *SIFs: Legal & Policy Reforms*, 321 JAMA 745 (2019). A SIF in Philadelphia was prohibited from opening by a federal appellate court in January 2021. *U.S. v. Safehouse*, 985 F.3d 225 (3rd Cir. 2021).

Thousands of claims among state, local, and tribal governments against opioid manufacturers and distributors were consolidated into a single, multidistrict case before the U.S. District Court for the Northern District of Ohio. Since 2019, multiple settlements have been reached. Pharma company, Endo International, agreed to pay $10 million. *Endo Announces Execution of Final Settlement Agreement*

& Release Resolving "Track 1" Opioid Cases, ENDO (Sept. 5, 2019). Opioid manufacturer, Johnson & Johnson®, settled some of its claims for $20.4 million. Sara Randazzo, *Johnson & Johnson Agrees to Settle Ohio Opioid Lawsuits for 20.4 million*, WALL ST. J., Oct. 1, 2019. Drug distributors, AmerisourceBergen®, Cardinal Health®, and McKesson®, along with drug maker Teva®, agreed to pay $260 million. Julie Carr Smyth & Geoff Mulvihill, *$260 Million Deal Averts 1st Federal Trial on Opioid Crisis*, AP NEWS (Oct. 21, 2019).

A $26 billion settlement involving Johnson & Johnson® and multiple distributors was finalized on February 25, 2022. Jan Hoffman, *Companies Finalize $26 Billion Deal With States and Cities to End Opioid Lawsuits*, N.Y. TIMES, Feb. 22, 2022. It included the creation of a free-standing entity to monitor shipments of opioid products among distributors as well as a national formula for allocating settlement proceeds among thousands of plaintiffs. *See* Revised Case Management Order for Track 3, at 5, In re: Nat'l Prescription Opiate Litigation, No. 1:17–md–2804 (N.D. Ohio Jan. 6, 2021).

In 2021, Purdue Pharma® proposed a settlement requiring members of the controlling Sackler family to pay in excess of $4 billion. *Purdue Moves to Unload Opioid Claims Via $10 Billion Plan (2)*, BLOOMBERG L., Mar. 16, 2021. Coupled with prior agreements for Purdue to file bankruptcy (and potentially switch to a nonprofit enterprise) more than $10 billion of settlement funds were projected. Following additional negotiations, settlement via bankruptcy proceedings seemed imminent until SCOTUS issued its decision in *Harrington v. Purdue Pharma, LP*, 144 S.Ct. 2071 (2024), on June 27, 2024. As part of the settlement terms, the Sacklers proposed to return billions in company funds only if they were released from all current and future opioid-related claims. In a 5–4 decision, Justice Gorsuch determined that U.S. bankruptcy law does not expressly authorize such extensive releases from liability. In dissent, Justice Kavanaugh lamented the immediate impacts of the Court's dismissal of the settlement arrangement for thousands who stood to recover. Conversely, *Harrington* preserves opportunities for affected victims to bring future fraud or injury claims against culpable parties in opioid or other mass litigation regardless of settlements with others.

Measuring these and other injuries and deaths across the country illustrates the tragic nature of preventable threats to the public's health. Multiple public health legal interventions are used or designed to help mitigate these impacts. As discussed in Chapter 10, for example, many injuries related to products are prevented through federal and state statutory and regulatory laws that directly intervene to alter the environment (e.g., building safer highways) or limit products or their uses (e.g., through consumer product safety agencies). When these or other legal interventions fail to sufficiently address the threats or result in viable policy options, such as evinced in response to the opioid epidemic, tort and criminal laws may be used to prevent and control injuries.

B. ADDRESSING HARMS VIA TORT LAW

Tort law encompasses various causes of action for civil wrongs (or "torts") that harm individuals or groups in some compensable way. Tort litigation includes actions brought by individuals or classes of persons for various physical, mental, and psychological harms caused by another's negligent or intentional acts. In most cases, the end result of successful claims in tort is monetary damages that are either *compensatory* (e.g., designed to pay an injured individual for actual costs plus pain and suffering) or *punitive* (e.g., designed to punish specific behaviors that led to individual harm).

Occasionally, damages may also include a court ordering a defendant to (1) pay additional costs for the injured person's litigation expenses, or (2) adjust its practices going forward through the court's power to cease one's actions. For example, a court may stop a governmental agency from selling real estate properties containing lead-based paint. *See City-Wide Coal. Against Childhood Lead Paint Poisoning v. Philadelphia Hous. Auth.*, 356 F. Supp. 123 (E.D. Pa. 1973).

In many ways, tort law is all about injury prevention. Tort cases constitute a substantial tool for preventing accidental or intentional acts that harm others. *See* Stephen P. Teret, *Litigating for the Public's Health*, 76 AJPH 1027 (1986). By providing recourse for individuals injured through risky behaviors or dangerous products, tort actions can discourage others from engaging in such behaviors, as well as encourage or require reform in entire industries (e.g., toys, vehicles) in the design, manufacture, or sale of products that may harm consumers. *See* Jon S. Vernick et al., *Role of Litigation in Preventing Product-related Injuries,* 25 EPIDEMIOLOGIC REVS. 90 (2003). These themes are illustrated through tort causes of action grounded in negligence, intentional acts, and strict liability, explained below.

1. NEGLIGENCE

Negligence refers generally to one's failure to conform to a standard of conduct, the consequences of which may result in injury to others. Proving a case of negligence sufficient to recover damages is not easy. It is not enough to suggest one acted carelessly or without regard for others' safety or health. Rather, a plaintiff must show via a preponderance (> than 50%) of the evidence that (a) there exists a duty of care; (b) which is breached by another; (c) causally resulting in harm; and (d) leading to actual damages. Successful claims in negligence thus include a 4-part showing of a duty, breach, causation, and damages, as explained below.

Duty. Individuals engage in all sorts of careless or flippant behaviors, many of which are not negligent because the law recognizes no underlying duty of care. A legal duty of care requires one to conform to a standard of behavior or conduct so as to protect others from unreasonable risks of injury or other harms. *See, e.g., Randi W. v. Muroc Joint Unified Sch. Dist.*, 929 P.2d 582 (Cal. 1997) (school must provide information of sexual misconduct of prior teacher in recommending the teacher for employment at another school).

Legal duties typically emanate from positive actions (i.e., what one does) but also sometimes from omissions (i.e., what one fails to do). Thus, an individual may owe another the duty to avoid driving erratically, but not to lend assistance to a stranger who succumbs to cardiac arrest on the street. However, in specific cases involving special relationships, one's duty to another may be heightened. A doctor may owe a legal duty to assist a patient if she suffers an injury in his office because of a recognized special legal relationship between physicians and their patients.

Breach. Once a duty is established, a plaintiff must show that the defendant failed to conform to it. Breaches of duties may be proven in several ways. A defendant may act contrary to what a "reasonable person" would do under the circumstances. This is a question of fact subject to varied outcomes. A breach may also be shown through a failure to follow customary practices or existing laws. Through what is known as *negligence per se*, a defendant may be adjudged to have breached a duty when he is shown to have acted inconsistently with statutory or regulatory laws. *See Martin v. Herzog,* 126 N.E. 814 (N.Y. 1920) (violation of a statute mandating the use of headlights for vehicles constituted *negligence per se* as to the duty one owes other travelers).

Causation. An action in negligence may only be warranted if it can also be shown that the defendant's breach reasonably caused one's injury. Courts tend to assess evidence based on whether the plaintiff's damages (a) would not have arisen "but for" the defendant's breach ("causation in fact") or (b) were a foreseeable consequence of the defendant's actions, or failures to act ("proximate cause"). This element can be difficult to prove in many cases, especially when injuries occur or are discovered some time after an incident. *See Fisher v. U.S.*, 705 F. Supp. 2d 57 (D. Mass. 2010) (finding in favor of a refrigerator repairman who developed epilepsy about a year after experiencing an electric shock from exposed wires in an uncovered junction box); *Izell v. Union Carbide Corp.*, 180 Cal. Rptr. 3d 382 (Ct. App. 2014) (allowing claim of a construction business owner who developed mesothelioma 33 years after exposure to asbestos).

Unless courts allow for the tolling of the statute of limitations (which bars tort claims after a set period of time) to the point of discovery of one's illness (instead the actual date in which the injury may have occurred), such claims may be rejected. *See, e.g., Field v. Gazette Pub. Co.*, 59 S.W.2d 19 (Ark. 1993) (dismissing claim based on lead exposure allegedly from unsafe work conditions due to statute of limitations that began from the date of exposure, not ascertainment); *contra Boldt v. Jostens, Inc.*, 261 N.W.2d 92 (Minn. 1977) (causal relationship between employee's disability and her prior exposure to glue at her workplace was allowed based on medical expert testimony).

Damages. Finally, a plaintiff must show actual damages or losses. In other words, the plaintiff must actually have been harmed by the breach of duty such that damages can be assessed. Courts do not require defendants to pay for plaintiffs' fictional damages (e.g., undocumented allegations of psychological trauma). "Real damages" in the form of calculable losses due to physical or mental injuries or death must arise. These might include medical costs of treatment for physical or mental injuries, loss of wages, or temporary or permanent disabilities. When acts of negligence cause the death of others (e.g., vehicular crashes), wrongful death claims may entail more extensive damages for the benefit of close family members.

2. INTENTIONAL ACTS

Some torts are not based on mere negligence, but rather involve intentional acts. Striking one intentionally in a fight may assuredly result in tort liability stemming from an assault even if the victim is injured only nominally. Unlike cases of negligence there is no need to show the defendant failed to conform to set standards. If the defendant intentionally commits an assault or other act causing another harm, he may be liable absent a sufficient defense.

George Zimmerman Case
George Zimmerman, a Florida volunteer neighborhood patrol who shot and killed an

unarmed Black minor, Trayvon Martin, claimed to be acting in self-defense in 2013. Zimmerman was acquitted of criminal charges, but later settled with the Martin family who brought a tort claim based in wrongful death. Martin's parents also settled a separate wrongful death claim against the homeowners' association of the neighborhood where their son was killed. *See* Lizette Alvarez, *Settlement is Reached in Slaying*, N.Y. TIMES, Apr. 5, 2013; Barbara Liston, *Trayvon Martin's Family Settles Wrongful Death Claim: Rep.*, REUTERS, Apr. 5, 2013.

Additional intentional torts include false imprisonment (unjustifiably holding someone against his or her will), infliction of emotional distress (causing mental harm to another), and invasion of privacy (infringing on an individuals' bodily privacy interests). W. PAGE KEETON ET AL., PROSSER & KEETON ON TORTS 33–107 (5th ed. 1984). To deter harmful conduct, courts may enter judgments including minimal compensatory payments as well as injunctions against further contact between the defendant and the person bringing the action.

3. STRICT LIABILITY

Under principles of strict liability, some defendants are held responsible regardless of whether they conform to standards of negligence or intend a specific harm. Sometimes the nature of one's activities or behaviors incur liability automatically when others are injured or killed. Persons may be strictly liable if (a) they knowingly engage in an abnormally dangerous activity; (b) resulting harms to foreseeable persons are proximately caused; and (c) the defendants are not otherwise insulated or immune from liability via statute or common law.

For example, a person engaged in transporting hazardous materials on public thoroughfares may be held strictly liable if some harm related to its movement occurs to others. It does not matter whether the defendant was negligent in transporting the materials. Strict liability is assessed as a sort of "cost of doing business" in abnormally-dangerous activities. *See Klein v. Pyrodyne Corp.*, 117 Wn.2d 1 (Wash. 1991) (pyrotechnic company strictly liable for damages from a detonated fireworks display); *Senator Linie Gmbh & Co. Kg v. Sunway Line*, 291 F.3d 145 (2nd Cir. 2002) (shippers of inherently dangerous goods strictly liable even without actual or constructive knowledge of the dangers); *Oil Re-Refining Co. v. Env't Quality Comm'n*, 361 Ore. 1 (2017) (refining company strictly liable for transporting and disposing of hazardous waste without a permit).

4. PRODUCTS LIABILITY

In the area of injury prevention, strict liability theories have their greatest application through product liability. Some products may be negligently manufactured or designed. Others may fail to meet manufacturers' own warranties. In either instance, resulting harms to users may lead to liability for the manufacturer. However, proving cases of negligence or breach of warranty is historically problematic and sometimes cost-prohibitive for injured parties.

Recognizing the limitations of claims in negligence or contract related to the manufacture or sale of products, state legislatures and courts apply strict liability principles to products (but not services) that are capable of injuring or killing individuals. This includes most defective products, such as vehicles or toys, that threaten the public's health through their potential to injure users. However, some inherently dangerous products, like alcohol, guns, and tobacco, are held to a higher standard of proof before courts may assess liability related to their sale or use due in part to historic acceptance of these products and their dangers in the marketplace.

Determining if a product is defective varies. Some courts assess whether a product is safe when used in an intended or reasonably foreseeable manner. Others balance whether predictable uses of a product outweigh its utility. While any product may conceivably be made safer, courts applying this latter standard balance the costs of safer construction or design against the product's hazards as currently manufactured. Some products, like prescription drugs, carry known risks, but also substantial benefits. They may be deemed "unavoidably unsafe" and thus protected from liability because they cannot be manufactured without some risk to users. *Grundberg v. Upjohn Co.*, 813 P.2d 89 (Utah 1991) (FDA-approved prescription drug, Halcion, for insomnia was deemed unavoidably unsafe).

As per Figure 7.4, product liability applies under 4 predominant themes (*see* LAWRENCE O. GOSTIN & LINDSAY F. WILEY, PUBLIC HEALTH LAW: POWER, DUTY, RESTRAINT 237–38 (3rd ed. 2016)).

Figure 7.4. Products Liability Themes

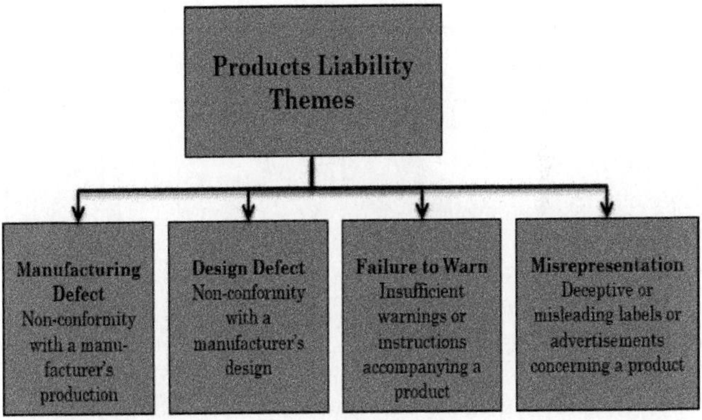

Manufacturing Defects. Some defects relate to non-conformances in manufacturing based on the maker's design. Products that do not conform to the manufacturer's plans may be dangerous to end users or others. Persons seeking recourse do not have to explain how the manufacturing defect occurred or why, only that it led to injury. From October 2015–June 2016, for example, 15 patients were treated at the University of Washington Medical Center for injuries caused by e-cigarette explosions due largely to manufacturing defects. Elisha G. Brownson et al., *Explosion Injuries from E-cigarettes*, 375 NEJM 1400 (2016).

Design Defects. Lawsuits brought against Tesla® in 2021 allege that its cars' autopilot systems malfunctioned as designed, leading to injuries and deaths when its vehicles crashed. Neal E. Boudette, *Tesla Accidents Deepen Concerns About Autopilot*, N.Y. TIMES, July 6, 2021.

Design Defects—School Bus

On a late night in the summer of 1988 outside Carrollton, Kentucky, a drunk driver collided with a school bus transporting mostly children back from a church field trip. The bus exploded, contributing to the deaths of 24 children and 3 adults. Parents sued Ford Motor Company® and a vehicle body manufacturer which supplied bus frames to Ford. The parents alleged that a design defect regarding the placement of an unprotected gas tank near the front of the bus contributed to their children's' injuries and deaths when the tank ignited on impact with the other driver's vehicle. JAMES S. KUNEN, RECKLESS DISREGARD: CORPORATE GREED, GOVERNMENT INDIFFERENCE, & THE KY SCHOOL BUS CRASH (1994). The parents settled reportedly for over $50 million. Chris

Kenning, *25 Years Later, Carrollton Bus Crash Survivors Still Struggle*, RETRO CINCINNATI, May 13, 2013.

Tragically, the Ford bus involved in the crash was built just days before implementation of new Federal Motor Vehicle Safety Standards, 49 C.F.R. § 571.301, requiring repositioning of gas tanks toward the middle of bus frames and encasing tanks in steel mesh to prevent punctures during crashes. James S. Kunen, *Two Families Fight to Make Ford Pay for the KY School-Bus Disaster That Killed Their Daughters*, PEOPLE, Oct. 31, 1988.

Not all manufacturers of defectively designed products are tagged with liability. In June 2013, the U.S. Supreme Court ruled against Karen Bartlett in favor of a generic drug manufacturer. Bartlett suffered irreparable skin damage and partial blindness after taking a generic medication to reduce her shoulder pain. The cause of harm related to the original design of the patented drug, and not its generic equivalent. The Court found that generic drug manufacturers are not liable for defective drug designs tied to their original developers. *Mutual Pharm. Co., Inc. v. Bartlett*, 507 U.S. 472 (2013); *see also Brusewitz v. Wyeth*, 562 U.S. 223 (2011) (limiting state torts claims for design defects against vaccine manufacturers).

Failures to Instruct or Warn. Sometimes manufacturers fail to provide sufficient instructions on how to use a product safely or warnings of its known risks. A failure to instruct or warn may arise where a manufacturer does not provide sufficient guidance on a product's proper and safe use. In *Technical Chem. Co. v. Jacobs*, 480 S.W.2d 602, 605 (Tex. 1972), the Texas Supreme Court defined a product as unreasonably dangerous or defective when an ordinary person would not have marketed the product without "supplying warning as to risk and dangers involved in using the product as well as instructions as to how to avoid those risks and dangers." *Id.* at 605.

Failure to Warn—Lawn Mowers

Failing to warn consumers about the dangers of placing hands or other appendages under a mower while its blade is operating contributed to thousands of injuries and related lawsuits over decades. *See, e.g., Ames v. Sears, Roebuck & Co.*, 514 A.2d 352 (Conn. App. Ct. 1986). As a result, manufacturers now provide ample warnings of these dangers. As well, mowers are made with "stop dead" safety switches or handles to help limit the possibility of injuries by cutting the motor instantly if the switch or handle is released. 16 C.F.R. § 1205.5 (2012) (requiring controls on walk-behind rotary power mowers).

Additional products have been modified following tort litigation to reduce consumers' risks of injury. *See, e.g., McCormack v. Hankscraft Co.*, 154 N.W.2d 488 (Minn. 1967) (faulty tip-proof vaporizer was redesigned to add stability); Jon S. Vernick et al., *Role of Litigation in Preventing Product-related Injuries*, 25 EPIDEMIOLOGIC REVS. 90 (2003).

In a slate of cases over the past several years, talcum powder manufacturers have been sued successfully on the premise that their products failed to warn of known potential harms of cancer risks related to long-term uses among consumers. In 2020, a Missouri appellate court awarded 20 women a total of $2.1 billion in damages against Johnson & Johnson® for failure to disclose that their talc products contained asbestos. *Slemp v. Johnson & Johnson*, 589 S.W.3d 92, 97 (Mo. Ct. App. 2019). Brent Kendall & Peter Loftus, *Supreme Ct. Won't Consider Johnson & Johnson Challenge to Baby Powder Judgment*, WALL ST. J. (June 1, 2021).

Misrepresentation. A product may also be deemed defective where a manufacturer labels or advertises it so as to give a false impression. Failing to disclose known risks of prescription drugs may constitute a claim for misrepresentation, as would advertisements or product packages that make false claims or intentionally conceal known facts about the product's dangers. In 2012, FDA ordered the removal of a television commercial sponsored by Mylan® for its EpiPen® product. The ad suggested that EpiPens® were a safe and effective preventive treatment for underlying allergies. FDA labeled the claim as "false and misleading." Mylan® had to issue a counter-statement that its product cannot prevent allergic reactions. Charles Duhigg, *Outcry Over EpiPen*

Prices Hasn't Made Them Lower, N.Y. TIMES, June 5, 2017.

A year later, in 2013, PepsiCo® paid $9 million and agreed to remove the words "all natural" from the labels of its Naked® juice products to settle claims the product contained synthetic ingredients. Candice Choi, *Pepsi to No Longer Call Naked Juices 'Natural,'* WALL ST. J. (July 26, 2013). However, in *Cosgrove v. Blue Diamond Growers*, No. 19 Civ. 8993, 2020 WL 7211218 (S.D.N.Y. 2020), a court dismissed claims of false and misleading advertising against a seller of vanilla almond milk. The product contained only trace amounts of vanilla, but tasted like it. Identifying a product as "vanilla" on the label implies taste, and not actual content, concluded the court, and thus its marketing was not legally deceptive. *See also Becerra v. Dr Pepper/Seven Up, Inc.*, 945 F.3d 1225 (9th Cir. 2019) (rejecting allegations that the company violated California consumer fraud laws by using "diet" in its product Diet Dr. Pepper® as promising weight loss or healthy weight management).

Misrepresentation—Fast Food

In *Pelman v. McDonald's Corp.*, 396 F.3d 508 (2d Cir. 2005), 2 obese teenagers and their parents sued McDonald's®. They alleged its ads and representations encouraged consumers to purchase unhealthy products through false, misleading, or incomplete information in violation of New York state law regulating deceptive business practices. The teens' claims were ultimately dismissed for failure to certify a class in 2011. Many states' legislatures subsequently passed "cheeseburger bills" prohibiting similar claims against fast food or other restaurants. Bonnie Hershberger, *Supersized America: Are Lawsuits the Right Remedy?*, 4 J. FOOD L. & POL'Y 71, 82 (2008).

Product liability actions can be used not only to compensate injured persons, but also to reform entire product lines. Once any court determines that a particular product is defective pursuant to an individual or class action, manufacturers have a strong incentive to immediately correct the defect to avoid future litigation. Sometimes this entails the complete removal of the product from the marketplace because a product cannot be made safer (e.g., lawn darts). Other times, the product is redesigned (e.g., vehicles), repackaged (e.g., cigarettes), or re-purposed (e.g., prescription drugs, like Viagra®, created for 1 condition (blood pressure), but marketed for another (erectile dysfunction)) to correct or address the defect.

Federal and state consumer product safety commissions also regularly monitor products that pose risks to users and issue recalls or recommendations for their removal or redesign based on similar bases. *See* Eileen Flaherty, *Safety First: The Consumer Product Safety Act of 2008*, 21 LOY. CONSUMER L. REV. 372, 377–78 (2009). CPSC has required for public health and safety reasons the recall of vehicles, tires, drugs, produce, electronic devices, and toys (*see* Chapter 9 for more information).

Finally, in some cases (e.g., tobacco, alcohol, guns), products that have known dangerous effects even when used by consumers as intended are allowed to remain on the marketplace based on legislative or other historic protections from liability. Tort litigation surrounding the sale, trade, or manufacture of guns is an example. For years, gun-related suits grounded in tort law percolated among state and local governments based on multiple theories. It was argued that guns were improperly designed because they (a) were easy to use, even for small children; (b) lacked clear indicators whether they were loaded; and (c) failed to use available technology to prevent unauthorized uses. *See, e.g.*, Stephen P. Teret et al., *Makings Guns Safer*, 14 ISSUES IN SCI. & TECH. 37 (1998).

While many of these cases failed, new theories emerged. Some sued gun manufacturers on the premise that their mass production of guns precipitated known sales to persons (e.g., felons, mentally-disabled) who cannot lawfully purchase them. If so, manufacturers may have breached a duty of entrustment, suggesting personal property owners owe a duty not to allow others to possess property if it is foreseeable they may use it in harmful ways. Handing a stick of dynamite to a known pyromaniac with a match might implicate the tort of negligent entrustment. As applied to gun makers, however, the theory largely fell flat. *See, e.g.*, *Hamilton v. Beretta*

U.S.A. Corp., 750 N.E.2d 1055 (N.Y. 2001); *contra Ileto v. Glock*, 349 F.3d 1191 (9th Cir. 2003). Additional cases grounded in public nuisance law also arose (*see* Chapter 10).

In partial response to this litigation in 2005, Congress passed the Protection of Lawful Commerce in Arms Act (PLCAA), 15 U.S.C. §§ 7901–7903 (2012). It forbids civil or administrative actions or proceedings against a gun manufacturer, seller, or trade association for damages, injunctions, abatement, or other relief resulting from the criminal or unlawful misuse of guns or other products, subject to several narrow exceptions. *Id.* at § 7903(5). PLCAA brought to an end virtually all litigation against gun manufacturers for harms to the public's health related to the criminal use of non-defective firearms protected by the 2nd Amendment. Jon S. Vernick et al., *Availability of Litigation as a Tool for Firearm Injury Prevention: Comparing Guns, Vaccines & Motor Vehicles*, 97 AJPH 1991 (2007).

C. CRIMINAL LAW & PUBLIC HEALTH

Tortious behavior can also be criminal in nature, allowing for dual causes of action (as per the George Zimmerman case noted above). One who drives negligently and causes a crash might only face a civil suit for injuries to the other driver or related property damages. One who engages in the same negligent acts under the influence of drugs or alcohol may face tort and criminal actions. This is because the person's behavior constitutes a civil wrong (harm to another driver) and an offense against the state (driving under the influence (DUI) of alcohol or drugs on public thoroughfares).

Criminal laws are typically set forth in statute at the federal or state levels. Local governments with sufficient home rule may also address criminal acts via ordinances. The nature and extent of government's ability to define and declare unlawful criminal acts exceed the scope of this text. However, at least part of the authority for criminal laws is the protection of the safety, health, and welfare of communities under government's "police powers," discussed in Chapter 2. *See, e.g., U.S. v. Skinner*, 973 F. Supp. 975 (W.D. Wash. 1997) (Washington law criminalizing a blood-alcohol level of .10% or higher within 2 hours of driving is consistent with state's police powers); *see also* Rachelle Blidner, *'They're going where they belong*, N. Y. DAILY NEWS (Dec. 9, 2014) (Tennessee woman plead guilty to 2nd degree murder and aggravated child abuse after forcing her 5-year-old stepdaughter to drink 2.4 liters of grape soda as punishment, leading to her death from hyponatremic encephalopathy).

At one time public health laws were tied to extensive criminal enforcement of acts deemed contrary to the public's health. LAWRENCE O. GOSTIN, PUBLIC HEALTH LAW: POWER, DUTY, RESTRAINT 151–53 (2nd ed. 2008). Not long ago, for example, attempted suicide was a criminal offense in most states. *See* 83 C.J.S. *Suicide* § 6 (2013). Charging individuals with a crime for attempted suicide can be pointless when their behaviors warrant public health or medical interventions, and not criminal sanctions.

Consequently, states have repealed these laws. *See* Catherine D. Shaffer, *Criminal Liability for Assisting Suicide*, 86 COLUM. L. REV. 348, 350 (1986) (noting that no state statutorily criminalizes attempted suicide although some punish assisted suicide).

Modern public health officials tend to disassociate positive legal interventions to protect the public's health with criminal penalties. This is due in part to prior abuses and adherence to the pervasive ethic of voluntarism throughout public health practice. Yet in the context of injury prevention and control, criminal law may still be used to prosecute and punish those who:

- commit domestic violence;
- abuse or abandon children;
- create dangerous or unsafe workplaces;
- engage in bullying in schools or workplaces;
- commit homicides, assaults, or batteries;
- cause mental health harms by intentionally exceeding noise pollution limits (*see* Jennna Russell, *In Rhode Island's Capital, 'Noise Is the New Smoking,'* N.Y. TIMES, June 24, 2024);
- fire guns in unsafe ways (e.g., in a heavily-populated environment);

- allow children access to loaded guns or dangerous weapons (*see* discussion re: prosecution of the Crumbleys in Chapter 7);

- distribute tobacco, alcohol, or drugs to minors;

- intentionally attempt to transmit HIV or other communicable conditions;

- distribute dangerous, illicit drugs (*see* Michael Corkery, *California Prosecutors Filing Murder Charges in More Fentanyl Deaths*, N.Y. TIMES, Mar. 15, 2024 (documenting prosecutions of persons in Riverside, CA and other locales who supply fatal doses of fentanyl to others); or

- sell or serve adulterated or tainted products (*see* RICHARD J. BONNIE ET AL., PUBLIC HEALTH LAW, ETHICS & POLICY 1046–1063 (2nd ed. 2021) (discussing deadly listeria outbreak in 1998 extending from a Michigan-based meat plant operated by Sara Lee Corp.®).

Stewart Parnell—2015

In 2015, Stewart Parnell, the former chief of Georgia-based Peanut Corporation of America, was sentenced to 28 years in prison for crimes related to his company's sale of salmonella-contaminated nuts that sickened hundreds and killed 9 Americans. Records revealed corporate knowledge of contamination prior to shipping products. Kevin McCoy, *Former Peanut Executive Gets 28 Years in Salmonella Case,* USA TODAY, Sept. 22, 2015.

Clearly government has the capacity, and sometimes the justification, to criminalize behaviors in the interests of injury prevention. In July 2017, hundreds of health care providers were charged with over-prescribing unnecessary opiate medications to thousands of patients and fraudulently billing federal programs. Kevin Johnson, *412 Charged in $1.3 Billion Opioid Fraud Takedown*, USA TODAY, July 14, 2017 (one group of 6 doctors in Michigan allegedly billed Medicare for $164 million in false claims). Provided it acts consistently with strong constitutional protections against unwarranted prosecutions, governments' powers to punish acts resulting in injuries to others are extensive. Whether criminal prosecution of these or other behaviors actually improves the public's health is less certain. *See, e.g.*, Julia F. Costich & Dana J. Patton, *Enforcement: Linking Policy & Impact in Public Health*, 53 JURIMETRICS J. 293 (2013).

In some cases, criminal laws may arguably deter behaviors sufficiently to the improvement of the public's health. DUI laws were significantly upgraded across states in the latter part of the 20th century in response to mounting evidence of the extensive role of excessive alcohol and drug use in driving violations and resulting crashes. Coupled with aggressive enforcement efforts, public incidence of DUI declined, along with related injuries and deaths. Thomas H. Nochajski & Paul R. Stasiewicz, *Relapse to Driving Under the Influence): A Rev.*, 26 CLINICAL PSYCHOL. REV. 179 (2006). Many credit the passage of DUI laws with lower rates of related crashes, but coextensive public health education campaigns and industry advertising also contributed substantially to reshaping societal views and behaviors concerning drinking and driving.

In other cases, criminal laws may not only fail to improve public health outcomes, they may actually worsen them. Aforementioned laws that rely on criminal prosecutions and incarceration to deter illicit drug use lack efficacy. Prior and recent studies have shown recidivism rates among those prosecuted for drug possession are reduced through drug treatment and rehabilitation programs in lieu of incarceration. *See* David B. Wilson et al., *A Systematic Rev. of Drug Court Effects on Recidivism,* 2 J. EXPERIMENTAL CRIM. 459 (2006).

Criminal laws designed to deter individuals' actions are sometimes deemed offensive (even if they work) or drive some behaviors underground. As to the former, motorcycle helmet laws passed in most states in the 1970s to address significant injuries and deaths among cyclists have been repealed in many states. Even though these laws are shown to reduce motorcycle-related deaths (in some cases by ½ in a given year), they have been criticized as overly paternalistic. *See Simon v. Sargent,* 346 F. Supp. 277 (D. Mass. 1972), *aff'd,* 409 U.S. 1020 (1972) (Massachusetts' motorcycle helmet law did not violate substantive due process); *see also Benning v. State*, 641 A.2d 757 (Vt. 1994) (Vermont's motorcycle helmet law upheld against a challenge that it infringed individuals' right to liberty).

Figure 7.5. Helmetless Motorcycler in the U.S.

Source: Wash. St. Dep't of Vet. Affairs: St. Vet. Cemetery.

As a result, motorcycle helmet laws have been statutorily repealed in many states (but not Massachusetts, 540 MASS. CODE. REGS. § 22.08 (2013), or Vermont, 23 VT. STAT. ANN. § 1256 (2013)). In 2019, only 71% of motorcyclists reportedly wore helmets in states without helmet laws. Even among those donning helmets in these states, only 56% of the head gear comply with federal safety regulations. NHTSA, MOTORCYCLE HELMET USE IN 2019—OVERALL RESULTS 2 (2020).

Correspondingly, motorcycle-related deaths in jurisdictions turning back helmet laws have risen. *See, e.g.*, Kristen J. Mertz & Harold B. Weiss, *Changes in Motorcycle-Related Head Injury Deaths, Hospitalizations & Hosp. Charges Following Repeal of PA' Mandatory Motorcycle Helmet Law*, 98 AJPH 1464, 1466 (2008) (number of Pennsylvanians dying from motorcycle-related injuries increased 40% after the state's helmet law was repealed). In partial response to these trends, New Mexico legislators considered a bill in 2015 to charge escalated rates for motorcycle registrations if riders sought to forego helmets. S.B. 308, 2015 Leg., 52nd Sess. (N.M. 2015).

One lesson of the Prohibition era was that criminalizing the possession and sale of alcoholic beverages nationally did not necessarily temper its use. Instead, it (1) shifted the venues for its consumption from public to private places, and (2) transformed sellers from known distributors to unknown "moonshiners" and "bootleggers." DWIGHT VICK & ELIZABETH RHOADES, DRUGS & ALCOHOL IN THE 21ST CENTURY: THEORY, BEHAVIOR & POL'Y 131–32 (2010). Countless Americans drank adulterated or unsanitary liquor as a result; others lost their lives trying to police those engaged in unlawful use and sales.

Criminal laws that are finely crafted, reflective of social norms, fairly enforced, and shown to be effective in lessening injuries or deaths without violating constitutional guarantees can help reduce injuries and deaths. Conversely, some criminal laws are bluntly constructed, impinge autonomy for purely paternalistic reasons, are improperly enforced largely against minorities or other protected classes, or unnecessarily impact individual rights (*see Ferguson v. City of Charleston*, discussed in Chapter 4). These criminal laws are poor substitutes for efficacious public health laws and policies better designed to prevent injuries and deaths.

As illustrated throughout Part II, public health agents possess many powers to address varied public health conditions with accompanying trade-offs inherent in balancing individual and communal interests. Mitigating injuries and deaths, whether intentional or otherwise, involves applications of tort and criminal laws. Responsible use and application of these laws against select parties may lend to improved public health outcomes. Conversely, over-zealous efforts among public and private actors to avert injuries and deaths via tort and criminal laws may lead to inapposite results.

	Chapter 7—Discussion Questions
?	1. How can laws & policies be used effectively to prevent injuries & related deaths?
?	2. What are the limits of legal liability grounded in negligence to address injuries?
?	3. How is product liability a potentially viable legal route to address injurious products?
?	4. How do inherently dangerous or harmful products like guns survive tort liability to remain on the market?
?	5. What are key ethical & legal concerns about using criminal law to deter injurious behaviors?

PART III

LAW & THE PROMOTION OF THE PUBLIC'S HEALTH

Part I sets the foundations for the field of public health law. Part II explores how law can be used effectively as a tool to prevent or control known or potential threats to the health of populations. Inexorable trade-offs between communal and individual interests in the theory and practice of public health law regarding the role of law to (a) authorize voluntary, mandatory, and compulsory public health powers; (b) allow government to tax, spend, and regulate to further community health; and (c) mitigate harms from injuries and deaths through tort and criminal laws.

Building on themes framed in prior chapters, Part III examines the scope and limits of law in promoting health outcomes in 4 areas. Chapter 8 explores the influence of law in managing public health information. Law is pivotal to privacy and security protections of modern public health surveillance, reporting, and data use practices. Chapter 9 examines legal issues in regulating public and private communications within society. How law impacts the built environment and use of private property is the focus of Chapter 10. In Chapters 11 and 12, some of the most dynamic and controversial issues in public health law are analyzed related to PHE legal preparedness and response to multiple emergencies, including the COVID-19 pandemic.

CHAPTER 8

PUBLIC HEALTH INFORMATION MANAGEMENT, PRIVACY & SECURITY

	Chapter 8—Learning Objectives
✓	1. Examine extensive facets of the universe of health information privacy laws
✓	2. Explore the scope, breadth & application of the HIPAA Privacy Rule
✓	3. Understand how state & local privacy laws interplay with federal protections
✓	4. Understand the meaning of a right to know & related law or policy requirements
✓	5. Assess the distinctions between public health practice & public health research

Data are the lifeblood of public health practice. Public health agencies gather and use an array of data for surveillance, epidemiologic investigations, and research. For decades, these practices have provided essential population-based information about the prevalence of communicable and chronic conditions, initial outbreaks of infectious diseases, and the rise of epidemics. Accurate public health data justify government interventions and support allocations of limited public health personnel, resources, and funds to improve communal health.

Sophisticated surveillance and other activities rely on data generated through legal reporting requirements. These laws obligate medical professionals and others to provide information to government based on tests, screens, diagnoses, treatments, or other findings about individuals. Such efforts are essential to monitoring the public's health, but they can also generate controversy. Much of the data collected via government are identifiable and often sensitive, including information about persons' sexual diseases (e.g., HIV/AIDS), genetics (e.g., Phenylketonuria), mental health status (e.g., Alzheimer's disease), and personal profile (e.g., victims of domestic violence or gunshots).

The acquisition, use, and disclosure of identifiable health and other data via public health agencies raise significant information privacy and security concerns, all of which must be balanced with public health purposes to achieve key communal objectives. Striking this chord is complicated by a legal patchwork of privacy laws and policies, public perceptions of the need for strong privacy protections, and politicized instances of privacy abuses that raise doubts whether public health agencies handle private data securely in all instances.

A. SURVEILLANCE & REPORTING

Public health surveillance is defined as the "systematic and continuous collection, analysis, and interpretation of data, closely integrated with the timely and coherent dissemination . . . and assessment to those who have the right to know so that action can be taken." DICT. OF EPIDEMIOLOGY 239 (Miquel Porta ed., 5th ed. 2008). Public health agencies conduct extensive surveillance largely at the state and local levels. Key information, sometimes in statistical form, is also shared with federal authorities like CDC to ascertain national or regional trends.

Each state maintains public health surveillance systems to monitor (a) notifiable disease conditions (e.g., measles, syphilis, cryptosporidium); (b) noninfectious conditions (e.g., injuries, cancers); and (c) public health indicators (e.g., behavioral risk factors). Together with additional governmental collections of vital records (e.g., birth and death records), federal, state, and local surveillance not only helps identify public health threats, it furthers nearly every other intervention in public health practice or research. *See* Stephen B. Thacker, *Surveillance, in* FIELD EPIDEMIOLOGY 16–32 (Michael B. Gregg et al. eds., 1996).

Methods of surveillance include:

(1) Gathering and monitoring available electronic data related to health risk behaviors (e.g., tobacco or alcohol use);

(2) Use of web-based or electronic surveys;

(3) Development of data registries for cancers or birth defects (among other conditions) based on screening programs, hospital discharges, worker compensation claims, or other sources;

(4) Assessment of syndromic data, such as spikes in 9-1-1 calls, emergency room visits, or purchases of over-the-counter medications (e.g., analgesics, antacids, naloxone) which may precipitate outbreaks of infectious or food-borne illnesses, rises in drug use, or acts of bioterrorism. *See, e.g.*, Wilfredo Lopez, *N.Y.C. & State Legal Authorities Related to Syndromic Surveillance*, 80 J. URB. HEALTH i23 (2003); and

(5) Environmental scans, such as ongoing assessments of wastewater discharge for various contaminants, traces of drug use, or infectious diseases. *See, e.g.*, Paulina Pineda, *Study Finds Traces of Opioids in Tempe Wastewater*, ARIZ. REP., Feb. 2, 2019, at 9A.

Surveillance data are predominantly collected through state- or local-based reporting of identifiable health information about varied conditions. *See, e.g.*, Terence L. Chorba et al., *Mandatory Reporting of Infectious Diseases by Clinicians*, 262 JAMA 3018 (1989). Legal reporting requirements vary across jurisdictions in relation to factors like:

a. ***Type & Number of Conditions Required for Reporting.*** Many states follow annual recommendations concerning approximately 120 reportable conditions from the Council of State and Territorial Epidemiologists (CSTE) based on modern case definitions it sets with CDC. *Surveillance Case*

Definitions for Current & Historical Conditions, Nat'l Notifiable Diseases Surveillance Sys., CDC (Oct. 4, 2022);

b. ***Persons or Entities Required to Report.*** In addition to doctors, nurses, and pharmacists, reporters may include diagnostic laboratories, schools, employers, law enforcement agencies, and others. Hospitals and other health entities, for example, are required to report health-care associated infections (HAIs) like Methicillin-resistant Staphylococcus aureus (MRSA) in multiple states. *See* David A. Hyman & Bernard Black, *Public Reporting of Hosp. Infection Rates: Not All Change Is Progress*, 53 JURIMETRICS J. 327 (2013);

c. ***Time Periods for Reporting Conditions.*** Persons or entities may be required to share information about a specific condition. In cases of active surveillance, reports may be legally required in real time when they are detected (e.g., bioterrorism agents, rabies, EVD, Rocky Mountain spotted fever). Concerning chronic or other conditions subject to more passive surveillance practices, reports may be requested bi-weekly, monthly, or even annually;

d. ***Agencies Receiving Reports.*** Not all public health reports are collected by public health agencies. Departments of consumer safety, education, emergency management, environment, housing, and transportation, among others, may actively receive, process, and share these data; and

e. ***Penalties for Failure to Report Conditions.*** While most state reporting laws include explicit sanctions like fines or licensure revocations against HCWs for failure to report, they are rarely invoked in modern times absent potential, significant public health consequences. In the late 1990s, California's medical board temporarily revoked the license of a doctor who neglected to report a food handler with a clear case of hepatitis. A community outbreak of hepatitis associated with the handler arose, resulting in 62 cases and 1 death. David P. Fidler et al., *Emerging & Reemerging Infectious Diseases: Challenges for Int'l, Nat'l & State L.*, 31 INT'L LAW. 773 (1997).

Rates of reporting compliance fluctuate depending on the type of condition, need for rapid public health responses, and other factors. Reporting of diseases like human rabies or Rocky Mountain spotted fever capture close to 100% of known cases, due in part to the need for quick interventions to prevent further significant harms or deaths to affected individuals. Actual reporting of Chlamydia, gonorrhea, or other STIs (*see* Chapter 4) might include fewer than 10% of cases. For these types of conditions, epidemiologists conduct periodic studies to (1) help validate the estimates of the completeness of reporting and (2) better calculate actual disease prevalence across the population. *See* Verla S. Neslund et al., *Legal Considerations in Public Health Surveillance in the*

U.S., *in* PRINCIPLES & PRACTICE OF PUBLIC HEALTH SURVEILLANCE (Lisa M. Lee et al. eds., 2010).

B. BALANCING INDIVIDUAL PRIVACY & COMMUNAL INTERESTS

Collecting some data for public health surveillance through ongoing lawful activities raises few objections. For example, gathering information about how many bottles of antacid are sold in a given day at local drug stores may help unveil the presence of a potential outbreak of food- or water-borne illness. Such data hardly invoke major privacy concerns among individuals so long as purchasers' names are not shared with local government officials. Significant interests arise, however, when names or other personal identifiers are disclosed as per many legal reporting requirements involving specific conditions.

Government seeks access to identifiable health data to further its mission to protect the public's health through surveillance and active interventions. Individuals want to maintain the privacy of their sensitive health information. Alternatively, others may claim a "right to know" of additional data (such as their exposure to infectious diseases) that may impact their own health despite the potential infringement on individual privacy expectations. As discussed later, one's right to know of exposure to conditions ranging from TB to HIV to COVID-19 infections can be compelling, but must be considered against the backdrop of assuring privacy of data acquired via health care or public health authorities.

As per Figure 8.1 below, the respective interests of government to acquire and use identifiable data and individuals seeking to limit their disclosure may seem inapposite. In reality, they are actually synergistic. Government must respect individual privacy interests when it acquires and uses identifiable data for public health purposes. Otherwise, people will evade health services such as testing, screening, partner notification, and even treatment when they sense (or experience) privacy infringements.

Figure 8.1. Privacy & Public Health Synergy

Prior to the use of anonymous testing for HIV in the 1980s, many at-risk adults would not be tested for fear of privacy invasions. *See, e.g.*, Carla Markhof Obermeyer & Michelle Osborn, *The Utilization of Testing & Counseling for HIV: A Review of the Social & Behavioral Evidence*, 97 AJPH 1762–74 (2007). For years, individuals impacted by opioid use needed a prescription to receive life-saving doses of naloxone in cases of overdoses (which is no longer the case as per Chapter 7). Yet, during this time, privacy concerns coupled with fears of prosecution kept many at-risk adults from seeking them. As a partial remedy, the New York City Department of Health and Mental Hygiene and other health departments issued standing orders granting licensed pharmacists authority to dispense naloxone to family members or friends of at-risk people to help alleviate privacy concerns. *Naloxone & Overdose Prevention in Pharmacies,* NYC HEALTH (2017).

Conversely, individuals must allow governmental authorities some reasonable access to their identifiable health data to protect the community's health (which, as noted in Chapter 1, is a core objective). Synergies between respecting individual privacy interests and promoting the public's health via surveillance and other activities help explain the extant legal environment underlying public health information management.

Most public health reporting laws do not require individuals' consent or authorization to share their identifiable health data with public health officials. Thus, a doctor who diagnoses a patient with TB does not need the patient's permission to report the patient's status to the local health department. Nor does the issuance of a named report by the doctor to a public health agency constitute a breach of the doctor's typical duty of confidentiality owed to her patients. As discussed below, public health reporting requirements represent an exception (among others) to a doctor's legal and ethical duty to maintain patient confidentiality.

Just because a public health agency may lawfully acquire identifiable health information about individuals, however, does not allow for unrestricted uses of the data. Consistent with privacy and security laws and policies (discussed below), public health agencies are limited legally in how they can use or disclose identifiable data. They may even face complications related to their use of these data for public health purposes because of incongruities among state statutory and regulatory laws that:

- feature poorly-worded or limiting provisions;
- apply highly-restrictive measures to certain types of data;
- fail to explicitly address or allow potential data uses or sharing;
- set unreasonable standards to allow basic public health data sharing; or
- are misinterpreted toward protecting privacy as an absolute.

James G. Hodge, Jr., *Editorial: Exchanging Identifiable Health Information Among Health Dep'ts* 107(8) AJPH e1 (2017). Consistent with principles of public health ethics supporting the use and confidentiality of identifiable health data (*see* Chapter 1), protecting privacy is a key objective of public health entities, but not an excuse for under-utilizing surveillance and reporting data for communal good.

C. PRIVACY, CONFIDENTIALITY & SECURITY

Protecting the privacy, confidentiality, and security of public health data reflects responsible data collection and sharing practices. Though sometimes used interchangeably, these terms have distinct legal and ethical meanings as summarized below.

Privacy
Broadly refers to the rights or interests of individuals to control acquisitions, uses, or disclosures of their identifiable health data.
Confidentiality
Denotes the obligations of those who receive such information, often through some legally-recognized relationship (e.g., doctor/patient), to respect individual privacy interests.
Security
Concerns technologic or administrative safeguards or tools to protect identifiable health data from unwarranted access, use, or disclosure.

Maintaining information security is challenging in an era of massive, digital exchanges within large electronic health databases and biobanks that can be hacked or infiltrated. Peter D. Jacobson et al., *Risk Governance & Pop. Health*, 53 JURIMETRICS J. 279 (2013). To counter these threats to privacy and security, e-surveillance systems incorporate sophisticated techniques to thwart unwarranted access. James G. Hodge, Jr., *Health Information Privacy & Public Health*, 31 JLME 663 (2004). Hospitals and health departments rely on comprehensive cybersecurity programs with loss prevention services, insurance coverage, breach resolution services, and technology tools designed to detect and block outsiders from interfering with information networks. *See, e.g.*, ASPR, HEALTHCARE SYS. CYBERSECURITY READINESS & RESPONSE CONSIDERATIONS (2021).

Various privacy and security laws and policies governing health data uses and disclosures underlie the fragmented nature of health information privacy protections. As noted in Chapter 3, neither constitutional principles nor common law concepts of duties of confidentiality support broad individual expectations of health information privacy.

In *Whalen v. Roe*, 429 U.S. 589 (1977), the U.S. Supreme Court considered a constitutional challenge to a New York state reporting requirement related to prescriptions of controlled substances (e.g., morphine). Unscrupulous physicians provided excessive prescriptions for these drugs to patients, which resulted in illegal street sales. In response,

New York's legislature mandated that all prescriptions for controlled substances be reported to the state health department. Such data were used to monitor potential public health abuses and kept offline in locked facilities to protect privacy.

Notwithstanding privacy safeguards built into New York's statutory requirements, doctors and patients sued, alleging violations of constitutional decisional privacy interests grounded in due process principles of liberty under the 14th Amendment. Rejecting their claims, the Court noted that so long as government shares "a proper concern with, and protection of, the individual's interest in privacy," including reasonable security measures (e.g., protections for stored data), public health reporting requirements are constitutionally-sound. *Id.* at 605.

SCOTUS' limited vision of the extent of health information privacy interests has been regularly challenged by lower courts. In *Dillard v. O'Kelley*, 961 F.3d 1048 (8th Cir. 2020), a federal appellate court observed how informational privacy is an amorphous constitutional right. Several persons claimed that police and other governmental actors violated their rights to privacy by disclosing reports of sexual abuse related to claims arising while they were minors and serving as cast members of a reality television show. Media members receiving the reports were able to connect the plaintiffs as victims of abuse. The court held the right to informational privacy had an "uncertain status" because it is only assumed to exist via interpretation by the Supreme Court but has never been definitively stated as a protected right. It concluded the right "does not clearly exist [and] cannot be clearly established."

Absent stronger constitutional and common law protections, a bevy of federal and state statutes and regulations comprises the dominant basis for health information privacy protections across the U.S. As per Figure 8.2, the universe of privacy laws extends across all levels of government, affects multiple entities, and covers various data. Collectively, these laws safeguard health information privacy while accommodating government interests in accessing identifiable data for public health purposes.

Figure 8.2. Universe of Health Information Privacy Laws

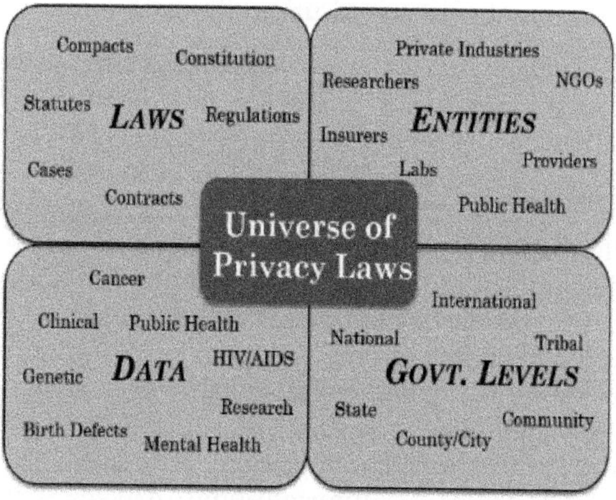

1. FEDERAL PRIVACY LAWS

Numerous federal laws protecting the privacy of health and other data apply to different types of information, persons, and entities. The Privacy Act of 1974, 5 U.S.C. § 552(a) (2012), governs collections of identifiable information, including medical data, by federal agencies. It protects individual privacy by:

- specifying when one's health information can be disclosed with (or without) consent;
- prohibiting government maintenance of identifiable data that are irrelevant and unnecessary to accomplish agency purposes;
- requiring agencies to publish a notice about the purpose of each record system and disclosures outside the agency; and
- mandating that agencies inform individuals of the statutory basis for collecting data, as well as consequences for not supplying the information.

The Freedom of Information Act (FOIA) of 1966, 5 U.S.C. § 552 (2012), requires federal agency records to be open and available to the public. On its face, FOIA seems to be the antithesis to assuring privacy, but its open door provisions are subject to several exceptions. Relevant examples include the Act's exemption for "personnel and medical files and similar files the disclosure of which would constitute a clearly unwarranted invasion of personal privacy." *Id.* at § 552(b)(6). These data do not have to be shared pursuant to "FOIA" requests from the public.

Rodriguez v. U.S. Dep't of Army

In *Rodriguez v. U.S. Department of Army*, 31 F. Supp. 3d 218, 235 (D.D.C. 2014), a former soldier sought judicial review of the Army's denial of his FOIA request for medical records of a child victim. The victim was the subject of a criminal investigation resulting in the soldier's conviction, confinement, and dishonorable discharge. The federal district court denied access to the documents under FOIA given an insufficient public interest to counter the significant privacy interests inherent in highly-sensitive medical data.

Additional federal privacy protections apply to research and other health data. The Public Health Service Act (PHSA), 42 U.S.C. §§ 201–300 (2012), protects identifiable information collected respectively by CDC/NCHS (§ 242m(d)) and HHS/AHRQ (§ 299c–3). Federal agencies can issue "assurances of confidentiality" to individuals and institutions that: "[n]o [identifiable] information . . . may be used for any purpose other than . . . for which it was supplied," absent consent (§ 242m(d)).

HHS may also grant "certificates of confidentiality" to researchers to protect participants from legally compelled disclosures of identifiable health information (§ 241(d)). Researchers generally seek these certificates when health data collected are so sensitive (e.g., related to sexual practices, mental health, or illegal conduct) that their subjects might not participate in the research or otherwise give false information.

Provisions of the E-Government Act of 2002, Pub. L. No. 107–347, 116 Stat. 2899 (2002), protect the confidentiality of federal government statistical collections of health or other identifiable information. The act restricts statistical data uses to the purposes for which they are gathered, penalizes unauthorized disclosures, and requires federal agencies to conduct privacy assessments before developing or procuring information technology.

The HITECH Act of 2009, 42 U.S.C. § 17935 et seq. (2018) authorizes HHS to establish programs to promote the public's health through electronic health records (EHRs). OFF. OF THE NAT'L COORDINATOR FOR HEALTH INFO. TECH., EHR ADOPTION & UTILIZATION: 2012 HIGHLIGHTS & ACCOMPLISHMENTS 1 (2012). Hospitals and other health care providers receive monetary incentives to follow regulations, including demonstrating that they are putting EHRs to "meaningful use" via requirements to:

- electronically capture health data in a standardized format;
- use EHRs to track key clinical conditions; and
- initiate reporting of health quality measures and public health information.

The goal is for providers to participate in a national health information exchange (HIE) that promotes efficient data uses to improve patient quality and safety. To date, that goal is unrealized.

Uptake of electronic data exchanges, however, has been plagued by multiple issues including industry failures to align systems, lending to profound interoperability gaps. Robert Pear, *Tech Rivalries Impede Digital Medical Record Sharing*, N.Y. TIMES, May 27, 2015. A lack of standardized policies and practices has further impeded HIE initiatives. *HIE Policy Issues*, AHRQ (2015). Federal and state efforts to address these practice, policy, and regulatory issues have been, at best, problematic. A 2016 national survey on state and community HIE efforts revealed a decrease in operational alignments coupled with a lack of funds and increased competition. Julia Adler-Milstein et al.. *The Number of HIE Efforts Is Declining, Leaving the Viability of Broad Clinical Data Exchange Uncertain*, 35 HEALTH AFFS. 1278 (2016). Additional pitfalls continue to impair national operability despite billions of federal dollars devoted to improvements over decades.

2. HIPAA PRIVACY RULE

Pursuant to the Health Insurance Portability and Accountability Act (HIPAA), Pub. L. No. 104–191, 110 Stat. 1936 (1996), Congress authorized HHS to create national standards for health information privacy protections. After years of drafting and significant compromises, the resulting regulations, known as the HIPAA Privacy Rule (or the Rule), 45 C.F.R. pts. 160, 164 (2004), took full effect on April 14, 2004. The Rule was later altered by the Genetic Information Nondiscrimination Act (GINA), Pub. L. No. 110–223, 122 Stat. 881 (2008), and the HITECH Act, and subsequently revised in 2013. 78 Fed. Reg.

5566–5702 (Jan. 25, 2013), amending 45 C.F.R. pts. 160, 164.

In December 2020, HHS' Office for Civil Rights (OCR) proposed additional modifications to the Rule to enhance individuals' right to access electronic health information, authorize more flexibility for disclosures in emergencies (such as the COVID-19 pandemic), and reduce administrative burdens. *HHS Proposes Modifications to the HIPAA Privacy Rule to Empower Patients, Improve Coordinated Care & Reduce Regulatory Burdens*, HHS (Dec. 20, 2020).

On April 26, 2024, HHS OCR finalized an amendment to limit disclosures of PHI regarding lawful reproductive health care following SCOTUS' rescission of the federal constitutional right to abortion in *Dobbs v. Jackson Women's Health Organization*, 597 U.S. 215 (2022). The premier objective was to disallow requests for PHI disclosures from abortion-hostile states seeking to target HCWs or recipients who have provided or obtained lawful reproductive health care in abortion-protective states. *See HIPAA Privacy Rule To Support Reproductive Health Care Privacy*, 89 Fed. Reg. 32976 (Apr. 26, 2024).

Despite ongoing reforms, the core functions of the Privacy Rule remain largely the same. The Rule:

- bestows individuals with greater control over their health information;
- sets boundaries on the acquisition, use, and disclosure of "protected health information" (PHI);

- establishes privacy and security safeguards that covered entities (e.g., health care providers, insurers, and data clearinghouses), their business associates, and others must follow; and
- provides guidance on how to keep electronic PHI secure against reasonably anticipated threats or hazards, as well as unwarranted uses and disclosures by health personnel.

45 C.F.R. pt. 164, at § 164.306(a) (2004).

By HHS' original design the Rule sets a national floor of health privacy protections (*see* preemption discussion in Chapter 2). To this extent, it does not preempt all state/local privacy laws. Salvatore Lucido et al., *HIPAA Privacy Rule & Public Health: Guidance from CDC & HHS*, 52 MMWR 1 (2003). State or local laws that protect the privacy of PHI to a lesser degree than the Rule are overridden. Those laws providing greater or enhanced coverage are not. These may include, for example, state-based genetics, mental health, cancer, or other condition-specific privacy laws conferring enhanced protections for what some policymakers view as "super-sensitive" data, such as Hawaii's law excerpted below.

Hawaii HIV/AIDS Privacy Law
Records of any person related to HIV/AIDS, "held or maintained by any state agency, health care provider or facility . . . , or any other agency, individual, or organization in the State shall be

strictly confidential." Such information "shall not be released or made public upon subpoena or any other method of discovery." HAW. REV. STAT. § 325–101 (2016).

The Rule draws no distinctions among health data; its provisions apply to all identifiable health information regardless of its content.

Under the Privacy Rule, in general, a covered entity must seek a written authorization from an individual to acquire, use, or disclose his or her PHI. As with many privacy laws, this requirement is subject to several exceptions. 45 C.F.R. § 164.508(a)(1) (2013). One concerns "standard transactions" (i.e., data exchanges between covered entities needed to treat, pay, or reimburse for care). These transactions are fundamental to the delivery of health services, and do not generally require individuals to consent (unless they pay for health care in full out of pocket). Thus, a hospital need not obtain a patient's written authorization to share her PHI with her health insurance company to seek reimbursement. These exchanges occur automatically without explicit patient authorizations under the Rule.

The Rule also allows covered entities to disclose PHI to a "public health authority" (PHA) without individual authorization. PHAs are broadly defined as any governmental agency, as well as entities working under a grant of authority from such agency, that is "responsible for public health matters as part of its official mandate." *Id.* at § 164.501. PHAs include agencies like HHS, CDC, FDA, and tribal, state, or local public health departments. Notably they also include entities under contract with such agencies, such as universities, data processing companies, or hospitals running chronic disease registries.

Thus, by design, the Rule allows covered entities to disclose PHI to PHAs pursuant to state or local reporting requirements without individual consent. Additional disclosures without authorization are also allowed by the Rule for specific public health purposes including to:

- maintain the quality, safety, or effectiveness of FDA-approved products;
- notify persons exposed to communicable diseases (a.k.a. partner notification discussed in Chapter 4);
- track work-related injuries (consistent with workers' compensation programs);
- report victims of abuse, neglect, or domestic violence;
- conduct health oversight activities;
- share school immunization information (in partial resolution of prior prohibitions of such data sharing stemming from the Family Educational Rights and Privacy Act (FERPA), 20 U.S.C. § 1232(g) (2012); 34 C.F.R. pt. 99 (2012), applying to student educational records); and

- prevent serious threats to persons or the public during emergencies (like the COVID-19 pandemic as per Chapter 12).

The Rule requires covered entities to limit the amount of information shared to the "minimum necessary" to achieve a specified goal. 45 C.F.R. § 164.514(d)(1). This requirement, however, does not apply to disclosures to PHAs pursuant to public health reporting laws. Covered entities can reasonably rely on a PHA's determination that the amount of PHI requested is the minimum needed for a public health purpose. *See* Lucido et al., *HIPAA Privacy Rule & Public Health.*

What is the impact of the Privacy Rule on public health surveillance and reporting practices? The answer is simple in theory. PHAs performing public health activities are not covered by the Rule. Reporting laws authorizing PHAs to collect data remain intact. As a result, covered entities must continue to supply identifiable health data to PHAs without individual authorization just the same as they did prior to the Privacy Rule.

In practice, however, the Privacy Rule impacts PHAs in external and internal ways. *Externally*, the Rule can stymie the flow of some data to PHAs. Despite the allowance for public health disclosures without individual written authorization, some covered entities battle PHAs over whether they can share PHI without individual consent. Hospitals may contest whether they have to provide all or part of a patient's medical record when requested by PHAs pursuant to a reporting requirement. In reality, the

Rule does not limit how much data PHAs may request nor does it authorize covered entities to deny PHAs access to such data.

Internally, while the Rule does not apply to PHAs engaged in public health activities, it may apply to PHAs performing "covered functions," or those functions that assimilate activities of covered entities. By way of an example, a local public health clinic may occasionally provide flu vaccines or other health services to the public for a minimal charge (for which it bills electronically). Concerning this specific activity, it may be engaged in a covered function and thus has to adhere to the Rule. This is true even though the PHA's underlying goal of its vaccination efforts is not so much to provide individual health services (a covered function), but rather to assure immunization rates remain high in the community (a public health objective).

To separate their public health and covered functions for purposes of compliance, many state or local PHAs designate themselves as "hybrid entities" through an assessment process created by HHS. *Id.* at 9–10. In this capacity, only that portion of the PHA which is engaged in covered functions needs to adhere to the Rule; other parts or divisions of the PHA do not so long as adequate safeguards are in place.

3. STATE & LOCAL PRIVACY LAWS

Many states' privacy laws assimilate federal protections. A few states' laws reflect the same broad themes of the HIPAA Privacy Rule. *See, e.g.*, LA.

STAT. ANN. § 40:1173.5 (2015); TEX. HEALTH & SAFETY CODE ANN. § 182.108 (West 2015). Most state privacy laws, however, tend to be more specific, applying to select data recipients (e.g., PHAs, health insurers); certain medical tests, diseases, or conditions (e.g., genetic tests, HIV status, mental disorders); or particular data sources (e.g., nursing or health care facilities). *See* James G. Hodge, Jr., *Health Information Privacy & Pub. Health*, 31 JLME 663 (2004). As a result, state and local PHAs are governed by multiple, inconsistent, and fragmented privacy provisions that differ (or are relatively silent) in the degree of privacy protections afforded, allow uses or disclosures outside PHAs, or are unclear about when disclosures may be made.

While state and local PHAs typically excel at assuring the confidentiality of their identifiable health records (despite sometimes limited legal guidance), well-publicized breaches of privacy can erode public confidence in public health data practices. In a notorious case in Pinellas County, Florida in 1997, a local public health official caused the names of 4,000 AIDS patients to be leaked to 2 newspapers and was accused of spreading the lists around gay bars. *Man Who Leaked AIDS List Gets 60 Days*, OCALA STAR-BANNER, May 15, 1997. An additional leak of HIV+ positive patients in Singapore by an American resulted in the subsequent online disclosure of over 14,000 records in 2019. Mike Ives, *Singapore Says an American Leaked Records of 14,200 H.I.V. Patients*, N.Y. TIMES, Jan. 29, 2019. In September 2020, a leak of over 10,000 COVID-19 test results were sent to an unauthorized user by a temporary public health employee in Delaware. *Delaware Division of Public Health Announces Data Breach Incident*, Delaware.gov (2020).

Developed with funding from CDC, the Model State Public Health Privacy Act of 1999 (MSPHPA) (later incorporated into the Turning Point Model State Public Health Act of 2003) provides affirmative privacy provisions for state and local PHAs. MSPHPA combines privacy safeguards for public health data with authority of PHAs to acquire and use identifiable health information for legitimate purposes. Several states have incorporated related provisions into their statutory or regulatory laws to guide appropriate access, uses, and disclosures of PHI (as defined in the act) for legitimate public health purposes, including "prevention of injury, disease, or premature mortality, or promotion of health in the community" (*see* Figure 8.3).

Figure 8.3. MSPHPA

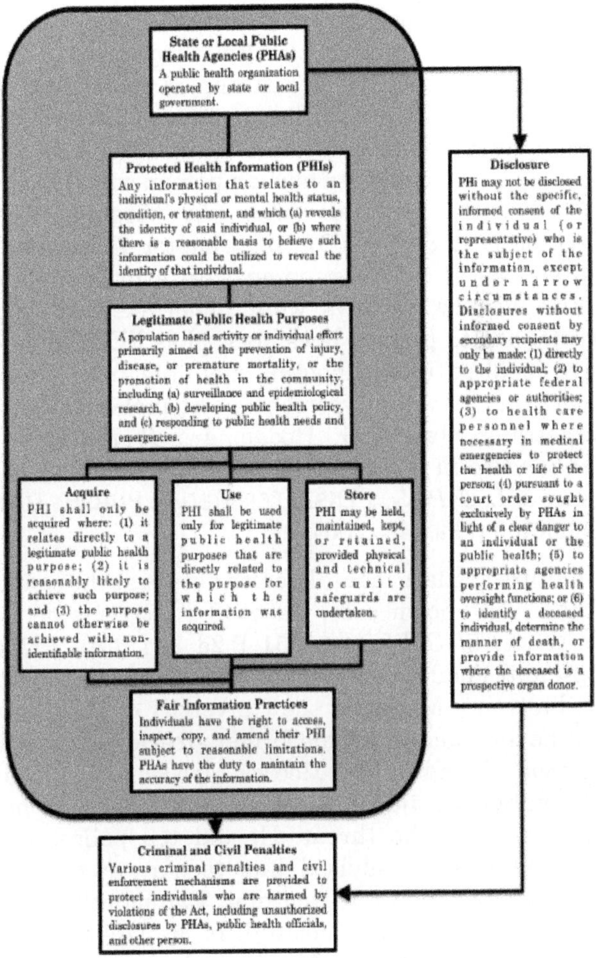

Source: Lawrence O. Gostin et al., *Informational Privacy & the Public's Health: MSPHPA*, 91 AJPH 1388 (2001).

D. PRIVACY & THE RIGHT TO KNOW

Protecting privacy is synergistic with accomplishing public health objectives, but sometimes privacy laws can impair public health efforts. Overly-strict disclosure provisions impinge legitimate exchanges of identifiable data between PHAs (e.g., sharing data about a person with TB who crosses state borders). After the Virginia Tech shooting tragedy in 2007 (*see* Chapter 7) involving the actions of a lone gunman with a prior mental health history, reviews were undertaken on how mental health privacy laws (as well as FERPA) may have resulted in withholding key data from public health and law enforcement personnel about the perpetrator. James G. Hodge, Jr., *Protecting the Public's Health Following the Virginia Tech Tragedy: Issues of L. & Pol'y*, 1 DISASTER MED. & PUB. HEALTH PREPAREDNESS S43 (2007).

Failure to share mental health data is at the center of the well-known case, *Tarasoff v. Regents of the University of California*, 551 P.2d 334 (Cal. 1976). Prosenjitt Poddar explicitly told his psychotherapist, Dr. Lawrence Moore, at the University of California that he intended to kill his former girlfriend, Tatiana Tarasoff. Despite Dr. Moore's awareness of this information, he did not directly warn Tarasoff or her parents about the threat. He did tell police, who detained Poddar, advised him to stay away from Tarasoff, and then released him. Two months later, Poddar murdered Ms. Tarasoff. *Id.* at 340–41. After her parents sued Dr. Moore and the California University system, California's Supreme Court held that mental health professionals have a "duty to warn" third parties of known, serious threats of violence by the professional's patients. *Id.* at 334.

Many courts initially followed the *Tarasoff* decision. *See Schuster v. Altenberg*, 424 N.W.2d 159 (Wis. 1988) (physician's duty is established when it is foreseeable that his patient may cause harm to another); *Alberts v. Devine*, 479 N.E.2d 113 (Mass. 1985) (physician owes his patient a duty not to disclose medical information without patient consent absent serious danger to patients or others).

In *Volk v. Demeerleer*, 386 P.3d 254 (Wash. 2016), the Washington Supreme Court considered whether a mental health professional owes a duty to protect the general public when a patient expresses violent, homicidal behaviors in non-specific ways. For 9 years, Demeerleer attended psychiatric sessions with Dr. Howard Ashby in Spokane for treatment of his depression and bipolar disorder. On multiple occasions, he expressed suicidal and homicidal ideas to Dr. Ashby, but never suggested specific persons were targets (unlike in *Tarasoff*). After Demeerleer later shot and killed his ex-girlfriend, Rebecca Schiering, and her 9-year-old son, Phillip, before killing himself, the Schierings' estate sued Dr. Ashby alleging failure to warn.

In his defense at trial, Dr. Ashby argued successfully that under Washington statute, REV. CODE WASH. § 71.05.120, he only owed a duty to warn reasonably-identifiable persons of a patient's threats. On appeal, the court reversed the lower court, holding that mental health providers could be required to warn "all foreseeable victims" in such cases as determined by the jury or other fact-finder. If so, mental health professionals may be negligent for failing to take reasonable measures to prevent the harm. While it is "unrealistic to expect perfection in all mental health diagnoses," concluded the court, professional standards to assess a "patient's dangerousness" are workable. *Id.* at 268.

Some state legislators have recognized a chilling effect of duties to warn on the doctor/patient relationship, and sought to respect traditional duties of confidentiality doctors owe to patients. Multiple state legislatures converted *Tarasoff's* judicial duty to warn into a statutory legal privilege (and then extended it to other HCWs in addition to mental health professionals). Thus, a HCW who is aware of a foreseeable danger posed by a patient may legally warn persons at risk, but does not have to do so in most states. *See, e.g.,* Lawrence O. Gostin & James G. Hodge, Jr., *Piercing the Veil of Secrecy in HIV/AIDS & Other STDs: Theories of Privacy & Disclosure in Partner Notification*, 5 DUKE J. GENDER L. & POL'Y 9 (1998).

State-recognized duties or privileges to warn in support of an individual's "right to know" extend beyond mental health contexts. Legal rights to know support individuals' knowledge of their exposure to infectious diseases through:

(1) an infected individual (i.e., such persons are legally-obligated to disclose their infectious condition to others at risk. *See, e.g., People v. Jensen*, 586 N.W.2d 748 (Mich. Ct. App.

1998) (state statute requiring HIV+ persons to disclose their status to all sexual partners does not violate constitutional free speech or privacy concerns));

(2) a medical professional (i.e., a doctor who unintentionally exposes a patient to a blood-borne pathogen). *See Brzoska v. Olson,* 668 A.2d 1355 (Del. 1995) (dentist who intentionally lied to patients about his HIV+ status faced fraudulent misrepresentation charges));

(3) a public health agent (i.e., via partner notification, discussed in Chapter 4); or

(4) a health provider (as seen in *Tarasoff* or *Volk*). A HCW may also be legally obligated to instruct a patient on how to limit the spread of the patient's infectious disease. *See Reisner v. Regents of the Univ. of Cal.*, 37 Cal. Rptr. 2d 518, 523 (Ct. App. 1995) ("a doctor who knows he is dealing with the '20th Century version of Typhoid Mary' ought to have a very strong incentive to tell his patient what she ought to do and not do and how she ought to comport herself in order to prevent the spread of [HIV].").

E. DISTINGUISHING PRACTICE & RESEARCH

Public health agencies need identifiable health data primarily for practice activities, including surveillance, epidemiological investigations, and evaluation and monitoring. Other public health activities involving identifiable information may constitute human subjects research (HSR). *See, e.g.*, WILLIAM W. LOWRANCE, PRIVACY, CONFIDENTIALITY & HEALTH RSCH. (2012).

HSR—Defined

"HSR" is defined in the federal Common Rule (governing federally-conducted or supported research) as "a systematic investigation, including research development, testing, and evaluation, designed to develop or contribute to generalizable knowledge" involving living humans or their private data.

Fed. Pol'y for the Protection of Human Subjects, 82 Fed. Reg. 12 (Jan. 17, 2017) (codified at 45 C.F.R. § 46).

For example, a PHA may conduct a double-blinded, controlled study to assess the efficacy of a new treatment among a randomly-selected group of persons. This research requires adherence to a series of research protections (e.g., individual informed consent absent a waiver) and procedures (e.g., review by an institutional review board (IRB)) to help maintain the health and safety of human subjects.

Privately-funded research may not have to meet these specific oversights, leading at times to controversial issues related to the publication of their results (e.g., concerning pandemic influenza or bioterrorism agents). *See, e.g.*, Vickie J. Williams, *The "Jurassic Park" Problem—Dual Use Rsch. of Concern, Privately Funded Rsch. & Protecting Public Health*, 53 JURIMETRICS J. 361 (2013).

Beyond clear practice and research activities is an array of public health efforts that are not so neatly characterized. Philip Amoroso & John Middaugh, *Rsch. vs. Public Health Practice: When Does a Study Require IRB Review?*, 36 PREVENTIVE MED. 250 (2003). Distinguishing between these activities is critical because:

(1) federal, state, and local laws and ethical principles governing HSR often require extensive and burdensome procedures that can delay or derail activities;

(2) the HIPAA Privacy Rule (and other privacy laws) employ different standards for the disclosure of PHI to PHAs depending on whether the underlying activity is public health practice or research. In general, it is more difficult to acquire PHI under the Rule for research purposes without individual authorization (although dual authorizations are allowed); and

(3) widespread methodological variations in distinctions between public health practice and research have led to inefficient and duplicative reviews among IRBs and PHAs.

There is no national consensus on how to distinguish public health practice and research activities. Even though the Common Rule, HIPAA

Privacy Rule, and other laws require these distinctions to be made, they traditionally provided little direct guidance on how to do so. However, in January 2017, new guidance was embedded in a revised version of the Common Rule issued by HHS' Office for Human Research Protections (OHRP). For the first time, the Common Rule defined HSR to explicitly exclude "public health surveillance" and similar activities. Fed. Pol. for the Protection of Human Subjects, 82 Fed. Reg. 12 (Jan. 17, 2017) (codified at 45 C.F.R. § 46). This regulatory language goes a long way toward resolving prior debates about whether some public health activities may constitute research. *See Attachment A—PHA & Surveillance Activities*, HHS/OHRP (Nov. 13, 2020).

Still, public and private entities may cling to inconsistent and divergent approaches for drawing distinctions. James G. Hodge, Jr., *An Enhanced Approach to Distinguishing Pub. Health Practice & HSR*, 33 JLME 125 (2005). To help resolve resulting incongruities CSTE proposed a comprehensive approach for distinguishing public health practice and research activities. CSTE, PUBLIC HEALTH PRACTICE V. RSCH.: A REPORT FOR PUBLIC HEALTH PRACTITIONERS 1–61 (2004).

CSTE defined *public health practice* as "the collection and analysis of identifiable health data by a PHA [to protect] the health of a particular community, where the benefits and risks are primarily designed to accrue to the participating community." *Id.* at 16. Conversely, *public health research* is defined as "the collection and analysis of identifiable health data by a PHA [to generate] knowledge that will primarily benefit those beyond the participating community who bear the risks of participation." *Id.* at 15.

Based on these core definitions, a dual-stage process for drawing distinctions was created. The initial stage refers to core foundational principles to classify "practice" or "research" activities in relatively easy cases. Where these core principles do not neatly distinguish a specific activity, a series of enhanced criteria (set forth below) should be considered for each part of a multi-faceted activity.

General Legal Authority. Sometimes specific legal authority exists for a public health practice activity (which often typifies it as practice). In other instances, PHAs may conduct activities pursuant to more general legal authorization. The TURNING POINT ACT § 5–102(a), for example, authorizes state or local PHAs to "collect, analyze, and maintain [information to] . . . accomplish or further the mission or goals of public health, or provide essential public health services and functions." Absent other criteria favoring a research classification, the activity is likely practice and not research.

Specific Intent. CDC and others have focused on intent underlying data collection as a distinguishing factor, but broad conceptions of intent could apply to either practice or research. CDC's revised guidance continues to rely on generalized notions of the underlying "purpose of the project," determined on a case-by-case basis, to make distinctions.

CSTE specifies the underlying intent of *research* is "to test a hypothesis and seek to generalize the findings or acquired knowledge beyond the activity's participants." The intent of *public health practice* is "to assure the conditions in which people can be healthy through public health efforts that are primarily aimed at preventing known or suspected injuries, diseases, or other conditions, or promoting the health of a particular community." CSTE, PUBLIC HEALTH PRACTICE V. RSCH., at 15.

Responsibility. In research, responsibility for the health, safety, and welfare of individual participants falls on specific individuals, typically principal investigators (PIs). In public health practice, responsibility for individuals' well-being is held typically by government entities via their legal and ethical duties.

Participant Benefits. Research is designed primarily to advance scientific knowledge. Participants may fail to receive any direct benefit from the activity or even be harmed by it. Whenever risks are imposed on participants to generalize the results, the activity is research. Conversely, public health practice activities are premised on providing some known or expected benefit to participants or the population of which they are members.

Experimentation. Unlike public health practice, research is experimental by design. Research may involve introducing something non-standard or unproven to subjects or to their identifiable health data. Although innovations are a part of public health practice, it is dominated by the use of standard, accepted, and proven interventions to address a known or suspected public health problem. Any activity that introduces experimental procedures is more likely research than public health practice.

Subject Selection. HSR is largely (though not exclusively) driven by the researcher's desire to test an underlying hypothesis. To reduce the possibility of bias, the PI may select human subjects randomly so that the results may apply to a larger group. Participants for practice activities are selected because they have, or are at risk of, a particular condition and can likely benefit from the activity. Thus, if an activity utilizes control groups to garner generalizable information or randomly selects its participants to eliminate bias, the activity is likely research rather than practice.

Despite greater clarification of these distinctions in the 2017 version of the Common Rule and via CDC, use of CSTE's process may help improve uniformity in difficult cases. The ultimate objective is to perform public health activities that respect and protect the privacy rights and interests of individuals while improving or promoting the public's health.

Significant legal interests arise related to how government acquires and uses health information about individuals. Balancing individual privacy and communal health objectives throughout the management of PHI is essential to the advancement of the public's health. In other ways, government seeks to manage information that is not about individuals, but rather is directed toward them in the greater marketplace of ideas, products, and services. In these instances, the legal focus shifts from respecting privacy to protecting free speech. And yet, as explored in Chapter 9, a central legal question remains: *when and how can government regulate information in the interests of promoting the health of populations*?

	Chapter 8—Discussion Questions
?	1. How is protecting health information privacy synergistic with public health promotion?
?	2. What is the preemptive effect of the HIPAA Privacy Rule on state & local laws?
?	3. How does the Privacy Rule impact PHAs internally & externally?
?	4. When do persons have a legal right to know about others' identifiable health data?
?	5. What are key factors to distinguish public health practice & research activities?

CHAPTER 9

REGULATING COMMUNICATIONS

	Chapter 9—Learning Objectives
✓	1. Assess the multiple, diverse ways that government regulates public health messages & communications
✓	2. Explore the tensions between public health messages & industry objections
✓	3. Examine how government assures industry messages are accurate & healthy
✓	4. Review commercial speech limitations regarding government infringements
✓	5. Determine the legal boundaries of public health promotion of core messages

Identifiable health data may be the lifeblood of public health surveillance, but another type of information is also core to public health interventions. Through public health education, required disclosures, and communications, information is wielded to apprise individuals and groups of key public health issues, change specific behaviors to ameliorate health outcomes, and avert or correct potentially misleading, deceptive, or fraudulent statements made in the marketplace. Regulating communications to promote positive messages (e.g., eating healthy) and diminish negative ones (e.g., using tobacco) is fundamental to the health of communities. *See, e.g.,* Harvey V.

Fineberg, *Public Health in a Time of Gov't Austerity*, 103 AJPH 47 (2013). It can also be highly contentious.

Governmental public health education efforts raise sensitive issues surrounding politically hot topics like sex, drugs, and guns that sometime trigger legal or political responses. Required disclosures in the form of product labels, warnings, or advisories lead to industry backlash. Freedoms of speech (noted in Chapter 3) are implicated when government attempts to control commercial marketing or advertising. *See, e.g.*, Micah L. Berman, *Manipulative Marketing & the 1st Amendment*, 103 GEO. L. J. 497 (2015). Hurdling these and other legal issues is a major challenge any time public health messages conflict with individual, commercial, or societal interests or expectations about the role of government in the larger marketplace of ideas.

A. PUBLIC HEALTH EDUCATION

Public health education conducted by governmental or private entities is widespread and varied. As per the public health messages underlying drug paraphernalia depicted in Figure 9.1, it may entail notices of information or warnings to at-risk individuals or their parents (e.g., annual school vaccination announcements); use of imagery (e.g., the physiological effects of tobacco or methamphetamine use) or symbols of support for specific causes or initiatives (e.g., pink ribbons for breast cancer awareness, red ribbons for heart disease awareness, and teal ribbons for sexual assault awareness).

Figure 9.1. Drug Paraphernalia Poster

Source: *Some Things You Don't Share With Anyone*, D.C. Dep't of Hum. Servs. (Mar. 2012).

Systematic, ongoing health campaigns are also used to promote public health. Each year WHO recognizes "World TB Day" to marshal educational and other efforts towards the eradication of the disease. CDC annually promotes "STD Awareness Month" to highlight information on the prevalence and spread of these diseases. The Utah Department of Health's "Got Vaxed?" campaign targets adolescents to remind them to get vaccinated for measles, rubella, varicella, and other diseases. Local public health officials in St. Louis conducted a "No Flu For You" campaign to increase influenza vaccination among HCWs. The National Institute of

Neurological Disorders and Stroke introduced its "Know Stroke" messaging to help educate the public about warning symptoms. Risks and prevention of heart disease among women are the targets of the "Heart Truth" campaign sponsored by the National Heart, Lung, and Blood Institute.

Other governmental entities and private sector companies also engage in public health education. NHTSA's "Click It or Ticket" campaign encourages drivers to wear seatbelts to reduce vehicular injuries and deaths. Playing off themes from Star Wars® movies, the Arizona Department of Motor Vehicles posted creative messages to drivers as per Figure 9.2. Fernanda Santos, *Lightspeeding Is Forbidden: Highways Turn to 'Star Wars,'* N.Y. TIMES, Dec. 22, 2015.

Figure 9.2. Star Wars Themed Road Messaging

Source: Arizona DOT (@ArizonaDOT), X (Dec. 15, 2015, 3:50 AM).

In 2013, several national cellular providers promoted the slogan, "It Can Wait," suggesting that young drivers refrain from using their cellular devices due to the dangers of distracted driving. Pharmaceutical companies and other medical providers' marketing campaigns can also highlight public health issues. In 2013, Merck & Company® ran its "One Less" advertisements promoting Gardasil® shots to prevent HPV (*see* Chapter 4). In 2017, Johnson & Johnson® ran a full page newsprint ad touting its commitment to "bring together the public and private sectors . . . to make a real difference in the world's health." Johnson & Johnson, *We Want the World to Be Ready*, N.Y. TIMES, July 7, 2017. Many educational campaigns, such as the "2min2x" (brush for 2 minutes twice a day) promotion for oral health in children, include public service announcements. AD COUNCIL, PUB. SERV. ANNOUNCEMENTS CATALOG (Q3 2013). Countless additional messages like these are circulated online via social media, such as the Biden Administration's 2021 efforts to encourage COVID-19 vaccination through TikToks featuring influential pop stars. Katie Rogers, *At the White House, Olivia Rodrigo Says Vaccines Are 'Good 4 U'*, N.Y. TIMES, July 14, 2021.

Collectively, public health education and promotion are thought to increase individuals' knowledge of conditions or risks resulting in changes in individual behaviors or choices to reduce harms. After 2 years of CDC's "VERB" campaign (encouraging children ages 9–13 to be physically active every day—*see* Figure 9.3), researchers positively correlated children who saw the campaign with improved cognitive and behavioral outcomes related to physical activity. Marian E. Muhman et al., *Evaluation of a Nat'l Physical Activity Intervention for Children: VERB Campaign, 2002–2004*, 32 AM. J. PREVENTATIVE MED. 38, 42 (2007).

Figure 9.3. VERB

Source: CDC, *Youth Media Campaign* (2004).

Population-based communications aimed at preventing cardiovascular disease in the U.S. and abroad from the 1970s through the 1990s have been shown to heighten awareness and improve risk-reducing behaviors, including dietary changes and lowering weight. *See* Melanie A. Wakefield et al., *Use of Mass Media Campaigns to Change Health Behavior*, 376 LANCET 1261, 1265 (2010).

Still, not all public health education efforts are proven effective. Some can actually have the opposite effects, offending specific groups or the public. A 2013 anti-pregnancy campaign in Chicago featured mock images of pregnant boys (*see* Figure 9.4 below). The campaign, aimed at reducing teen pregnancy and

STD transmissions, was objected to by the transgender community. Rheana Murray, *Boys, Not Girls, Are Pregnant in Chicago's Shocking Campaign to Reduce Teen Pregnancy*, N.Y. DAILY NEWS (June 10, 2013).

Figure 9.4. Healthy Chicago "Unexpected"

Source: CHI. DEP'T OF PUB. HEALTH (2013).

An anti-obesity campaign in Atlanta ("Stop Sugarcoating It, Georgia") used billboard and television ads to portray overweight children asking "Mom, why am I fat?" and stating, "Being fat takes the fun out of being a kid." Potential stigmatization of obese children and adults led some to criticize the campaign and question its effectiveness. Carrie Teegardin, *Grim Childhood Obesity Ads Stir Critics*, ATLANTA J. CONST. (Dec. 21, 2011); *see also* Chapter 4 for discussion of ADA-related concerns.

Former New York City's Mayor Michael Bloomberg and the City's Health Department's campaign against the sale of large-container SSBs was meant to deter their consumption through education and restricted portion controls. On March

11, 2013, a local court blocked implementation of the City's portion size proposal, which was affirmed on appeal on July 30, 2013. *N.Y. Statewide Coal. of Hisp. Chambers of Com. v. N.Y. Dep't of Health & Mental Hygiene*, 970 N.Y.S.2d 200 (App. Div. 2013).

Beyond the use of specific taxes on SSBs (discussed in Chapter 6), public health-supported efforts to restrict soda consumption, particularly among minors, extend further. In May 2015, the City of Davis (CA) ordained that milk and water become the "default choices" for kids' meals offered in restaurants. *See* Claire Doan, *Davis Makes Water, Milk Default in Kids' Meals,* KCRA.COM (May 28, 2015); Jane E. Brody, *Prudent Ways to Fight Childhood Obesity*, N.Y. TIMES, June 23, 2015.

San Francisco's City Council approved ordinances in 2015 designed to curb soda consumption through warning labels ("WARNING: Drinking beverages with added sugar(s) contributes to obesity, diabetes, and tooth decay.") on soft drink advertisements, ad bans on city-owned property, and prohibition of purchases of soft drinks with city funds. Tamara Audi & Mike Esterl, *Soda's New Enemy: San Francisco,* WALL ST. J., June 9, 2015.

A resulting lawsuit challenging the measures on 1st Amendment grounds was filed by the American Beverage Association. Sam Frizell, *Big Soda Sues San Francisco Over Beverage Warnings*, TIME, July 27, 2015; *Am. Beverage Ass'n v. S.F.*, No. 16–16072 and 16–16073 (9th Cir. 2017). San Francisco argued that its required warning is constitutional because it is factual, accurate, and reasonably related to its public health and information interests. After the lower court denied the Association's preliminary injunction, a federal appellate court reversed. It found that the 1st Amendment challenge to San Francisco's ordinance was likely to succeed in part because smaller warnings on SSB packages than prescribed by law would be just as effective. *Am. Bev. Ass'n v. S.F.*, 916 F.3d 749 (9th Cir. 2019).

Public health education may help inform the populace of health risks, but it can also lead to public distrust when it lacks transparency. Examples include stealthy attempts via government to manipulate messages in the private sector, compensate people or programs to issue specific information favorable to the public's health, or promote information that is poorly-supported by, or inconsistent with, scientific data. *See* LAWRENCE O. GOSTIN, PUBLIC HEALTH LAW: POWER, DUTY, RESTRAINT 340–41 (2d ed. 2008).

In *NRA v. Vullo*, 602 U.S. 175 (2024), SCOTUS unanimously clarified that while government officials may share their personal opinions they cannot use their powers to "punish or suppress views that the government disfavors," even in promotion of the public's health. As superintendent of the N.Y. Department of Financial Services, Maria Vullo allegedly claimed she would look past underwriting companies' infractions if they ceased gun-related business with NRA. As the Court reasoned, to the extent her actions were intended to "selectively to punish or suppress speech through private intermediaries" she violated NRA's 1st Amendment rights *Id.*

B. REQUIRED DISCLOSURES OF PUBLIC HEALTH INFORMATION

Government does not have to rely solely on education and positive messaging to counteract negative societal behaviors or trends. It can also require disclosures of information regarding products or services. Two prominent examples of government mandated disclosures of public health information include (1) warnings or advisories on products and services; and (2) posting of calories (and potentially other data) on restaurant or food service menus.

1. WARNINGS & ADVISORIES

Product or service information conducive to population health may be voluntarily provided via industry practices or stem from tort-related claims (*see* Chapter 7). Figure 9.5 re-creates an actual warning posted on early 20th century farming equipment notifying users of risks of its operation.

Figure 9.5. Farm Machinery Industry Warning

Federal and state public health agencies can also legally require manufacturers and service providers to label products or services with warnings, advisories, or other messages. Some of this information is designed to equip consumers with adequate data to make healthy choices (e.g., ingestion of low-fat products), avoid use of specific products (e.g., tobacco), or understand the hazards of certain services (e.g., potential for injury related to recreational activities or amusement rides). Other mandated information is designed to relay accurate data (e.g., contents of food) so consumers can properly assess risks unique to their consumption of products or use of services.

Service providers are not immune from government regulation. In June 2024, U.S. Surgeon General Dr. Vivek H. Murthy called for warning labels to be posted among social media platforms to provide parents with information about the mental health risks for children engaged in extended use of such sites. Vivek H. Murthy, *Opinion: Social Media Platforms Need a Health Warning*, N.Y. TIMES, June 18, 2024. The Surgeon General's recommendation was coupled with other law and policy reforms needed to limit harmful effects of rampant access to social media especially among adolescents. Congressional legislation would be needed to implement a warning label requirement.

Dr. Murthy's call to action immediately preceded SCOTUS' decision in *Murthy v. Missouri*, 144 S.Ct. 1972 (2024) on June 26, 2024. During the COVID-19 pandemic, multiple federal agencies and officials urged social media platforms to remove misleading or false content. *See* S. L. Myers, *Appeals Court Rules White House Overstepped 1st Amendment on Social Media*, N.Y. TIMES, Sept. 8, 2023. Even though these platforms largely agreed previously to delete false or misleading content, Missouri, Louisiana, and other parties alleged that government "pressure" to cleanse their sites of misinformation amounted to censorship in violation of 1st Amendment freedoms of expression.

Justice Amy Coney Barrett for the Supreme Court's majority determined that states and other claimants lacked standing in failing to demonstrate any current or future injuries tied to alleged federal "censorship." In an era of increased reliance on social media and the emergence of artificial intelligence propagating sites, these issues are bound for reconsideration via law- and policy-makers, as well as courts. *See, e.g.*, James G. Hodge, Jr. et al, *Public Health Legal Protections in an Era of Artificial Intelligence*, 114(6) AJPH 559 (2024).

At the federal level, multiple, additional agencies play significant roles in issuing warnings and advisories including CPSC, FDA, and FTC, as summarized below.

Consumer Product Safety Commission. CPSC was established via Congress in 1972 to "assist consumers in evaluating the comparative safety of . . . products." Consumer Product Safety Act (CPSA), 15 U.S.C. §§ 2051–2089, at § 2051(b)(2) (2012). It is authorized generally to investigate potentially-dangerous products, as illustrated below.

Lumber Liquidators

In May 2015, CPSC launched an investigation of the national chain, Lumber Liquidators®, which allegedly sold flooring imported from China with excessive levels of the carcinogen, formaldehyde. Long-term exposure to formaldehyde may lead to asthma, skin allergies, headaches, nausea, and, in some cases, nose or throat cancer. *Formaldehyde*, Am. Lung Ass'n (Nov. 2, 2023). Lumber Liquidators® later agreed to stop selling these questionable products. Rachel Abrams, *Lumber Liquidators' Founder Steps In as Chief Resigns*, N.Y. TIMES, May 22, 2015.

CPSC can also require warnings or instructions for various products (except food, drugs, cosmetics, tobacco, and alcohol, which are regulated under other federal laws). 15 U.S.C. at § 2052(a)(5). With some exceptions, packaging of any toy with small parts for children between the ages of 3–6 must feature the following information: "WARNING: CHOKING HAZARD—Small parts. Not for children under 3 yrs." CPSC also regulates toxic, corrosive, flammable, or other hazardous products via the Federal Hazardous Substances Act, 15 U.S.C. §§ 1261–1278 (2012). Labels on such materials feature words like DANGER, WARNING, or CAUTION, precautionary measures, and instructions on how to deliver first aid. *Id.* at § 1261(p)(1).

The CPS Improvement Act of 2008, Pub. L. No. 110–314, 122 Stat. 3016, authorizes CPSC to re-examine the effectiveness of existing warning labels particularly for children's products. 15 U.S.C. § 2056b (2012). In November 2012, CPSC recalled an inflatable children's waterslide and ordered its manufacturer to update the warning labels to include age and weight restrictions. CPSC, Sportspower Recalls Children's Waterslides Due to Injury Hazard (Recall 13–502) (2012). In 2016, CPSC issued warnings about the safety of "hoverboards" based on dozens of reports of exploding or flammable batteries. Letter from Robert Howell, Acting Dir., Off. of Compliance & Field Operations, CPSC, *Manufacturers, Importers & Retailers of Self-Balancing Scooters* (Feb. 18, 2016). In 2021, CPSC required Fisher-Price® to recall its 4-in-1 Rock' n Glide Soother after the product was linked to reports of several child deaths. Jesus Jimenez, *Fisher-Price Recalls Rockers After 4 Deaths*, N.Y. TIMES, June 7, 2021.

Food & Drug Administration. FDA regulations of food, drugs, and cosmetics include the authority to require appropriate warning labels or other information. Food, Drug & Cosmetic Act of 1938, Pub. L. No. 75–717, 52 Stat. 1040. FDA may consider such products misbranded if they fail to include material information on their use (21 U.S.C. § 321(n)), and consequently mandate warning labels. Cosmetics, for example, are subject to several warning requirements including that they have not been properly tested for all uses. 21 U.S.C. § 740.10 (2012). FDA concerns about the presence of Bisphenol A (BPA) in babies' plastic bottles led industry to abandon its use in their manufacture.

Leila Barraza, *A New Approach for Regulating BPA for the Protection of the Public's Health*, 41 JLME 9 (2013). FDA's oversight of prescription and over-the-counter drugs entails extensive required disclosures (as per the text box example below).

Aspirin Labels
Aspirin labels must state the following: "It is especially important not to use aspirin during the last 3 months of pregnancy unless definitely directed to do so by a doctor because it may cause problems in the unborn child or complications during delivery." 21 C.F.R. § 201.63 (2012).

Following testing and approval, most prescription drugs carry a consumer warning of their unintended uses or potential side effects, which may be summarized in commercial advertisements. Such requirements do not apply to products classifiable as nutritional supplements, like herbal remedies, because they are not definable as "drugs." Peter Goldman, *Herbal Medicines Today & the Roots of Modern Pharmacology*, 135 ANNALS INTERNAL MED. 594, 598 (2001).

Drug-related warnings are not always geared toward protecting consumers directly. Sometimes the intended targets of such warnings include HCWs or others responsible for their dispensing or administration. In *Hubbard v. Bayer Healthcare Pharmaceuticals, Inc.*, 983 F.3d 1223 (11th Cir. 2020), for example, a federal appellate court denied a woman's claim against Bayer® that it insufficiently warned that its birth control pills (marketed as Beyaz®) could cause blood clots leading to stroke. Under Georgia state law, persons must show a breach of a duty to warn that proximately caused the injury. The court determined that Bayer's® duty to warn extended only to the prescribing physician, not to the actual user.

Most packaged foods for direct sale to consumers are clearly labeled with basic information pursuant to the Nutritional Labeling and Education Act of 1990 (NLEA), 21 U.S.C. § 343 (1990). Foods generally do not require warnings *per se*, subject to some notable exceptions. *See, e.g.*, Noah Lars, *The Imperative to Warn: Disentangling the "Right to Know" from the "Need to Know" About Consumer Products*, 11 YALE J. ON REG. 293, 315 (1994). Since 1974, package labels of the sweetener, aspartame, have included warnings about its ingredient, phenylalanine, which some persons cannot metabolize. 21 C.F.R. at § 172.804; *see also* Harriet H. Butchko & W. Wayne Stargel, *Aspartame: Scientific Evaluation in the Postmarketing Period*, 34 REG. TOXICOLOGY & PHARM. 221, 222 (2001). Dietary supplements containing iron warn against its accidental overdose, which "is a leading cause of fatal poisoning in children under 6." 21 C.F.R. at § 101.17(e)(1).

Caffeinated products have received additional regulatory attention. Related deaths from caffeine over-consumption are exceedingly rare, but possible. In May 2017, the Richland County (SC) coroner determined that caffeine-induced arrhythmia due to excessive ingestion was the official cause of death of a 16-year-old teen with no underlying heart conditions. The teen consumed a café latte, large Mountain Dew®, and 16-oz energy drink within a 2 hour period. Cleve R. Wootson Jr., *A Teen Chugged a Latte, a Mountain Dew and an Energy Drink. The Caffeine Binge Led to His Death*, WASH. POST, May 16, 2017.

In 2018, a 21-year-old Australian lost consciousness and died after consuming a caffeinated protein shake. A coroner determined the cause of death to be a caffeine overdose. Gabby Landsverk, *A 21-Year-Old Died After Drinking a Protein Shake with a Caffeine Supplement So Powerful It Knocked Him Unconscious*, INSIDER (July 9, 2019). In January 2021, a 29-year-old personal trainer in North Wales drank a high caffeine drink prior to a work-out. He experienced heart palpitations and suddenly expired. A pathologist found he had 392 milligrams of caffeine per liter of blood and determined "caffeine toxicity" as the cause of death. Aime Gordon, *Personal Trainer, 29, Died Shortly After Drinking Pre-Workout Shake Containing up to 200 Times More Caffeine Than a Normal Cup of Coffee, Inquest Hears,* DAILY MAIL, Mar. 30, 2021.

Despite these rare cases, FDA has traditionally recognized the safety of caffeine as an additive to carbonated soft drinks, 21 C.F.R. § 182.1180(c)), issuing only minor recommendations regarding daily consumption of caffeine (e.g., no more than 400 milligrams per day, or approximately 4 cups of coffee,

10 sodas, or 2 energy shots). Some studies even suggest positive health benefits from regular consumption of highly-caffeinated products like coffee. Jane E. Brady, *Wake Up to Good News About Coffee*, N.Y. TIMES, June 15, 2021. However, caffeine's presence in other products (e.g., ice cream, yogurt, gum, candies, syrup, bottled water) presents new and under-studied risks. *See* Brady Dennis, *Slew of New Caffeinated Food Products Has FDA Jittery*, WASH. POST, June 1, 2013.

Caffeine sold in a powdered form has led to deaths due to unintended overdoses and public calls for stronger regulations. Murray Carpenter, *Caffeine Powder Poses Deadly Risks*, N.Y. TIMES, May 18, 2015. As noted on FDA's website, 1 teaspoon of pure powdered caffeine (as well as liquid concentrations) have the equivalent amount of caffeine as 20–28 cups of coffee. "These are toxic amounts that can have serious health consequences." FDA, *Purely & Highly Concentrated Caffeine* (July 15, 2021). FDA cautioned against their production, sale, and use in 2018. FDA, GUIDANCE FOR INDUSTRY: HIGHLY CONCENTRATED CAFFEINE IN DIETARY SUPPLEMENTS (2018).

Energy Drinks

The sale and marketing to children of energy drinks, once classified by manufacturers as "dietary supplements," led San Francisco to sue a producer to stop its advertising and promotions tailored to kids. *Herrera v. Monster Beverage*

Corp., No. CDC–13–531161, 2014 WL 4810141 (Cal. Super. Ct. Mar. 5, 2014); *see also* Barry Meier, *Suit Claims Monster Markets to Children*, N.Y. TIMES, May 7, 2013. In 2016, the California Superior Court determined that the scope of relief sought in the case would be statewide. *Herrera v. Monster Bev. Corp.*, No. CGC–12–531161, 2016 Cal. Super. LEXIS 5871 (May 23, 2016).

In 2023, Panera® was sued over sales of its large-size "Charged Lemonade," which contains 390 mg of caffeine—more than an 18-ounce Monster® and 12-ounce Red Bull® combined. Nik Popli, *Panera Bread Faces Second Wrongful Death Lawsuit Over Caffeinated 'Charged Lemonade'*, TIME, Dec. 6, 2023). At least 2 Americans, a 21-year old college student and a 46-year old man, died allegedly after consuming the product. In another case, a 28-year old woman experienced permanent heart issues. *Katz et al. v. Panera Bread Company*, 2:23–cv–04135–TJS (E.D. Pa. Oct. 23, 2023); *Brown v. Panera Bread Company*, N23C–12–001 (Del. Super. Ct. Dec. 4, 2023); *Skerritt v. Panera Bread Company*, No. N24C–01–107 (Del. Super. Ct. Jan. 16, 2024). Following the filing of these suits, Panera® heightened its warning label for the drink and sold it behind counters away from other beverages.

Federal Trade Commission. FTC supplements FDA's regulation of tobacco products through its enforcement of the Federal Cigarette Labeling and Advertising Act of 1965, 15 U.S.C. §§ 1331–1340

(2012). Government regulation and industry acquiescence have resulted in progressively stronger warnings on tobacco products, notably cigarettes. What was once a fairly non-specific warning (e.g., "Caution: Cigarette Smoking May Be Hazardous to Your Health") has evolved into more affirmative warnings such as "Smoking can kill you." *Id.* at § 1333(a)(1).

In 2011, FDA called for new graphic warnings on cigarette packaging (like those featured in Australia and other countries). Required Warnings for Cigarette Packages and Advertisements, 76 Fed. Reg. 36628–01 (June 22, 2011). As discussed below, however, FDA's regulation was struck down by at least 1 federal court. *See R.J. Reynolds Tobacco Co. v. FDA*, 696 F.3d 1205 (D.C. Cir. 2012).

The Alcoholic Beverage Labeling Act (ABLA) of 1988, 27 U.S.C. §§ 213–219 (2012), addresses "health hazards that may result from the consumption or abuse of alcoholic beverages." *Id.* at § 213. All alcoholic beverage containers must include the following: "GOVERNMENT WARNING: (1) According to the Surgeon General, women should not drink alcoholic beverages during pregnancy because of the risk of birth defects. (2) Consumption of alcoholic beverages impairs your ability to drive a car or operate machinery, and may cause health problems." *Id.* at § 215(a). Beyond this warning, the Act may allow additional state-based requirements on the labeling of alcoholic beverages. *See, e.g., Bronco Wine Co. v. Jolly*, 95 P.3d 422 (Cal. 2004). In 2013, the federal Alcohol and Tobacco Trade and Tax

Bureau approved voluntary use of nutrition-like labels on all packaged alcohol products. Mary Clare Jalonick, *Nutritional Labels May Be Coming on Some Alcoholic Drinks*, WASH. POST, June 4, 2013. In 2024, federal public health authorities posited a potential warning label modification for alcohol tied to its known cancer risks.

2. MENU LABELING

For years, select state and local governments including New York City, Seattle-King County, California, and Massachusetts required restaurants and other vendors to post calorie data about their products on menus. The overriding public health goal of menu labeling is to help people make healthier choices when they eat out to reduce their calorie intake and improve health outcomes. Together with increased physical activity and other measures, reducing the amount of calories Americans consume is central to addressing the obesity epidemic (*see* Chapter 6).

In 2010, FDA was required pursuant to the ACA to issue regulations to implement menu labeling nationally. ACA, Pub. L. No. 111–148, 124 Stat. 119 § 4205 (2010). On December 1, 2014, FDA published a final rule requiring covered establishments to list calorie information for standard menu items. Food Labeling; Nutrition Labeling of Standard Menu Items in Restaurants & Similar Retail Food Establishments, 79 Fed. Reg. 71155 (Dec. 1, 2014) (codified at 21 C.F.R. §§ 11, 101). A separate final rule already requires vendors owning or operating 20 or more vending machines to disclose calorie information on the products they sell. Food Labeling; Calorie Labeling of Articles of Food in Vending Machines, 79 Fed. Reg. 71259 (Dec. 1, 2014).

FDA's regulations require restaurants or other retail food establishments with more than 20 locations to post caloric information on menus, menu boards, and drive-thrus. Posted menu data must be in a similar font, size, and color as used to describe menu items and their prices. Variable menu items offering different choices or size options, like combination meals, must include an accurate calorie range (e.g., 500–650 calories).

Though extensive, FDA's regulations are limited in their coverage. They do not apply to foods intended for consumption by more than 1 person purchased in many retail food establishments. Nearly 65% of the nation's restaurants are not covered (because they are not chains), nor does the rule apply to hotels, movie theaters, or other entities whose primary business is not food service (although they often sell foods similar to those sold in restaurants). T.R. Goldman, *The FDA's Menu-Labeling Rule (Updated)*, HEALTH AFFS. (July 13, 2015).

Even among chain restaurants that are covered by the rule, only standard menu items prepared on site, self-serve salad bars, and beverage dispensers must feature posted calories. Postings are not required for condiments, alcoholic beverages, pre-packaged foods (e.g., salad dressing), or temporary or "test" items that appear on the menu for 90 days or less per year (e.g., specialty drinks or appetizers). Due to purported space limits more extensive nutritional data (e.g., fat, sugar, and salt content) are not required. Menus may include brief statements about USDA's daily calorie standard and how consumers can access additional nutritional data.

State and local efforts to require menu labeling were initially litigated based on several grounds, including that they were preempted by the NLEA. *See* Lainie Rutkow et al., *Preemption & the Obesity Epidemic*, 36 JLME 772 (2008). Though once opposed, the National Restaurant Association ultimately endorsed FDA's regulations due in part to their preemptive effect. Press Release, Nat'l Restaurant Ass'n Statement on Proposed Menu Labeling Regul. (Apr. 1, 2011). FDA regulations preempt contrary state and local rules applying to covered restaurants.

Even as menu labeling practices nationalize, their efficacy as a public health preventive measure is debated. Some data suggest that posting calories positively alters consumer habits and vendor practices. Siyi Shangguan et al., *A Meta-Analysis of Food Labeling Effects on Consumer Diet Behaviors & Industry Practices*, 56 AM. J. PREV. MED. 300 (2018) (food labeling information decreased total intake of fat by 10.6%, unhealthy options by 13.0%, and calories by 6.6%, while increasing vegetable consumption by 13.5%). Calorie postings on menus increase transparency and may also heighten restaurants' accountability for the foods they serve.

Other researchers suggest that menu labeling has little or no effects on consumers' behaviors. Some studies suggest that adults and children dining at fast food restaurants with calorie-labeled menus consume similar amounts of calories as patrons of the same restaurants without them. Tara Parker-Pope, *After Menu Labels, Parents & Kids Order Same Foods,* N.Y. TIMES, Feb. 16, 2011. Menu labels may have no effect on calorie consumption even when they include recommendations for calorie consumption per meal in addition to the calorie count of the particular menu item. Julie S. Downs et al., *Supplementing Menu Labeling With Calorie Recommendations to Test for Facilitation Effects*, 103 AJPH 1604 (2013); Susan E. Sinclair et al., *The Influence of Menu Labeling on Calories Selected or Consumed: A Systematic Rev. & Meta-Analysis*, 114 J. ACAD. NUTRITION & DIETETICS 1375 (2014).

In recognition of these limits, as well as the preemptive effect of FDA's regulations, some support alternative models of menu labeling or at least allowing greater experimentation at the state or local levels. Peggy J. Liu et al., *A Test of Different Menu Labeling Presentations*, 59 APPETITE 770 (2012); James G. Hodge, Jr. & Lexi C. White, *Supplementing Nat'l Menu Labeling,* 102 AJPH e11 (2012). Including interpretative symbols, such as a traffic light (denoting when specific levels of fat, sodium, or sugar exceed daily recommendations for single menu items), may help reduce consumer calorie selection and consumption (*see* Figure 9.6).

Figure 9.6. Menu Traffic Light Image

C. CONTROLLING COMMERCIAL COMMUNICATIONS

As noted above, government efforts to conduct or fund public health education campaigns can raise political debates and arguments. Whether government is empowered legally to speak directly on public health issues is fairly well-settled. It can issue its own messages, even if people do not always like their content. Less clear is government's power to restrict when, where, and how individuals and companies market their products. Government interference with the advertising, marketing, or promotion of products or services ignites allegations of infringement of freedoms of speech, specifically commercial speech, under the 1st Amendment.

Public health agencies can absolutely proscribe advertising of illegal products (e.g., cocaine) or services (e.g., illicit drug sales). They can also prohibit advertising of information about lawful products that is false (e.g., medications claiming to cure HIV/AIDS or COVID-19) or misleading (e.g., "low tar cigarettes are better for your health"). As explained below, none of these forms of commercial speech is entitled to any protection under the 1st Amendment.

While there is no inherent legal right to sell dangerous or harmful products in the private marketplace, government's ability to restrict the sale of products must be separated from its interference with commercial expressions about lawful products or services. For example, government may be able to ban the sale of highly-caffeinated beverages to minors, but not prohibit their advertising generally so long as the product remains lawful for other consumers.

Furthermore, public health agencies can set reasonable, "content neutral" limits on commercial (or other) speech. In *Ward v. Rock Against Racism*, 491 U.S. 781 (1989), the Supreme Court observed that "government may impose reasonable restrictions on the time, place, or manner of protected speech provided restrictions are 'justified without reference to the content of the regulated speech, that they are narrowly tailored to serve a significant governmental interest, and that they leave open ample alternative channels for communication of the information.'" *Id.* at 791 (citing *Clark v. Cmty. for Creative Non-Violence*, 468 U.S. 288, 293 (1984)).

As a result, public health measures that restrict the *time* (i.e., when a message may be displayed, such as outside the hours of children's broadcast programming), *place* (i.e., where it may be displayed, such as within or near schools), and *manner* (i.e., how it is displayed, such as billboard ads vs. point of sale ads) of commercial advertisements may be lawful so long as alternative channels for communication are available. LAWRENCE O. GOSTIN, PUBLIC HEALTH LAW: POWER, DUTY, RESTRAINT 357 (2nd ed. 2008).

Since 1976 when SCOTUS recognized commercial speech protections in *Virginia State Board of Pharmacy v. Virginia Citizens Consumer Council, Inc.*, 425 U.S. 748 (1976) governmental attempts to (1) restrict advertising of legal products, or (2) require commercial entities to provide truthful information through warnings or counter information may raise constitutional arguments. In the former case, government may be limiting truthful speech (which the Court disdains). In the latter case, government is forcing an entity to speak through compelled warnings or data postings which it might not otherwise choose to state.

The freedom to speak under the 1st Amendment also includes the freedom not to speak (*see, e.g.*, *Wooley v. Maynard*, 430 U.S. 705 (1977)) or subsidize speech with which one does not agree, other than through general taxes (*see, e.g., U.S. v. U. Foods*, 533 U.S. 405 (2001) (federal act mandating assessments on handlers of fresh mushrooms to fund advertising and other initiatives violated freedom of speech)). These and other potential infringements of commercial speech are often examined under the Supreme Court's *Central Hudson* test stated below.

Central Hudson Commercial Speech Test

In *Central Hudson Gas & Electric Corp. v. Public Service Commission of New York*, 447 U.S. 557, 566 (1980), SCOTUS set forth a 4-step test to assess potential infringements of commercial speech. Courts must ask whether:

1. the speech concerns lawful activity and is not misleading; *and*
2. the asserted government interest is substantial; *if so, then whether*
3. the law directly advances the governmental interest asserted; *and*
4. it is not more extensive than is necessary to serve that interest.

Step 1 of the *Central Hudson* test is largely perfunctory. If commercial speech concerns an unlawful activity (e.g., sale of alcohol to minors) or is patently misleading (e.g., "chewing tobacco is safe for one's gums"), government can restrict it entirely because the speech is unprotected. Determining the line between information that is merely suggestive as contrasted with misleading can be specious. Nuanced issues arise related to commercial speech that intimates behaviors contrary to the public's health, but is not directly misleading, which some label as "manipulative marketing." Micah L. Berman, *Manipulative Marketing & the 1st Amendment*, 103 GEO. L. J. 497 (2015) (suggesting that these types of non-informational marketing practices are not entitled to any 1st Amendment protection). While industry ads depicting healthy people smoking cigarettes, consuming liquor, eating fast food, or driving carelessly may all invoke negative behaviors that lead to preventable morbidity and mortality, the ads are not considered legally misleading or deceptive under current jurisprudence.

Still, this did not stop 2 pastors in Washington, DC from bringing a lawsuit against Coca Cola® and others in July 2017 alleging fraudulent advertising practices. Mary Brophy Marcus, *Coca-Cola gets served a lawsuit by 2 pastors*, CBS NEWS (July 14, 2017). In October 2019, the D.C. Superior Court dismissed most of the claims. *Praxis Project v. Coca-Cola Co.*, No. 004801 B, 2019 D.C. Super. LEXIS 17 (Oct. 1, 2019). Later, Coca-Cola® pledged to offer drinks in smaller sizes and reduce sugar amounts in many of its beverages. Emily Field, *Coke Must Face DC Pastors' Deceptive Marketing Suit*, LAW360, Oct. 2, 2019.

Provided commercial speech subject to regulation survives inquiry under the 1st step, the 2nd part of the *Central Hudson* test asks whether government's interest is substantial. Government cannot simply restrict commercial speech because it does not like a product, service, or corresponding message. It must have some basis for doing so. Protection of the public's health, especially the health of minors, is routinely agreed by courts to qualify as a substantial governmental interest, particularly when state or local government acts to curtail commercial speech.

The more difficult assessments arise in steps 3 and 4 of the Court's test. To survive scrutiny, government's interests in protecting the public's health must be directly advanced by its chosen intervention and be no more extensive than necessary. Early in its commercial speech jurisprudence, the Supreme Court generally accepted government arguments that its interventions directly advanced public health interests consistent with judicial deference of legislative findings under separation of powers (discussed in Chapter 2). This is no longer the case. The Court has clarified that government must demonstrate a strong nexus between its restriction of commercial speech and its public health objective. Public health agencies must increasingly produce evidence of efficacy for specific interventions negatively impacting commercial speech.

In *44 Liquormart, Inc. v. Rhode Island*, 517 U.S. 484 (1996), the Court struck down Rhode Island's attempt to ban advertising of the price of alcohol (other than at the point of sale) to help lower consumption. Concerned about significant limitations of otherwise truthful advertising, Justice John Paul Stevens clarified that the state must show that its restriction will advance its public health interest "to a material degree." *Id.* at 505. The Court concluded:

(1) there was no "reasonable fit" between Rhode Island's abridgement of speech and the reduction in alcohol consumption. *Id.* at 507;

(2) just because the state could ban the sale of alcohol altogether does not mean it can restrict truthful advertising about such products; and

(3) application of lesser standards for protections of commercial speech related to "vice" products like alcohol is unwarranted. *Id.* at 513–14.

D. COMMERCIAL SPEECH & TOBACCO

Restrictions on commercial advertisements of tobacco are central to governmental efforts to reduce consumption of products that collectively remain a leading cause of preventable deaths in the U.S. (*see* Chapter 6). Some restrictions are authorized via federal statute. The Family Smoking Prevention and Tobacco Control Act (FSPTCA) of 2009, 21 U.S.C. § 387 (2009), put aside prior federal preemptive measures to allow states and localities to regulate the time, place, and manner of tobacco promotion or advertising, but not the content.

Other advertising limitations were negotiated as part of the Master Tobacco Settlement Agreement of 1998 between big tobacco companies and 46 states and 6 U.S. territories. NAT'L ASS'N OF ATTYS. GEN., MASTER SETTLEMENT AGMT. (1998). In addition to paying hundreds of billions of dollars to the jurisdictions through 2025, tobacco companies agreed to restrict large outdoor ads such as billboards and use of cartoon characters (e.g., Joe Camel®), as well as limit merchandising and sponsorship of sporting venues (which the FSPTCA now expressly prohibits).

Some states have sought additional tobacco advertising restrictions. In *Lorillard Tobacco Co. v. Reilly*, 533 U.S. 525 (2001), Justice Sandra Day O'Connor (*see* Figure 9.7) applied the *Central Hudson* test to a series of restrictions on tobacco ads proffered by the Massachusetts Attorney General.

Figure 9.7. Justice Sandra Day O'Connor

Of particular concern was the attempt to prohibit outdoor ads of smokeless tobacco products and cigars within 1,000 feet of any school or playground. While each of the 3 initial prongs of the *Central Hudson* test were satisfied, Justice O'Connor found the regulation failed the final element because it was more extensive than necessary to advance governments' interest in reducing tobacco use. Implementation of the outdoor ban would have broadly curtailed multiple forms and types of speech, including in-store ads and oral communications. As well, there was no attempt, alleged the Court, to tailor the prohibition to different settings in urban, suburban, or rural communities.

The Court also invalidated Massachusetts' requirement that no advertisements of smokeless tobacco or cigars be placed lower than 5 feet from the floor in establishments within the same 1,000 feet radius of schools and parks. Designed to limit kids' exposure to these ads, Justice O'Connor rejected the measure as failing to advance the Commonwealth's interests. Restrictions on the use of self-service displays and placement of such products outside the reach of minors were allowed as these interventions were not considered advertisements. They were approved because they were narrowly tailored to limiting access to children and left open other channels of communication.

Tobacco Power Walls

Undecided in *Lorillard* is whether courts would approve a ban on prominent tobacco displays known as "power walls." These displays tend to be directly behind counters at convenience stores or other locales, feature multiple brands of cigarettes or other tobacco products, and often display specific products (e.g., Marlboro®) in large print. Some U.S. municipalities have considered bans on these displays as have several foreign countries. National retailers like Target® and CVS®, removed tobacco power walls from their premises because they no longer sell tobacco products.

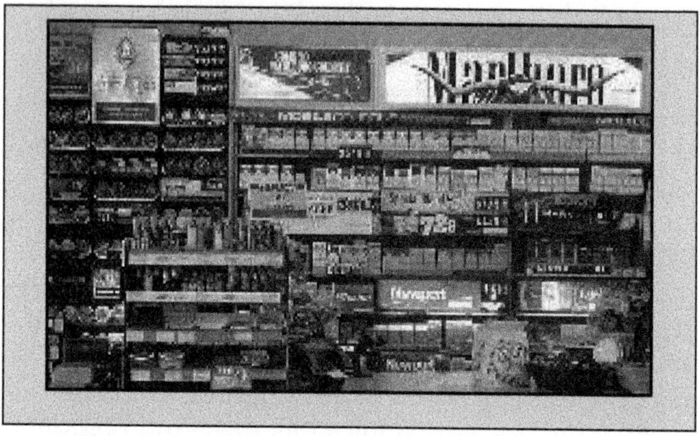

Tobacco advertisements remain a divisive area of Supreme Court jurisprudence with many lessons applying to other commercial speech restrictions in the interests of the public's health. In an interesting exposé, researchers examining information housed in the Truth Tobacco Industry Documents archive (part of the 1998 Master Settlement agreement noted above) uncovered explicit evidence of how tobacco companies used similar advertising to attract children to consume SSBs like Kool-Aid® and Hawaiian Punch® beginning in the 1960s. *See* Andrew Jacobs, *Big Tobacco Hooked Them Young, on Sugar*, N.Y. TIMES, Mar. 15, 2019.

Concerning tobacco ads specifically, FDA (authorized by the passage of the FSPTCA) proposed a series of additional anti-tobacco initiatives in 2011, including a requirement that the fronts of cigarette packs feature graphic color depictions of the negative health impacts of smoking. Required Warnings for Cigarette Packages & Advertisements, 76 Fed. Reg.

36628–01 (June 22, 2011). Soon after reviewing FDA's proposed images (some of which were visually disturbing in their depiction of the harms of tobacco use), several tobacco companies challenged FDA's regulations in federal court on 1st Amendment (and other) grounds.

In *Discount Tobacco City & Lottery, Inc. v. U.S.*, 674 F.3d 509 (6th Cir. 2012), *cert. denied sub nom. Am. Snuff Co. v. U.S.*, 569 U.S. 946 (2013), the 6th Circuit Court of Appeals upheld the constitutionality of FDA's proposed graphic warnings for cigarette packs (but rejected a restriction that tobacco advertising be produced only in black and white). Largely bypassing the *Central Hudson* test, the court found "[a]mple evidence establishes that current warnings do not effectively inform consumers of the health risks of tobacco use and that consumers do not understand these risks." *Id.* at 569. To the extent FDA's regulations require graphic and textual warnings that convey the "factual health risks of smoking," the court held they were "reasonably related to the government's interest in preventing consumer deception and are therefore constitutional." *Id.*

Six months later in 2012, another federal court of appeals found inapposite to the 6th Circuit decision. In *R.J. Reynolds Tobacco Co. v. FDA*, 696 F.3d 1205 (D.C. Cir. 2012), the D.C. Circuit Court of Appeals held that FDA's proposed graphic images failed to meet the 3rd prong of *Central Hudson*. The court suggested FDA lacked any evidentiary support linking use of graphic imagery with lowering tobacco use. *Id.* at 1219. FDA's evidence relying on use of similar imagery in other countries was rejected on the basis that it showed only that consumers thought more about the health implications of smoking, but generally did not quit. *Id.* at 1220.

Undeterred, FDA proceeded to develop proposed graphic warnings with new images. When it failed to complete its rule in 2016, multiple public health and medical groups sued to force compliance. A federal court in Massachusetts ordered FDA to issue a final rule by March 15, 2020. *Federal Court Orders FDA to Issue Final Rule Requiring Graphic Cigarette Warnings*, TRUTH INITIATIVE (Mar. 6, 2019). FDA complied, issuing its final rule in March 2020. *Cigarette Labeling & Health Warning Requirements*, FDA (June 4, 2021). As per Figure 9.8, it featured 11 new required warnings containing images showing cancers and other negative impacts of smoking.

Figure 9.8. Select FDA Required Warnings for Cigarette Labels

U.S. tobacco companies have sought multiple delays in enforcing FDA's rule, arguing irreparable harms. Jacqueline Thomsen, *Fifth Circuit Asks if Cigarette Graphic Warnings Are 'Shocking,'* BLOOMBERG L., Dec. 5, 2023. More than 4 years after the rule was issued, it had still not yet taken effect due to ongoing litigation. *R.J. Reynolds Tobacco Co. v. FDA*, 23–40076 (5th Cir. Feb. 6, 2023).

Judicial decisions in tobacco advertising and other modern commercial speech cases have the potential to set a dangerous threshold for government regulation of communications in the interests of health promotion. Requiring government to unequivocally link proposed regulations of commercial speech with public health objectives may protect commercial speech interests against unwarranted restrictions, but at what cost?

In furtherance of commercial speech protections, courts may stop public health agencies from restricting negative commercial messages or requiring mandatory product or service disclosures unless they have a strong evidentiary basis of efficacy. Unfortunately, this basis may not exist until an implementation is tried and assessed. Requiring high levels of proof of effectiveness for public health entities to intervene dampens the sharing of truthful, positive messaging on the potential harms of commercial products and services for which the public may be largely unaware. One need only revisit the unscrupulous tobacco ads of the 1950s–1970s to understand the potential harms of unregulated commercial advertisements, which the Supreme Court recognizes as a social failure. In response to current political and judicial trends, public health authorities and scholars are strategizing on how to alter the existing legal environment favoring commercial speech over communal health.

	Chapter 9—Discussion Questions
?	1. Can governments promote their own public health messages without limitation?
?	2. What legal or other objections may extend from aggressive public health education campaigns?
?	3. How has SCOTUS' assessment of commercial speech protections changed over time?
?	4. What are primary legal challenges to greater restrictions of negative commercial messages contrary to the public's health?
?	5. Why are commercial messages antithetical to health promotion not always legally restricted?

CHAPTER 10

MONITORING PROPERTY & THE BUILT ENVIRONMENT

	Chapter 10—Learning Objectives
✓	1. Explore the legal routes to promoting health through the built environment
✓	2. Understand the powers of government to require inspections & abate nuisances
✓	3. Weigh the tensions underlying these powers pursuant to individual property rights & interests
✓	4. Distinguish core governmental efforts & responsibilities related to abating nuisances & taking property
✓	5. Assess the historic & modern roles of local zoning in promoting healthy environments

Interventions to ameliorate health risks stemming from uses of public and private property and the built environment are prolific across all levels of government. Their extensive authority to inspect real property (e.g., land and improvements) helps protect public health and safety. Overseeing the production and shipment of foods, drugs, and other consumables is the mission of thousands of governmental and private sector actors. Abating nuisances through regulatory actions as well as private litigation can negate general or particular risks to the community's health.

Altering the built environment to promote safer, healthier communities is supported by federal conditional grants and state legal requirements requiring quality construction of buildings, schools, and playgrounds. Through zoning laws, local officials separate industrial and residential areas, encourage inclusion of biking or walking trails, and even restrict the types and numbers of businesses (e.g., alcohol or tobacco outlets, fast food restaurants) that may locate in specific areas such as near schools.

All of these measures (plus other extensive environmental laws related to clean air, water, and land covered outside this text) seek to balance public health legal authority with individual and corporate property interests, principally concerning searches (via the 4th Amendment) and takings (via the 5th Amendment), as discussed initially in Chapter 3.

A. INSPECTIONS & OVERSIGHT

Government agencies are empowered to conduct extensive inspections to ensure the safety, health, and welfare of the public. Federal statutes authorize USDA's Food Safety and Inspection Service and FDA to inspect businesses' premises, facilities, inventories, operations, and records. Federal agents inspect domestic and foreign facilities producing meat, poultry, and eggs via a slate of Congressional legislation focused on proper sanitation. *See, e.g.*, Federal Meat Inspection Act of 1906, 21 U.S.C. §§ 601–625 (2013); Poultry Products Inspection Act of 1957, 21 U.S.C. §§ 451–472 (2013); Egg Products Inspection Act of 1970, 21 U.S.C. §§ 1031–1056 (2013).

Pursuant to the Food, Drug & Cosmetic Act, 21 U.S.C.S. §§ 301–399 (2013), HHS prioritizes inspections and other efforts concerning "high risk facilities" with known safety risks, negative compliance histories (e.g., food recalls, outbreaks of foodborne illness, or violations of food safety standards) or other criteria. *Id.* at § 350j(a)(1). In 2010, the Food Safety Modernization Act, 21 U.S.C. §§ 2201–2252 (2013), called for HHS to increase the frequency of all inspections. In 2013, FDA issued new regulations requiring food importers to assure the safety of products they receive from abroad following multiple outbreaks stemming from contaminants in produce and other foods. *See, e.g.*, Mary Clare Jalonick, *FDA Plan Would Put Food Safety on U.S. Importers*, ARIZ. REP., July 27, 2013, at D4. Imported foods with known safety risks must be certified consistent with known safety standards. FDA, INT'L FOOD SAFETY CAPACITY-BUILDING PLAN 4 (2013).

States and localities authorize other types of health inspections of public buildings, private residences, and businesses through statute or regulation. During the Zika virus outbreak in 2016, for example, localities across the southern U.S. conducted inspections of private property to assure compliance with mosquito abatement policies. Lawrence O. Gostin & James G. Hodge, Jr., *Is the U.S. Prepared for a Major Zika Virus Outbreak?*, 315 JAMA 2395 (2016).

Many state and local laws are generally-worded to allow public health inspections based on reasonable grounds as per the language from the City of Baltimore health code in the text box below.

Baltimore Health Inspection Law

Baltimore's city code provides that the health commissioner may enter "at all reasonable times . . . any structure or premises within the City . . . whenever the Commissioner has reason to believe that a health hazard [or] nuisance [or any other violation]" has occurred on the property. BALTIMORE HEALTH CODE § 2–107 (2013).

In many cases, inspectors arrive without advance notice and search any public spaces (e.g., restaurant or business lobbies or service areas) directly or based on available surveillance. *L.R. Willson & Sons v. OSHRC*, 134 F.3d 1235 (4th Cir. 1998) (surveillance videotape of common areas in hotels can be used for inspection purposes by OSHA).

Public health authorities in many states are explicitly directed to inspect public eating establishments, particularly restaurants, on a regular basis. *See, e.g.*, R.C.N.Y. tit. 24, ch. 23, § 23–03 (2013). Based on information illustrated below in Figure 10.1, each restaurant violation in Maricopa County (Phoenix), Arizona, is assessed a certain number of points. The more the points, the worse the grade for the establishment. Points and grades for each establishment are published online and select newsprint.

Figure 10.1. Maricopa County Restaurant Grading Sys.

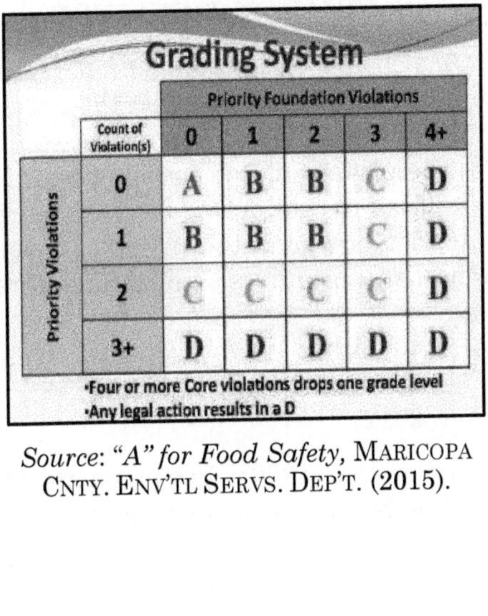
Grading System

		Priority Foundation Violations				
	Count of Violation(s)	0	1	2	3	4+
Priority Violations	0	A	B	B	C	D
	1	B	B	B	C	D
	2	C	C	C	C	D
	3+	D	D	D	D	D

•Four or more Core violations drops one grade level
•Any legal action results in a D

Source: *"A" for Food Safety*, MARICOPA CNTY. ENV'TL SERVS. DEP'T. (2015).

States like South Carolina also require prominent posting of inspection grades at the restaurant's premises. 38 S.C. CODE. REGS. 61–25 (2014).

While many state and local laws grant extensive authority to inspect premises, there are legal limits. Texas state law prohibits health inspections at private residences without permission from an adult occupant or an authorization by a magistrate or court finding a "probable violation of a state health law, a control measure . . . or a health ordinance." TEX. HEALTH & SAFETY CODE ANN. § 161.011 (2013). Pennsylvania statutes limit the time in which commercial inspections may be conducted to "hours of operation and other reasonable times." PA. FOOD CODE § 46.1101 (2013).

B. SEARCH & SEIZURE

Public health inspections and property oversight are essential environmental health interventions, but they have the potential for abuse, particularly related to the privacy of one's residence or economic interests related to conducting lawful businesses. To protect against unwarranted privacy invasions, the 4th Amendment prohibits "unreasonable searches and seizures" of one's personal effects, residences, businesses, or other real property. RUSSELL L. WEAVER ET AL., PRINCIPLES OF CRIMINAL PROC. 92–100 (4th ed. 2012).

Prior to the late 1960s, governments conducted routine public health inspections of commercial and private premises without much, if any, advance warning to occupants. Courts tended to approve these unannounced inspections, except in truly egregious scenarios, on the premise that temporary intrusions were necessary to accomplish legitimate, public health ends. LAWRENCE O. GOSTIN, PUBLIC HEALTH LAW & ETHICS: A READER 445 (2002).

However, in 2 companion cases, *Camara v. Municipal Court of San Francisco*, 387 U.S. 523 (1967), and *See v. City of Seattle*, 387 U.S. 541 (1967), the U.S. Supreme Court rejected long-standing arguments that government interests in public health inspections automatically outweigh privacy concerns. It determined that the 4th Amendment requires advance warrants for even purely administrative public health inspections of personal residences (*Camara*) and commercial property (*See*). Following these 2 cases, only under special exceptions were warrantless searches without advance notice for public health purposes allowed.

Twenty years later, the Court reconsidered its application of warrant requirements to public health inspections. In *New York v. Burger*, 482 U.S. 691 (1987), it held that warrantless searches of businesses are permissible provided there is sufficient statutory authority and oversight. Burger ran a vehicle junkyard and dismantling business in Brooklyn. After he was charged with possession of stolen property, he sought to exclude key evidence based on a warrantless search of his real property by officials acting under New York state law. The Court disagreed, upholding the statutory authority for administrative warrantless searches concerning businesses operating in "closely regulated industries." *Id.* at 700.

As the Court noted, businesses that are engaged in dangerous activities (e.g., ballistics plants) or are traditionally heavily regulated (e.g., health care facilities) have reduced expectations of privacy related to their operations. As a result, regulatory schemes allowing inspections of commercial establishments without a warrant may be constitutional so long as (1) government's interests are substantial; (2) warrantless inspections are "necessary to further [that] regulatory scheme;" and (3) the inspection program has a "constitutionally adequate substitute for a warrant." *Id.* at 692.

Search and Seizures—Players, Inc.

In *Players, Inc. v. City of New York*, 371 F. Supp. 2d 522 (S.D.N.Y. 2005), each of SCOTUS' 3 requirements in *Burger* was considered regarding warrantless public health inspections concerning tobacco use. Players, Inc., a private social club, challenged a New York state law allowing warrantless searches of commercial premises to enforce smoking bans. A federal district court upheld New York's statutory authority for these inspections because:

(1) government has a substantial interest in ensuring the health and safety of restaurants against the risks of exposure to tobacco smoke;

(2) warrantless inspections are necessary since advance knowledge of the date, time, and purpose of the inspection may allow restaurateurs to hide or mask violations; and

(3) the state-based regulatory scheme provided sufficient notice to business owners that they are subject to inspections.

Additional applications of the Court's standards in *Burger* authorize warrantless inspections and searches for public health purposes of private residences and various businesses including:

- restaurants (*Contreras v. City of Chi.*, 119 F.3d 1286, 1288 (7th Cir. 1997));
- pawn shops (*S&S Pawn Shop Inc. v. City of Del*, 947 F.2d 432 (10th Cir. 1991));
- adult stores (*Allno Enters., Inc. v. Baltimore Cnty.*, 10 F. App'x 197, 200 (4th Cir. 2001));
- animal dealers (*Hodgins v. USDA*, 238 F.3d 421 (6th Cir. 2000));
- nursing homes (*Blue v. Koren*, 72 F.3d 1075, 1079 (2nd Cir. 1995)); and
- day care centers (*Rush v. Obledo*, 756 F.2d 713 (9th Cir. 1985)).

Still not all warrantless public health inspections pass constitutional muster. In *Gordon v. City of Moreno Valley*, 687 F. Supp. 2d 930 (C.D. Cal. 2009), a federal district court invalidated "raid" style inspections of barber shops by the Moreno Valley

(CA) health department and city police. The searches were unreasonable because the officers entered establishments brandishing weapons, explored non-public areas, and directly questioned customers. In *Tucson Woman's Clinic v. Eden*, 379 F.3d 531, 538 (9th Cir. 2004), a federal appellate court invalidated Arizona's law requiring abortion clinics to submit to unannounced, warrantless searches of the facilities, physicians' offices, and patients' medical records.

C. NUISANCE ABATEMENT

Nuisance law arises from the legal adage that "every person should use [one's] property as not to injure the property of another." *Pendergrast v. Aiken*, 236 S.E.2d 787, 798 (N.C. 1977). In the realm of public health law, nuisance has distinct meanings. The aforementioned TURNING POINT ACT § 1–102(36) (*see* Chapter 8) defines nuisance as "a condition, act, or failure to act that unreasonably interferes with the health or safety of the community by endangering life, generating or spreading infectious diseases, or otherwise injuriously affecting the public's health."

Nuisances may take on many forms and impact the public's health in different ways. They may be public or private by nature. Government tends to intervene to abate public nuisances, while individuals or corporate entities litigate to address private ones. As discussed below, laws supporting the abatement of public and private nuisances authorize direct interventions to mitigate health-related harms to the public.

1. PUBLIC NUISANCE

In its broadest conception, a public nuisance is "an unreasonable interference with a right common to the general public." RESTATEMENT (2ND) OF TORTS § 821B (1979). State and local public health agencies' long-standing powers to abate public nuisances often apply where uses of one's property (e.g., accumulating trash, creating noxious smells) produce clear and obvious health risks for others.

Arizona, for example, authorizes abatement of "[a]ny condition or place . . . that constitutes a breeding place for flies, rodents, mosquitoes and other insects that are capable of carrying and transmitting disease-causing organisms. . . ." A.R.S. §§ 36–601(A)(1), 49–141(A)(1). In 2016, Chicago's city council ordained that homeowners who failed to keep their outdoor premises free of trash attracting rodents may be fined up to $500. Aamer Madhani, *Metro Areas See Surge of Rats*, USA TODAY, Apr. 24, 2016. In July 2017, New York City announced a $32 million plan to abate rats, spurred by multiple public health concerns. J. David Goodman, *With $32 Million Plan, de Blasio Is Latest Mayor to Wage a Rat War*, N.Y. TIMES, July 13, 2017.

Source: Design by Avery M. Hodge

On Long Island, local officials attempted to use their emergency health and safety laws to require a property owner to remove accumulated junk for what the owner claimed were purely aesthetic reasons. Alan Feuer, *Messy Yard Pits a Mechanic Against a Town on the Rise*, N.Y. TIMES, May 16, 2016.

Summit County Board of Health v. Pearson

In *Summit County Board of Health v. Pearson*, 809 N.E.2d 80 (Ohio Ct. App. 2004), the Pearson family kept lions, tigers, leopards, bears, foxes, pigeons, dogs, and an alligator on its property in Copley Township, Ohio. When the local health department inspected the property following complaints of foul odors, it found unsanitary collections of blood, feces, urine, and decomposing animal bones. Among other potential sanctions, it issued an advisory to the family to remove offending materials.

After the Pearsons failed to comply, the property was found to be a public nuisance via an administrative hearing. Following their failed appeal, the Pearsons were required to abate the nuisance by cleaning the property at their own expense.

As per the *Pearson* case, so long as government follows statutory or regulatory procedures it may abate nuisances in the interests of protecting the community's health. Under § 5–11 of the TURNING POINT ACT, state or local public health agencies may immediately and thoroughly investigate any suspected nuisance upon receipt of a complaint or when there is probable cause to believe that a nuisance exists within the agency's jurisdiction. If confirmed, the agency may issue an order to "avoid, correct, or remove, at the owner's expense" any property or condition that constitutes a nuisance within a reasonable period of time.

Non-compliance with such orders allows the public health agency to remove or abate the nuisance at the owner's or occupant's expense. In cases of nuisances on real property, abatement expenses may be attached to the property through a court-ordered lien. *See, e.g., City of Bellingham v. Chin*, 988 P.2d 479 (Wash. Ct. App. 1999) (abatement expenses attached as lien to tavern that constituted a drug-dealing nuisance). In other instances, judgments may be entered against offending persons for the costs incurred by government in abating the nuisance directly.

Outside traditional uses of nuisance abatement laws to clean up real property or destroy contaminated personal property is the potential to address multiple, other types of offenses. In *City of New York v. Milhelm Attea & Bros., Inc.*, 550 F. Supp. 2d 332 (E.D.N.Y. 2008), the city brought a public nuisance action against tobacco wholesalers who sold untaxed cigarettes to tribal reservation retailers. It claimed these cigarettes were being resold at prices below market to the detriment of the public's health. Allowing the City's claim to proceed, the court broadly conceived public nuisance as "conduct or omissions which offend, interfere with or cause damage to the public in the exercise of rights common to all. . . ." *Id.* At 349–50 (citing *Copart Indus. Inc. v. Consol. Edison Co.,* 41 N.Y.2d 564, 568 (1977)). The parties later settled.

Public Nuisance—City of Chicago
In 2004, consistent with other local government lawsuits, the City of Chicago sued gun manufacturer, Beretta®, claiming its weapons were a public nuisance because they led to the deaths and injuries of police, medical personnel, and residents. *City of Chi. v. Beretta U.S.A.*, 821 N.E.2d 1099 (Ill. 2004). The city alleged that Beretta "intentionally and recklessly" designed, marketed, distributed, and sold firearms that it "should know" would be used illegally with direct harms to the community. *Id.* at 361–62. The Illinois Supreme Court dismissed the claim, finding (1) there was no legal duty applicable to Beretta; and (2) a lack of proximate cause for gun-related injuries or deaths in the community. *See also* Chapter 7 for additional discussion of gun-related litigation and PLCAA.

Additional actions in public health nuisance beyond traditional property clean-ups have been brought to:

- control the gathering of street gangs in California (*People ex rel. Gallo v. Acuna*, 929 P.2d 596 (Cal. 1997));
- limit emissions among power plants and automobiles in Connecticut (*Am. Elec. Power Co. v. Connecticut*, 564 U.S. 410 (2011));
- stymie drug-related activities in Ohio (*State ex rel. Rothal v. Smith*, 783 N.E.2d 1001 (Ohio Ct. App. 2002));
- recoup damages from exposure to lead paint in Rhode Island (*State v. Lead Indus. Ass'n*, 951 A.2d 429 (R.I. 2008));
- eliminate offensive chili odor and irritants causing physical harm and discomfort (*City of Irwindale v. Huy Fong Foods, Inc.*, No. BC525856, 2013 WL 5813088 (C.D. Cal. Oct. 28, 2013)), later dismissed. *See* Jolie Lee, *Sriracha Factory Freed of Public Nuisance Label*, USA TODAY, May 29, 2014;
- limit the supply of prescription opiates through major distributors and retailers to stem the tide of mass over-consumption (Scott Higham & Lenny Bernstein, *Cherokee Tribe Sues Opioid Distributors*, WASH. POST, Apr. 21, 2017;
- Target ENDS companies for deceptive marketing practices involving minors. (*State*

of Minnesota v. Juul Labs, Inc., 27–CV–19–19888 (D. Minn. 2023));

- Lessen mental health impacts on youth fueled in part by social media companies like Facebook, Instagram, and Tik Tok. *Social Media Created Public Nuisance, Schools Say*, LAW360, Mar. 5, 2024; and
- Require PepsiCo® to alter its one-time use of plastic packaging in light of its accumulation in the Buffalo River in New York State. *N.Y. sues Pepsi over river-clogging plastics*, WASH. POST, Nov, 16, 2023.

2. PRIVATE NUISANCE

Unlike public nuisances, a private nuisance refers to the non-trespassory invasion of another's use and enjoyment of land. RESTATEMENT (2ND) OF TORTS § 821D (1979). Private nuisances may arise from facts similar to traditional public nuisance cases, but entail private rights of action usually through tort litigation to correct the offense (other than physical trespassing, which is addressed under different legal theories).

As in *Pearson*, odor is the main source of the nuisance in *Pestey v. Cushman*, 788 A.2d 496 (Conn. 2002). After years of tolerating increasingly offensive odors, the Pesteys brought a private nuisance claim against their neighbors, the Cushmans, who operated a dairy farm. In many cases, farmers are allowed greater leeway regarding natural odors from their crop or livestock production. In this case, however, the Pesteys claimed successfully at trial that the odor stemmed from the Cushmans' negligent operation of the farm.

On appeal, the Connecticut Supreme Court considered whether: (a) the odorous conditions had a "natural tendency to create danger and inflict injury upon person or property;" (b) resulting harms were continuous; (c) the Cushman's use of the land was unreasonable or unlawful; and (d) the nuisance was the proximate cause of injuries and damages. *Id.* at 504 (*citing Walsh v. Stonington Water Pollution Control Auth.*, 736 A.2d 811, 815–16 (Conn. 1999)). A jury found in favor of the Pesteys and required the Cushmans to pay $100,000 in damages.

Private Nuisance—Hale v. Ward County

In *Hale v. Ward County*, 818 N.W.2d 697 (N.D. 2012), the Hales owned land outside Minot, North Dakota, near Ward County's shooting range used to train law enforcement officers. They brought a private nuisance claim against the County, alleging harms from hazards from the shooting range in proximity to their land.

The North Dakota Supreme Court dismissed Hales' claims under very different standards than the court relied on in *Pestey,* including assessment of:

a. whether the Hales knew (or should have known) about the activity when they purchased the land;

b. the utility of the shooting range conduct balanced against harms to the Hales;

c. how the Hales attempted to accommodate the County's use of the land; and

d. whether the Hales timely sought relief.

Another type of interference on the use of private property was litigated in *Lucero v. Trosch*, 121 F.3d 591 (11th Cir. 1997). Dr. Lucero performed abortions at a clinic in Birmingham, Alabama. Anti-abortion protestors outside of the clinic shouted loud enough to disturb activities within the clinic, as well as intimidate patients and medical staff. Dr. Lucero sought to enjoin the protesters' activities via a private nuisance claim. The 11th Circuit Court of Appeals weighed the protesters' freedoms of speech under the 1st Amendment with the interests of Dr. Lucero, his staff, and patients to engage in lawful activity without excessive interference. Ultimately, the appellate court ruled in favor of the clinic. Not only did the protesters interfere with Dr. Lucero's business, they also infringed on government's interests to allow patients to seek abortions, ensure public safety and order, respect residential privacy, and protect "captive" audiences from targeted picketing. *Id.* at 602 (citing *Madsen v. Women's Health Ctr., Inc.*, 512 U.S. 753 (1994)).

Conversely, in 2022, the 6th Circuit Court of Appeals found that city ordinances imposing a 10-foot "buffer zone" outside the entrance of all healthcare facilities infringed the 1st Amendment rights of pro-life protestors. *Sisters for Life, Inc. v. Louisville-Jefferson Cnty.*, 56 F.4th 400 (6th Cir. 2022). Scrutinizing the buffer zone ordinance as overly broad, the court noted that the ordinance "makes things 'substantially more difficult' for Sisters for Life's members to conduct 'close, personal conversations' with people attempting to enter the clinic since members must stand several feet away from them . . .". *Id.* at 407.

D. TAKINGS

The power to abate nuisances includes the ability to shutter or evacuate residences or businesses temporarily or permanently. Most of the time the exclusion is not physical *per se* (i.e., an individual is not forcibly removed from the premises), but rather a person or corporation may be required to obviate conditions (at their own expense) or be prevented from engaging in activities on the premises that resulted in a nuisance. In the select cases above, for example, the Pearsons were required to clean up the nuisance created by housing animals on their property and the Cushmans had to alter their dairy farm practices (and compensate their neighbors).

Applications of nuisance laws that negatively impact property owners' possession, use, or commercial interests raise questions related to whether government has taken private property without just compensation in violation of the 5th Amendment of the U.S. Constitution. As discussed initially in Chapter 3, a taking may occur whenever government (1) physically occupies a premises to the exclusion of a private owner or (2) permanently deprives a property owner of all economic value via regulation or other interventions. If takings are lawfully occurred, private property owners must be compensated for their property losses.

Establishing a "physical" taking is relatively easy to show. If government takes a person's land for public purposes (e.g., to build a highway) pursuant to its power of eminent domain, it must provide just compensation. However, as per the *Kelo* case (545 U.S. 469 (2005)) noted in Chapter 3, determining what constitutes a legitimate public purpose sufficient to justify uses of eminent domain powers can be tricky.

Proving what is known as a "regulatory taking" is even more difficult because there is almost always some economic value left in the property affected by the law or regulation. In *Lucas v. S.C. Coastal Council*, 505 U.S. 1003 (1992), SCOTUS determined that a property owner who lost the entire economic use of only part of his land still retained some value. The predominant approach in assessing when regulatory takings require compensation entails 3 factors:

(1) the economic impact on the property owner;

(2) the "character of the governmental action;" and

(3) "interference with distinct investment-backed expectations."

Penn Central Trans. Co. v. N.Y.C., 438 U.S. 104, 124 (1978).

For example, in *Rose Acre Farms, Inc. v. United States*, 559 F.3d 1260 (Fed. Cir. 2009), USDA implemented regulations to control the spread of salmonella on poultry farms. These included restrictions on the interstate sale of poultry and eggs and allowing the confiscation, killing, and testing of some chickens on farms with a history of positive salmonella tests. After salmonella outbreaks were traced back to Indiana-based Rose Acre Farms, USDA restricted several of its properties and removed large numbers of potentially infected hens. Rose Acre Farms alleged that application of the regulations effected a taking of its property. The court found that:

- the economic impact was not severe;
- the character of the regulations directly advanced public health and safety; and
- to the extent the regulations were based on new science, Rose Acre Farms could not have reasonably expected changes to its farming practice.

Still, on balance the court concluded that the regulations did not constitute a taking.

Compare another court's finding, however, in the case, *In re Upstream Addicks and Barker (Texas) Flood-Control Reservoirs*, 146 Fed. Cl. 219 (2019). The Court of Federal Claims found that the U.S. Army Corps of Engineers was liable for damages to properties flooded outside Houston following Hurricane Harvey in August 2017. The Corps' failure to control overflowing reservoirs despite long-term knowledge of risks of flooding of surrounding properties constituted a taking for which reasonable compensation was due to hundreds of property owners. The Corps argued that the flooding was the result of a natural disaster and that it was compelled to allow the reservoirs to overflow to protect downstream properties. The court determined, however, that the Corps' inaction was actually a primary cause of harm.

At first glimpse, the 5th Amendment Takings Clause seems to have the potential to require government to compensate owners for the use or occupation of their property or deprivation of their economic interests to further the public's health. Takings requiring compensation to property owners, however, should not be confused with nuisance abatements to protect the public's health. Compensation is not required under the 5th Amendment when government exercises its power to stem public health nuisances for the benefit of the community. *See, e.g., Harms v. City of Sibley*, 702 N.W.2d 91, 95 (Iowa 2005) (abatement of a nuisance created by dust, noise, traffic, and lighting issues at a concrete plant does not constitute a taking).

When private uses of land or other property offend the public's health, as per the cases above, government may enter and inspect the property, remove the offending issues (or require the owner to remove them), or condemn the property. *Lawton v.*

Steele, 152 U.S. 133, 136 (1894); *Arcara v. Cloud Books, Inc.*, 478 U.S. 697 (1986). Government does not have pay property owners for such entry. To the contrary, it may attach fines, or levies, to the property (as previously noted).

E. ZONING & THE BUILT ENVIRONMENT

The built environment directly impacts the health of communities. Research illustrates how decisions related to the (1) creation and layout of neighborhoods, (2) engineering and building of houses and commercial structures, and (3) design of communities can affect the public's health, both positively and negatively. *See* Shobha Srinivasan et al., *Creating Healthy Communities, Healthy Homes, Healthy People*, 93 AJPH 1446 (2003). In an era of global climate change and significant shifts in migration, development of sustainable communities has been prioritized at the federal, state, and local levels. HUD ET AL., PARTNERSHIP FOR SUSTAINABLE COMMUNITIES, 3 YEARS OF HELPING COMMUNITIES ACHIEVE THEIR VISIONS FOR GROWTH AND PROSPERITY (2012).

Public health interventions, including a focus on HIAP and increased uses of HIAs (noted in Chapter 1), help to assess potential or actual negative impacts of community design and other factors within the built environment. *See, e.g.*, Joe Gose, *Construction That Focuses on Health of Residents*, N.Y. TIMES, Mar. 6, 2013 (describing use of HIAs in developing or revitalizing housing districts). Many municipalities harness their local zoning authority (defined below) to effectuate changes in promotion of the public's health.

Zoning Defined

Zoning refers generally to a local government's ability to set conditions on the use of public or private property within its jurisdiction. Zoning laws authorize local governments to (1) create various districts for industrial, commercial, residential, and farming uses; and (2) set specifications for density of buildings and lot sizes, with reasonable variances for different uses within each district. Variances may be "grandfathered" in (because their use pre-existed implementation of the zoning requirement), or allowed in some specific applications. Osborne M. Reynolds, Jr., *The "Unique Circumstances" Rule in Zoning Variances—An Aid in Achieving Greater Prudence & Less Leniency*, 31 URB. LAW. 127 (1999).

One of the primary historic foundations for zoning laws, dating back to their origination in large U.S. cities predominantly in the early 20th century, is protecting the public's health. Joseph Schilling et al., *The Public Health Roots of Zoning: In Search of Active Living's Legal Genealogy*, 28 AM. J. PREVENTIVE MED. 96, 99 (2005). In 1926, the U.S. Supreme Court affirmed that (1) comprehensive zoning laws were permissible pursuant to state-based police powers and (2) protecting the public's health was legitimate bases for zoning measures. *Village of Euclid v. Ambler Realty*, 272 U.S. 365 (1926) (approving zoning ordinance preventing a landowner from using his land for industry). For decades, public health zoning measures, coupled with building and fire codes, have:

- separated industrial uses from residential areas;
- required sufficient distance between built structures;
- mandated mixed-use developments; and
- assured adequate egress in the interests of public safety.

As suburban sprawl crept across the U.S., local governments began to require developers to set aside space for parks and community recreation. Sidewalks, playgrounds, and running trails that encourage outdoor activity consistent with a "complete streets" focus are commonly featured in zoning applications for new projects or revitalization efforts. David Wilson, *Malden Takes Complete Look at Street Safety*, DAILY ITEM (May 29, 2017).

To the extent aggressive uses of zoning to alter the built environment limit land uses or add costs for developers and owners, legal challenges inevitably surface. In *Dolan v. City of Tigard*, 512 U.S. 374 (1994), Tigard (Oregon) considered the issuance of a zoning permit to a business owner, Florence Dolan, to redevelop her plumbing/electrical supply store. The City sought to condition the permit on Dolan's agreement to allow space for a greenway that would assist in water drainage and provide a bike/pedestrian pathway. Following a series of legal challenges, the U.S. Supreme Court found that the City did not adequately prove that the exaction was reasonably related to the public purposes of improved drainage and decreased vehicle traffic.

In addition to creating recreational spaces and safer neighborhoods, some local communities experiment with zoning uses to change consumer behaviors in other ways. They seek to restrict access to unhealthy foods by limiting the number, placement, or design of fast food and other restaurants. JULIE SAMIA MAIR ET AL., THE USE OF ZONING TO RESTRICT FAST FOOD OUTLETS: A POTENTIAL STRATEGY TO COMBAT OBESITY (2005).

Local zoning laws can be used to help create a healthier retail food marketplace by:

- banning the placement of new fast food, or "formula" (i.e., franchised or chain) restaurants;
- rezoning residential areas to restrict developments of fast food restaurants;
- limiting the density of fast food restaurants or convenience stores, especially near elementary or secondary schools; or
- providing incentives for developers to offer healthy food outlets. *Id.*

San Francisco prohibited "formula retail uses" (including franchised fast food restaurants) in 1 of its historic districts. *Id.* Detroit proposed that certain fast food restaurants may not be built within 500 feet of a school. Seattle restricted the placement of mobile food trucks within its borders. Other communities rely on local zoning ordinances to limit the number or placement of fast food outlets for aesthetic reasons or installations of drive-thrus in the interests of public safety. *Id.*

Defining Fast Food Restaurants

A local zoning ordinance in Concord, Massachusetts defines a "drive-in or fast-food restaurant" as:

> any establishment whose principal business is the sale of foods or beverages in a ready-to-consume state, for consumption within the building or off-premises, and whose principal

> method of operation includes: (1) sale of foods and beverages in paper, plastic or other disposable containers; or (2) service of food and beverages directly to a customer in a motor vehicle.
>
> CONCORD, MASS., ZONING BYLAW § 4.7.1 (2002).

In Los Angeles, a zoning law prohibited the opening and remodeling of stand-alone fast food restaurants. L.A., CAL. ORDINANCE 180103 (July 29, 2008). It was accompanied by financial incentives to increase South L.A.'s produce markets and sit-down restaurants. COMMUNITY HEALTH COUNCILS, INC., FAST FOOD RESTAURANT REP. (2011). Despite the ordinance, researchers determined between 2007–2012 that the prevalence of obese or overweight persons in the area increased at a faster rate than the rest of L.A. Fast food consumption increased as well. Roland Sturm & Aiko Hattori, *Diet & Obesity in L.A. Cnty. 2007–2012: Is There a Measurable Effect of the 2008 Fast-Food Ban?*, 133 SOCIAL SCI. & MED. 205, 205–11 (2015). These deleterious findings contrary to the intended goals of L.A.'s ordinance may be due to the limited number of fast food restaurants affected by the ban as well as delays in implementation.

Courts typically uphold public health exercises of zoning laws on varied grounds so long as government has a rational basis for its measure or decision (and there are no other invidious foundations for the measures). For example, in *Bellas v. Planning Board of Weymouth*, 778 N.E.2d 30 (Mass. App. Ct. 2002), a Massachusetts appellate court approved the denial of a zoning permit to a franchised doughnut shop that sought to include a drive-through window on its premises. The drive through, observed the court, would generate increased traffic that could negatively affect the safety of school children or others. *See also Bess Eaton Donut Flour Co., Inc. v. Zoning Bd. of Rev. of Town of Westerly*, No. 99–0209, 2000 WL 276818, at 1 (R.I. Super. Feb. 15, 2000) (approving zoning denial of a bake shop with drive-through because it would adversely impact the neighborhood); *contra In re Westbury Trombo, Inc. v. Bd. of Trs.*, 763 N.Y.S.2d 674 (App. Div. 2003) (invalidating local zoning law restricting fast food businesses from operating during certain hours).

Public health powers to monitor property and alter the built environment are limited. Fourth Amendment privacy protections and 5th Amendment requirements to compensate for takings of private property necessitate careful implementation of laws authorizing public health agents to inspect property and abate nuisances. Creation of healthier communities can contravene some commercial interests and generate related economic objections. Whether grounded in constitutional law or local politics, arguments against property-based interventions to advance the public's health reflect the type of tradeoffs that must be accommodated with sufficient guidance and planning.

	Chapter 10—Discussion Questions
?	1. How have courts altered their assessment of the legality of public health inspections?
?	2. What are the key differences between public/private nuisances & how they are abated?
?	3. When must government compensate owners after taking property for public health purposes?
?	4. What are some practical limitations to the use of zoning to promote a healthy environment?
?	5. What other legal opportunities exist to promote health through the built environment?

CHAPTER 11

PUBLIC HEALTH EMERGENCY LEGAL PREPAREDNESS & RESPONSE

	Chapter 11—Learning Objectives
✓	1. Examine the legal environment for responding to diverse PHEs
✓	2. Explore the multi-faceted roles of federal, state & local governments in emergency preparedness & response
✓	3. Identify federalism implications entailed in interjurisdictional emergencies
✓	4. Analyze key preparedness issues extending from changes in the legal environment
✓	5. Consider contentious legal & policy debates concerning liability protections for HCWs & entities

One of the most sensational and difficult areas of public health practice is emergency preparedness and response. During pandemics, acts of bioterrorism, natural disasters, or other public health crises, public and private sector entities and individuals must make critical choices in real-time that can affect the lives and health of entire populations. In making these choices they must adapt to a new (albeit temporary) paradigm that prioritizes the health of the community (versus the health of the individual) as the consummate goal. James G. Hodge, Jr. et al., *Practical, Ethical & Legal Challenges Underlying CSC*, 41(s1) JLME 50 (2013).

The law adapts as well. As the Arizona Supreme Court observed in a case assessing emergency powers in response to the Spanish flu pandemic over 100 years ago, "Necessity is the law of time and place, and the emergency calls into life the necessity for the operation of law. The emergency calls forth the occasion to exercise the power to protect the public health." *Globe Sch. Dist. No. 1 v. Bd. of Health*, 175 P. 55 (Ariz. 1919).

By design, modern federal, state, tribal, or local emergency declarations change the legal landscape to further the public's health. Specifically after the terrorist attacks on September 11, 2001 ("9/11") and ensuing anthrax incidents, a series of significant legal reforms emerged to:

- revamp governmental organization and response efforts;
- create new preparedness classifications centered on declaration of "public health emergencies (PHEs);" and
- revise existing legal norms to clarify roles and responsibilities of public and private actors in emergency response efforts.

As per Figure 11.1, the role of law in emergencies is essential to effective preparedness and response on multiple levels of government, across diverse topics, and involving an array of private sector entities and individuals.

Figure 11.1. Emergency Legal Preparedness Topics

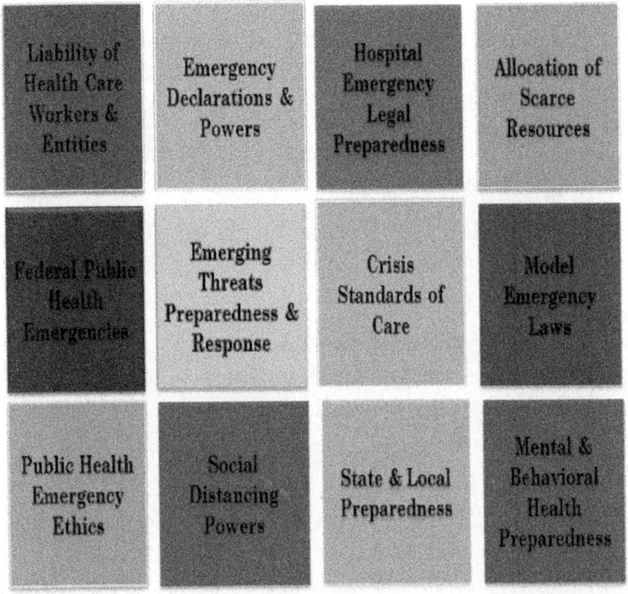

While law is critical to obviating public health harms, it can also be highly controversial. Eloisa C. Rodriguez-Dod, Aileen M. Marty & Elena M. Marty-Nelson, *Tears in Heaven: Religiously & Culturally Sensitive Laws for Preventing the Next Pandemic*, 66 CATH. U. L. REV. 117 (2017); Sheri Fink, *Whose Lives Should Be Saved? To Help Shape Policy, Researchers Ask the Public*, N.Y. TIMES, Aug. 22, 2016.

Additional PHE threats since 9/11 notably include:

- infectious diseases like SARS (2003), H1N1 flu (2009/2010), EVD (2014), Zika virus (2016), and COVID-19 (2020–2023) (*see* Chapter 12);
- natural disasters like hurricanes Katrina (2005), Isaac (2012), Sandy (2012), Harvey (2017); Idalia (2023), and Beryl (2024);
- wildfires in California (2020) and Hawaii (2023–2024);
- heat-related deaths or blackouts in Phoenix, AZ and other hot climates following one of the hottest years on record (2023); and
- varying threats like the impacts of racism, gun violence, vaccine hesitancy, blackouts and lack of access to health services.

See, e.g., Sheera Frenkel, *Black & Hisp. Communities Grapple with Vaccine Misinformation*, N.Y. TIMES, Mar. 10, 2021; Sheryl Gay Stolberg, *Can New Gun Violence Rsch. Find a Path Around the Pol. Stalemate?*, N.Y. TIMES, Apr. 2, 2021; Christopher Flavelle, *Blackouts Are Growing Threat to U.S. Cities*, N.Y. TIMES, May 4, 2021; Noah Weiland, *Heat-Related Hospital Visits Rose in 2023, Study Finds*, N.Y. TIMES, Apr. 19. 2024.

Each of these examples and others have revealed legal pitfalls and myths in diverse areas of emergency preparedness law and policy. As discussed below, these issues include: (1) duplicative and, at times, counter-productive roles of federal, state, and local governments, (2) challenges in real-time legal decision-making, and (3) concerns over liability protections for HCWs, emergency responders and entities. This chapter lays out core theories and applications of emergency legal preparedness and response, beginning with the scope and definition of PHEs. Assessing and understanding these key themes are critical to exploring the extraordinary legal issues surfacing during the COVID-19 pandemic, largely discussed in Chapter 12.

A. DEFINING PUBLIC HEALTH EMERGENCIES

Traditionally, frontline preparedness and response efforts have largely been the responsibility of state and local governments pursuant to their police powers (*see* Chapter 2). Federal public health agencies like HHS and CDC provided national guidance and resources, but lacked extensive legal authority or manpower to address specific local public health needs in mass casualty events.

The terrorist attacks and anthrax exposures in 2001 changed everything. Thousands were killed instantly on 9/11, and over 15 people were infected with anthrax and 5 died later that Fall. As per the text box below, the specific source and cause of the anthrax bioterrorism attack remain uncertain.

FBI Investigation—Anthrax Bioterrorism

Concerning the source of the 2001 anthrax bioterrorism attacks, FBI alleged that Dr. Bruce Ivins, who took his own life in 2008, was the lead culprit. However, at least 1 former FBI agent, Richard Lambert, sued the Bureau suggesting potential discrepancies in its investigation, leading to significant questions as to whether Dr. Ivins was in fact the lead (or sole) bioterrorist. Scott Shane, *Former FBI Agent Sues, Claiming Retaliation Over Misgivings in Anthrax Case*, N.Y. TIMES, Apr. 9, 2015.

National security concerns arising from these events revolutionized federal preparedness and response efforts. *See, e.g.*, David Fidler, *Constitutional Outlines of Public Health's "New World Order,"* 77 TEMP. L. REV. 247 (2004). The federal government alone is constitutionally vested with supreme authority to act in defense of the nation and address matters of national security. U.S. CONST. art. 4, § 4. Federal efforts to investigate criminal acts of terrorism intersected with state and local efforts to protect the public's health from known or potential anthrax exposures. Significant questions surfaced as to who exactly was in charge of controlling bioterrorism threats and on what legal basis.

Federalism questions like these in public health have arisen routinely over decades, but the stakes were considerably higher in the "post 9/11" era. As

President Obama (Figure 11.2) noted in 2011, integrated, interjurisdictional coordination across all levels of government is essential to effective emergency responses. Nat'l Preparedness, 8 PRES. POL. DIRECTIVE (Mar. 30, 2011).

Figure 11.2. President Barack Obama

During the administrations of Presidents Obama and George W. Bush, an increasing array of PHEs were classified as national security threats or priorities, including diseases like SARS, MERS, MDR-TB, and pandemic influenzas. In 2014, even antibiotic-resistant bacteria was identified as a national security priority via an Executive Order from President Obama, which outlined cross-sector efforts and investments to prevent and control outbreaks. Exec. Order No. 13,676, 3 C.F.R.§ 13676 (2014).

On September 22, 2006, DHS' Secretary issued a material threat determination for EVD on the grounds that the viral agent directly affects national security. This designation helped allocate federal aid through military operations and funding for public health research, supplies, and biosurveillance. A decade later, on February 26, 2016, HHS' Secretary Sylvia Burwell stated that Zika virus has "significant potential to affect national security or the health and security of United States citizens living abroad . . . ." 81 Fed. Reg. 10,878, 10,879 (Mar. 2, 2016). *See* James G. Hodge, Jr. & Kim Weidenaar, *PHEs as Threats to Nat'l Sec.*, 9(1) GEO. NAT'L SEC. L. & POL. 81 (2017).

Even as federal efforts focused on investigating the perpetrators of the 9/11 terrorist acts, state and local preparedness officials and leaders were concerned about a new type of bioterrorism emergency stemming from the anthrax exposures. Long-standing, existing state-based "emergency" or "disaster" declarations were traditionally crafted to address "all hazards" (including epidemics), but used typically in response to natural disasters (e.g., fires, floods, earthquakes, hurricanes). Unlike these disasters, bioterrorism events have an unpredictable potential for systemic and widespread disability and death in the population over extended periods. Searching for new legal responses to address public health threats, state and local policymakers called for legal reforms in late 2001.

With support from leading national public health associations and CDC, the Centers for Law and the Public's Health at Georgetown and Johns Hopkins Universities developed the MODEL STATE EMERGENCY HEALTH POWERS ACT (MSEHPA) in December 2001. Based in part on existing core principles and guided by national input and commentary, MSEHPA features a cohesive series of model provisions for state, tribal, and local governments considering how to respond to bioterrorism or other public health threats. Lawrence O. Gostin et al., *MSEHPA: Planning & Response to Bioterrorism & Naturally Occurring Infectious Diseases*, 288 JAMA 622 (2002). The text box below diagrams key provisions of MSEHPA.

MSEHPA Key Provisions	
Article I: Title, Findings, Purposes & Definitions	
§ 101	Short title
§ 102	Legislative findings
§ 103	Purposes
Article II: Planning for a PHE	
§ 201	PHE Planning Commissions
§ 202	PHE Plan
Article III: Measures to Detect & Track PHEs	
§ 301	Reporting
§ 302	Tracking
§ 303	Information Sharing
Article IV: Declaring a State of PHE	
§ 401	Declaration
§ 402	Content of declaration
§ 403	Effect of declaration
§ 404	Enforcement
§ 405	Termination of declaration
Article V: Management of Property	
§ 501	Emergency measures concerning facilities & materials

MSEHPA Key Provisions	
§ 502	Access to & control of facilities and property
§ 503	Safe disposal of infectious waste
§ 504	Safe disposal of human remains
§ 505	Control of health care supplies
§ 506	Compensation
§ 507	Destruction of property
Article VI: Protection of Persons	
§ 601	Protection of persons
§ 602	Medical examination & testing
§ 603	Vaccination & treatment
§ 604	Isolation & quarantine
§ 605	Procedures for isolation & quarantine
§ 606	Collection of laboratory specimens; performance of tests
§ 607	Access to & disclosure of PHI
§ 608	Licensing & appointment of health personnel
Article VII: Public Information Regarding PHEs	
§ 701	Dissemination of information
§ 702	Access to mental health support personnel

MSEHPA balances individual and communal interests underlying modern responses to a PHE, defined as "an occurrence or imminent threat of an illness or health condition that:

(1) is believed to be caused by . . . bioterrorism; the appearance of a novel or previously controlled or eradicated infectious agent or biological toxin [or other causes]; . . . and

> (2) poses a high probability of . . . a large number of deaths . . . ; serious or long-term disabilities . . . ; or widespread exposure to an infectious or toxic agent that [presents] a significant risk of substantial future harm to a large number of people in the affected population."

MSEHPA § 104(m), Ctrs. for Law & the Public's Health (2001).

Though this definition was criticized initially by some as overly-broad, the scope of what constitutes a PHE is actually considerably more limited than most existing state-based definitions of emergency or disaster (which are also used often to respond to public health crises as seen especially during the COVID-19 pandemic as per Chapter 12). Under MSEHPA, a PHE declaration may be issued only when it can be shown that an act of bioterrorism or other public health threat poses a "high probability" of a large number of deaths, disabilities, or exposures to agents that could cause future harms. These statutorily-defined limits are designed to confine PHE declarations to instances necessitating rapid and effective public health responses like SARS or smallpox, but not the slow, global spread of conditions like obesity (for which rapid legal responses may not be efficacious despite prevalent rates of obesity among the world's population). *See, e.g.*, Matt Richtel, *Over 10% of World's Population Is Obese, Study Finds*, N.Y. TIMES, June 12, 2017.

Since the introduction of MSEHPA, however, some states and localities have declared PHEs to address an array of threats well outside the initial context of pandemic illness or bioterrorism. For example, in 2013, the City of Boston and New York State issued separate declarations of PHEs for short periods in response to annual flu outbreaks. *See* James G. Hodge, Jr., *The Changing Nature & Scope of PHEs and Response to Annual Flu,* 11 BIOSECURITY & BIOTERRORISM 142 (2013). Other declarations of PHEs have been issued for a host of conditions or occurrences including:

- Contamination of public water supplies (Alamosa County, CO);
- Localized measles outbreaks (Pima County, AZ);
- Release (and potential further release) of amphibole asbestos (Libby and Troy, MT);
- Drinking water contamination (Black Falls and Grand Falls, Navajo Nation);
- Dramatic increases in reports of domestic violence (Nassau County, NY);
- Shortages of affordable, safe medical cannabis (Oakland, CA);
- Impacts of racism (multiple states and localities);
- Severe storms and tornadoes (MO);
- Food insecurity (County of Hawai'i, HI);
- Lead in drinking water (Flint, MI);

- Opioid-related morbidity and mortality (multiple states and localities); and
- West Nile Virus outbreaks (Dallas County, TX).

See James G. Hodge, Jr., Sarah A. Wetter & Erica N. White, *Legal Crises in Public Health*, 47 JLME 778 (2019).

2015 HIV/AIDS Outbreak in Indiana
In March 2015, former Indiana Governor (and former Vice President) Mike Pence declared a state of PHE to respond to a localized spike in the numbers of HIV infections in rural Scott County. *Indiana to Declare PHE Over HIV Outbreak*, CHI. TRIB., Mar. 26, 2015. Governor Pence's declaration authorized the temporary implementation of a needle exchange program (NEP) to counter the spread of HIV to over 160 people largely infected through intravenous drug use of the prescription opioid, Opana®, which was later withdrawn from the market. Shari Rudavsky, *Scott County, Health Dep't Working on NEP*, INDYSTAR, Mar. 27, 2015. Indiana's former health commissioner (and later U.S. Surgeon General) Dr. Jerome Adams noted how "[IDUs are] getting HIV because they're addicted." Alan Schwartz & Mitch Smith, *Needle Exchange Is Allowed After HIV Outbreak in an Indiana County*, N.Y. TIMES, Mar. 27, 2015.

In 2016, Congress lifted its long-standing ban on use of federal funds for NEPs to help prevent HIV spread among IDUs. *See* Laura Ungar, *Congress Removes Funding Ban on Needle Exchanges*, USA TODAY, Jan. 8, 2016.

For more information, *see* the table and accompanying information in JAMES G. HODGE, JR., ET AL., EMERGENCY MED. SERVICES & MED. SURGE: ESSENTIAL LEGAL ISSUES 1 (2015).

B. STATE & LOCAL PUBLIC HEALTH EMERGENCY POWERS

Following the completion of MSEHPA, legislatures or agencies in nearly all the states and D.C. introduced dozens of legislative bills or regulations based in whole or part on the Act. By 2006, 39 state legislatures passed bills related to MSEHPA. CTRS. FOR L. & THE PUBLIC'S HEALTH, MSEHPA: STATE LEGIS. ACTIVITY 2–20 (2006). Thirty-four states and D.C. have legislatively defined PHEs, or like terms. NETWORK FOR PUB. HEALTH L., EMERGENCY DECLARATION AUTHORITIES—TABLE (2016). In addition, several MSEHPA provisions are reflected in other model public health acts, including the TURNING POINT ACT and UNIFORM EMERGENCY VOLUNTEER HEALTH PRACTITIONERS ACT (2007) (focused on emergency deployment and use of volunteer health providers).

Through these and other legislative or regulatory reforms, a new legal platform for PHE response efforts emerged, particularly at the state and local levels. A declaration of PHE triggers a series of optional, expedited public health powers for governmental public health agents to respond in concert with public safety and emergency management actors. While these powers vary across jurisdictions, state and local public health officials are authorized generally during PHEs to expeditiously:

- Close roads, businesses, or other places;
- Implement curfews or other social distancing measures;
- Evacuate "at risk" places or populations where justified;
- Collect specimens and implement safe handling procedures for the disposal of human remains or infectious wastes;
- Test, screen, vaccinate, and treat exposed or infected persons;
- Separate individuals exposed (quarantine) or infected (isolation) with communicable conditions from others to prevent further transmission;
- Abate public health nuisances and destroy dangerous or contaminated materials;
- Take private property with just compensation as needed to care for patients or protect the public's health;
- Seek assistance from out-of-state health care volunteers through licensure reciprocity (i.e.,

recognizing the license of an out-of-state volunteer in good standing as if it were issued in-state during the PHE);

- Immunize select public and private actors (including volunteers) from legal claims grounded in negligence (discussed further below);

- Reimburse private sector contributors for emergency response efforts; and

- Inform the population of public health threats in accessible, understandable, and culturally-relevant ways.

In many states, the Governor (or other politically-appointed actor such as a state health commissioner) may also waive specific statutory or regulatory laws that impede response efforts for the duration of a PHE (e.g., licensure regulations, scope of practice limitations, or procurement codes that may hamper resource acquisitions). *See* Daniel G. Orenstein, *When Law Is Not Law: Setting Aside Legal Provisions During Declared Emergencies*, 41 JLME 73 (2013). Political actors may also:

- coordinate services among public health and emergency actors (e.g., authorizing state public health departments to work closely with emergency management and law enforcement personnel);

- reallocate state resources (e.g., state agents, supplies, drugs, equipment); and

- expend finances to effectuate emergency response efforts (with opportunities later for a full accounting).

See James G. Hodge, Jr., *The Evolution of Law in Biopreparedness*, 10 BIOSECURITY & BIOTERRORISM 38 (2012).

C. FEDERAL PUBLIC HEALTH EMERGENCY POWERS

While much of the action in PHE preparedness is exerted by state and local actors on the frontlines of response efforts, the federal government is deeply embedded in preparedness through multiple legislative and regulatory reforms and related programs arising after 9/11. The slate of federal emergency preparedness laws include:

- The Federal Public Health Security & Bioterrorism Preparedness & Response Act of 2002, Pub. L. No. 107–188, 116 Stat. 594 (2002) authorizing (1) implementation of the National Disaster Medical System (NDMS) to coordinate rapid deployment of specialized response teams; and (2) ASPR's Strategic National Stockpile (SNS) to distribute pre-stocked essential medicines and supplies within hours of an event anywhere nationally.

- The Project BioShield Act of 2004, Pub. L. No. 108–276, 118 Stat. 835 (2004), which allows FDA to issue emergency use authorizations (EUAs) during declared chemical, biological, radiological, or nuclear (CBRN) emergencies. 21 U.S.C. § 360bbb–3(a)(1) (2013).

- The Homeland Security Act of 2002, Pub. L. No. 107–296, 116 Stat. 2135 (2002), and Public Health Threats & Emergencies Act of 2000, Pub. L. No. 106–505, 114 Stat. 2314 (2000), which create and empower the Department of Homeland Security (DHS).

- Additional federal reforms authorizing emergency waivers of provisions of the Emergency Medical Treatment & Active Labor Act (EMTALA), 42 U.S.C. § 1320b–5 (2008). In non-emergencies, EMTALA typically requires hospitals to provide emergency care to persons seeking treatment. In addition, through what are known as "§ 1135 waivers," CMS eligibility requirements for Medicaid and Medicare programs can be temporarily suspended. 42 U.S.C. § 1320b–2 (2013). Waivers of EMTALA or CMS requirements can be essential during real-time PHEs when adherence to normal requirements is impossible.

Beyond these core federal laws, many explicit federal PHE powers are concentrated in 4 federal laws depicted in Figure 11.3. Collectively, these laws authorize the federal government to declare (and renew) states of general emergency, disaster, and PHE.

Figure 11.3. Major Federal Emergency Acts

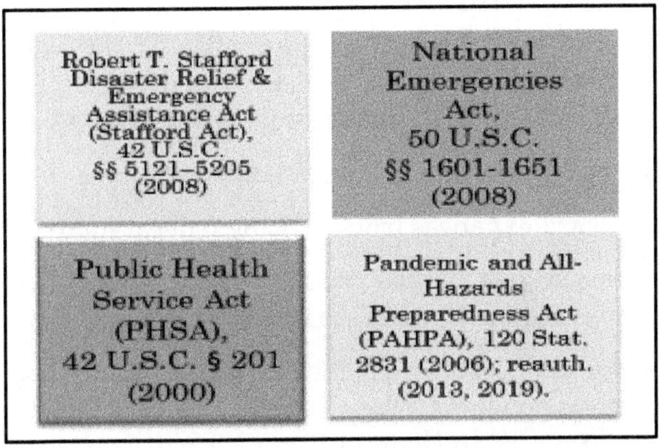

Emergency and disaster declarations may be made by the President via the Stafford Act or the National Emergencies Act (NEA) for relatively short or longer durations. A NEA declaration made initially by President George W. Bush after 9/11 was extended for over 15 years. Stafford Act declarations are issued typically pursuant to a request of a state Governor for federal assistance following natural disasters (e.g., tornados, ice storms, floods, fires, or hurricanes) or man-made emergencies (e.g., civil unrest, oil or chemical spills, bombings, explosions, bridge collapses, or blackouts).

While corresponding federal emergency or disaster powers are broad, they are not tailored *per se* to PHEs involving the spread of infectious diseases or bioterrorism agents. *See, e.g.*, EDWARD C. LIU, CONG. RSCH. SERV., RL34724, WOULD AN INFLUENZA PANDEMIC QUALIFY AS A MAJOR DISASTER UNDER THE

STAFFORD ACT? (2008). As a result, PHSA expressly authorizes HHS' Secretary to declare a PHE in response to "significant outbreaks of infectious diseases or bioterrorist attacks." 42 U.S.C. § 247d (2008). Federal PHE declarations allow HHS to:

- rapidly execute grants or contracts;
- award expenses from existing federal funds;
- investigate the cause, treatment, or prevention of a disease or disorder; and
- waive certain federal laws (including provisions of the HIPAA Privacy Rule (discussed in Chapter 8)).

Congressional passage of PAHPA in 2006 (as subsequently reauthorized) significantly facilitates the use of medical countermeasures (MCMs) for various public health threats. As former HHS Secretary Kathleen Sebelius noted in 2010, "[o]ur Nation must have the nimble, flexible capacity to produce MCMs rapidly in the face of any attack or threat, known or unknown, including a novel, previously unrecognized, naturally occurring emerging infectious disease." ASPR, PHE MCM ENTERPRISE REV. 3 (2010). Her comments proved prescient against the backdrop of the COVID-19 pandemic a decade later (*see* Chapter 12).

Federal legislative reforms also enhanced FDA's ability to issue EUAs. EUAs allow use of unapproved medical products or unapproved uses of approved products leading up to or during an emergency in the absence of adequate and available alternatives. 21

U.S.C. § 360bbb–3 (2013). FDA can issue EUAs based on any of the following:

- Determination by HHS' Secretary of a PHE (or its significant potential) that may affect national security or the health and security of U.S. citizens living abroad;
- Determination by DoD's Secretary of a military emergency (or its significant potential) involving a heightened risk of attack;
- Determination by DHS' Secretary of a domestic emergency (or its significant potential) involving a heightened risk of attack; or
- Identification of a material threat by DHS' Secretary sufficient to affect national security or the health and security of U.S. citizens living abroad.

FDA guidance on EUAs clarifies their issuance and revocation leading up to and during declared emergencies; substantive content; bases for their approval or denial; intersection of EUA applications with routine drug or product approval processes; and prescribing practices, shelf-life extensions of specific drugs, and preemptive effects. *See* EUA of Medical Products & Related Authorities; Draft Guidance for Industry & Pub. Health Stakeholders, 81 FED. REG. 19191–01 (Apr. 4, 2016). Extensive availability of EUAs (especially during the COVID-19 pandemic) has led some drug and device providers to consider the route as a legal path of first resort to developing and distributing their products with potential utility in emergencies.

EUAs During Ebola, Zika & COVID-19

FDA has issued several EUAs related to the use of field tests to detect EVD, Zika, and COVID-19:

- An Enterovirus D68 (EV–D68) outbreak in late 2014 prompted FDA to issue an EUA for limited use of a lab assay to detect strains of EV–D68 in individuals exhibiting symptoms. EUA of an In Vitro Diagnostic Device for Detection of EV–D68, 80 Fed. Reg. 37625–33 (July 1, 2015).
- Several EUAs were issued in 2016 regarding new tests to detect Zika virus infection more rapidly and accurately, especially among pregnant women. EUA of an In Vitro Diagnostic Device for Diagnosis of Zika Virus Infection, 81 Fed. Reg. 17170–01 (Mar. 28, 2016).
- During the 3 year PHE surrounding the COVID-19 pandemic, numerous EUAs were issued to respond to PPE and ventilator shortages, as well as for new diagnostic tests, vaccines, and plasma treatments. *EUAs*, FDA (Mar. 4, 2024).

D. EVOLVING EMERGENCY LEGAL ENVIRONMENT

Substantial legal reforms have completely altered the emergency legal environment since 9/11, but major law and policy conflicts remain. Three premier challenges in emergency legal preparedness, discussed below, include (1) assessing the respective roles of federal, state, and local governments arising from multiple emergency declarations and response efforts; (2) engaging in "legal triage" during real-time emergencies; and (3) protecting practitioners and entities from liability during crises.

1. INTERJURISDICTIONAL ROLES IN EMERGENCY PREPAREDNESS

The extensive array of emergency laws at all levels of government leads to the potential for overlapping emergency declarations and authorities. In response to Hurricane Katrina, for example, federal states of emergency and major disaster were initially declared pursuant to the Stafford Act on August 27, 2005 and August 29, 2005, respectively. HHS' Secretary also declared a PHE for Louisiana on August 29 as flood waters rose in New Orleans.

Responding to multiple declarations, DHS officials were unsure how best to deploy their resources. Major gaps in services resulted from a lack of inter-agency collaboration, leading to additional legislative reforms. As noted above, PAHPA stripped DHS from its primary role in PHEs, replacing it with HHS. SARAH A. LISTER, CONG. RSCH. SERV., RL33579, THE

PUBLIC HEALTH & MED. RESPONSE TO DISASTERS: FEDERAL AUTHORITY & FUNDING 6 (2007).

State and local emergency declarations can also overlap. PHE reforms based on MSEHPA, for example, are layered on top of existing "emergency" and "disaster" frameworks. Like federal authorities, states sometimes issue dual declarations for the same event. In 2005, Louisiana's Governor Kathleen Blanco issued states of emergency and PHE following Hurricane Katrina. So did Maryland Governor Martin O'Malley in response to the H1N1 pandemic in 2009.

Duplicate emergency declarations are not only redundant and potentially confusing, they can create legal conflicts. For example, similar emergency powers to evacuate or close premises may be vested in different governmental agents (e.g., departments of health and emergency management), resulting in potentially divergent orders when states of emergency and PHE are simultaneously invoked. *See, e.g.,* James G. Hodge, Jr. & Veda Collmer, *A Legal Duty To Evacuate Health Care Facilities in Emergencies*, 25(3) ABA HEALTH LAW. 20 (2013).

Coordination breakdowns in preparedness and response efforts within and across jurisdictions can waste scarce resources through duplicative or conflicting efforts that negatively impact the public's health or erode public confidence in communal safeguards. During the 2014 Ebola outbreak, multiple states (e.g., CA, FL, NJ, NY, TX) legally refused to follow specific CDC social distancing guidance concerning HCWs returning from "hot zone" clinics in affected West African countries. James G. Hodge, Jr., *Legal Myths of Ebola Preparedness & Response*, 29 NOTRE DAME J. L., ETHICS & PUB. POL. 355 (2015). Resulting approaches varied across states as to how best to handle risks related to these returning HCWs, as per the isolation case of nurse Kaci Hickox (*see* Chapter 5).

2. PRACTICING LEGAL TRIAGE

Emergency laws ideally authorize a clear set of powers to facilitate emergency responses. In actuality, real questions arise as to what public or private actors can do in emergencies pursuant to constitutional, statutory, or regulatory laws, as well as contracts and other agreements. Framed often in sweeping terms and subject to multiple interpretations, emergency laws offer lots of options. Yet, key choices must be made by public health and emergency management leaders and their private sector partners, lending to the need for resiliency-training and preparedness exercises before and after major events.

These and other real-time factors necessitate rapid and substantial legal decision-making in an altered landscape, as well as enhanced public health governance. Lance A. Gable, *Evading Emergency: Strengthening Emergency Responses Through Integrated Pluralistic Governance*, 91 OR. L. REV. 375 (2012). Yet the practice of PHE legal preparedness and response is non-standardized, under-studied, and, at times, poorly executed. Peter D. Jacobsen et al., *The Role of Law in Pub. Health Preparedness:*

Opportunities & Challenges, 37 J. HEALTH POLITICS, POL. & L. 297 (2012) (noting that frequent misperceptions of laws could implicate morbidity and mortality in emergencies).

Through "legal triage" (depicted as the intersection of manifold factors in Figure 11.4 below) public and private health practitioners, emergency responders, and their legal counsel at all levels of government must prioritize legal issues and solutions in real-time to facilitate legitimate PHE responses.

Figure 11.4. Legal Triage

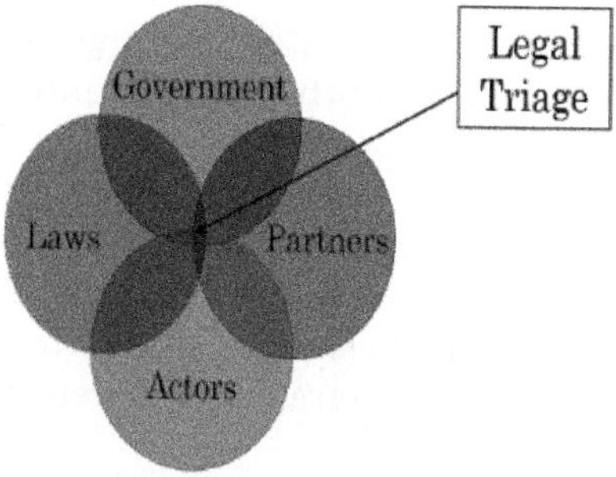

Practicing legal triage entails:

- identification of legal issues that may facilitate or impede public health efforts;
- assessing and monitoring changing legal norms;
- crafting innovative, legally-sound solutions to known or purported barriers to public health responses;

- explicating legal conclusions through effective, tailored communications; and
- regularly revisiting the utility and efficacy of legal guidance to improve public health outcomes.

James G. Hodge, Jr. & Evan D. Anderson, *Principles and Practice of Legal Triage During PHEs*, 64 N.Y.U. ANN. SURV. AM. L. 429 (2008). These objectives are not easily met (as illustrated repeatedly during the COVID-19 pandemic as per Chapter 12), but can be as essential to effective emergency responses as medical or other practices designed to obviate or limit public health impacts.

3. EMERGENCY LIABILITY PROTECTIONS

One of the most contentious issues related to emergency response efforts involves personal and entity liability. Governments and some quasi-government entities may largely be immune from claims grounded in failures to act to prevent the spread of infectious diseases or other PHEs. Even direct harms caused by these entities may not result in liability. In 2016, for example, a federal court of appeals held that that the United Nations (U.N.) is immune from a class action lawsuit brought by thousands of families of victims of a cholera outbreak in Haiti. The outbreak was most likely caused by U.N. peacekeeping forces on assignment after the devastating earthquake in Haiti in 2010. Jonathan M. Katz, *U.S. Court Upholds UN's Immunity in Cholera Suit*, N.Y. TIMES, Aug. 18, 2016.

Conversely, private health care practitioners, volunteers, and others in the U.S. fear their potential liability for medical malpractice or other claims leading to injuries or deaths during emergencies. Considerable evidence exists revealing the scope of diagnostic and other errors in the provision of intensive care in routine and emergency settings. Andrew D. Auerbach et al., *Diagnostic Errors in Hospitalized Adults Who Died or Were Transferred to Intensive Care*, JAMA INTERNAL MED., Jan. 8, 2024. Hospitals, clinics, and nonprofits are understandably anxious about their potential liability for negligent acts or omissions of their staff.

Concerns over liability in emergencies can diminish HCWs' participation in response efforts to the detriment of the public's health. *See* IOM, CSC: A SYS. FRAMEWORK FOR CATASTROPHIC DISASTER RESPONSE 59 (2012). Such unease can also impact their direct provision of care in emergencies (and non-emergencies). *See, e.g.,* Emily R. Carrier et al., *High Physician Concern About Malpractice Risk Predicts More Aggressive Diagnostic Testing In Office-Based Practice*, 32 HEALTH AFFS. 1383 (2013) (physicians worried about malpractice risks are significantly more likely to practice defensive medicine with some patients).

Some suggest HCWs' concerns are unwarranted because extensive or unscrupulous liability claims during and after public health crises are uncommon. George J. Annas, *Standard of Care—In Sickness & in Health & in Emergencies*, 362 NEJM 2126 (2010). This may not be true related to liability claims extending from the COVID-19 pandemic. Harris Meyer, *How Likely Are Malpractice Lawsuits From Treating COVID?*, MEDSCAPE (Jan. 25, 2021). Initial analyses suggest the number of medical malpractice claims filed in 2020 was lower than in 2019 due, in part, to social distancing measures during the pandemic. Robert E. White Jr., *Malpractice Claims from the COVID-19 Pandemic: More Questions Than Answers*, TDC GROUP (Apr. 9, 2021).

Anticipated rises in medical malpractice claims after the pandemic may be due to suspensions of non-essential procedures, HCW burnout, heightened hospital safety scores, and long-COVID impacts. Maura Keller, *Hardening Med. Malpractice Rates, a Slew of COVID Claims & What It All Means for the Healthcare Sector*, RISK & INS. (June 7, 2021); Tara Bannow. *Medical Malpractice Lawsuits, Delayed by the Pandemic, Are Hitting Hospitals Harder Than Expected*, STAT (Dec. 5, 2022); Shannon Young, *It's Still Unclear How the Covid-19 Pandemic Will Shape Malpractice Claims*, HEALTHCARE BREW (Nov. 22, 2023).

Health practitioners and entities also point to exceptional liability claims that have previously arisen following attempts to handle patients with limited resources in crises. *See* Michelle Carpenter et al., *Deploying & Using VHPs in Response to Emergencies*, 3 AM. J. DISASTER MED. 17 (2008). For example, following Hurricane Katrina Dr. Anna Pou (*see* Figure 11.5) faced multiple criminal charges related to the alleged euthanasia of 4 patients (aged 61–90) by nurses under her supervision at the flooded and largely inoperable Memorial Medical Center in New Orleans.

Figure 11.5. Dr. Anna Pou

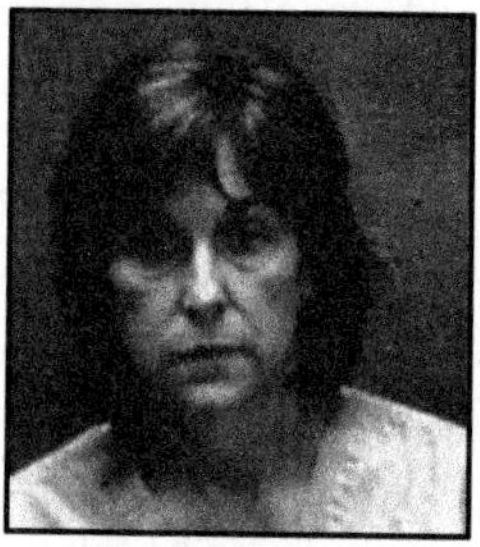

Source: Russell McCulley, *Charges Dropped in Katrina Hosp. Deaths*, REUTERS: HEALTH NEWS (July 25, 2007).

Criminal charges were later dropped, but civil litigation brought by 3 families against Dr. Pou ensued. Christopher Drew & Shaila Dewan, *Louisiana Doctor Said to Have Faced Chaos*, N.Y. TIMES, July 20, 2006. The cases settled for undisclosed terms. SHERI FINK, 5 DAYS AT MEMORIAL: LIFE & DEATH IN A STORM-RAVAGED HOSP. 467 (2013).

In a separate case, Tenet Health Systems, which operated Memorial Medical Center where Dr. Pou was employed, settled claims in 2011 brought by Hurricane Katrina victims for a reported $25 million. *Everett v. Tenet Health Sys. Mem'l Med. Ctr., Inc.*, No. 20067948 (La. Orleans Parish Civ. Dist. Ct. 2010). The victims' claims were grounded not only in negligence for Tenet's failure to respond, but also for its failure to properly plan and prepare for the hurricane and city-wide flooding. James G. Hodge, Jr. & Erin F. Brown, *Assessing Liability for Health Care Entities That Insufficiently Prepare for Catastrophic Emergencies*, 306 JAMA 308 (2011).

Weeks after Dallas' Texas Presbyterian Hospital admitted that its staff's failures to properly diagnose and treat Thomas Eric Duncan for EVD (including possible data entry errors) may have contributed to his 2014 death, the hospital settled with his family for an undisclosed amount. Assoc. Press, *Texas: Ebola Victim's Family to be Paid by Hosp.*, N.Y. TIMES, Nov. 12, 2014. One of 2 nurses, Nina Pham, who became infected with EVD while treating Duncan, separately sued the hospital for current and future injuries. She alleged in part that the hospital's preparedness failures to safely treat Ebola patients through adequate protections for HCWs led to her own infection and injuries. Jennifer Emily, *Dallas Hosp.'s Owner Says Ebola Nurse Nina Pham's Lawsuit Should be Dismissed*, DALL. MORNING NEWS (April 3, 2015). A Texas Court of Appeals later denied Pham recovery for any of her claims. *Tex. Health Res. v. Pham*, No. 05–15–01283–CV, 2016 Tex. App. LEXIS 8336 (Aug. 3, 2016).

Nationally-publicized cases and other factors affect practitioners' attitudes. Multiple studies attest to the unwillingness of many HCWs to serve during emergencies when faced with the threat of potential liability. *See, e.g.*, Jonathan Ives et al., *Healthcare Workers' Attitudes to Working During Pandemic Influenza: A Qualitative Study*, 9 BMC PUB. HEALTH 56 (2009); Braylee Grisel et al., *The Ethical*

Obligation to Treat Infectious Patients: A Systematic Review of Reasons, CLINICAL INFECTIOUS DISEASES, Apr. 24, 2024. As a result, IOM recommended in 2009 that "state and local governments should explicitly tie existing liability protections (e.g., through immunity or indemnification) for health care practitioners and entities to crisis standards of care [CSC]." IOM, GUIDANCE FOR ESTABLISHING CSC FOR USE IN DISASTER SITUATIONS 49 (2009); *see also* IOM, CSC: A TOOLKIT FOR INDICATORS & TRIGGERS (2013).

Despite prevalent liability concerns and national recommendations, there is no comprehensive liability protection for HCWs, volunteers, or entities in all emergency settings. Instead, an array of federal and state liability protections apply selectively to practitioners and entities—particularly volunteers and government entities and officials—who act in good faith. Sharona Hoffman, *Responders' Responsibility: Liability & Immunity in PHEs*, 96 GEO. L. J. 1913 (2008). These laws, including EMAC (below), immunize or indemnify actors or entities from specific claims or monetary damages.

EMAC
All states and D.C. have executed the Emergency Management Assistance Compact (EMAC), Pub. L. No. 104–321, 110 Stat. 3877 (1996). EMAC provides strong liability protections for state or local agents (and deputized private actors) during declared emergencies. Additional protections stem from limited emergency waivers of sanctions or

fines for failing to comply with federal or state statutes.

The Public Readiness and Emergency Preparedness (PREP) Act, 42 U.S.C. § 247d–6d (2012), addresses liability risks in distributing or implementing federally-approved MCMs (e.g., medicines, vaccines, supplies). Upon a PREP Act declaration by HHS' Secretary, liability immunity is extended to covered persons, including federal officials, manufacturers, drug distributors, pharmacies, and state and local program planners, involved in the development, distribution, and administration of MCMs. The PREP Act also creates a compensation fund for individuals injured from the administration or use of covered MCMs.

Though broad, PREP Act liability protections apply for a limited period of time and only to acts that are negligent in nature, not intentional or criminal. A lower court decision in New York suggested that PREP Act liability protections do not immunize a school system or health practitioner involved in the alleged "bad faith" administration of the H1N1 vaccine to a minor student whose parents did not provide their consent. The case was reversed on appeal. *Parker v. St. Lawrence Cnty. Pub. Health Dep't*, 954 N.Y.S.2d 259 (App. Div. 2012); *see also Kehler v. Hood*, No. 4:11 CV 1416 FRB, 2012 WL 1945952 (E.D. Mo. May 30, 2012) (PREP Act barred product liability and failure to warn actions against vaccine manufacturer when the employer failed to obtain informed consent prior to administration of the H1N1 vaccine).

In *Garcia v. Welltower OpCo Group LLC*, No. SACV 20–02250(KESx), 2020 WL 492581 (C.D. Cal. Feb. 10, 2021), a federal court in California determined the PREP Act provided immunity in a suit against a nursing facility alleging elder abuse and neglect, wrongful death, and intentional infliction of emotional distress after a high-risk patient expired at the facility due to COVID-19 infection. The nursing facility argued it was shielded from liability. The court agreed, finding the defendants' actions fell within the scope of the PREP Act's immunity provisions.

In an Oregon case, the 9th Circuit Court of Appeals determined that PREP Act liability protections even negate federal constitutional claims under 42 U.S.C. § 1983 for alleged improper distributions of COVID-19 vaccinations. The claims centered on failures to distribute vaccines to prison inmates even through corrections workers in the facilities received doses. As per the court's decision in *Maney v. Brown*, 91 F.4th 1296 (9th Cir. 2024), "Congress intended to expressly immunize covered persons from § 1983 actions for claims covered by the [PREP] Act, even if [they] are federal constitutional claims."

Other courts have reached inapposite judgements, finding that the PREP Act does not preempt all claims, notably those grounded in state law. Richard H. Hughes, et al., *COVID-19 PREP Act Litigation: The Tip of the Liability Iceberg*, HEALTH AFFAIRS FOREFRONT (2023). For example, in *Saldana v.*

Glenhaven Healthcare, a family member of a nursing home resident raised state-based claims (e.g., elder abuse, willful misconduct, negligence, and wrongful death) alleging the facility failed to protect Saldana from COVID-19. The 9th Circuit determined that the PREP Act did not intend to "completely preempt all state-law claims related to the pandemic." *Saldana v. Glenhaven Healthcare*, 27 F.4th 679, 688 (9th Cir. 2022). *See also Manyweather v. Woodlawn Manor, Inc.*, No. 3:21–CV–1317 (U.S. Dist. Ct. W. Dist. La. 2022); *Estate of Joseph Maglioli v. Alliance HC Holdings, LLC*, No. 2:20–CV–06985 (3rd Cir. 2021).

Though inconsistent, the patchwork of federal, state, and local laws provides liability protections covering hundreds of thousands of practitioners, volunteers, and entities for acts of ordinary negligence under a collective umbrella (*see* Figure 11.6).

Figure 11.6. Umbrella of Liability Coverage

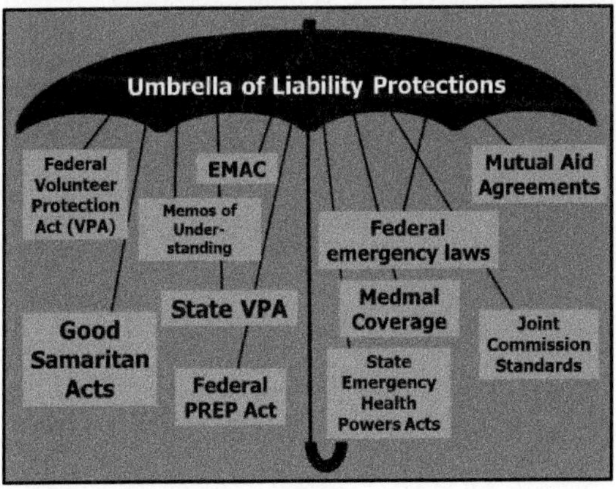

Like the PREP Act, virtually no liability protections immunize or indemnify practitioners or entities for acts that constitute gross negligence, willful or wanton misconduct, or crimes. In addition, fewer protections cover hospitals, clinics, pharmacies, and other health entities. TFAH, READY OR NOT?: PROTECTING THE PUB. HEALTH FROM DISEASES, DISASTERS & BIOTERRORISM 38–39 (2008).

Existing liability protections have neither satisfied all HCWs seeking complete immunity nor dissuaded patient-rights advocates wanting to preserve access to legal remedies for injuries or deaths arising from negligence. HCWs have consistently asked Congress to pass national, uniform liability protections that apply widely in declared emergencies, including during the COVID-19 pandemic.

Good Samaritan Health Professionals Act

The Good Samaritan Health Professionals Act, H.R. 1733, 113th Cong. (2013), was introduced initially on April 25, 2013, reintroduced in H.R. 865, 114th Cong. on February 11, 2015, and then again in 2017. H.R. 1876, 115th Cong. (2017). The Act would limit the liability of volunteer HCWs responding to a federal disaster, emergency, or PHE if they act on a "good faith belief" that a treated individual needed health care.

As federal and state governments implemented various liability protective laws, regulations, and executive orders during the COVID-19 pandemic, opposition resurfaced. Some commentators suggested medical malpractice immunity "threaten[s] the safety of our most vulnerable" by diluting HCWs' "sense of responsibility." Kay Van Wey, *COVID-19 Medical Malpractice Shield Laws Endanger Patients*, LAW360 (Aug. 24, 2020). Others questioned whether pandemic-related liability protections for HCWs should extend to treatment involving non-COVID patients. Betsy J. Grey & Samantha Orwoll, *Tort Immunity in the Pandemic*, 96 IND. L.J. SUPP. 66, 74 (2020); Tony Pugh & Lydia Wheeler, *Push to Expand Doctors' Legal Immunity for Virus Draws Ire*, BLOOMBERG L. (June 25, 2020). Extending the scope of protections to nursing facilities during the pandemic intimated they would be unaccountable later. Abigail Abrams, *'A License for Neglect.' Nursing Homes Are Seeking—& Winning—Immunity Amid the Coronavirus Pandemic*, TIME, May 14, 2020. Despite these views, the overwhelming majority of federal and state legislators and policymakers favor strong liability protections for HCWs (and even health care entities) during declared emergencies including the COVID-19 pandemic.

Following 9/11, biopreparedness legal reforms have transformed how all levels of government and private sector actors prepare for and respond to PHEs. Federal, state, and local government agencies reorganized. New classifications of PHEs emerged and were utilized. Emergency public health powers were clarified. Public health officials, emergency managers, and civil libertarians continue to debate the premises of existing and potential legal reforms.

Despite these efforts, emergency legal preparedness and response were "put to the test" during one of the greatest public health crisis in U.S. history—COVID-19. Consequently, profound legal and policy issues covered in Chapter 12 provide a capstone to the study and practice of emergency public health laws and policies for the 21st century.

	Chapter 11—Discussion Questions
?	1. How has the legal environment in emergency preparedness changed drastically since 9/11?
?	2. Why are interjurisdictional issues so prevalent concerning PHE preparedness & response efforts?
?	3. How do federal & state laws intersect or conflict during PHEs?
?	4. What are the primary roles for government in the practice of legal triage?
?	5. What are the ethical & legal ramifications of protecting HCWs from liability in PHEs?

CHAPTER 12

COVID-19 PANDEMIC: PUBLIC HEALTH EMERGENCY LAW & POLICY RESPONSES

	Chapter 12—Learning Objectives
✓	1. Examine unprecedented societal impacts of the COVID-19 pandemic
✓	2. Assess major law & policy challenges underlying one of the most significant public health crises in U.S. history
✓	3. Analyze core legislative, executive & judicial responses to protect the public's health from a highly infectious disease
✓	4. Consider pandemic legal responses on key issues including social distancing powers, vaccine allocation & CSC
✓	5. Explore potential shifts in U.S. emergency legal preparedness & response post-pandemic

As examined in Chapter 11, PHE preparedness and response present some of the most dynamic law and policy issues in the field of public health law. Prior PHEs like EVD, Zika virus, H1N1, and Hurricane Katrina raised difficult legal conundrums requiring real-time responses within the realm of legal triage. However, nothing approached the magnitude of PHEs like the COVID-19 pandemic of 2020–2023.

As the costliest public health threat ever in the U.S., the COVID-19 pandemic was *unprecedented.* On her retirement from CDC during the pandemic in 2021, U.S. Public Health Service Rear Admiral Dr. Anne Schuchat observed "[t]he COVID-19 pandemic has been as large a disrupter as a world war, and its effect on life expectancy exceeds any threat we have faced since the last 'great' pandemic of 1918." Anne Schuchat, *Op-ed: What I Learned in 33 Years at the CDC*, N.Y. TIMES, June 11, 2021.

Even as the virus at the source of the pandemic continues to mutate lending to its endemic status projected for years ahead coupled with occasional new outbreaks, core lessons have emerged. Dani Blum, *Covid Virus Continues to Evolve*, N.Y. TIMES, May 14, 2024. Critical legal and policy responses to COVID-19 exceed prior PHE responses, providing key observations and lessons in modern preparedness and response. Although severe politicization of public health legal interventions among U.S. political actors across all levels of government underscore the pandemic, these issues are largely covered outside this text.

A. UNPRECEDENTED PUBLIC HEALTH CHALLENGES & RESPONSES

Not since the Spanish flu pandemic in 1918–1919 had the world been impacted so extensively by an emerging infectious condition as COVID-19 (*see* Figure 12.1).

Figure 12.1. Coronavirus

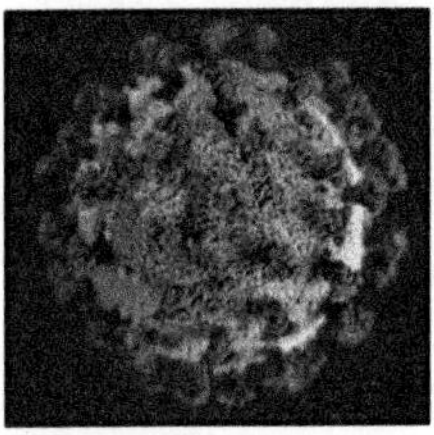

Arising from unidentified sources initially in Wuhan, China as early as late 2019, the COVID-19 pandemic began spreading globally in early 2020. Initial cases in the U.S. were believed to have emerged in specific locales as early as November 2019. Confirmed cases in cities like Seattle, New York, Phoenix, and Los Angeles were detected in January 2020, with rapid spread across the country commencing in February 2020.

COVID-19 is the disease caused by one of several deadly coronavirus strains. At the inception of the pandemic, its epidemiologic characteristics were indeterminate. This substantially affected global and national responses. Only through real-time epidemiologic assessments did the risks of COVID-19 transmission and infection materialize. As an infectious condition, it was more easily spread through airborne and other means than most strains of annual influenza. Gabriel G. Katul et al. *Global Convergence of COVID-19 Basic Reproduction Number & Estimation From Early-time SIR Dynamics*, 15(9) PLOS 1-e0239800 (2020). COVID-19 could also be transmitted through other routes, including via surface or other contacts.

About 80% of persons infected had no or mild symptoms, even though they were capable of transmitting the virus to others. Zunyou Wu & Jennifer M. McGoogan, *Summary of a Rep. of 72314 Cases from the Chinese Ctr. for Disease Control & Prevention*, 323 JAMA 1239 (2020). Symptomatic persons experienced reactions similar to annual flu, including extended periods of coughs, aches, fatigue, fever, and sore throats. Most persons' symptoms dissipated relatively quickly, generating a level of immunity along the way.

The extent to which COVID-19 infections may lead to long-term health complications years later is not fully known. CDC estimated that up to 20% of symptomatic persons had extended bouts of the disease, labeled "long" COVID-19 cases (*see* Figure 12.2). These persons suffered repeated cycles of illness, fatigue, mental impacts (e.g., depression, brain fog), and diminished physical capacities (e.g., loss of smell/taste, heart palpitations, respiratory distress). Additional concerns related to post-COVID conditions including increased risks for dementia, strokes, gastrointestinal, pulmonary, and other disorders have since emerged years after initial infections. Sumathi Reddy, *Mini-Strokes, Gut Problems: Scientists See Links to an Old Bout of Covid*, WALL ST. J., July 2, 2024. Why a subset of COVID-19 patients experienced these more extensive symptoms and outcomes is not medically clear, although some suggest these conditions may extend from inflammation caused initially by the virus.

Figure 12.2. Long COVID-19 Symptoms

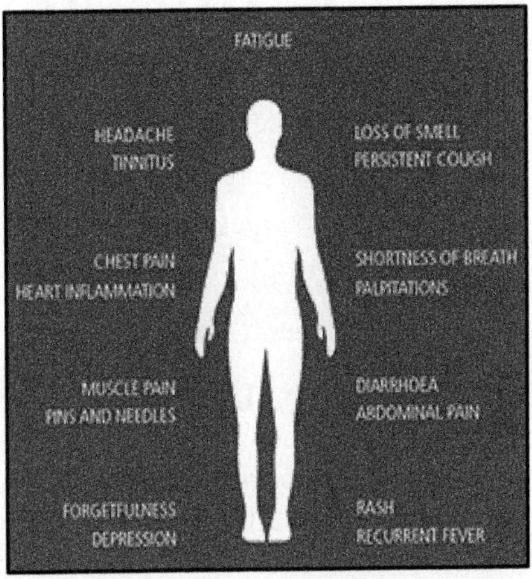

Source: WHO Reg'l Office for Eur. (2021).

Among symptomatic cases, millions of Americans suffered considerably greater health impacts, especially the elderly and persons with pre-existing conditions. Roughly 7% of infected persons required extended hospitalization. Lacking accurate tests, diagnoses, and efficacious treatments at the inception of the pandemic, patient surges quickly soared. WHO's Director-General Tedros Adhanom Ghebreyesus (Figure 12.3) formally declared COVID-19 a pandemic on March 11, 2020, signaling that this emerging infectious disease was a stealthy, global killer.

Figure 12.3. Dr. Adhanom Ghebreyesus

As documented below, U.S. public and private sector response efforts to quell COVID-19 were unparalleled. The numbers alone underlying the pandemic across America illustrate the magnitude of impacts and help explicate the scope and extent of law and policy interventions. Societal impacts of the COVID-19 pandemic in the U.S. included:

- Over 103 million cases and 1.184 million American deaths confirmed since February 2020—actual numbers of cases were likely far higher;
- COVID-19 related deaths in the U.S. occurred among every age range from 0–85+ years, with nearly 80% of deaths among persons aged 65 and older;
- Over the course of the pandemic, COVID-19 death rates among Black, Latino, and Indigenous Americans were more than twice the rate of White Americans;
- In 2020 and 2021, COVID-19 was the 3rd leading cause of mortality in the U.S. (after

heart disease and cancer). In 2022, COVID-19 was still 4th on this list despite widespread availability of vaccines;

- Approximately 17% of all confirmed COVID-19 deaths worldwide occurred in the U.S. even though it accounts for just over 4% of the global population;
- Over 6.88 million Americans required short-or-long-term hospitalization due to their COVID-19 infections;
- Approximately 750 million COVID-19 tests were distributed;
- Over 315 million Americans were placed under stay-home orders in April 2020 alone;
- Tens of millions of Americans were subjected directly to quarantine or isolation orders;
- Approximately 40% of Americans reported suffering mental health issues during the pandemic due in part to extensive social isolation;
- Among the U.S. public health workforce, 53% report suffering at least 1 significant mental health condition tied to the pandemic;
- More than 335 million doses of vaccines were administered in less than 7 months between January–July 2021, with 230 million Americans fully inoculated;

- U.S. economic losses were estimated to exceed $16 trillion, including direct federal expenditures;
- Direct infusions of federal stimulus funds to booster the economy and pay at risk Americans totaled more than $5.6 trillion;
- Over 1 million business closures occurred across the U.S.;
- More than 87 million Americans lost their jobs from January 2020 through May 2021;
- Nearly 86 million former workers in the U.S. sought unemployment benefits;
- Greater than 8 million U.S. households were unable to pay rent due to the pandemic;
- Over 50 million Americans experienced food insecurity at the height of the pandemic, resulting in unrivaled demands at food pantries;
- Average life expectancy of Americans dropped by over 2 years from 2019 (78.8 years) to 2021 (76.4 years) due largely to the pandemic, with greater decreases among racial and ethnic classes and vulnerable communities; and
- The highest annual increase in the U.S. overall mortality rate ever recorded (16%) occurred in 2020, exceeding even that of World War II and the 1918–1919 pandemic.

Extensive impacts from a singular infectious disease source in such a truncated period of time led to the most sensational emergency public health law and policy responses ever undertaken in the U.S., as described further below.

B. INVOCATION OF EMERGENCY PUBLIC HEALTH DECLARATIONS & POWERS

As the threat of morbidity and mortality from COVID-19 quickly escalated in early 2020 governments at all levels issued an extensive array of emergency declarations and measures never before employed in unison in the U.S. *See, e.g.*, Michelle M. Mello et al., *Legal Infrastructure for Pandemic Response: Lessons Not Learnt in the US*, 384 BMJ 1 (2024). The litany of emergency declarations began on January 31, 2020 when HHS declared a national PHE. Press Release, Alex Azar, HHS, Secretary Azar Declares PHE for U.S. for 2019 Novel Coronavirus (Jan. 31, 2020). This 90-day declaration was renewed 13 consecutive times until it was officially terminated on May 13, 2023 by President Biden facing pressure from Congress.

Coextensively, Secretary Azar initiated a separate declaratory process to invoke the federal PREP Act, providing extensive liability and other protections for persons and entities implementing federally-approved MCMs. *Declaration Under the PREP Act for MCMs Against COVID-19*, 85 Fed. Reg. 15198 (Mar. 17, 2020). PREP Act emergency measures were subsequently amended multiple times to include new guidance responding largely to developments surrounding COVID-19 vaccinations via Operation Warp Speed (discussed below).

By March 13, 2020, with significant public health and political pressures mounting as COVID-19 cases escalated exponentially, President Trump (Figure 12.4) issued concurrent emergency declarations under the Stafford Act and National Emergencies Act (*see* Chapter 11) authorizing manifold federal public health powers, substantial assistance to states and territories, and extensive economic remedies.

Figure 12.4. President Donald J. Trump

On March 20, President Trump also invoked the Defense Production Act, 50 U.S.C.A. § 4511(a) (2015), to allow federal control over specific manufacturing and distribution capacities in the private sector for certain products (e.g., ventilators, personal protective equipment). Later, on August 6, 2020, he clarified via Executive Order that COVID-19 was a national security threat. Exec. Order 13944, Combating PHEs & Strengthening Nat'l Security by Ensuring Essential Medicines, MCMs & Critical Inputs Are Made in the U.S., 85 Fed. Reg. 49929

(Aug. 6, 2020). Each of these federal emergency measures was renewed, recognized, or sustained for months, including after President Joe Biden (Figure 12.5) took office midstream through the pandemic in January 2021.

Figure 12.5. President Joseph R. Biden

State, territorial, tribal, and local governments declared their own series of emergencies. As illustrated in Figure 12.6 below, by the end of March 2020, every state Governor had concurrently issued emergency, disaster, or PHE declarations (*see* Chapter 11 for more information on these distinctions). As in prior events, some declared multiple types of emergencies. This marked the first time in U.S. history that all states were united in formally-declared states of emergency.

Figure 12.6. State and Territorial Emergency Declarations in Response to COVID-19

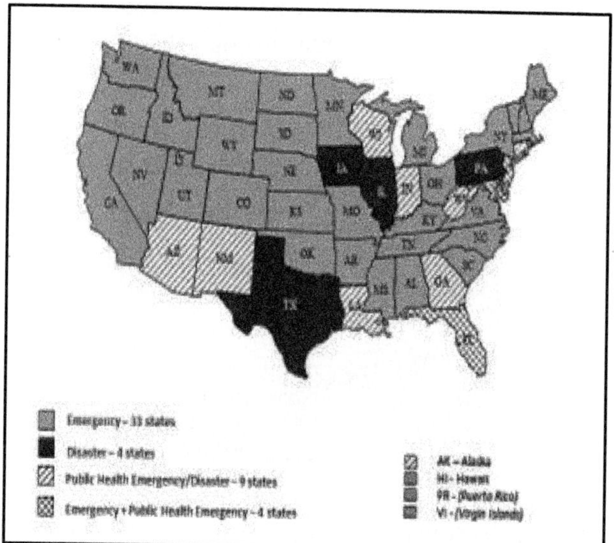

Source: JAMES G. HODGE, JR., COVID-19 EMERGENCY LEGAL PREPAREDNESS PRIMER (2021).

These declarations directly authorized a broad array of emergency legal authorities, supplemented by incident response plans, gubernatorial executive orders, real-time rule-making, and legislative proposals. James G. Hodge, Jr. et al., *COVID's Constitutional Conundrum: Assessing Individual Rights in PHEs*, 88 TENN. L. REV. 837 (2021). Efficacious public health interventions involving testing, screening, surveillance, contact tracing, treatment, and research were conducted extensively through expedited means. Essential supplies were secured through government contracts or select takings of private sector inventories.

Health care and public health responders were mobilized via interstate licensure allowances or waivers to work directly or via telemedicine in other states. Specific liability protections crafted in real-time during the pandemic provided immunity or indemnity for HCWs, volunteers, and entities against claims of ordinary negligence (*see* Chapter 11). *Liability Protections for Health Care Professionals During COVID-19*, AMA (Apr. 20, 2020).

As discussed below, medical standards of care shifted to accommodate crisis modes in hospitals, clinics, and other facilities. NASEM, RAPID EXPERT CONSULTATION ON STAFFING CONSIDERATIONS FOR CSC FOR THE COVID-19 PANDEMIC (July 28, 2020). Routine statutory or regulatory requirements governing health care, housing, transportation, employment, and other impacted sectors were eased or temporarily set aside to support emergency response efforts.

Among the most dynamic public health response powers, however, were those directly altering personal and social behaviors. As per Figure 12.7, a bevy of social distancing measures (referenced initially in Chapter 5) were legally-authorized and heavily used initially and then for varying intervals throughout the pandemic.

Figure 12.7. Social Distancing Measures

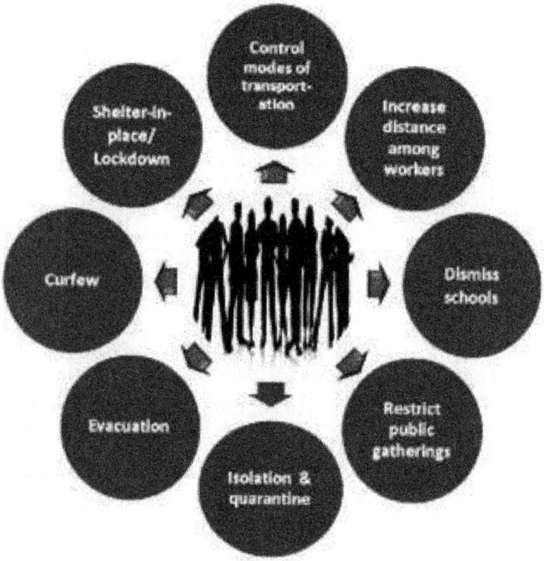

Each of these interventions was intended to create safe distances or spaces among persons who might otherwise unwittingly spread COVID-19. Every American was directly affected in their daily activities by these measures, including extensive closures in public and private sectors. Stay-at-home orders were issued for weeks in the Spring 2020 consistent with CDC guidance advising against social gatherings larger than 10 persons. CDC, INTERIM GUIDANCE: GET YOUR MASS GATHERINGS OR LARGE COMMUNITY EVENTS READY FOR COVID-19 (2020).

The collective impacts of these social distancing requirements were characterized by some policymakers and media as "lockdowns," although they never approached the level of social distancing measures deployed in other countries. In China, for example, tens of millions of persons were essentially roped off from society for months through heavily-enforced restrictions of their movements in 2020. K.H. Wan et al., *The End of 'Cordon Sanitaire' in Wuhan: The Role of Non-Pharmaceutical Interventions Against COVID-19*, 185 PUB. HEALTH 6, 6–7 (2020). Nevertheless, from early Spring to Summer 2020, Americans were asked or required to stay home, refrain from unnecessary travel, wear masks, and avoid most social contact. Non-essential businesses, schools, religious institutions, and other entities were temporarily shuttered or subjected to limited, non-contact operations.

At the inception of the pandemic when efficacious treatments and widespread vaccinations were unavailable, utilization of social distancing powers unquestionably tamped down infections and saved American lives. David Rubin et al., *Ass'n of Social Distancing, Population Density, & Temperature with the Instantaneous Reproduction Number of SARS-CoV-2 in Counties Across the U.S.*, 3 JAMA NETWORK OPEN, July 23, 2020, at 1–2. Researchers analyzing data from March–August 2020 positively associated social distancing measures with saving between 866,350 to 1,711,150 American lives. Olga Yakusheva et al., *Lives Saved and Lost in the First 6 Months of the US COVID-19 Pandemic: A*

Retrospective Cost-Benefit Analysis, 17 PLOS ONE 1 (Jan. 1, 2022).

Yet, widespread social distancing also led to profound political, judicial, and legislative responses among persons and entities objecting to perceived or actual infringements of their freedoms, rights, and economic interests. A resulting melee of legal challenges, discussed below, obfuscated emergency response efforts and redefined the challenges of legal triage in extended, real-time, catastrophic PHEs.

C. JUDICIAL CHALLENGES TO PHE INTERVENTIONS

Aggressive social distancing measures to combat COVID-19 were countered initially through substantial litigation. In *Wisconsin Legislature v. Palm*, 942 N.W.2d 900 (Wis. 2020), the state's supreme court invalidated the authority of the state's Secretary of Health (at the behest of the Wisconsin legislature) to issue stay-home and other emergency orders at the height of the pandemic. Under the court's reasoning, the Secretary failed to comply with proper administrative procedures despite being authorized by a prior executive order issued by Governor Tony Evers. Still, the order was deemed unconstitutional and state-wide restrictions were lifted (although Milwaukee and other larger municipalities maintained specific closure orders under their home rule). As a result, COVID-19 cases in Wisconsin escalated in the following weeks. *See* Nicholas Reimann, *Wisconsin Sees Coronavirus*

Spike 2 Weeks After Abrupt Reopening, FORBES (May 28, 2020).

American businesses and individuals filed thousands of cases in courts nationally to directly challenge PHE powers on multiple grounds. *See, e.g.*, Linda A. Sharp, *COVID-19 Related Litigation: Constitutionality of Stay-at-Home, Shelter-in-Place, and Lockdown Orders*, 55 A.L.R. FED. 3D ART. 3 (2020). They argued that extensive applications of social distancing powers infringed an array of constitutionally-protected interests including:

- **Religious free exercise rights:** *Tandon v. Newsom*, 593 U.S. 61 (2021) (rejecting California's restriction barring meetings of more than 3 families to worship in a private home as infringing 1st Amendment free exercise rights under strict scrutiny);
- **Establishment Clause:** *Calvary Chapel of Bangor v. Mills*, 459 F. Supp. 3d 273 (D. Me. 2020) (upholding executive orders limiting the size of religious gatherings to 10 people against 1st Amendment Establishment Clause challenge);
- **Freedom of speech:** *Geller v. de Blasio*, 613 F. Supp.3d 742 (S.D.N.Y. 2020) (affirming New York City's executive order banning non-essential gatherings against free speech challenge);
- **Rights to assemble:** *Ramsek v. Beshear*, 468 F. Supp. 3d 904 (E.D. Ky. 2020) (enjoining Kentucky Governor Andy Beshear's executive

order prohibiting mass gatherings as contrary to the 1st Amendment);

- **Freedom of association:** *Lebanon Valley Auto Racing Corp. v. Cuomo*, 478 F. Supp.3d 389 (N.D.N.Y. 2020) (upholding New York Governor Andrew Cuomo's executive order allowing racetracks to operate by limiting access to essential personnel);

- **Right to bear arms:** *Brandy v. Villanueva*, No. CV 20–02874–AB (SKx), 2020 WL 3628709 (C.D. Cal. Apr. 6, 2020) (denying request for a temporary restraining order based on 2nd Amendment objections of California emergency closure order applied to gun shops in Los Angeles);

- **Right to travel:** *Roberts v. Neace*, 457 F. Supp. 3d 595 (E.D. Ky. 2020) (enjoining a gubernatorial executive order restricting travel into and out of the state);

- **Reproductive rights:** *Preterm-Cleveland v. Att'y Gen. of Ohio*, 456 F. Supp. 3d 917 (S.D. Ohio 2020) (stopping Ohio COVID-19 restrictions on surgical abortions, concluding they unduly burdened the right to abortion);

- **Right against cruel and unusual punishment:** *Richard v. Pritzker*, No. 1:20–cv–0209, 2020 WL 1648584 (N.D. Ill. Apr. 2, 2020) (challenging Illinois Governor J.B. Pritzker's alleged failure to take necessary precautions to limit COVID-19 impacts in prisons as violating the 8th Amendment);

- **Right to privacy:** *Machovec v. Palm Beach Cnty.*, 310 So. 3d 941 (Fla. Dist. Ct. App. 2021) (allowing enforcement of a mask mandate in public places against a right to privacy challenge);
- **Equal protection:** *World Gym, Inc. v. Baker*, 474 F. Supp. 3d 426 (D. Mass. 2020) (upholding Massachusetts Governor Charlie Baker's order closing non-essential businesses against equal protection claim by business owners);
- **Takings challenges:** *Schulmerich Bells, LLC v. Wolf*, No. 2:20–cv–01637, 2020 WL 1486677 (E.D. Pa. Mar. 26, 2020) (arguing that Pennsylvania Governor Tom Wolf's executive order closing non-essential businesses violated the 5th Amendment takings clause);
- **Substantive and procedural due process:** *Xponential Fitness v. Arizona*, No. CV–20–01310–PHX–DJH, 2020 WL 3971908 (D. Ariz. July 14, 2020) (rejecting procedural due process arguments against Arizona Governor Doug Ducey's executive order closing fitness centers); and
- **Economic due process:** *Cnty of Butler v. Wolf*, 486 F. Supp.3d 883, 919–20 (W.D. Penn. 2020) (concluding that Pennsylvania's orders closing "non-life-sustaining" businesses violated due process. *See also* Jennifer L. Piatt, *A Balancing Act: Public Health,*

COVID-19 & the Economic Due Process "Right to Work," NEB. L. REV. BULL. (2021).

Overwhelmed by the volume, scope, and extent of claims, courts attempted to adjudicate them while implementing their own social distancing efforts to conduct safe proceedings during the pandemic. See, e.g., Michelle M. Mello et al., *Judicial Decisions Constraining Public Health Powers During COVID-19: Implications For Public Health Policy Making*, 43(6) HEALTH AFFAIRS 1 (2024). As per the cases listed above, their judgments varied drastically, but are generally classifiable in 2 distinct categories (*see* Figure 12.8).

Figure 12.8. Constitutional Approaches to COVID-19 Litigation

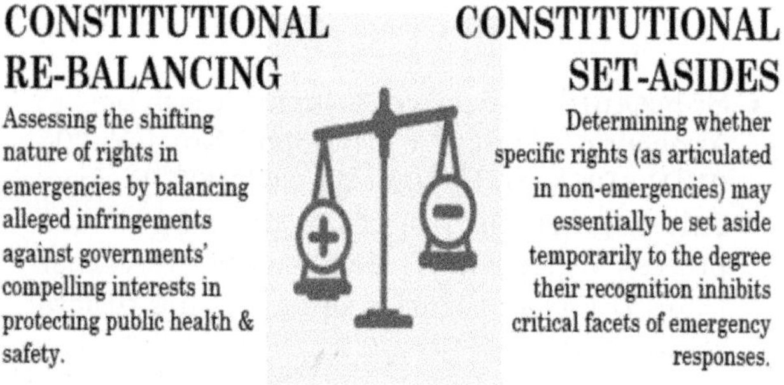

(1) *Constitutional re-balancing.* Most courts weighed assessments of individual rights against compelling governmental interests supporting public health efforts to respond to COVID-19. Judges attempted to re-conceive or re-calibrate individual

rights under emergency circumstances. They recognized that rights are not absolute, but rather subject to manifold restraints especially in emergencies. As a federal district court in California explained, "[t]he right to expressive association is not an absolute right and can be infringed upon if that infringement is: (1) unrelated to the suppression of expressive association; (2) due to a compelling government interest; and (3) narrowly tailored." *See Givens v. Newsom*, 459 F. Supp. 3d 1302, 1312–1315 (E.D. Cal. 2020) quoting *Legacy Church v. Kunkel*, 455 F. Supp. 3d 1100, 1159 (D.N.M. 2020).

Within the broader classification of re-balancing efforts, courts diverged considerably on whether to apply: (a) deferential tests to assess alleged rights-based infringements due to COVID-19 public health interventions via the Supreme Court's prior guidance in *Jacobson v. Massachusetts* (*see* Chapter 3) or other emergency assessments; or (b) traditional tiered analyses, reviewing infringements under rational basis, intermediate, or strict scrutiny (*see* Chapter 2). Some jurists incorporated traditional scrutiny along with *Jacobson*-themed analyses in their decisions. *See, e.g.*, *Ass'n of Jewish Camp Operators v. Cuomo*, 470 F. Supp. 3d 197, 217 (N.D.N.Y. 2020) (rejecting due process and free exercise challenges to executive orders prohibiting overnight summer camp operations during the pandemic).

(2) *Constitutional set-asides*. A select, minority of courts took a different approach in assessing COVID-19 legal challenges, concluding that some individual rights may be temporarily set-aside in emergencies.

In the appellate case, *In re Abbott*, 954 F.3d 772, 778 (5th Cir. 2020), *vacated as moot by Planned Parenthood v. Abbott*, 141 S. Ct. 1261 (2021), Texas Governor Greg Abbott issued executive orders limiting surgical procedures, including most abortions, during the pandemic. After a series of constitutional challenges were dispensed by the lower court, the 5th Circuit Court of Appeals in New Orleans (Figure 12.9) reviewed and permitted the temporary regulations. In declared emergencies, surmised the court, all constitutional rights may be "reasonably restricted."

Figure 12.9. 5th Circuit Court of Appeals

In *Binford v. Sununu*, No. 217–2020–CV–00152, at 15 (N.H. Super. Ct. Mar. 25, 2020), New Hampshire Governor Chris Sununu's social distancing orders prohibiting gatherings of more than 50 people were challenged on 1st Amendment freedom of assembly and free exercise grounds. In a terse decision the court rejected traditional tiered scrutiny analysis. Instead it deferred to a prior decision, *Smith v. Avino*,

91 F.3d 105, 109 (11th Cir. 1996) *abrogated on other grounds by Steel Co. v. Citizens for a Better Env't*, 523 U.S. 83 (1998). In *Smith*, a federal appellate court analyzed the constitutionality of an emergency curfew in Florida during Hurricane Andrew in 1992. It found that an executive agent's good faith action taken with some factual basis supported by necessity is constitutional even if individual freedoms are temporarily restricted. The court in *Binford* concurred, finding Governor Sununu's order "sufficiently analogous to a curfew in response to a riot or natural disaster," *Binford* at 15, and thus in alliance with 1st Amendment principles. Under the court's view, these rights were not outweighed by necessity. Rather, they were simply put aside. In response to the decision, the New Hampshire legislature passed a bill to disallow emergency suspensions of any civil liberty guaranteed under federal or state constitutions. H.B. 440, 2022 Reg. Sess. (N.H. 2022). It was signed into law on April 4, 2022. N.H. REV. STAT. ANN. § 4:45.

Judicial attempts to assess complex and sometimes novel constitutional claims challenging emergency response efforts during the COVID-19 pandemic were problematic. Courts setting aside constitutional arguments in the throes of the emergency had little precedential support. As the U.S. Supreme Court acknowledged in *Jacobson*, constitutionally-protected rights cannot be ignored or obliterated during emergencies. 197 U.S. at 31. During the COVID-19 pandemic, the Court clarified how constitutional norms remain intact even in crises. *S. Bay U. Pentecostal Church v. Newsom*, 140

S. Ct. 1613 (2020) [hereinafter *South Bay I*]. Contrary decisions among lower courts created opportunities for warrantless governmental interventions inviolate of individual freedoms and unmoored from science, best practices, or efficacy.

Courts attempting to re-balance individual constitutional rights during the pandemic faced other shortcomings. Litigants often argued claims based on fixed notions of what rights mean outside the emergency context. In *Carmichael v. Ige*, 470 F. Supp. 3d 1133, 1145 (D. Haw. 2020), litigants claimed Hawaii Governor David Ige's emergency quarantine order infringed their rights to travel. The federal district court demurred, admonishing litigants for "characteriz[ing] the 14-day travel quarantine as a travel ban when it is not."

Courts attempting to balance emergency powers and individual rights also became embroiled in second-guessing the emergency expertise of public health agencies, implicating separation of powers principles (*see* Chapter 2). Resulting complexities were illustrated in a series of cases decided by the U.S. Supreme Court beginning in mid-2020. On May 29, 2020, the Court held in *South Bay I* that California's COVID-19 temporary limitations on religious assemblies outweighed congregants' 1st Amendment religious freedoms. As Chief Justice John Roberts noted:

> "Our Constitution principally entrusts '[t]he safety and the health of the people' to the politically accountable officials of the States 'to guard and protect.' . . . [T]hey should not be

> subject to second-guessing by an 'unelected federal judiciary,' which lacks the background, competence, and expertise to assess public health and is not accountable to the people."

140 S. Ct. 1613–14 (quoting *Jacobson*, 197 U.S. 11, 38 (1905)). On July 24, 2020, the Court denied an emergency petition in a similar claim by a religious institution in Nevada. *Calvary Chapel Dayton Valley v. Sisolak*, 140 S. Ct. 2603 (2020).

Yet, just 4 months later on November 25, the Court (with newly-arrived Justice Amy Coney Barrett) struck down a New York State measure impacting places of worship as contrary to the free exercise of religion. *Roman Catholic Diocese of Brooklyn v. Cuomo*, 592 U.S. 14, 20 (2020). "Even if the Constitution has taken a holiday during this pandemic," concurred Justice Gorsuch (Figure 12.10), "it cannot become a sabbatical." *Id.* at 23.

Figure 12.10. Justice Neil Gorsuch

Then, on February 5, 2021, the Court declared unconstitutional California's prohibition of indoor religious services, essentially reversing its Opinion in the same case just months earlier. *S. Bay U. Pentecostal Church v. Newsom*, 141 S. Ct. 716 (2021) [*South Bay II*].

The Court's decision in *South Bay II* greatly limited the capacity of states or localities to apply closure orders to religious institutions similar to other assemblies. Just days after its issuance, California officials lifted assembly limits applied solely to religious entities while retaining restrictions on similar gatherings outside the protection of the 1st Amendment. David G. Savage & Alex Wigglesworth, *Some California Churches Will Reopen Sunday After Supreme Court Lifts Ban on Indoor Services*, L.A. TIMES (Feb. 6, 2021).

Consequences of the Court's mid-pandemic reversal of its approach to balancing 1st Amendment free exercise rights and PHE powers were telling. As Justice Kagan (Figure 12.11) observed in dissent, "[i]t is difficult enough in a predictable legal environment to craft COVID policies that keep communities safe. That task becomes harder still when ' "adrift" ' officials must guess which restrictions this Court will choose to strike down." *South Bay II*, 141 S. Ct. at 723 (2021) (Kagan, J., dissenting).

Figure 12.11. Justice Elena Kagan

In the end, as courts sought to navigate their way through rights-based claims against PHE interventions, utilization of divergent tactics led to unpredictable outcomes obscuring the scope and execution of emergency powers. As courts struggled to cope with the enormity of legal issues they faced during the pandemic, they produced a body of non-uniform decisions with varying precedential impacts on future executions of PHE powers. *See, e.g.*, James G. Hodge, Jr. et al., *State PHE Powers in Response to COVID-19*, 113 AJPH 275 (2023).

D. LEGAL OBJECTIONS TO CRISIS STANDARDS OF CARE

Through multiple waves of infections over the course of the COVID-19 pandemic, hospitals and other health care providers were repeatedly overwhelmed with an influx of patients. Robert D. Truog et al., *The Toughest Triage—Allocating Ventilators in a Pandemic*, 382 NEJM 1973, 1973–75 (2020). Especially in U.S. urban areas where COVID-

19 cases were initially concentrated, patient surges had the capacity to shift hospitals from conventional/contingency standards of care to implementation of "crisis standards of care," or CSC (*see* Figure 12.12).

Figure 12.12. Shifting to CSC

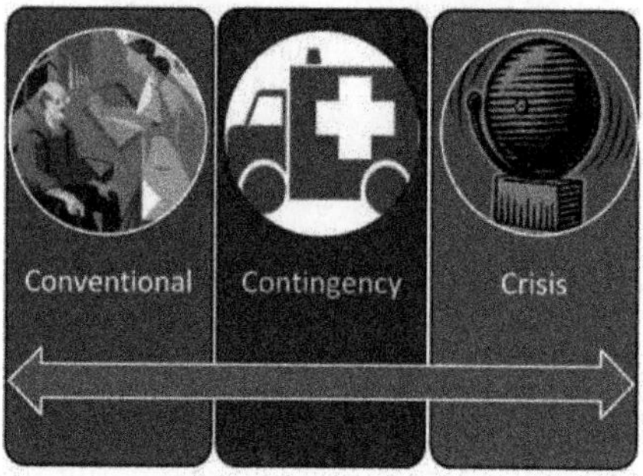

In 2009 IOM defined CSC as a "substantial change in usual health care operations and the level of care it is possible to deliver," typically triggered by a formally declared pervasive or catastrophic disaster. IOM, *Guidance for Establishing CSC for Use in Disaster Situations* (2009). In the ensuing decade, most states, many large urban areas, and specific hospitals crafted CSC plans for use in declared emergencies. While selective CSC plans in specific jurisdictions were invoked previously, extensive implementation of CSC emerged during the pandemic. Hospitals and other health entities struggling to determine appropriate allocations of scarce resources in treating scores of patients during the COVID-19 pandemic turned to these plans for explicit guidance. As they did, resulting disparities in treatments led to substantial legal and ethical issues.

Lacking uniform, express federal guidelines for rationing care in emergencies, state CSC plans and policies included specific provisions for allocating ventilators (a.k.a. "vents") or other resources when demand exceeded supply. The goal was to allocate these limited resources to save lives in emergencies based on affirmative, medically-sound guidance. Allocation decisions regarding vents and other scarce resources (e.g., ECMO machines) were wrenching. Smaller U.S. hospitals lacking vents were forced to make critical choices early on in the pandemic. Even in larger, well-supplied hospitals, shortages of trained staff meant there were fewer persons to operate vents or other medical interventions. U.S. HHS, OFF. INSPECTOR GEN., HOSP. EXPERIENCES RESPONDING TO THE COVID-19 PANDEMIC: RESULTS OF A NAT'L PULSE SURV. MAR. 23–27 (2020).

In March 2020, several major U.S. hospitals resorted to using alternative oxygen devices to help COVID-19 patients breathe. Mark Maremont, *Lacking Ventilators, Hosp. Seek Out Alternative Device*, WALL ST. J. (Mar. 25, 2020, 2:39 PM). COVID-19 case surges in early summer 2020 led Arizona's health department to amend and activate its CSC plan on June 29 as hospitals faced dire shortages of ICU beds. Stephanie Innes, *Arizona Hosp. Have COVID-19 Surge Plans, But Do They Have the Staffing & Supplies?*, AZ CENT. (June 15, 2020).

Determining which patients received vents—literally "life or death" decisions—led to highly-divergent approaches. Some CSC plans required doctors to "color code" who received vents based on their likelihood of survival and manifold other factors. Doctors in other settings assessed at-risk COVID-19 patients pursuant to their Sequential Organ Failure Assessment (SOFA) scores (*see* Figure 12.13). *See, e.g.*, Emily C. Cleveland Manchanda et al., *CSC in the USA: A Systematic Review & Implications for Equity Amidst COVID-19*, J. RACIAL & ETHNIC HEALTH DISPARITIES, Aug. 13, 2020, at 1, 8.

Figure 12.13. SOFA Scoring Sys.

Organ System, Measurement	SOFA Score				
	0	1	2	3	4
Respiration PaO_2/FiO_2, mmHg	Normal	<400	<300	<200 (with respiratory support)	<100 (with respiratory support)
Coagulation Platelets $x10^3/mm^3$	Normal	<150	<100	<50	<20
Liver Bilirubin, mg/dL (µmol/l)	Normal	1.2-1.9 (20-32)	2.0-5.9 (33-101)	6.0-11.9 (102-204)	>12.0 (<204)
Cardiovascular Hypotension	Normal	MAP<70 mmHg	Dopamine ≤5 or dobutamine (any dose)**	Dopamine >5 or epinephrine ≤0.1 or norepinephrine ≤0.1	Dopamine >15 or epinephrine >0.1 or norepinephrine >0.1
Central Nervous System Glasgow Coma Score	Normal	13-14	10-12	6-9	<6
Renal Creatinine, mg/dL (µmol/l) or Urine output	Normal	1.2-1.9 (110-170)	2.0-3.4 (171-299)	3.5-4.9 (300-440) or <500 mL/day	>5.0 (>440) or <200 mL/day

Source: ASPR TRACIE, SOFA Score: What It Is & How to Use It in Triage 4 (2020).

Other CSC plans proposed lottery systems. Joanne Kenen, *A Lottery for Ventilators? Hosp. Prepare for Ethical Conundrums*, POLITICO (Mar. 27, 2020). Some hospitals and other health systems essentially allocated vents or other resources on a "first-come, first-served" basis or via other *ad hoc* approaches.

Many CSC plans, however, attempted to prioritize patients based on their survivability using factors including age, disability status, SOFA scores, or other measurable factors. As hospitals and health professionals implemented CSC plans, allegations quickly surfaced that existing approaches violated antidiscrimination protections via the ADA, Rehabilitation Act, ACA, and other federal or state anti-discrimination laws. George P. Smith, II, *CSC & Triage: Medico-Legal Conundrums*, 128 PENN. ST. L. REV. 751 (2024). Legal complaints were filed with HHS/OCR largely by entities representing disabled persons in multiple states (e.g., AL, AZ, CT, KS, MA, PA, TN, UT, & WA).

Alabama's Emergency Operations Plan included provisions (crafted prior to the pandemic) to allocate vents in PHEs. ALA. DEP'T PUB. HEALTH, ANNEX TO ESF 8 OF ALA. EMERGENCY OPS. PLAN, CRITERIA FOR MECHANICAL VENT TRIAGE FOLLOWING

PROCLAMATION OF MASS-CASUALTY RESPIRATORY EMERGENCY (2010). The protocol listed several health conditions, including heart failure and respiratory failure, for which providers should "not offer mechanical ventilator support." *Id.* at 7–9. It also explicitly stated that "persons with severe mental retardation, advanced dementia or severe traumatic brain injury may be poor candidates for ventilator support." *Id.* at 8. After disability rights entities complained to OCR in March 2020 that persons with intellectual disabilities were expressly excluded from receiving vents, Alabama health authorities quickly altered the plan. *See OCR Reaches Early Case Resolution with Alabama After It Removes Discriminatory Ventilator Triaging Guidelines*, HHS (Apr. 8, 2020).

In Tennessee, specific patients with metastatic cancer, dementia, traumatic brain injuries, or advanced neuromuscular disease requiring assistance with activities of daily living or chronic vent support could be denied access to critical care. TENN. ALTERED STANDARDS OF CARE WORKGROUP, GUIDANCE FOR THE ETHICAL ALLOCATION OF SCARCE RESOURCES DURING A COMMUNITY-WIDE PHE 5 (2016). Challenges to plans like these centered on the possibility that hospitals could remove or deny vents from disabled patients with varying conditions, lending to negative health repercussions or death.

Guidance distributed by the Washington State Department of Health recommended triage teams consider transferring hospital patients with "loss of reserves in energy, physical ability, cognition and general health" to outpatient or palliative care. Age, underlying diseases, and likelihood of survival may be used to determine which patients receive full access to care versus mere "comfort care." WASH. STATE DEP'T OF HEALTH & N.W. HEALTHCARE RESPONSE NETWORK, SCARCE RESOURCE MGMT. & CSC 3–5 (2020). Disability rights advocates alleged the guidelines illegally discriminated against people with disabilities in setting priorities to treat younger, healthy persons.

On March 28, 2020, OCR issued guidance on civil rights laws applying during the COVID-19 emergency. *Bulletin: Civil Rights, HIPAA & the Coronavirus Disease 2019*, HHS OCR (Mar. 28, 2020). Multiple, additional investigations were launched of state-based CSC plans potentially contravening federal law. Sheri Fink, *U.S. Civil Rights Office Rejects Rationing Medical Care Based on Disability, Age*, N.Y. TIMES, Mar. 28, 2020. Classifying some CSC measures as "ruthless utilitarianism," OCR sought immediate adjustments in several state plans (as noted above) and issued ongoing guidance to correct others. *Id.* For example, OCR worked with Utah state authorities to legally adjust its CSC plan, including:

- Disallowing use of a patient's long-term life expectancy, resource-intensity, and duration of need as allocation factors;
- Removing categorical exclusion criteria on the basis of age, disability, and functional impairment in favor of "an individualized assessment based on the best available objective medical evidence;"
- Reasonable modifications for considering patients with underlying disabilities;
- Protecting against "steering" patients into agreeing to withdrawals or withholdings of life-sustaining treatment;
- Providing patients or their surrogates with information on treatment alternatives;
- Prohibiting blanket "Do Not Resuscitate" policies due to limited resources, or requiring patients to consent to specific plans; and
- Eliminating hospitals' re-allocations of personal vents brought by disabled patients for their own use.

OCR Resolves Complaint with Utah After It Revised CSC to Protect Against Age & Disability Discrimination, HHS (2020).

While disability rights were at the forefront of initial concerns among advocates, allegations of discrimination based on age, race, color, national origin, limited English proficiency, and sex also arose, leading to specific, additional OCR guidance and substantial modifications by states, localities, and hospitals. *See* Jennifer L. Piatt & James G. Hodge, Jr., *Issue Brief, CSC: Legal Issues Underlying Key Decisions Regarding Scarce Resources*, NETWORK FOR PUB. HEALTH L. (June 29, 2021).

E. REAL-TIME DEVELOPMENT & DISTRIBUTION OF VACCINES

One of the greatest achievements in response to the COVID-19 pandemic came through Operation Warp Speed. This multi-agency program aligned public and private sectors to research, develop, test, and authorize effective vaccines. *Trump Administration Announces Framework & Leadership for 'Operation Warp Speed,'* HHS (2020). In less than 8 months, pharmaceutical companies including Pfizer,® Moderna,® and Janssen,® a division of Johnson & Johnson®, produced multiple safe and efficacious COVID-19 vaccines. FDA issued several EUAs making these vaccines available to Americans beginning in December 2020. Allocating and administering the vaccines nationally became the central challenge, as well as monitoring them for safety and efficacy through the federal Vaccine Adverse Event Reporting System.

Under President Biden's national COVID-19 strategy, beginning in January 2021 the U.S. engaged in the most extensive vaccine campaign in its history through national efforts to inoculate eligible Americans (e.g., most persons over 12 years old). WHITE HOUSE, NAT'L STRATEGY FOR THE COVID-19 RESPONSE & PANDEMIC PREPAREDNESS (2021).

FEMA opened dozens of vaccine clinics. HHS aligned with national drug store chains to distribute vaccines. *See, e.g.*, James G. Hodge, Jr. et al., *Legal Challenges Underlying COVID-19 Vaccinations*, 49(3) JLME 495 (2021).

Massive federal distributions of free vaccines to states, tribal governments, and localities were doled out with expectations they would follow pre-existing ethical guidance issued by NASEM and relied on heavily by CDC. *A Framework for Equitable Allocation of Vaccine for the Novel Coronavirus*, NASEM (Sept. 1, 2020). Multiple jurisdictions, however, deviated from ethical guidelines, resulting in political battles and legal challenges.

For example, in *Maney v. Brown*, No. 20–cv–00570, 2021 WL 354384 (D. Or. Feb. 2, 2021), a federal district court ruled that inmates in Oregon must be offered COVID-19 vaccines at the earliest date for eligibility in the states' vaccination plan assimilating federal guidance. Failing to inoculate inmates, even as corrections employees and persons living and working in congregate care settings were offered vaccines, reflected deliberate indifference to the serious risk of harm faced by inmates in violation of the 8th Amendment.

Despite distributing and administering hundreds of millions of doses of vaccines ahead of schedule between January–June 2021, nearly ½ the U.S. population (and approximately ¼ of HCWs) still remained unvaccinated as of July 1. Recognizing a downturn in inoculations, President Biden pled further with Americans to get vaccinated, but refused to back mandates (even for the military or federal workers) or support passports. Michael D. Shear & Noah Weiland, *Biden Calls for Door-to-Door Vaccine Push; Experts Say More Is Needed*, N.Y. TIMES, July 7, 2021. These and other law and policy issues severely threatened U.S. efforts to reach herd immunity as vaccine uptake tapered off in mid-Summer 2021 (*see* Figure 12.14) even as new strains of coronavirus spread nationally.

Figure 12.14. U.S. COVID-19 Vaccine Uptake Jan.–June 2021.

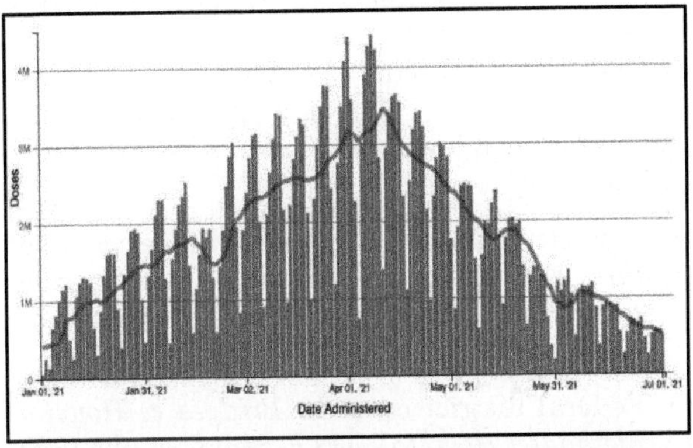

Source: CDC, COVID Data Tracker: Trends in Number of COVID-19 Vaccinations in the U.S. (July 6, 2021).

Controversial legal issues surrounded employer-based vaccine mandates. These mandates can be highly effective in increasing vaccinations, especially in health care industries. Reed Abelson, *More Hospitals Are Requiring Workers to Get COVID Vaccines*, N.Y. TIMES, July 22, 2021. Though contested at times, employer vaccine mandates were largely determined to be lawful consistent with EEOC approvals. *What You Should Know About COVID-19 & the ADA, the Rehabilitation Act & Other EEO Laws*, EEOC (May 28, 2021). Still, some employees objected on grounds that COVID-19 vaccines were not fully approved by FDA, and thus could not be legally-mandated.

The Food, Drug, and Cosmetic Act, 21 U.S.C.A. § 360bbb–3(e)(1)(A)(ii)(III) (2017), expressly allows Americans to refuse EUA vaccines. This provision, however, generally refers to avoiding compulsory, non-consensual vaccine measures. To the extent that employer-based vaccine requirements incentivize participation, and do not physically compel inoculations, employers may lawfully issue mandates as per the opinions of the:

- U.S. Department of Justice (*Whether § 564 of the FDCA Act Prohibits Entities from Requiring the Use of a Vaccine Subject to an EUA*, 45 Op. O.L.C., July 6, 2021); and
- Federal district court in *Bridges v. Houston Methodist Hospital*, 543 F. Supp. 3d 525 (S.D. Tex. 2021), *aff'd sub nom. Bridges v. Methodist Hosp.*, No. 21–20311, 2022 WL 2116213 (5th Cir. 2022) (rejecting employee's arguments that her hospital's COVID-19 vaccination mandate was unlawful).

Based in part on these legal interpretations, surging levels of infections, and sluggish vaccination rates, President Biden, federal agencies, and multiple state governors issued vaccine mandates for governmental employees, HCWs, employees of larger businesses, military, and others beginning in the latter part of 2021. Michael V. Shear, *Biden to Require COVID Vaccine or Regular Testing for Federal Employees*, N.Y. TIMES, July 29, 2021.

In January 2022, SCOTUS ruled that OSHA lacked regulatory authority to require large employers to ensure the vaccination status of millions of workers (despite OSHA's mandate allowing employees to opt-out). *Nat'l Fed'n of Indep. Bus. v. OSHA*, 595 U.S. 109 (2022). Simultaneously, the Court sustained a similar mandate issued via CMS for HCWs as a valid exercise of federal spending powers. *Biden v. Missouri*, 595 U.S. 87 (2022). Separate legal challenges to the President's capacities to mandate COVID-19 vaccines for employees and the military were never fully resolved as the federal PHE declaration ended in May 2023, rendering the cases moot.

Some governments and private industries turned to "vaccine passports" to require proof of inoculation as a prerequisite to the provision or receipt of services. Vaccination verification is common in many settings, including international travel. Vaccine passports related to COVID-19, however, were problematic. The federal government refused to expressly adopt vaccination passports or systems. While states like California and New York generated online vaccine passports for residents and businesses to use, Americans' concerns over privacy and autonomy contributed to legislative bans of passports in Alabama, Florida, Texas, and other states.

Requiring COVID-19 vaccines within schools and universities implicated other legal issues. As noted in Chapter 4, every state annually requires children in schools, daycares, and other settings to be vaccinated for various conditions (e.g., measles, mumps, rubella). Requiring vaccinations for COVID-19, however, was legally complicated by the tentative status of the vaccines as FDA-authorized, but not approved. Some states like Arkansas legislatively forbid school-based COVID-19 vaccine mandates. H.B. 1547, 93rd Gen. Assemb., Reg. Sess. (Ark. 2021).

Among American colleges and universities, COVID-19 vaccine requirements varied extensively ahead of the Fall 2021 semester. The American College Health Association fully recommended COVID-19 vaccine requirements (with specific exemptions) for on-campus students. Hundreds of higher education institutions set vaccine mandates for faculty, staff, and students, but others were reticent to follow. Elizabeth Redden, *Vaccine Politics*, INSIDE HIGHER ED (Apr. 30, 2021). Arizona Governor Ducey and the state legislature jointly pursued legal actions to prohibit such requirements. *See* James G. Hodge, Jr. et al., *Vaccinating Urban Populations in Response to COVID-19: Legal Challenges & Options*, 49 FORDHAM URBAN L. J. 1 (2021).

On July 18, 2021, a federal district court judge in Indiana denied a request for a preliminary injunction by several students challenging Indiana University's vaccination requirements. *Klaassen v. Trs. of Ind.*

Univ., 549 F. Supp.3d 836 (N.D. Ind. 2021). Judge Damon R. Leichty rejected students' claims of infringements of liberty interests under the 14th Amendment due process clause, as well as 1st Amendment violations of religious free exercise interests, extending from the university's vaccine mandate. After exploring the risks of COVID-19 infection, utility and safety of available vaccines, and the merits of students' arguments, the court determined the university can "pursue a reasonable and due process of vaccination in the legitimate interest of public health." *Id.* at 843. A subsequent appeal was later denied as moot. *Klaassen v. Trs. of Ind. Univ.*, 24 F.4th 638, 640 (2022).

Even as employer mandates, passports, or school requirements for COVID-19 vaccines took hold, they constitutionally exempted persons at direct risk of harm from vaccination (e.g., persons who are allergic or immuno-compromised). The U.S. Supreme Court clarified this liberty-based exception to general vaccine requirements in *Jacobson v. Massachusetts* (*see* Chapter 3). As discussed in Chapter 4, religious, philosophical, or other exemptions from vaccine requirements are largely a matter of law and policy, and not constitutional requirements. Failures to abide by religious exceptions, however, engendered constitutional challenges under 1st Amendment free exercise principles. Courts differed in their approaches related to religious exceptions. To date SCOTUS has not affirmed that the 1st Amendment requires religious exemptions to neutral vaccine requirements.

Long-standing, engrained notions of vaccine hesitancy among Americans (discussed in Chapter 4) resurfaced over perceived safety risks and personal liberty violations underlying the COVID-19 vaccine campaign. Fueled by false or misleading messaging largely by anti-vax entities via social media, widespread resistance to COVID-19 vaccines directly tamped down their uptake. *See, e.g.*, Jennifer L. Piatt & Erica N. White, *Misinformation Overload & the New Legal Landscape Surrounding COVID-19 Vaccines*, 19 SCITECH LAWYER 4 (2023). In July 2021, U.S. Surgeon General Dr. Vivek Murthy called on social media outlets to address rampant misinformation on their sites. Sheryl Gay Stolberg & Davey Alba, *Misinformation of Health Is Called an 'Urgent Threat,'* N.Y. TIMES, July 16, 2021.

Governments wielded specific educational efforts toward younger persons and others politically-disinclined to seek vaccines. These efforts, however, carried additional risks. When Tennessee's top immunization official, Dr. Michelle Fiscus, urged teens to get vaccinated through media campaigns and other messaging, she was dismissed allegedly due to pressure from state legislators. Rick Rojas, *Tennessee Virus Official Who Urged Shots for Teens Says She Was Forced Out*, N.Y. TIMES, July 14, 2021. She joined dozens of other leading state and local health officials across the nation who quit, resigned, retired, or were fired during the pandemic amid political or public pressure. Nadia Kounang, *The Pandemic Has Pushed More Than 250 Public Health Officials out the Door*, CNN HEALTH, May 23, 2021.

Public and private sectors also implemented a novel series of innovations to encourage vaccinations. These included direct payments, gifts, event tickets, raffles, and giveaways as well as dispensing liquor (LA, NJ) and even marijuana joints (AZ, WA) in exchange for persons willing to be vaccinated. Like other states (e.g., CA, CO, OR), Ohio established a "vaccine lottery" offering several $1 million payouts or full-ride in-state college scholarships to individuals newly seeking COVID-19 immunizations. Sarah Mervosh, *Who Wants to be a Millionaire? In Ohio, You Just Need Luck & Covid Vaccine*, N.Y. TIMES, June 3, 2021. Whether lotteries encouraged sufficient numbers of reluctant persons to get vaccinated, however, was unclear. Allan J. Walkey et al., *Lottery-Based Incentive in Ohio & COVID-19 Vaccination Rates*, JAMA, July 2, 2021, at E1, E2.

Potential liability for COVID-19 vaccine-related injuries captured policymakers' concerns and media attention as vaccines rolled out to states and territories. These concerns were largely dispelled through strong federal and state emergency liability protections. The afore-mentioned federal PREP Act insulated persons or entities from liability claims related to the manufacture or administration of vaccines and other MCMs, except in cases of willful misconduct. Declaration Under the PREP Act for MCMs Against COVID-19, 85 Fed. Reg. 15,198 (Mar. 17, 2020). Americans (or their families) suffering a serious physical injury or death directly related to their vaccination were eligible for select benefits through the federal Countermeasures Injury

Compensation Program so long as requests were filed within 1 year of receiving the vaccine. Apoorva Mandavilli, *Could the Covid-19 Vaccines Have Caused Some People Harm*, N.Y. TIMES, May 5, 2024.

F. PUBLIC HEALTH EMERGENCY LAWS IN THE 21ST CENTURY

As the numbers of Americans who were fully vaccinated rose, epidemiologic trends began to slowly improve despite emerging new strains of COVID-19. By May 2023, President Biden ended the national PHE in place for over 3 consecutive years. Most states followed suit, rescinding their declarations of emergency by the close of summer 2023. Yet, repercussions of the pandemic were still reverberating across the U.S. *See, e.g.*, James G. Hodge Jr., *"Out Like a Lion:" Terminating the COVID-19 National PHE*, 51(2) JLME 443 (2023).

Over the course of the pandemic, select state legislatures (especially in more conservative U.S. jurisdictions) proposed dozens of bills to strip PHE powers of state and local agencies, limit the duration of future emergency declarations, curtail local "home rule" powers, subject exercises of PHE powers to advance legislative reviews or strict judicial scrutiny, or restrict health officials from limiting religious assemblies or mandating masks or vaccinations. *See* James G. Hodge, Jr. & Jennifer L. Piatt, *COVID's Counterpunch: State Legislative Assaults on PHE Powers*, 36 BYU J. PUB. L. 33 (2021); James G. Hodge, Jr., Lauren T. Dunning & Jennifer L. Piatt, *State*

PHE in Response to COVID-19, 113(3) AJPH 275 (2023).

Michigan's Republican-dominated legislature, for example, introduced several bills to strip emergency powers from Governor Gretchen Whitmer (Figure 12.15) and the state Department of Health and Human Services. Governor Whitmer successfully vetoed several bills. Dave Boucher, *Whitmer Vetoes Bill that Would Strip Emergency Powers*, DETROIT FREE PRESS (Mar. 24, 2021). Ultimately, her emergency powers were curtailed by the Michigan Supreme Court via challenges brought by legislators and others. *Midwest Inst. of Health, PLLC v. Gov. of Mich.*, 506 Mich. 332 (2020).

Figure 12.15. MI Governor Gretchen Whitmer

In New York, Democratic lawmakers restricted Governor Cuomo's emergency powers after his administration provided incomplete reporting of nursing home-related deaths. Jesse McKinley & Luis Ferré-Sadurní, *Cuomo Faces Revolt as Legislators Move to Strip Him of Pandemic Powers*, N.Y. TIMES, Mar. 5, 2021. Ohio Governor Mike DeWine's veto of

Senate Bill 22, including a series of PHE power limits and legislative oversight provisions he described as unconstitutional, was overridden by the legislature. Cindy Abrams, *Ohio General Assembly Overrides Veto of Senate Bill 22,* OHIO HOUSE OF REPS. (Mar. 24, 2021). And in Kentucky, after state lawmakers passed 3 limiting bills over Governor Beshear's veto, he sued successfully in state court to declare them unconstitutional. Bruce Schreiner, *Judge Temporarily Blocks New KY Law on COVID-19 Rules*, AP, Feb. 3, 2021.

Public health agencies and authorities were openly concerned about the extended impacts of legislative efforts to reign in emergency and routine public health powers (despite the fact that most of the bills were never enacted). Even in states where legislative efforts to limit public health authority succeeded, counter legal options surfaced. Expanded use of federal national security, interstate commerce, and spending powers, as well as preemptive efforts at the national level, may circumvent or negate some lower-level governmental limitations on emergency responses.

For example, CDC used its disease control regulations to impose an eviction moratorium affecting non-commercial renters on September 4, 2020. Temporary Halt in Residential Evictions to Prevent the Further Spread of COVID-19, 85 Fed. Reg. 55, 292 (Sept. 4, 2020). CDC's novel order was framed as a public health protectionary measure against the prospect of millions of Americans losing their housing for their inability to pay rent due to pandemic hardships. It was quickly opposed in numerous cases. Landlords and others challenged CDC's underlying authority to issue the moratorium.

Multiple courts reached inapposite decisions. *Compare Brown v. Azar*, 497 F. Supp. 3d 1270, 1299 (N.D. Ga. 2020), *appealed*, No. 20–14210–H, 2020 WL 7641876 (11th Cir. 2020) (denying plaintiffs' petition for a preliminary injunction) *with Terkel v. CDC*, No. 6:20–CV–00564, 2021 WL 742877 (E.D. Tex. Feb. 25, 2021), *appealed*, No. 21–40137, 2021 WL 1794993 (5th Cir. Apr. 26, 2021) (nullifying CDC's order as beyond federal interstate commerce authority). On August 26, 2021, SCOTUS blocked further extensions of CDC's eviction moratorium after allowing it to continue for months. *Alabama Assoc. of Realtors v. HHS*, 594 U.S. 758 (2021). It determined that CDC had clearly exceeded its authority under the federal PHSA.

An additional example of federal prominence in emergency preparedness and response extended from PREP Act preemption. Even as states rescinded their emergency declarations, CDC clarified that HHS' invocation of the PREP Act would continue along with preemptive measures related to administration and distribution of vaccinations and other MCMs. One CDC official noted that even among states that end formal declarations of emergency, "state and local authorities may not prohibit or effectively prohibit [qualified persons] from ordering and administering [MCMs]. . . . The PREP Act contains an express preemption provision [that is] still applicable regardless of state laws and regulations." Letter from Margaret Honein, Incident Manager, CDC, to Colleague (July 2, 2021).

Constitutional counter-challenges grounded in separation of powers, due process, preemption, and other themes may also stymie enforcement of overly-restrictive state legislation limiting public health emergency powers. In addition, several states' legislatures introduced bills during the pandemic supporting emergency preparedness and response. *See* Dawn Hunter et al., *Strengthening Pub. Health Authority to Contain & Prevent Communicable Disease*, NETWORK FOR PUB. HEALTH L. (June 17, 2021). New model state law provisions on the scope of PHE powers may also stymie legislative affronts. *See, e.g., Model PHE Authority Act*, UNIF. L. COMM'N (Oct. 3, 2023). Additional state- or local-level executive options offer other strategic opportunities to bolster public health powers.

Substantial legal lessons learned during the COVID-19 pandemic have already reshaped anticipated PHE responses for the 21st century. *See, e.g.*, Michelle M. Mello et al., *Legal Infrastructure for Pandemic Response: Lessons Not Learnt in the US*, 384 BMJ 1 (2024). As Professor David Fidler forecasted over 2 decades ago, the "federalization of public health governance" has established "*de facto*" primacy or federal emergency preparedness and response over state and local governments. David Fidler, *Constitutional Outlines of Public Health's "New World Order,"* 77 TEMP. L. REV. 247, 255–56 (2004). Major shifts in federal accountability and corresponding response efforts mid-pandemic between the Trump and Biden Administrations revealed an enhanced role for federal authorities to address "national security threats." *See* WHITE HOUSE, NAT'L SEC. MEMO. ON U.S. GLOBAL LEADERSHIP TO STRENGTHEN THE INT'L COVID-19 RESPONSE & TO ADVANCE GLOBAL HEALTH SEC. & BIOLOGICAL PREPAREDNESS (2021).

Congressional interventions during the pandemic substantially enhanced federal public health powers through an extensive series of legislative enactments including the:

- *Families First Coronavirus Response Act*, Pub. L. No. 116–127, 134 Stat. 178 (2020);
- *CARES Act*, Pub. L. No. 116–136, 134 Stat. 281 (2020);
- *Paycheck Protection Program & Healthcare Enhancement Act*, Pub. L. No: 116–139, 134 Stat. 620 (2020);
- *Consolidated Appropriations Act*, Pub. L. No: 116–260 (2020); and
- *American Rescue Plan Act*, Pub. L. No. 117–2, 135 Stat. 2 (2021).

Collectively, these laws directly authorized federal public health interventions and provided unprecedented economic relief to individuals and businesses, alleviating some correlated risks to physical and mental health. *See* James G. Hodge, Jr., *National Legal Paradigms for PHE Responses*, 71(1) AM. U. L. REV. 65 (2021).

Perhaps most importantly, at the forefront of the COVID-19 pandemic were revelations of massive inequities in U.S. health care and public health responses. Americans' experiences during the pandemic were drastically different based on their race, ethnicity, social-economic class, and location (e.g., urban v. rural, tribal v. local). While millions of Americans gained new access to health services through the ACA, free vaccines, telehealth or other publicly-supported efforts during the pandemic, gross health disparities reflected across society contributed directly to preventable cases, injuries, and deaths.

Rectifying these outcomes from one of the worst public health crisis in U.S. history is not easy. *See* Sheryl Gay Stolberg, *Sept. 11 Investigator Lays Groundwork for Impartial Pandemic Inquiry*, N.Y. TIMES, June 17, 2021. There is strong potential for substantial, systemic reforms to assure U.S. responses to future global health threats do not repeat failed efforts during the COVID-19 pandemic. Just as with the national responses to 9/11, improving U.S. PHE preparedness and responses entail law and policy reforms guided by science, ethics, and sound policy. *See, e.g.*, James G, Hodge,

Jr. et al., *Post-COVID U.S. Legal Reforms Promoting Public Health & Equity*, 48 JLME 784 (2020). Assuring improved health outcomes for all Americans during the 21st century is an achievable goal through enhanced emergency legal responses, but also via the administration, funding, and de-politicization of routine public health activities and health care services at every level of government. *See, e.g.*, NASEM, EMERGING STRONGER AFTER COVID-19: PRIORITIES FOR HEALTH SYS. TRANSFORMATION (2021).

	Chapter 12—Discussion Questions
?	1. How did U.S. legal preparedness & response efforts during the COVID-19 pandemic differ from prior PHEs?
?	2. What are the premier legal challenges arising from COVID-19 that contributed to excess morbidity & mortality in the U.S.?
?	3. What specific skills or knowledge extending from the pandemic may enhance legal triage efforts during future PHEs?
?	4. How has the legal environment underlying public & private sector efforts to PHEs changed due to the pandemic?
?	5. How may policymakers & courts better address constitutional issues arising during extended PHEs based on lessons learned during the COVID-19 pandemic?

INDEX

References are to Pages
